SPIRITUAL WELL-BEING
Sociological Perspectives

Edited by
David O. Moberg

116126

University Press
of America™

Copyright © 1979 by

University Press of America, Inc.™

4710 Auth Place, S.E., Washington D.C. 20023

Printed in the United States of America

ISBN: 0-8191-0765-4

Library of Congress Catalog Card Number: 79-52191

ACKNOWLEDGMENTS

Special acknowledgment is made to the following for permission to reprint their copyrighted material:

Bookcraft Publishers, Salt Lake City, Utah, for excerpts from NO MORE STRANGERS, Vol. 1, by Hartman Rector, Jr., and Connie Rector, copyright 1971 (quotations in Chapter 13).

New York International Bible Society, New York City, for passages from the NEW INTERNATIONAL VERSION, copyright 1978 (quotations in Chapter 5 and several inserts between chapters).

THE PARACLETE, for permission to reprint Chapter 17 by Renetzky from volume 4, no. 2, Winter 1977.

SOCIOLOGICAL ANALYSIS for permission to reprint Chapters 1 and 24 by Moberg (with adaptations), Chapter 6 by Garrett, and Chapter 19 by Kauffman, all from volume 40, no. 1, Spring 1979.

In recognition of their indirect contributions to this book through sponsorship of the programs from which these papers came, all royalties after recovery of non-subsidized production expenses will be divided equally between the Association for the Sociology of Religion and the Sociology of Religion Research Committee of the International Sociological Association.

CONTENTS

PREFACE

During the 1970's there has been a remarkable increase of interest in "the spiritual." This surge of attention has been evident in "non-religious" as well as religious contexts, among people of Eastern and "new" religions as well as Christians, among Marxists and their ideological opponents, and in numerous nations across the face of the earth, not just in the United States of America where it perhaps has received the most attention.

A primary goal of most religious groups is to awaken, develop, and sustain the spiritual well-being of their constituents. To be sure, diverse concepts are used to reflect and express that objective, and among many it is more implicit than explicitly stated. The distinguishing features, components, and criteria of spiritual well-being often are only indirectly evident, and formal definitions of it, whatever the rubric used to label it, typically are lacking. It overlaps considerably with concepts of "good mental health," and some persons and groups reduce it to nothing but a psychological phenomenon. Serving human needs for spiritual health or analogous concepts consequentially constitutes an objective of numerous agencies and professions inside and outside the religious realm which are attempting to meet the total needs of people.

In spite of its central significance to the sociology of religion, the phenomenon of spiritual well-being has received very little direct attention within that discipline. This pioneering work constitutes a major step toward changing that unfortunate situation. Chapter 1 sketches some of the historical events associated with the emergence of this concept as it begins to vie for a position within the mainstream of sociology, particularly in the micro-sociological areas of social psychology and the sociology of religion.

The papers included in this volume comprise an impressive body of work upon which interested scholars, researchers, theorists, educators, administrators, planners, and organization leaders can build. It will be of relevance not only to sociologists in numerous areas of specialization, but also to teachers, researchers, and students in related disciplines like the psychology of religion, social gerontology, religious education, ecclesiology, religious studies, philosophy of religion, theology, and all of the major health-related areas of study. Researchers working on related

vii

topics in those disciplines and in such interdisciplinary areas as
religion and health, wholistic health care, the quality of life and
social indicators movements, mental health, and life cycle studies
can gain significant insights, suggested topics for study, and
methodological clues by reading these papers. Pastors, priests,
and rabbis, chaplains, counselors, clinical psychologists, psychia-
trists, nurses, social workers, and other members of the "helping
professions" can increase their understanding of the spiritual nature
and needs of people and of ways in which to help satisfy them by
perceptively reading this book. In other words, even though this
book is by sociologists, it deals with an interdisciplinary subject
(see Moberg, 1978b), and it can contribute to all the other disciplines and professions concerned with the spiritual domain of life.

As is inevitable in a book to which many authors have contributed,
numerous theoretical, methodological, ideological, and conceptual
perspectives are evident. Indeed, one of the ways in which it can
be studied is to make lists of the implicit or explicit definitions
of spiritual well-being and cognate concepts which are used by the
respective authors, of the research methods they use or advocate
for further study, of the theoretical orientations they reflect,
and of the implications for action which they identify or intimate.

Sociologists are not a homogeneous group. The light they cast
upon a complex subject like spiritual well-being is one of numerous
diffused rays shedding their beams from many sources, not that of a
single, powerful beacon shining in one direction and from but one
source.

This, of course, implies that neither I nor any of the contributors necessarily agrees with the other writers. To agree with all
would be impossible, for significant differences of perspective and
of ideological values lie beneath, as well as on, the surface of the
various chapters. We do all agree upon one thing at least -- that
this subject deserves explicit attention within our profession,
so it is worth devoting our time and energy in order to stimulate
discussion and study by publication of these papers.

Specifically, these contributions have come from two professional
meetings, both of which were international in scope. The first was
the Association for the Sociology of Religion (ASR). Its annual
meeting in Chicago, Illinois, September 3-4, 1977, included two
sessions with eleven papers on spiritual well-being. It is represented here in the chapters by Benson, Bourg, Christy and Lyon,
Fichter, Garrett, Hynson, Kauffman, Marcum, McNamara and St. George,
and Renetzky. (The ASR paper by Brewer was succeeded by another in
the 1978 program, which is included instead.) The other chapters
were presented originally at the quadrennial meeting of the International Sociological Association in Uppsala, Sweden, August 14-19,
1978. They constituted two of the five research-reporting sessions
of the Sociology of Religion Research Committee at the Ninth World

Congress of Sociology. Several of the papers have been modified considerably by their authors since the original presentation, and all have been edited for inclusion in this book.

As the organizer and moderator of all of the four program sessions in which these papers originally were given, as well as by being both the content and copy editor, I have had a much stronger personal interest in this book than might normally be true of an edited symposium. I have labored over many of these papers just as much as if they were my own, always with clarity of communication by the authors to the readers as the primary objective.

The quotations from resources which are inserted on pages between chapters which otherwise would be blank were selected as representative samples of thought-provoking materials which can stimulate reflection and help readers to find relevant materials from sources outside Sociology.

In the interest of unity and consistency, I have applied American standards of spelling, punctuation, and style (the last following the current conventions of most sociological journals). This has irked some of the authors from countries in which "the Queen's English" is standard. As one of them wrote in private correspondence to me,

Although my purist English...upbringing makes me shiver with horror at American spelling and even -- particularly! -- punctuation, I have learnt over the years to grin and bear (most of) it with the traditional stiff upper lip.

I trust that both they and our readers from English-speaking (in contrast to American!) countries will forgive the "distortions" of this book which, after all, is published in the United States of America.

Many of the papers use "man," "he," and similar words to refer generically to the totality of humanity, male and female. For the most part, I did not edit these to the more clumsy "she/he," "men/women," and analogous forms. Neither the authors nor I have any "sexist" intent in retaining that simpler, though "old-fashioned," wording!

The authors have agreed, again with reluctance in some instances, to having a single composite set of references for all chapters instead of separate, often overlapping, and frequently difficult to locate lists for each chapter. Wherever a date accompanies the name of an author in the text, the full reference to the work is found under that name and date in the list at the end of the book. If more than one by the same writer are cited for a particular year, letters are added to differentiate the respective works. The numbers which sometimes follow the date of a publication indicate the specific pages quoted or cited.

To list every person, organization, and agency which has contributed to the "well-being" of this book at Marquette University and in the other institutions and agencies represented by the editor and authors would be an impossible task. Many of these are mentioned in the acknowledgement notes accompanying the respective chapters. Particularly noteworthy are the Department of Sociology and Anthropology and the Graduate School of Marquette University, which have provided most of the secretarial services, translation fees,postage, supplies, and other costs associated with editing and production of this book. Mary Magestro and others in the Department provided many of the secretarial services. To all who have shared in this task -- including the unmentioned audience members at the professional meetings whose comments led to improvements of the respective papers -- we express our hearty thanks.

We are thankful also to Sociological Analysis, the journal of the Association for the Sociology of Religion, for permission to reprint the papers by Garrett, Kauffman, and Moberg; to Paraclete, the journal of the National Association of Christians in Social Work, for permission to reprint Renetzky's paper; to Bookcraft of Salt Lake City, Utah, for permission to include the extensive quotations from Rector and Rector (1971) in Duke's paper, and to the New York Bible Society International for permission to include quotations from the New International Version of the Bible.

In recognition of the important role played by the two professional associations which made possible the programs leading to this book, all royalties after recovery of direct, non-reimbursed editorial costs will be assigned in equal proportions to the Association for the Sociology of Religion and to the Sociology of Religion Research Committee of the International Sociological Association.

I believe I can speak for all of the authors in saying that we will be glad to receive constructive criticism, supplementary perspectives, copies of pertinent papers, reports of research, and similar materials related to our subject from readers. Therefore I have included mailing addresses of the authors in the List of Contributors at the end of the book. I hope many readers will communicate directly with me and the respective authors whenever they can share research findings or other pertinent theoretical, methodological, or substantive data.

In other words, I hope that this book will be a beginning, not an end -- the beginning of significant investigations related to the spiritual well-being of people in numerous nations, cultures, and subcultures in all parts of the world, not the end of a relatively minor set of events in the late 1970's. But even that dreamed-for goal can be seen as a means toward the end of enhancing the spiritual well-being of humanity, both individually and collectively.
                              -- David O. Moberg
                                 Milwaukee, Wisconsin
                                 February 23, 1979

PART I. INTRODUCTION

Chapter 1

THE DEVELOPMENT OF SOCIAL INDICATORS OF SPIRITUAL WELL-BEING FOR

QUALITY OF LIFE RESEARCH*

David O. Moberg

From numerous perspectives the times are ripe for the sociological
investigation of spiritual well-being. The word "spiritual"is
becoming an "in" word in American society. Not only has it returned
to a position of favor within the "mainline" religious bodies, but
it also is used in numerous non-religious contexts. News reports
about music, the effects of physical exercise, preservation and
appreciation of the environment, many political issues, and the satisfactions provided by a wide range of occult and therapeutic groups
are often described in the U.S.A. by using "spiritual" and related
words (Moberg, 1978c). The high level of incidence of alienation and
anomie in contemporary society, the search for personal fulfillment
and inner peace, the "identity crisis," the rise of "the new consciousness" (Glock and Bellah, 1976), and the search for meaning,
security, significance, and purpose are among the alleged sources of
increased concern for spiritual phenomena.

This interest is not limited to capitalistic societies. A four-
page section of the bibliography of Soviet Sociology distributed at
the Eighth World Congress of Sociology was devoted to "Sociological
Problems of Spiritual Life" (Express Information, 1974: 24-27).
Pravda, the Communist Party newspaper, has called for a crackdown
on individualism because it hampers development of "the new man."
The basic duty of the Communist Party is reported to be the shaping

*This chapter is reprinted with minor adaptations from Sociological
Analysis, vol. 40, no. 1, Spring 1979. The work reported was partially supported by a sabbatical leave from Marquette University and
a fellowship from the Institute for Advanced Christian Studies. Its
perspectives and conclusions are the author's and do not necessarily
represent those of either Marquette University or IFACS. The author
gratefully acknowledges assistance in various portions of the research by Karen Moore Bothel, Regina Marcum, OSF, Patricia Brusek,
Theresa Schreiber, Jamie Lee, and students in his 1976 Practicum in
Sociology.

of a new man who combines "spiritual richness and moral purity" (United Press International, 1974).

Although the meanings attached to the word "spiritual" vary considerably from one context of use to another, the fact that it receives such widespread attention indicates a broad interest in the spiritual nature and well-being of people. It also indicates the need to analyze the respective definitions and types of use of the word as a means of furthering genuine communication.

Spiritual well-being is not a synonym for religion. In many respects it is a much more specific concept, but in others it is even broader because it is not limited to the domain of religion. Its functional definition pertains to the wellness or "health" of the totality of the inner resources of people, the ultimate concerns around which all other values are focused, the central philosophy of life that guides conduct, and the meaning-giving center of human life which influences all individual and social behavior (Moberg, 1974a). (Other definitional approaches are discussed below and in the other chapters of this book.)

SOCIAL INDICATORS AND THE QUALITY OF LIFE

One of the most significant developments among policy makers and the supporting social sciences over the past decade has been the rapid growth of the social indicators movement. It has been stimulated by demands for evaluation, social accounting, monitoring, and reporting, as well as by the growing concern for social justice, effectiveness and efficiency in the use of public resources, and the correction of abuses in governmental bureaucracies. In the attempt to move beyond economic indicators, which are based primarily upon monetary values, various indicators related to health and illness, social mobility, public order and safety, education, social participation, mental health, and alienation were incorporated into the movement. A social indicator was

...defined to be a statistic of direct normative interest which facilitates concise, comprehensive, and balanced judgments about the condition of major aspects of a society. It is in all cases a direct measure of welfare and is subject to the interpretation that, if it changes in the "right" direction, while other things remain equal, things have gotten better or people are "better off" (U.S. Dept. of Health, Education, and Welfare, 1969: 97).

An important development within the social indicators movement has been the incorporation of various measures of the Quality of Life (QOL). The QOL indexes incorporate data relevant to suicide, drug addiction, juvenile delinquency, crime, alcoholism, physical and mental health, housing conditions, parks and playgrounds, and many other relatively objective components. Some also have used subjective measures like happiness (McCall, 1975), psychological well-being (Bradburn, 1969; see Cherlin and Reeder, 1975), and life satisfaction (Campbell et al., 1976).

An individualist approach to QOL stresses the achievements of persons, their dominance over circumstances, ability to overcome adversity, freedom from constraint, and fulfillment of individual aims. The transcendentalist approach emphasizes complementarity of interest and function, the importance of solidarity, and the primacy of the community over the individual. An interactionist-phenomenological approach implies that QOL is in constant flux as part of a continuing process of negotiation generated between individuals and society which leads to definitions of the QOL in terms of the outcomes of negotiations relevant to money, time, skill, and sentiment (Gerson, 1976).

Because of the significance of religion in human society, as well as the important role it has played in the theoretical development of the Sociology of Religion, we would expect various measures of religiosity to play a significant role in the QOL movement. To this date, however, it is a relatively neglected topic (Moberg and Brusek, 1978). In addition to political, philosophical, and theoretical reasons for the almost complete omission of religion from the QOL movement, the lack of adequate measuring instruments for indicators and the conceptual problems associated with definitions are major reasons for this neglect. Research to develop social indicators of spiritual well-being is essential if this hiatus is to be filled.

The Need for Spiritual Well-Being Indicators

Research to construct social indicators of spiritual well-being is relevant in a wide range of contexts. In the area of research methodology, it constitutes the specification and operational definition of a concept that currently has no standardized definition in sociology. It thus will facilitate a wide range of other basic research which, in turn, could contribute to many wholesome developments in the realm of sociological theory. Conditions, programs, and influences which are alleged to contribute to spiritual well-being then could be tested to determine whether or not they actually do. Relationships between physical health, mental health, and spiritual health could be analyzed. The ways in which spiritual well-being is related to the various "invisible" religions of modern society (Luckmann, 1967) could be tested. The relationships among varying kinds of value commitments with their complex bundles of assumptions, postulates, beliefs, values, and personal-social covenants could be analyzed to determine their impact upon spiritual well-being. Comparisons could be made of the relative impact of disengagement versus activity during the later years of the life cycle, and many other theoretical assumptions and constructs could be investigated if we had a valid and reliable index of spiritual well-being.

3

To help satisfy the rising demand for evaluation research, such an instrument also would make it possible to measure the spiritual components of the QOL of various populations. The possibility of comparing the levels of spiritual well-being of various ethnic, religious, institutional, program-centered, and other groups is very attractive to people who have a scientific mentality, but it is likely to be repugnant to religious leaders who fear the findings that might emerge from such investigations. They need to recognize that promoting the spiritual well-being of their people is a primary goal of most religious and "spiritual" groups. Currently accountability for attaining that goal has not been systematized but remains on a crude, pre-scientific level.

Often it is assumed that when an institution, such as a church, prospers in terms of membership, attendance, baptisms, confirmations, or fiscal "success," then it is attaining its ultimate goals. Recent revelations of the fact that theologically conservative churches in the U.S.A. are growing, while others are tending to decline in membership and financial strength, has called attention to the fact that the conservative groups attempt to keep spiritual values central and that this orientation is valued by most church members (Kelley, 1977). Only after an appropriate index of spiritual well-being has been constructed will it be possible to determine whether, in fact, there is a difference between the levels of spiritual health of the members of the conservative churches and those of the theologically more liberal mainline parishes and congregations. Indeed, only after such an instrument has been constructed will it be possible to determine scientifically whether involvement in religious faith and church activities does more harm than good to the human spirit.

A very significant area for evaluation research pertains to holistic health. As recognition grows that health care relevant to physical needs must also give attention to the mental and spiritual components of health, it will become increasingly important to include activities to promote spiritual well-being in all of the "helping professions" related to health, welfare, education, counselling, social work, pastoral care, clinical psychology, and other human service occupations (Moberg, 1977b). The evaluation of the levels of spiritual well-being of institutionalized populations in total-care institutions which profess to meet all human needs can be evaluated to determine whether or not a satisfactory level of spiritual well-being prevails among the residents. Before and after measures of programs and projects designed to promote the spiritual health of people can determine whether the desired outcomes actually were obtained. While this is particularly important for religious groups which explicitly attempt to obtain such goals, it applies as well to other cultural, social, educational, and therapeutic agencies which profess to promote spiritual maturity or health.

An index of spiritual well-being can also serve as a diagnostic tool for clergy and clinicians in the various helping professions.

Through its help, major areas for in-depth interviews with and investigations on behalf of clients can be identified with only a brief expenditure of time. In other words, like the numerous psychological and socio-psychological tests which are used extensively by clinical psychologists, social case workers, marriage and family counselors, chaplains, and other professional people, such an index will not replace professional care, but it will constitute an important tool to improve its efficiency.

AN OVERVIEW OF PROGRESS TO DATE

A pair of papers at the 1965 annual meetings of the American Catholic Sociological Society (Moberg, 1967a) and the American Scientific Affiliation (Moberg, 1967b) presented the need for the behavioral sciences to consider the spiritual nature of man. They indicated that a "spiritual" component of religiosity is the essence of a religious life, the kind of thing that Sturzo (1947) labeled "the true life" in his "Sociology of the Supernatural." Many philosophical, theological, and existential evidences support the hypothesis that man has a spiritual nature; it was concluded that some of these may be susceptible to scientific tests. A _verstehende_ research approach exploring self-reports of inner experiences, case studies of believers, the grasping by people for some kind of ultimate commitment or concern, and even tests of the validity of religious experience used by various religious groups in screening their members can all contribute to development of this subject in a sociological frame of reference.

The 1971 White House Conference on Aging devoted one of its major sections to spiritual well-being (Moberg, 1971b). The National Interfaith Coalition on Aging (NICA), which emerged out of it, has engaged in research on contributions of the religious sector to meeting the needs of the aging, including their contributions to spiritual well-being (Cook, 1977). NICA also developed a working definition of spiritual well-being which is intended for use in all religious bodies, each adapting it to fit its own history, theology, and organizational structure:
Spiritual Well-Being is the affirmation of life in a relationship with God, self, community and environment that nurtures and celebrates wholeness (National Interfaith Coalition on Aging, 1975).
Although this is not a scientific operational definition, it can be used phenomenologically and rhetorically within religious bodies. It is consistent with concepts of holistic well-being and definitions of good mental health. It provided a basis for organizing NICA's National Intradecade Conference on Spiritual Well-Being of the Elderly in April 1977, which included over eighty presentations on the subject. (Many will be published in Cook and Thorson, 1979.)

In a roundtable discussion at the 1974 meeting of the American Sociological Association (Moberg, 1974a) the possibilities of sociological research on the subject of spiritual well-being were explored. Numerous opportunities and problems pertinent to research on the topic were identified. It was concluded that such research would be just as legitimate as that on many relatively intangible concepts which already have been incorporated into sociology, psychology, and social psychology, such as alienation, anomie, attitudes, authoritarianism, happiness, the id, ego, and superego, intelligence, morale, motivation, pain, and values. Numerous methodological approaches could be used in various components of such research.

During the spring semester of 1975-76 I taught the Practicum in Sociology at Marquette University for senior students who were learning how to integrate theory and research methods by investigation of a specific topic. We worked on the problem of developing indicators of spiritual well-being. On the basis of insights and impressions drawn from numerous interviews with a fairly wide range of people, we concluded that NICA's definition does not constitute a good operational definition for research. As a first step toward constructing an index, our efforts culminated in an exploratory questionnaire which asked opinions about spiritual well-being, characteristics of spiritual health, influences upon it, and similar topics.

Questionnaire Findings

The questionnaire was administered by Practicum students to many individual research subjects and later by the instructor to students in four classes of three private midwestern colleges. A total of 121 questionnaires were completed, 52% by males and only 11.5% by persons aged 25 or over. By response to the question, "What is your present or most recent denomination?," 49% were Protestant, 45% Catholic, 5% Jewish, and 1% other. Our purpose in reporting a few selected findings is not to generalize to any larger population but rather to examine relationships between selected variables and the subjective evaluation of the respondents' spiritual well-being in response to the question, "Do you personally have SWB?" Surprisingly, 65% professed to have it, 26% were not sure or did not know, and only 9% answered "No" to the question.

As indicated in Table 1, most respondents believed that it is possible for a person to know whether or not he or she has spiritual well-being, and a majority believed it is possible to know whether somebody else has it. Most of them believed that everybody can have spiritual well-being, but that only "a few" or "about half" actually possess it. They tend to see it as a continuous rather than a discrete variable; that is, most saw it as something of which some people have more than others, although many viewed it also as a condition one either has or does not have. They interpreted it as something one can possess, then lose, and as a process of growth and development.

All categories of respondents agreed that finding meaning in life,

Table 1. Beliefs About Spiritual Well-Being by Self-Evaluated
Spiritual Well-Being (in percentages)

Questions and Response Categories*	Do you personally have SWB?			
	Yes	Not sure	No	Don't know
It is possible for a person to know whether he or she has SWB.				
Agree	99	96	92	80
Disagree	1	4	8	20
It is possible for people to know whether someone else has SWB.				
Agree	68	70	67	20
Disagree	32	30	33	80
How many people can have SWB?				
Everybody	82	73	64	80
Most people	18	27	18	0
About half	0	0	0	0
A few people	0	0	9	20
Nobody	0	0	9	0
How many people do have SWB?				
Everybody	7	5	0	0
Most people	24	18	0	20
About half	24	27	36	20
A few people	45	45	55	60
Nobody	0	5	9	0
SWB is a condition which one either has or does not have.				
Agree	52	44	64	40
Disagree	48	56	36	60
Some people have more SWB than others do.				
Agree	90	89	83	80
Disagree	10	11	17	20
SWB is something one can have and then lose.				
Agree	78	81	83	80
Disagree	22	19	17	20
SWB is a process of growth and development.				
Agree	95	96	83	80
Disagree	5	4	17	20
Number of Respondents (=100%)**	(78)	(26)	(12)	(5)

*Agree combines the responses of Strongly Agree, Agree, and Tend to
Agree. Disagree combines Strongly Disagree, Disagree, and Tend to
Disagree.
**The totals for the question on how many people do have SWB are 71,
22, 11, and 5, respectively. All others had either zero or only one
non-response.

7

Table 2. Selected Characteristics and Correlates of Spiritual Well-Being by Self-Evaluated Spiritual Well-Being (in percentages)

Questions and Response Categories		Do you personally have SWB?			
		Yes	Not sure	No	Don't know
Indicate whether each of the following items is essential to have SWB, most likely to be present if one has SWB, most likely to be absent, or not related at all to SWB:					
Peace with God:	Essential	73	62	67	80
	Present	21	27	8	0
	Absent	0	8	8	0
	Not related	6	4	17	20
Inner peace:	Essential	67	73	67	60
	Present	27	23	25	40
	Absent	1	4	0	0
	Not related	5	0	8	0
Faith in Christ:	Essential	53	50	42	40
	Present	26	27	42	0
	Absent	3	4	0	20
	Not related	18	19	17	40
Good morals:	Essential	32	38	9	40
	Present	55	42	64	20
	Absent	5	4	9	20
	Not related	8	15	18	20
Faith in people:	Essential	28	35	17	20
	Present	64	58	67	80
	Absent	1	4	0	0
	Not related	6	4	17	0
Helping others:	Essential	26	31	25	20
	Present	62	62	42	80
	Absent	3	4	17	0
	Not related	10	4	17	0
Good physical health:	Essential	5	15	25	0
	Present	36	35	42	60
	Absent	9	4	17	0
	Not related	49	46	17	40
Being successful:	Essential	3	4	25	0
	Present	32	46	33	80
	Absent	9	4	8	0
	Not related	57	46	33	20
Number of Respondents (=100%)*		(78)	(26)	(12)	(5)

*Occasional discrepancies in subcategory totals are due to the rounding of figures. Missing observations from non-responses to items vary from 0 to 2.

having harmony with one's self, happiness, and being good to others were either "essential" or "most likely to be present" if one has spiritual well-being. As noted in Table 2, the characteristics with the highest level of "essential" ratings were peace with God, inner peace, and faith in Christ, with those who claimed personally to have spiritual well-being ranking the explicitly religious items higher than did the others. They also differed in their evaluations of the role in spiritual well-being of good morals, helping others, and faith in people. All groups felt that good physical health. and being successful were not essential to spiritual well-being, but those who felt they personally lacked spiritual well-being were more likely to interpret these as essential or most likely to be present.

All agreed that their own spiritual well-being had not been influenced by the mass media, government, social clubs, having a good occupation or job, monetary savings, angels, demons, or their astrological sign and horoscope. They also agreed that their friends, family, and to some extent personal crises like illness, the death of a family friend, and participation in Holy Communion had affected their spiritual well-being. Table 3 summarizes some of these influences, giving particular attention to items related to the role of organized religion. While it may be hypothesized that spiritual well-being is distinct from "religiosity," it is evident that among these respondents a distinct relationship prevailed between believing they possess spiritual well-being, participating in church-related activities, and practicing personal pieties like praying and Bible reading, which typically are encouraged by Christian churches.

The respondents also indicated their belief that spiritual well-being gives meaning to life, that it is not closely correlated with physical health and illness, that the wealthy are no more likely than the poor to possess it, that it aids in making decisions, and that belief in oneself, in life after death, in a Supreme Being, in Jesus Christ is one's own Savior, and in the goodness of all people are necessary in order to possess spiritual well-being.

These results indicate that most of the people studied have rather definite ideas about the characteristics associated with, influencing, and affected by spiritual well-being, even though they have difficulty in providing a definition of it.

Interview Data

Three main categories of interviews have been included in this project. One of these consisted of discussions with Roman Catholic religious leaders about the nature of spiritual well-being and the criteria which indicate its presence or absence. The predominant perspective among these persons was that mental health is so closely related to spiritual well-being that there is no significant distinction between the two. A holistic perspective on human growth prevails among them, so they emphasize that spiritual maturity is a

Table 3. Influences on Spiritual Well-Being by Self-Evaluated Spiritual
Well-Being (in percentages)

| | Do you personally have SWB? | | | |
Questions and Response Categories	Yes	Not sure	No	Don't know
Most of the time an organized religion (church, synagogue, temple, etc.) hinders SWB more often than it helps it.				
Agree	27	23	42	80
Disagree	73	77	58	20
Are you a member of a church or synagogue?				
Yes	91	84	50	60
No	9	16	50	40
How often do you attend religious services in a church or synagogue?				
At least once a week	62	27	17	0
Once or more a month	15	46	25	20
Several times a year	17	19	17	60
Once a year or less	5	4	33	0
Never	1	4	8	20
How often do you attend or take part in other religious activities, such as Bible studies, religious discussions, prayer groups, etc.?				
At least once a week	25	4	0	0
Once or more a month	19	8	9	0
Several times a year	18	12	27	20
Once a year or less	19	31	18	40
Never	18	46	45	40
Please check how much each of the following affects or has affected your own SWB:				
Church: Very much, or Much	65	50	25	40
Some	15	38	33	20
A little, or Not at all	19	11	42	40
Attending church: Very much, or Much	50	31	42	0
Some	17	35	17	40
A little, or Not at all	33	35	42	60
Friends: Very much, or Much	77	77	50	80
Some	14	15	42	20
A little, or Not at all	9	8	8	0
Praying: Very much, or Much	72	46	25	40
Some	15	38	33	20
A little, or Not at all	13	15	42	40
Bible reading: Very much, or Much	45	23	25	0
Some	24	19	25	40
A little, or Not at all	31	58	50	60
Number of Respondents (=100%)	(78)	(26)	(12)	(5)

*Occasional discrepancies in subcategory totals are due to the round-
ing of figures. Missing observations from non-responses range from
0 to 2.

process of growth. Belief in one's self as a person, knowing who one is, being in relationship to God and Christ, putting one's self in the hands of God, coping effectively with life, relating wholesomely with other people, showing interest in them, and possessing traits like happiness, peacefulness, steadiness, radiance, poise, zest for living, self-worth, and self-determination are among the criteria by which its presence is indicated. The lack or loss of spiritual well-being is reflected in complaining, manipulating other people, taking without giving, going away from love, refusing to make decisions, carrying unnecessary guilt, bitterness, anger, and giving up on life, one's self, or one's personal appearance.

A second category of interviews was with Evangelical Protestant clergy and professional people. They viewed spiritual well-being as equivalent to spiritual health but considered spiritual maturity as somewhat different, pertaining to growth and a developmental process. They felt that the spiritual pervades the entire life of a person and includes such characteristics as commitment to Christ, communication with God, trusting God for guidance and the future, being open in one's relationships with Him and with other people, helping others, participating in Christian fellowship, joy, the other "fruits of the Spirit," loyalty to one's convictions, ability to benefit from criticism of others, and facing one's defeats, depression, and problems instead of running away from them, besides a large number of similar characteristics. Most of them felt that the perception of spiritual well-being tends to fluctuate somewhat, but the spiritually healthy person tends to grow in spiritual maturity, rising by irregular stages to ever-higher levels of spiritual health. None of them believed that people can attain absolute perfection in this life, and all felt that commitment to Jesus Christ is an absolutely essential beginning. For many this is so important that they felt persons who have not made such a commitment do not have spiritual well-being at all, regardless of those people's feelings. Others, however, felt that persons who are faithful in the context of Judaism and possibly even other religions could have spiritual well-being. All tended to differentiate between the perception of possessing it and the reality of actually doing so.

The third group of interviewees consisted of persons who were alleged by others to possess spiritual well-being. None of these felt that they had attained a 100% perfect position on a scale of spiritual well-being. They believed that the process of spiritual development or growth never ends in this life. Most of them could point to an explicit conversion experience, and many could identify significant events which had contributed to their own growth in spiritual maturity. Prayer, Bible reading, participation in Christian groups and activities, helping other people, serving in the church, and lessons learned from the chiding or correction of others were among the experiences which had contributed to their spiritual development.

11

The apparent discrepancies related to the conceptual definition and operational criteria of spiritual well-being may be a consequence of genuine differences, but it is more likely that they result from intervening variables. For example, they might reflect diverse linguistic patterns and semantic interpretations of the various speech communities. Theological and historical differences within each of the major Christian traditions also could result in contrasting definitions of the essence of spiritual life. Another possibility is that the frequent use of concepts like "spirituality" in the formation process of many Catholic religious communities has made it natural for their members to interpret analogous concepts like "spiritual well-being" in the context of the total process of religious socialization with its emphasis upon cultivating spiritual maturity.

It is possible, however, that the most important source of divergent perspectives from our interview data is methodological. The sample is small and unrepresentative; the Catholic leaders consisted of three priests and two sisters; the Protestants were eight clergy and lay leaders plus one interview with a group of seven, and there were only eight in-depth case studies of persons reputed to have spiritual well-being. All of the interviews were relatively unstructured, seeking only to explore each respondent's personal perspectives on the subject rather than to compare their opinions. The interviews with Catholic leaders were conducted by various graduate research assistants. The others by me as the principal investigator generally involved lengthier interviews and deeper probing. An additional round of interviews structured to probe answers to identical questions would be necessary in order to determine more precisely the degree to which and manner in which the three categories of respondents agree or disagree with each other.

For reasons such as these, the initial conclusions based upon these exploratory interviews and case studies must be interpreted as suggestive only; further investigation may confirm, modify, or dissipate the apparent differences noted above.

Sociologists' Perspectives

The 1977 annual meeting of the Association for the Sociology of Religion included two sessions devoted to papers on spiritual well-being. Of the eleven presentations, ten are published in this book, the eleventh being succeeded here by a 1978 paper by its author, Earl Brewer. They reflected a rather broad range of implicit and explicit definitions. Some of these were relatively conventional Christian concepts, viewing spiritual well-being as spiritual maturity, having a personal relationship to an indwelling spiritual being, being tuned in to "the power beyond one's self," drawing closer to God, or developing a right relationship with God which provides reconciliation and forgiveness for sin. Close to such definitions is the concept that spiritual well-being consists of being in a state of meaningful, purposeful relationship with God through one's relationships with man. Somewhat less conventional was the perspective that its foundation is the need of persons and groups to transcend themselves. Spiritual well-being also was viewed as one dimension of a role-set for persons who occupy the status of member within a religious organization. As such, it is always in a process of becoming.

Among the indicators of spiritual well-being used or reflected in those papers were healthy self-concepts, faith, belief in the bigness of God, unselfish giving to another person, following the life-style of Jesus, religion as the domain of life which yields satisfaction, intrinsic religiosity, coming to terms with sin, and moral character.

A similar but wider range of definitions and an even broader scope of criteria of spiritual well-being were reflected in the papers of the two major sessions on "Religion and Spiritual Well-Being" at the Ninth World Congress of Sociology in Uppsala, Sweden, in August 1978. They also are included in this volume, so readers can personally examine the nature and range of their diverse perspectives.

Any arrangement of contents in a volume by as many authors as are represented here must necessarily be somewhat arbitrary. The next section (Part II) presents conceptual studies, which center around definitional issues and criteria for discerning or identifying spiritual well-being. These are followed in Part III by papers which relate chiefly to past and present sociological theories. Qualitative research (Part IV) and quantitative studies (Part V) present the findings of original research relevant to our subject. My concluding chapter (Part VI) suggests the riches which can emerge from further theoretical, empirical, qualitative, and action-oriented studies on the subject.

Obviously, much content of theoretical importance is found in the sections of this book which deal with conceptual investigations, as well as in those which report the findings of research. They, in turn, are not at all devoid of conceptual and theoretical significance. In a very real sense, all parts and chapters are highly interrelated, even though all were written independently by authors of diverse theoretical, philosophical, linguistic, ideological, and methodological perspectives.

After reading this book, I think all will agree that "spiritual well-being" is a highly significant concept for scientists and practitioners in all of the disciplines and professions that deal with the quality of human life in the contemporary world.

THE PERVASIVENESS OF SPIRITUAL WELL-BEING

... the definition of "spiritual" is not so clear and rigidly fixed that it can be separated from the physical, psychological, material, and other aspects of human existence. Instead it is a component or dimension of man which runs through all of the person and his behavior, providing an orientation and focus which pertains to all of the positively valued joys and experiences of living and all of the negative problems and fears of life and death. ...

Because the spiritual is interwoven with all material and other aspects of human life, none of man's other needs can be fully resolved without including attention to his spiritual well-being. The needs related to income, nutrition, physical and mental health, housing, transportation, employment, retirement, education, and social roles all overlap with such aspects of the spiritual as ethical and moral values, the philosophy of life of the elderly and of those who plan (or refuse to plan) programs and services for them, the hidden agenda of anxieties and fears which lurk beneath the surface of collective decision-making in legislatures and community organizations, the estimates of the worth of people who have lost their normal claims to pride, viewing human life as sacred, and expecting God's judgment or rewards for one's behavior now and in a life beyond the grave.

Failure to recognize that man is a spiritual being and refusal to use his resources for service just because he is "too old" rank high among the indignities suffered by many people in their later maturity. A lack of spiritual well-being among the young as well as the old lies behind this problem. -- Background Paper on Spiritual Well-Being for the 1971 White House Conference on Aging (Moberg, 1971b: 14-15).

14

PART II. CONCEPTUAL STUDIES OF SPIRITUAL WELL-BEING

Chapter 2

INDIVIDUATION, INTERIORITY, AND SPIRITUAL TRADITIONS

Carroll J. Bourg

Spiritual well-being is not an easy topic to discuss within the
public language of sociology. The difficulty stems from a variety
of circumstances. One, the literature about spiritual well-being
is more extensive in histories of spiritual traditions, or in theological inquiries into spiritualities. Even contemporary religious
studies, while broader in scope than theology or history, frequently
rely on the more immediate expressions of religious leaders or spokesmen. These expressions are not restricted to the more refined distinctions among the disciplines of psychology, sociology, and anthropology. They often make use of poetry, rhetorical flourishes,
biblical notions, and metaphors, none of which easily translates
into the sociological lexicon.

A further difficulty is the evident paucity of inquiries into
these matters by sociologists. One can find a more abundant literature by psychologists who have investigated religious experiences,
mysticism, ecstasy, peak experiences, and the like. But even here
the unusual or extraordinary experience attracts more attention than
the ordinary spiritual well-being of the ordinary person.

Moreover, the sacred, sacralization, and its perhaps always concomitant process of secularization -- surely notions most prominent
in sociological inquiries -- usually have not been analyzed as they
bear upon spiritual well-being. A recent notable exception is to be
found in Mol's Identity and the Sacred (1976), but even there much
remains implicit. I shall attempt a preliminary sociological discussion in analyzing these important matters. Let me begin with
the terms in the title -- Individuation, Interiority, and Spiritual
Traditions -- but in reverse order.

SPIRITUAL TRADITIONS

The first characteristic of spiritual traditions is that there
are so many of them. They are sometimes referred to as spiritualities
or simply included as cultural elements. Since one might think it
appropriate to explore that variety at the outset, it should be

made clear that I do not intend to develop a typology or to present a comparative history of them. Far better to refer to them more concretely in the persons and traditions that they spawned.

As an aid toward clarification, I am deliberately limiting myself to selected spiritual traditions in the Catholic Christian history. An abundant literature contains descriptions and analyses of them. They would serve well to illustrate important components of spiritual traditions.

Many spiritual traditions have stemmed from the work of remarkable individuals like Benedict, Francis, Dominic, Ignatius, and others. While the historical circumstances of their peculiar developments are immensely important and worthy of serious study, each gradually developed emphases and orientations which became distinct disciplines. The spiritual disciplines combined both a learning and a rule, fidelity to which would help to cultivate special virtues. By virtue is meant a facility in acting and in dealing with specific and pragmatic resolutions of dilemmas and predicaments.

All the remarkable individuals I have mentioned also founded religious orders, but the important emphasis here is their attraction of followers who submitted themselves to the special discipline. The histories of Benedictines, Dominicans, Cistercians, Franciscans, and Jesuits give detailed analyses of those disciplines; one could find much sociological understanding of them by identifying the sociological circumstances within which the new orientations were developed, struggled to take hold, and eventually became significant spiritual traditions.

The multiple spiritual traditions had their own characteristic disciplines about the issues of working and praying, action and contemplation, knowing and willing, mobility and stability, and many more. One element that was common to these distinctive spiritual traditions was a sense of being bound by some rule, together with the learning that promoted and protected the rule. All of them acknowledged the difference between the "ideal" to be pursued and the "real" situation of the participants. But the discipline served the aspirant in his or her search for the appropriate action in changing circumstances.

A second element common to the diverse spiritual traditions was the concern for being linked to the collectivity. That linkage may have been exemplified again in the "holy rule," in the person of the "spiritual father" (abbot), in the Bishop, or in a link to the gospel or more generally to the Catholic tradition. The historically specific modes of being linked or connected to the collective have surely varied. But a consistent theme in the Catholic spiritual traditions has been the requirement to respect the collective and to justify one's relationship to it.

16

A third common element is the deeply sacramental or symbolic character of all intentions and actions. The rich notion of "intentio" was more than mere wishing or wanting. It included the idea of informing a behavior in such a way that it contained and thus carried meaning beyond its merely material composition; the intention informed the act or the work. It became symbolic. Much of the "world" as confronted in these traditions would be considered neither good nor evil. The subjectivity of the actor informed and thus made the neutral to be good or evil. The action itself thus could become sacramental or its opposite; that is, it would contribute to the development or to the damage of spiritual life.

But a fourth component, a corollary of the preceding, was the conviction that even the making of the symbolic carried a connection with the collective. There were corporate practices which somehow had been previously guaranteed or certified. In minor matters, the individual exercised the symbol-making power unencumbered by the collective. In so-called major matters, the various disciplines or rules provided boundaries, broad as they may have been, to the symbol-making of the individual.

While there are other elements common to the diverse Catholic spiritual traditions, I have emphasized the discipline or being bound by the rule, the concern for being linked to the collectivity, the sacramental or symbolic power of human intentions, and the collective character of the symbolic imagination. Amid many differences in historical circumstances and developments, these common components provided the manner and mode of negotiation and adaptation for those who submitted themselves to the variant spiritual disciplines.

INTERIORITY

The language of the spiritual life is not wholly alien to certain psychologies of human development. Existentialists have written widely about the contrast between interiority and exteriority; even about the struggle to achieve a life of greater interiority although surrounded and bombarded by exterior pulls and pushes. Henri Bergson (1935) distinguished between knowing a man from within -- his interior disposition and fundamental orientation -- and from without, the things about him, the exterior characteristics and circumstances. Kurt Wolff (1974, 1976) distinguishes between "being" and "leading a life." And Abraham Maslow (1962) dealt with a similar distinction in discussing the ways in which the human individual would achieve greater self-actualization.

Spiritual well-being, it seems to me, is to be found and measured in terms of greater interiority, of acting rather than merely reacting, of being a source, an origin, an initiator. One might develop measures of "integrity" in which the emphasis would be on interiority, that is, being gathered rather than scattered. Moreover, the power to "complete" or to "perfect" what has begun or has been done, half done, prevented, or perverted, is a peculiar power of the person who possesses heightened interiority.

One searches for appropriate ways of discerning spiritual well-being. Some components in the various spiritual traditions I have referred to would give the following emphases: there would be joy rather than sadness or acedia; openness to change rather than being fixed, rigid, or set in one's ways; a dealing with life and the living rather than with death and the dying; a growing sensuousness (tasting, touching, hearing, seeing, smelling) as opposed to the excessively rational, analytic, mere thought; an involvement in objects of life rather than in objects of mere study; participants in the cosmos rather than mere spectators who are occupied merely in gawking; a feeling of being bound by major symbols as opposed to being unbound or not bound by any symbols.

One need not immediately use the language of functional alternatives to discern that surely the paths toward achieving many of these modes of spiritual well-being are not to be confined to a few spiritual traditions. And surely there are now developing ways of achieving these results through means that seem to be merely psychological. But I insist that we must explore in much greater detail what the phenomenon is before becoming preoccupied with what is religiously unique about it, if anything at all.

I would emphasize the notes of joy, growing sensuousness, and being bound by symbols as the central components of spiritual well-being in the diverse Catholic spiritual traditions. These would serve as indicators of interiority.

INDIVIDUATION

The sociological inquiry into spiritual well-being in our time is most appropriately directed to considerations of individuation. This is particularly the case in assessing the predicaments and dilemmas of Catholic spiritual traditions, but it undoubtedly has pertinence for the more general situation.

Simmel's (1950, 1971) essays on individuality in the 18th and 19th centuries provide the basic ingredients for the analysis. He had noted that individuality in the 18th century exemplified singleness, with emphasis on the individual's being equal and free. In the 19th century, the equality of man is underscored but now mainly characterized by uniqueness. An outcome of these developments was that individual development and perfection was becoming separated from the development and perfection of society. The release from constraints which has ushered in the new freedom and the recognition of the equality of all men soon provided the context in which individual perfectibility no longer was closely associated with the perfection of society.

18

On this score, as Robertson (1976) has pointed out, Durkheim's insistence on the collective as being an integral component in the development of the individual seems quite different from Weber's analysis in which the individual grows by opposition to, even by escaping from the controlling character of, society.

I would advance the argument a step further by suggesting that individuality in the 20th century has taken on additional qualities which Simmel (1971) implied but did not discuss. It seems to me that in our time there has been a widespread blurring of collective boundaries so that the Weberian individual finds himself without a clearly defined target for his opposition; and further, the indistinct boundaries undermine the haven in which the Durkheimian individual can develop. In this situation, the individual becomes plural either in fact (already so for many) or in possibility. The separation of individual perfection from society's perfection becomes even more pronounced. In effect, the individual in the 20th century becomes a symbolic migrant.

Instead of looking at religion merely in the continuing argument about its contribution to the stability or change of society, it might well be more profitable to study society's troubles or predicaments through the troubles or predicaments manifested by religion. This suggestion carries a Durkheimian flavor, but it also reflects a perennial conviction in Catholic spiritual traditions. In none of them was spiritual development divorced from the concern over society's situation and perfection. It may well be that in the study of religion today we find evidence that the individual has become a symbolic migrant.

By symbolic migrant I mean to say that there is no single, over-arching collectivity which commands the allegiance of the individual; further, there is no collectivity which can exercise total control over the individual except, of course, in instances of totalitarian coercion. The individual becomes plural through his multiple belongings and thereby controls his allegiances and can refuse the controls of each collectivity.

For some, the notion of plural man sounds no different than the notion of multiple roles stemming from multiple social positions. But role analysis is inadequate in understanding the individual. Let me suggest a richer approach in which I would then distinguish three levels: (1) The most basic is the level of fundamental options (l'option fondamentale) in which orientations to the world are shaped. In earlier periods of history, a fundamental option may have occurred a few times in an individual's life, but most often it was rare. Because of more widespread migrations, both physical and symbolic, there may be more frequent "fundamental options" in the life course of the individual. If significant change occurs at all, it usually happens when the individual is freer and less determined. (2) A second level is role analysis in which are identified first the social positions and then the behaviors expected from those who occupy the positions, with of course considerable refinements about whose expectations they are. (3) The third level is more superficial, that is, on the surface, in the face of things. Goffman (1959, 1969) has perhaps written the most extensively about the situational determinants and typical behaviors in public places.

The first, deeper level, is less frequently changing, but its transformation is more profound. The second level is more visible but is still difficult to measure because many sociologists now recognize that roles are constantly being negotiated. I think it more obvious that the multiplicity of roles (not merely role-set) could be referred to as some form of pluralization. Nevertheless, it is at the deeper (first) level that pluralization is also occurring. It is happening at the level of consciousness and conscience,and it frequently manifests the dynamics of cultural conflicts and inter-civilizational encounters.

It is at this deeper level that the interiority-exteriority dialectic takes place. There is the pull toward a scattering of one's spiritual world and thus the basis for one's spiritual well-being. There is also the push toward the merely competitive processes, but now with weak and weakened social rewards and sanctions, both powerful supports in the formation and exercise of conscience. The individual is more on his own. In his autonomy there is no single, surely no total, and frequently no clear moral culture. The individual has been more fully liberated from constraints but is ambivalent about what appears to be an empty world. There is as a consequence a continuing search for symbol and symbol system to which one feels bound -- not captured and imprisoned, but bound.

The Catholic spiritual traditions have been particularly conducive to the development of spiritual disciplines, which in turn became models for large populations. In our time there seems to be no spiritual discipline for advanced industrialized society. We are currently unsure about scarcity and abundance, and about their connections in economic orders. We are unstuck; there is no center, or at least the center does not hold. We are, in effect, symbolic migrants, searching for more or taking what we can get.

SYMBOLIC MIGRATION

It is curious that the 20th century has been the century of displaced persons, individuals who because of wars, revolutions, political independences, or dramatic changes in agriculture have been uprooted and forced to move elsewhere to make a home. What is becoming more evident is the extent of symbolic migrations, the uprootings and displacements that stem from the absence of an abiding moral universe or of a recognized religious world.

Victor Turner's (1974) work is of course central; a recent statement of it appeared in 1977. His use of van Gennep's Rites de passage has been creative and suggestive. Although he has only recently begun to deal with modern or advanced societies, he recognizes the need to adapt the simpler notions of segrégation, marge et reaggrégation. The notion of the liminal -- from the Latin limen meaning threshold -- is central to an understanding of social and cultural migrations. The preliminal, the liminal, and the postliminal all address the issue of boundaries and passages from one status to another, from one social and moral universe to another. (Some contemporaries may prefer the revolving door, betwixt and between, neither inside nor outside, however much in motion.)

We may well be in a situation of permanent liminality. And a more general theory of religious behavior may have to address the systems of meaning, the modes of identity, and the definitions of reality in the widespread circumstance of liminality. Communitas in Turner's (1974, 1977) meaning -- at first a mode of anti- structure -- is pregnant with possible meaning. It may suggest liminality in the interstices of structure, or marginality at the edge of structure or inferiority from beneath structure. One could argue that communitas is to solidarity as Bergson's (1935) open morality is to closed morality.

While Catholic spiritual traditions may never be fully satisfied with the extant Protestant solutions to identity and to systems of meaning, many individuals within them are now seizing the available models in their symbolic migrations. So we find Catholic fundamen- talists, charismatics, pentecostals, high church, thomists, revival- ists, rationalists, mere ethicists, and so on; all of this adds on to the previous diversity. It is, indeed, taking place in a world in which the boundaries among religious bodies are becoming indistinct and in which there are myriad pilgrimages to other moral universes, to other spiritual worlds. What is not evident is the emergence of a spiritual discipline which will take up the new knowledges and new possibilities in our advanced technical civiliza- tion, so that everyday life may be guided, at least in broad out- line, by some clearly identifiable sets of ideals, aims, purposes, meanings, practices.

SOCIETY AND SPIRITUAL WELL-BEING

Let me refer briefly to a possible connection between society and spiritual well-being. Some authors have raised the issue of spiritual well-being in its sociological aspects by tracing the recent history of efforts at developing measures of quality of life. I have found most measures of quality of life to be only remotely connected with spiritual well-being. I would suggest, however, that a fruitful approach would be to analyze those societal conditions which make individual spiritual well-being easier or more difficult. Among other candidates I suggest the following:
1. The importance of language. Situations in which the integrity of

21

words is respected and there is usually truthfulness in statements, especially by public officials, are conducive to the individual's efforts at achieving interiority and integrity. It is surely more difficult for one who is surrounded by manipulations, deceits, lies, and deceptions.

2. The quality of <u>conversations</u> in families, churches, workplaces, and so on, as opposed to the Babel (to use the biblical term) or the cacophony of strident voices.

3. Whether members of the society are truly <u>participants</u> in political processes or merely alienated members of a mass society. It is important to note that Catholic spiritual traditions have tended to be preoccupied with political participation rather than with involvement in economic orders.

4. The availability of <u>music and poetry</u> that is truly expressive of the people and not merely the ceaseless production of narcissistic postures and performances.

These passing references do no more than suggest the importance of a language that communicates truth, conversations with mutual respect, participation in the politics of the people, and collective expressions of and for the people. They also imply the corresponding corruptions of the culture.

Their extreme absence renders difficult the achievement of spiritual well-being. The void they would leave requires more forceful initiative by the individual who is without a congenial environment for achieving joy, and without a sense of being bound by symbols which enrich as well as express his life.

Chapter 3

SPIRITUAL WELL-BEING AS A VARIETY

OF GOOD MORALE

Harold Fallding

This paper will attempt to develop an idea that I have
broached previously in several places (Fallding, 1958; 1968:
95-97, 122; 1974: 3-30, 183-186, 194-196). This is the notion
that "spiritual experience" is essentially the thing we sometimes
also call good morale, in that it is a case of the shedding of
self-consciousness and self-concern, the release, that comes
through losing oneself in some system of order. In the 1958
paper I was concerned with definition. One observation I made in
the 1968 book is that this same kind of experience can result
from immersion in systems at quite different levels of experience.
Thus, without denying that they are different experiences, we can
acknowledge that they comprise one class of experiences. To me
it seems important that we always keep in mind both the likeness
and differences of experiences in this class. As I put it:
    People can find "delight" in art and "fun" in games
    because they are the sort of creatures that can find
    "service" in institutions and "blessing" in religion.
    These are not the same things by any means, but they
    are the same kinds of things. Their achievement rests
    on the same kinds of conditions. It is a precarious
    prize always, but it is a prize that is taken when a
    set of persons surrender to rules that immerse them in
    a system where they "lose themselves" (Fallding, 1968:   122).
In my 1974 book I elaborated on and illustrated the ways in which
this kind of release is sought in religion specifically: it is
sought differently in the religion of natural need fulfillment
from the way in which it is sought in salvation religion (or
what I think can also be called the religion of spiritual satisfaction). In the former, the morale in question is born from the
confidence that all one's natural needs will be supplied. It
is the repose in providence as expressed, for example, in asser-
ting "The Lord is my shepherd, I shall not want." The morale
in salvation religion is more the confidence we demand once our
need for spiritual release becomes self-conscious. It is the

confidence that one will always stay high -- if I may put it
that way. That is, regardless of fluctuations in personal fortune, moods, merit, and the like, the person is confident that
he will remain immovably taken out of himself.

Both because spiritual well-being is sought at these different
levels in the evolution of religious culture and because it is
sought by different means in the different ways of salvation,
we need criteria of spiritual well-being that are trans-faith
and trans-cultural. Some would question whether such criteria
can ever be found. They will argue, probably, that it is from
the religions themselves that any knowledge of such criteria
comes to us. So in adopting criteria we will simply be taking
directions from the religions and, moreover, will most likely be
choosing between them, since some may appeal to us more. Yet,
even if it be true that religious thinkers have provided much
of what we choose to use, I do not think that prevents an independent scientific approach. What is necessary for that approach
is that we give a reasoned defense of the criteria we propose,
as being coherent among themselves and able to discriminate between
cases in the relevant way. This scientific approach will not
only make comparison across faiths possible, but it will bring
a liberating provisionality to our thinking. For, in science,
such criteria are acknowledged to be simply conventions, and
could well be replaced by others if we came to see reason for
that. Nor would the validity of such criteria necessarily be
suspect if they showed, for example, that the followers of some
religious traditions are more likely to score high than the
followers of others. Since the surviving religions are forced
into a controversy among themselves as to where the greater truth
lies, it is not unlikely that the criteria implicit in some of
them could show a closer matching to the scientific ones.

There is one further preliminary. I must make clear where I
see a discussion of this kind dove-tailing into the completer
output of scientific labor. This is a theoretical discussion
of the criteria appropriate for isolating a concept, not an
operationalization of indices for making empirical measurements.
Operationalization is, I believe, the absolutely indispensable
next step. But that next step can be taken only with concrete
research situations in mind. I doubt that one can operationalize
many concepts in general, as if one were to set up to compile a
student's compendium of operational indices from one's arm-chair
and send it out for general use around the globe. On the other
hand, one may discuss theoretical criteria in general. It is my
belief that one should always make a considerable pause at this
point before plunging into the empirical phase of the work, since
one runs a definite risk of adopting inappropriate indices if
one does not. Now the broadest criterion of spiritual well-
being which I propose to use is a confidence in facing life's

realities. In a way, this may be taken to sum up the whole matter. But it is itself made recognizable by and can be factorized into four subordinate criteria, viz. : (i) a life-facing realism, (ii) a surrender to the control of the inclusive unity, (iii) a stable purposiveness and identity gained, and (iv) a shedding of self-consciousness and self-concern. We shall consider each of these in turn.

I think it is fair to say that these criteria exemplify the four facets of morale that have been recognized to be quite general, to be present regardless of the situation. For there is always (i) a challenge and this is met by (ii) a unified or cohesive effort to which the person is subordinated. Then (iii) the purposes developed in the course of that effort become the person's own, while (iv) the support drawn from the combined effort and the confidence inspired by its effectiveness relieve the person of anxiety over the challenge being met. The concept of morale itself has not been as carefully examined in sociology as one would like, even though studies making use of it have been undertaken in contexts as diverse as industry and war. It was mainly the group dynamics movement that gave recognition to morale as a group-generated force, and it was generally assumed that a cohesive group is a high morale group. Studies showed that individuals identified with groups that effectively secured their interests, and they were willing to accept whatever group control was needed to make them productive at the level that the group required. Relationships in such groups were structured cooperatively rather than competitively, and a consensus in perceptions and commitments was developed through democratic procedures where that was the expected way or, as in the case of the army, through acceptable leadership. (For behavioral studies involving considerations of morale see Berkowitz, 1956; Deutsch, 1973; Gerard and Rabbie, 1961; Kahn and Katz, 1953; Roethlisberger and Dickson, 1961; Schachter, 1959; Schachter et al., 1951; Seashore, 1954; Shils and Janowitz, 1948; Triplett, 1898; White and Lippitt, 1960.)

A LIFE-FACING REALISM

A rock-bottom element of concern in religion, irrespective of the tradition, is that any morale one can muster is to be enjoyed only in the full face of life's realities. It is not to be had by entertaining illusions or evading unpleasant, disturbing, or exacting aspects of life but, on the contrary, in full cognizance of them. Indeed, it could be because life contains seriously threatening and disconcerting contingencies that the religious concern is born.

To measure spiritual well-being, then, we need to distinguish this life-facing realism from Polyanna optimism. It would supply a kind of base measure to know whether the person himself has measured life's cup of bitterness to the full -- not necessarily

to have drunk it, but to know and feelingly accept as fact all
that it contains. Buddhism's frank concentration on the fact of
suffering and Christianity's on the fact of sin illustrate what
I mean. On the other hand, the alternative possibility of evasion
might be illustrated in the evasion of a recognition of death
recently observed in North America. The same evasion is also
illustrated there in that heartless farewell where people assure
each other that nothing untoward will happen to them, pledging
not to as much as admit that it could. Contrary to the religious
conviction that some have won, that whatever happens will be for
the best, the sentiment here is that only the best can be contem-
plated to happen.

There is typically an opposition between the religious and
other attitudes over this very question of how much reality to
face. Other attitudes defend a norm of not looking too deeply
at either the "gloomy" or "puzzling" aspects of life, of adaptation by evasion. But the religious attitude considers this short-
sightedness a false expediency. It considers that the long-
sightedness that takes everything into account is the true awareness, and that this will lead in turn to the true practicality.
It is determined to be radical at any cost, in the original
meaning of the word; that is, to forestall false starts by going
directly to the root of things. One thing its honesty brings
it to is the arrestment experienced before paradox, for it finds
life too big to be gotten around by any simple accounting. It
is brought to humor for the same reason. Since the honest accounts
of life's separate aspects will never entirely cohere, their dis-
continuities generate incongruities. I shall suggest that the
realism we are discussing is equivalent to seriousness. Yet
it is a seriousness that in no way excludes humor; on the contrary,
humor is indispensable to it.

We have Hamlet's (Shakespeare, 1953: 1017) list of provoca-
tions for one itemization of life's threatening and disconcerting
realities. He questioned whether suicide might even be nobler
than enduring them. What he was naming in his renowned soliloquy
was inescapable features of the human condition. It is simply
a fact that such features of our life as these can be known
through reflection on it; yet people vary in their awareness and
acceptance of them, and the lives they live vary greatly in
consequence. We can name more even than Hamlet names. Perhaps
such contingencies could be arranged systematically in a classification, although it would be difficult to make it exhaustive.
Death, aging, sickness, accident, and disaster remind us of the
frailty and temporality of everyone's very existence. The
limited nature of all individual abilities reminds us of our
dependence on human cooperation, itself difficult to achieve,
precarious, and limited in turn in what it can accomplish. The
limitation of natural resources leaves the threat of scarcity
and want ever-present and exacerbates competition.

Because of these limitations, and because we must so often
act in ignorance, as well as for other reasons, there is the
possibility of frustration and failure in all personal and collective undertakings. In addition, things constructed through
great labor and cost, whole civilizations in fact, can fall into
ruin. Within us are warring inclinations, and our ability to
master them is not certain. Willfully or wantonly we can be the
perpetrators of crimes and sins, and we can be the victims of
those committed by others: of ingratitude, deception, theft,
violence, brutality, and much besides. We can both contribute
to and suffer from the ravages of war, anarchy, or government-
achieved injustice and tyranny.

My point is not to make a trite recapitulation of self-evident
truths. Rather it is that there is a certain awakening when a
person acknowledges, feelingly, that these are the kind of realities that constrain him. But the attitude taken toward them is
just as much a part of the awareness in that awakening. I want
to call it an accepting attitude, yet I do not want to be misunderstood. It is not pretending that evil is good but acknowledging
it as a given that must be taken into account. It is not an
indifference that neglects the improvements that can be made,
but an acknowledgment that there is a limit to the improvement
possible and that human life is a mixture of control over circumstances and being controlled by them. The realization pursued
in Zen Buddhism is very much this awareness. The Jewish insistence
that man should remember his creatureliness before God is also.
The same insistence is in Christianity, for the yoke that is easy
and the burden that is light, which Jesus offers to share, are
the yoke and burden of the humility in this realization. But
possibly the thing that is more distinctive of Christianity in
this connection is the insistence that one come to the conviction
of sin. It is made possible to acknowledge oneself a sinner
with this same kind of acceptance, because grace is shown to
mean that God himself is thus accepting.

These considerations will show that if we make this reality-
acceptance a part of our measure of spiritual well-being, we will
be giving points to those who have learned from a variety of traditions, as well as to others, perhaps, who have realized the awareness independently. What that awareness imparts is a particular
poise, the beauty of seriousness. Yet this poise, and the awareness of the problems inherent in reality that allows it, are no
more than the foundation of the confidence in facing the life in
which those problems inhere. It is that confidence, rounded to
its completeness, that makes the good morale of spiritual well-
being.

A SURRENDER TO THE CONTROL OF THE INCLUSIVE UNITY

It is essentially a confidence that none of life's shadows or

27

negatives, if I may call them that, can be undoing in any final
sense. They cannot prevent the successful attainment of the positive good, and they may even be turned to good account in reaching
it. For, real though all these shadows are, they are not everything. There is a larger pattern of which they are but a part
and in which the person himself is also immersed. That larger
pattern makes a system of order, a unity, and that unity has the
ultimate control -- including a control over the person. Life's
dire contingencies belong to the foreground where his own exercise
of control tries its limits and experiences frustration. In
the background beyond are the forces to which he can only surrender,
and within whose grasp he is simply held. To live uninjured by
life's dire contingencies, he must pass into the control of these
forces that have also mastered them. In relation to these ultimate
realities, then, he is primarily passive, a recipient of what
they have to give. To rest properly in their lap a certain discipline expressing a due respect for them is required; but,
that given, he is taken hold of, mastered and made secure. To
find himself thus anchored and located gives meaning to his life
and release. He knows that he does not have to anxiously and
feverishly strive on his own account, but is taken care of.

One way in which this self-inclusion in a background is realized
is through affirming dogmatic belief; this belief will be more or
less systematic. One could illustrate very simply with two
increments in this filling in of background in the early development of the Hebrew tradition: in the aftermath of the flood
(The Bible, Genesis 6-9) and in the experience of Abraham (Genesis
12-25). The flood was understood as a punishment for widespread
sinfulness, for only Noah had been good in his time. But after
the flood God is found promising to fasten mankind secure in his
mercy and to never again put the earth under a curse because of
what man does. The rainbow he sets in the sky is the sign of
his covenant to cause a regular succession of seasons for the
ripening of crops, so sustenance needs will be guaranteed for as
long as the earth remains. This belief obviously put a supporting
frame around the life of the individual who cherished it. A
similar but more specifically detailed support was derived from
a later covenant. God pledges to be the God of Abraham and his
descendents, to make them prosper in a land of their own, and to
make Abraham the father of many nations. Every male child born
under the provisions of this covenant is to be circumcised as an
an acknowledgment of the security that has been guaranteed.

However, while we can indeed see a larger context for a self-
inclusion effected through specific measures like these, it
finds its fullest expression in that total cosmos that the individual takes for the background of his life. It is quite characteristic of developed religious thought-systems to take in that
total sweep, to sketch in existence from its beginning to end,
and to bid the individual live out his career against this.

28

The Jew is enjoined to adhere to the people that God has chosen to show the nations that he is a merciful savior and righteous judge. The Christian's and Muslim's career is a phase in the great unfolding leading from creation to judgment, and to a realm beyond judgment where faithfulness is vindicated. The Hindu's and Buddhist's career is part of the great cosmic movement of creatures through the cycle of rebirths, and of an eventual extrication from this. It is inclusion within such all-inclusive schemes that brings the person meaning and release from anxiety, and it is the person's profiting from such a scheme that measures of spiritual well-being would need to tap.

But we can encounter an alternative expression of the self-inclusion we are discussing in the mystical experience of union. Mainline orthodoxies have characteristically been ambivalent about the mysticism practiced amongst their following. Possibly this is because mystical experience can be set up as normative, to the great consternation of those among the faithful who are not capable of it. Mysticism has many degrees, of course; the direct apprehension of one's inclusion in reality's unity is one of the most advanced. Even persons who are able to reach lesser mystical states on occasion may never reach this. It is therefore understandable that the status to be accorded to mystical experience should become an issue in the religious community. But it is just as much an issue for anyone attempting a scientific assessment of spiritual well-being, for we will need to know whether we are to make it a requirement for spiritual well-being, or whether we are to treat it as being, in some sense or another, optional or additional.

My own inclination is to regard the capacity for mystical experience as one of our individual differences, just as intelligence and musical and mathematical ability are individual differences. A person who has it and cultivates it possesses a means of apprehending directly the unity that may otherwise be apprehended through dogma. This may enhance his own assurance and make him more willing to come under that unity's control. But it may do much the same for others in the community if the mystic communicates his discoveries to them; for we may presume that his gift can work to their benefit as much as to his own. If mysticism is evaluated in this way, we see that it is not, in itself, either equivalent to spiritual well-being or necessary for it in the individual case. Thus we can proceed to measure for spiritual well-being leaving it out of account, while acknowledging that in some cases it may have been a means through which that well-being was attained. An analogy might be helpful. Muscular strength is not, in and of itself, physical health. Some persons have considerably more muscular strength than others, but they are not necessarily healthier because of it, even though the health they achieve will partly depend on exercising the muscles they have. We may therefore compare measures of health, leaving

measures of strength out of account. As a matter of fact, it
might be worth adding that the adulation sometimes accorded to
mysticism seems to me quite out of proportion. The capacity
for mysticism is sometimes taken to comprise the pinnacle of
human ability. But, at best, it is only one among diverse
gifts whose benefits must be shared if members of a believing
community are to mature in faith.

Whether realized with the assistance of mysticism or without
it, the sense of being located in a controlling ground is sufficiently the same in different cases for us to name some of its
properties. And, although I use the term "ground" for my generalizing, I will not necessarily mean what it is sometimes made
to mean, namely that abyss or desert of Godhead by which mystics
like Tauler (1901: 93-106, 321-324), Ruysbroeck (1916: 167-
178), and Saint John of the Cross (1908) characterize God negatively
at the apex of contemplation. In the sense of self-location
that I have in mind, there can be a more widely shared set of
ingredients. Accounts of everyday religious experience refer to
them repeatedly; I think especially of the accounts given in
hymns and other more mater-of-fact religious writing like that of,
say, George Fox (1911), John Wesley (1909-16), Charles Wesley
(1762), John Bunyan (1970a, 1970b), John Donne (1912, 1953-
62), Gerard Manley Hopkins (1967), and T.S. Eliot (1970). There
can, for example, be an overwhelming sense of relief. There can
be a profound subduing and composure, a deeply-breathing peace.
There can be a sense not of seeking but finding, of a once-and-
for-all coming home. There can be a sorrowing repentance for
having resisted and shut oneself out. There can be a welling
confidence, not in oneself but in that which has taken control.
There can be an ardor in selfgiving to it, and a thrill of fulfillment in finding that it was for outpouring that one was made.
There can be a sense of unsurpassable significance from the
greatness of that to which one is given. There can be a sense of
wholeness from the singleness of devotion it compels. There can
be a weightlessness from the loss of self-importance before it.
There can be a sense of cleanliness from knowing, from one's
acceptance, that one's sins are forgiven. There can be a sense
of openness from being made generous and forgiving in turn. There
can be a joy without measure in knowing all good possessed.

It seems to be a human universal to quest for happiness, and
it has also been common to report that it is not to be found where
one at first supposed. Coveted pleasures have a tendency to cloy
and become distasteful and enslaving. Some people make a distinction by speaking of true and lasting happiness, and then insist
on that. Not everyone reaches this level of discrimination,
however, and many continue unchecked to seek happiness where
others would say it cannot be found: in hedonism, for instance,
or in things like success, wealth, power, and distinction.
Amsterdam, when I visited it in 1978, was described to me as a

Mecca of modern pleasure-seekers. I found it hard to believe
that those in its streets were any more intent on happiness than
other people are, but there were evidences that many had settled
for it in what some would call passing pleasure, and that some
were its slaves. A guided tour not long before had taken me
into the gambling halls at Monte Carlo, and I saw faces there
wearing the same fixed weariness as I saw on certain faces in
Amsterdam. But I have also seen the same tortued hardness on
the faces of the ambition-driven in academia and in places of
finance and business. The seeker after lasting happiness is one
who refuses to rest in entanglements like those. He claims
that it is a different thing altogether -- true happiness --
when he surrenders control and lays down his burdens in spiritual
release.

He may also call it lasting happiness and this has its own
significance. For this happiness has a peculiar way of linking
past, present, and future for the person who finds it. Spiritual
release seems to him transcendent, so the present moment assumes
eternal significance for him. Yet he finds that what he has now
continues unabated through each subsequent "now." As a result,
in retrospect he is able to recall having it before and, in prospect, can anticipate having it still. But this happiness is
lasting in a profounder sense as well. For it is the rising of
desire itself, the very awakening of thirst, that brings the
returning waves of unhappiness that ruffle the erstwhile silenced
sea. Now these waves no longer come, for desire cannot rise
above the surfeit of satisfactions already offered. The person
cannot thirst again, and his peace and joy stem from that. Desire
has been extinguished, not by attacking it to eradicate it,
buy by a blessedness exceeding all that it can ask. Life after
this discovery is oriented so differently from life without it
that the person can only be said to have been converted. Yet
a few observations need to be made concerning the status that is
to be given to the actual conversion experience. The same circum-
spection has to be exercised regarding this as in regard to mysticism.

I think it is objectively true that anyone who makes this
discovery has been converted. But the actual conversion experience, the actual initiation that is, can be very variable. It
is possible that the person may be completely unconscious of the
conversion even though he cannot remain unconscious of what he
is converted to. On the other hand, the conversion itself may
be an intense experience, having both height and depth to it,
exhilaration and disturbance. The actual unfolding depends
partly on the temperament and training of the person, but also on
the preparation for entry that he has undergone and the state
of mind into which that preparation has brought him. For such
reasons I think we can leave the actual conversion experience
out of account when we measure spiritual well-being, just as we
can leave mystical experience out of account. Once again, an

analogy may help us. Everyone on a street-car has the benefit
of the ride, irrespective of the door by which they enter or
whether they waited an hour to catch it or jumped in breathless
from a chase.

Some may ask if there is anything left by which to measure
this factor of being under control, if we bracket out the conversion experience of initiation to it and the mystical experiences
that may be incidental to its growth. I think there is still
much to take note of, and there are four sides to it. First,
there is the discipline the person exercises in order to put
himself in the place where the power beyond him takes control.
Secondly, there are his various specific sensings of the control
impinging on him, of the kinds that I have itemized. Thirdly,
the person will have his own way of describing the object of
control that is impinging on his life, be it in dogmatic or mystical terms or a combination of these. But we are clearly reckoning
with the faith factor here; to explore the fourth aspect we will
need a probe that tries to lay that bare. For the believing
person can have no conclusive proof of the unity and its control,
yet he is prepared to be provisional about it and to act as if it
were sure.

A STABLE PURPOSIVENESS AND IDENTITY GAINED

While superficial thinking might lead us to suppose that the
surrender or engulfment just described dissolves the self totally,
the opposite is the case. It achieves a firmness and distinctness
unknown before; this would seem altogether credible if we think
of it as the internalization of the unity in which it rests.
Some mystical writing suggests the dissolution of the self, and
there is a sense in which that does occur, since the former ego
and its importance disappear. But the completer account of mystical
union testifies to another self being securely realized, and
dogmatic religion speaks of the salvation of the soul. We can
therefore take the strength of such a self as a further measure
of spiritual well-being.

It might be pertinent at this point to say that I consider
projection to be the mechanism involved in the realization both
of this self and of the ground we have just been discussing.
That is to say, the person gives content to the unity that con-
strains him through an idealization of the actual social relations in which his life is lived. His sense of a self is then
his confident expectation that this ideal will be actualized in
his experience. Already present to him as potentiality, he
believes it will eventually be present as actuality, and he has
a sense of continuity through being headed in that same direction
through all the time taken to attain it. It is in this sense
that he becomes what he is and continues to be what he was. But
this projection aspect of the self I have dealt with in another

paper (Fallding, 1978), and my Sociology of Religion (1974) enlarges on projection as it relates to the ground. It is therefore not necessary to go into this here.

Yet we do need to bear in mind here the part that purposiveness plays in giving content to the self. What am I? I am those satisfactions that I first chose and then have succeeded in enjoying, either in the past or present, as well as those chosen satisfactions I confidently expect to enjoy. We think of an identity when we think of a self, and it is with satisfaction that we identify. Presumably this is because satisfaction is an indication to us of some kind of fulfillment attained: a matching has taken place between what we were made to have and what has been secured. Satisfaction, in thus showing us what we were made to have, draws a profile of us that we would not have otherwise. But there is an intervening matching in addition, for what intervenes is an appropriate choice. I chose to seek the satisfaction I found, and in so far as the object chosen was capable of yielding satisfaction, my choice rightly divined my need. The self, then, could be likened to the density that comes into the profile line when three sheets of rice paper, bearing identical drawings, are superimposed and the drawings made to coincide. The need-outline, chosen-goal-outline, and satisfaction-outline lie one above the other, reinforcing the solidity of the line I see.

We have also, of course, to take account of the evolutionary factor here: it is simply a question of what is sufficient to satisfy. What satisfies the less evolved consciousness is no longer sufficient in itself to satisfy the more evolved -- identity is invested in a different thing accordingly. This is the variability I drew attention to toward the beginning of this paper. At first, as was indicated, it is the fulfillment of the natural needs that satisfies. At that level, the ground in which one rests is seen as the supplier of such needs, and it is relied upon as an active providence. The more evolved consciousness wants this still, but more besides. It now wants the assurance of remaining immovably taken out of itself by permanent absorption into the ground. At this point the ground is relied upon as an active savior. My reason for referring to this again here is to point out that this variability in the content of the self will have to be allowed for when measuring the strength of identity as an index of spiritual well-being. But how is that strength to be recognized?

This self has a unity of organization that reflects the unity of that within which it lives; this means that its elements are harnessed to the same purpose. Indeed, its purpose is given to it by that unity: it can generate no availing purpose from itself. What is its own particular contribution to that wider, cosmic purpose? It is a dedication to securing its needs as it understands them at its own particular level of evolutionary understanding, and assisting its fellows to secure theirs. Strategically placed to secure the needs of itself and of selves near it, this self seeks to have all these selves freed from want, or, later, it seeks their salvation. It seeks nothing else besides, and that economy gives it purity. True to self in this sense, not lured away by temptations or deflected by distractions, it has integrity. It also has a constancy, persevering through time with great patience against every obstacle in its one endeavor. More than this, it has a vibrant expectancy, which is what hope means when understood theologically. For it is assured that the perfection of satisfaction that is not yet attained will come to it at last. There is a principle of life itself in hope for human beings: we are alive to the extent that we live in eager anticipation of the yet-to-be. The presence or absence of this anticipation is what distinguishes, for instance, between one aged person and another: if we say an aged person is still youthful, it is because he or she still looks forward eagerly to the future.

If this expectancy factor seems to contradict what was said concerning present happiness, it is only because language is limited. It is true that spiritual well-being means happiness attained in the present. But it is equally true that present happiness includes the anticipation of a development to come. Moreover, this expectancy may exact a prodigious frustration from the self while it awaits the consummation. Some who maintained spiritual well-being have had their powers frozen through prolonged imprisonment, or impaired through illness, or shadowed through lack of recognition or rejection, or cut off entirely through early death. For as long as they lived they were able to persevere and, if need be, adapt their course drastically, confident that nothing can eclipse the effectiveness of authentic living eventually. It seems, indeed, that this self finds much of its realization only through suffering; this fact should prevent us from construing the happiness we spoke of as any frothy freedom from trouble and pain. Partly through knowing its own costliness, then, this is a self-valuing self, respecting itself and loving itself. It is, as well, a self-relishing self that enjoys itself, a richly pasturing self that feeds deeply on its own fulfilled inwardness and will not give it in exchange for the entire world. Put all this together, and it is not inappropriate to say that it is a stable purposiveness and identity gained. People everywhere acknowledge the need for purposiveness, of course. But, just as there is a disagreement between the religious and other attitudes over true awareness and true happiness, so is there a disagreement over the true purposiveness. Other attitudes will let purposes multiply out of anxious cares, like a garden given back to the wilderness, thereby expecting to fill life full. Only religious purposiveness displays the austere pruning of seeking nothing save what the cosmos seeks -- selves that were destined to be; thereby seeking the fullness of life by the narrow way.

If its looking to its own need makes this seem a reprehensibly
selfish self to some readers, all I can suggest is that a self
could scarcely conceive a care for other selves without having
conceived a care for itself. It is that care that it is able to
extend to the other. Furthermore, without a concern for its own
satisfaction, it can hardly be motivated to move and so come to a
self. Religions have never considered it unworthy to seek one's
daily bread and one's own salvation. Kierkegaard (1941) made a
right willing to be oneself the cure for the spiritual sickness
that leads to spiritual death. Jesus inveighed against people who
labored for the food that perished, but still expected them to
labor for the food that did not. Food was an image of satisfaction
enjoyed, and he said his own food was to do the will of the Father
(The Bible, John 4: 31-34; 6: 25-59). He found satisfaction in
pursuing that will, and he is represented in the Epistles as having
endured the cross for the sake of the joy that was set before him
(The Bible, Hebrews 12: 2). Indeed, it is hard to believe that the
seeking of fulfillment which I have depicted -- for oneself and for
others -- can be anything other than doing the will of God. One
would think God must will this: certainly Jesus' "good works"
largely consisted of seeking this for people, and he summarized
the Decalogue teaching as love of God, neighbor, and self (The
Bible, Matthew 22: 34-40). People often talk, sometimes crypti-
cally, about knowing and doing the will of God when presented with
alternatives. But, whatever the resolution is in terms of a particular action chosen, I would expect it must be an action furthering
this fulfillment.

But someone might still insist asking, how does the often-
applauded attitude of sacrifice relate to this self-seeking?
What is entailed in sacrifice requires careful examination. It
would not involve any gratuitous self-mutilation that denies
the person fulfillment when it is possible, whether that mutila-
tion be material, mental, or spiritual. What it could entail is
a renunciation of what one does not need, in order to divert
this surplus to people who are in need. Mainly, though, it seems
to entail the idea that the self is realized only by pursuing
the socially constructive course of action; that is, by securing
its place in the controlling ground rather than by "seeking its
own." Thus, sacrifice is not any perverse renunciation of one's
own good, but a realization that we can only come to the good
together. This means that there has sometimes to be some post-
ponement or marking time on one's own good, until the co-bene-
ficiaries are brought in or brought in line. The theological
idea that we cannot come to final salvation until we come to it
together supplies an instance of this. The sacrifice made by
the Mahayana Buddha, in his refusing to enjoy enlightenment alone,
supplies another instance. So also does Jesus' giving his life
for the salvation of the world -- before taking it up again
with enhanced force. Laying-down-one's-life-for-one's-friend is
scarcely a daily routine with us, except, figuratively, in the

pouring out of effort on the friend's behalf. Those crises where it actually occurs are forced by extreme situations where it is impossible that both should live. But we can still read in such actions an affirmation of the importance of self-fulfillment, since this is what one desires for the friend. There is, in any case, no repudiation of its desirability for both, but simply an acknowledgment that it is not possible for both under the circumstances. In short, the self that we have been considering is part of the life that is gained by losing it: it presupposes the repudiation of the self-sufficient ego and surrender to greater control that we have already discussed.

Before concluding this section of the paper, we ought to refer to the Atman or Overself of Hinduism and the Holy Spirit of Christianity, since these are two of the most developed notions of human subjectivity to be found in the religions. Different though these are from one another, they are alike in three ways. They both locate within the individual a principle of life that is not the phenomenal ego. For both of them, this life is the same from one individual to another. For both of them, it is a life that is also found beyond the human individual, being identical with divinity itself.

The stable identity we have been examining would seem to have very similar features, for it provides the person with a new self, rather than leaving him with nothing when the former ego crumbles. In addition, it should appear from our analysis that this is much more a self in which the person stands, so to speak, as representative man, in which he affirms himself by what his created nature contains in common with others. Without forgoing its individuality, then, this self has a universality that distinctly resembles that ascribed to the Atman and the Holy Spirit. And if, as I suggested, we view it as an internalization of the ground with which the person is encircled, then it must become in some sense a copy of the divine, and be itself divine to that extent.

A SHEDDING OF SELF-CONSCIOUSNESS AND SELF-CONCERN

We come finally to a consideration of the abandonment or shedding of self-consciousness and self-concern, the exhilaration, that is to be found in spiritual well-being, due to the confidence that one's need will be supplied. Analogies exist in the effects of solidarity in a family, a fellowship group, a business firm, a sport's team, a military unit, a nation; these will help to indicate the kind of thing I want to draw attention to now. If such groups are particularly effective in what they can accomplish through cooperation, the individual member is relieved of concern on his own behalf to that extent. He is not relieved of effort, since he is expected to be a contributor to the group. But his effort is proportioned to his capacity, so he is not

strained by being overburdened. At the same time, the benefits
coming to him exceed what he could produce alone, and they are
guaranteed. Most important of all, then, he is relieved of
anxiety and made secure. As a result, in his producer capacity
he identifies more with the "we" than the "I": I-consciousness
is eclipsed in we-consciousness. It is in this way that esprit-
de-corps induces exhilaration and takes the person out of himself.

Yet this shedding of self-consciousness because of a shedding
of self-concern in no way abolishes the self that is savored
which was just discussed. Language once again seems to fail us.
We use the expression "self-consciousness" to indicate a variety
of states. The self-consciousness lost here is more that painful
state induced when some remark has caused us to become, as we
say, "self-conscious," and embarrassed us. It is the consciousness that we have had attention drawn to us in such a way as to
isolate us. We hate to be singled out like that, and dispropor-
tionate public praise and deserved public blame seem equally able
to do it. This self-consciousness of self-isolation is acutely
painful and inhibiting. In the extreme case it can seem to be
crushing, since it leaves us with the insecure feeling that everything depends on us alone, whereas we know we are not capable of
everything. That self-consciousness is taken away in the exhilaration born of solidarity.

The exhilaration attendant on spiritual union is the same as
this. The person is not exempted from striving according to his
limited capacity, but he knows that the necessary supplementation
of that effort is certain. He knows that it is through his root-
ing in a supporting ground that his every practical need will
be met and, in the case of the person of advanced consciousness,
his offences cancelled and his soul saved. This is nothing other
than a kind of liberty -- "true freedom" the religious person
might call it to distinguish it from the thousand other things
to which the word has been applied. As we have seen, it is not
the freedom of constraint thrown off, for the person is brought
under control. But it is freedom from care: for the burden of
our own importunate ego weighs us down, its narrowness suffocat-
ingly shuts us in. This "true freedom" is admission into the
larger horizon, the infinite horizon indeed, of release from this
always finite care. Yet it is a misunderstanding of this liberty
for the person to drop tools and make no provision for his material
needs. The lesson that Jesus draws from the Heavenly Father's
provision for the birds and lilies is that we should have no
anxiety over our needs being met, not that we should neglect to
work and plan as our contribution toward it (The Bible, Matthew
6: 25-34; Luke 12: 22-31). The antinomianism of forgoing moral
constraint because one is saved by grace shows a misunderstanding
of one's liberty at another level. Since such misunderstandings
are possible, we should perhaps take warning. In attempting to
identify this factor in spiritual well-being, we will need to be

37

discriminating. Certain attitudes that resemble this abandonment will not be the genuine article. Not all the debonaire
are trusting in the Lord. Being unprepared, neglectful, resource-
less, inept, indifferent, careless, casual, and simplistic can all
give a spurious impression of this abandonment; drugs and dis-
traction can, while they last, banish care.

Gratitude for and a cherishing and stewardship of one's resources is a more likely index of what we are after. There will
be an acknowledgment that one certainly does not enjoy them
through work and merit alone. There will be a disposition to
assume that the sufficiency of today guarantees a sufficiency for
tomorrow. There is a still more exquisite poise to identify if
we are to find those who are trusting that their spiritual need
will be met, their sins pardoned, and their souls saved. Again,
they will not be indifferent to their spiritual well-being nor
neglectful of measures to insure it. But their life will be
free from self-justification. The good they do will not be done
for that; it will be an outpouring of gratitude for the inflowing
grace.

There is a certain gaiety in the lives of those who live with
this abandonment, even a playfulness, if I may put it that way
without inviting misunderstanding. I do not mean that the person
abolishes the distinction between play and work, much less that
his attitude to life is not a serious one. What I mean, rather,
is that he conducts himself as one who knows that the part that
depends on him is definitely limited. All the resources and
conditions necessary for the performance are supplied: his
part is to make the moves. He takes a delight in making them
with skill, and his whole life thereby can become an expressive
activity of worship and praise. He travels very, very lightly.
All his baggage having been freighted by air, his walk can turn
to dancing.

Possibly it is because of this detachment that such an acute
tension can arise between the political and religious attitudes.
A person who is political to the exclusion of religion can be
scandalized because the religious person enjoys life in the present, in a world that abounds with injustice and cries out for
reform. It is indeed possible that a religious person can let
himself be anaesthetized from the painful call to action by his
spiritual intoxication. But that is hardly the authentic attitude
of the person experiencing true abandonment. What spiritual
intoxication does for that person is to give him a due sense of
proportion in his political undertakings. One would expect to
find him working for greater justice, knowing that justice will
still be imperfect when change has been made, and also knowing
that the more important spiritual good is equally available in all
degrees of the world's imperfection.

CONCLUSION

It is of the essence of scientific procedure to isolate variables unequivocally from one another and then inspect for relationships between them. I have been striving for that sharp isolation of spiritual well-being. If we can achieve it, and then operationalize the factors in it, we will be able to note how it correlates with a variety of other interesting things, some of which are quite close to it and yet strictly distinguishable from it.

I have already pointed out the possibility of noting differences in spiritual well-being among adherents of the different religions. It will also be possible for adherents of the sects and denominations within any one religion to be compared for their spiritual well-being. A variety of spiritual disciplines are also canvassed within any one religion, so we could compare the spiritual well-being of persons adopting different ones.

As we have seen, genuineness is of the essence of religious practice -- so much so that the charge of hypocrisy seems to carry its greatest opprobrium there. We could, then, compare actual spiritual well-being with the claim made to it. Some people are much more explicit and vocal in their religious profession than others: we could see how this religious talkativeness correlates with spiritual well-being. Some people have a much more elaborately thought-out religious position; we could see how this religious thoughtfulness relates. We could examine how spiritual well-being relates to different expressions of practical morality and political involvement, it being one consideration to explore the issue already noted; that is, to ask whether it is ever associated with indifference or withdrawal or, alternatively, with involvement that shows a certain detachment. It is possible that the invisible religion that Luckmann (1967) documented, the religion that is not yet dogmatically formulated in any standard way, can bring spiritual well-being, and we could inspect for that. It is possible that the person who is professedly irreligious could be in a state of spiritual well-being, perhaps because his concern for truth and integrity has been thus rewarded, and we could inspect for that. Indeed, it would be an important part of my own understanding of the usefulness of a measure of spiritual well-being that it should be applied to the population at large, not simply to those who are religious by profession.

There are, finally, two whole classes of correlations that it would be particularly interesting to explore. One class consists of the correlations between spiritual well-being and what are commonly taken to be expressions of well-being at other levels. Physical health and mental health would make two of these. Spiritual well-being is by no means an exact equivalent of mental health as a psychologist would define it, even though it might be contributory to it. (For, certainly, its realism would seem to forestall the perceptual distortion of schizophrenia, its firmness of purpose the emotional exaggeration of mania and depression, and its security the anxious compulsiveness of neurosis.) Material well-being in achieved sufficiency and wealth could be correlated with spiritual well-being; also manual, mental, and artistic giftedness; also occupational fulfillment, professional success, social status, and public recognition; also the enjoyment of refined living through having intellectual and aesthetic cultivation and opportunities to exercise these.

The second especially interesting class of correlations are those between spiritual well-being and the other varieties of morale. Fun in games, delight in art, service in institutions, and morale in social contexts like those referred to in the immediately preceding section of the paper might all be examined. Is there any tendency for good morale in one of its varieties to be made to compensate for the person's not finding it in another? Alternatively, is there any tendency for the person who finds morale in one context to find it in many; is there a generalized disposition to be a morale finder? Again, whether they find it or not, is there any general tendency for some persons to be morale seekers, willing to observe the conditions for securing it in diverse contexts? If we find there are people who consistently give their priority to seeking morale, could we not say their values are spiritual values?

The reader will note how, in particular, I have felt constrained to distinguish spiritual well-being from mysticism, conversion, and mental health. It is tiresome how quickly discussion of spiritual well-being can be diverted into discussion of these other things -- and then left without attention itself. But if we attend only to other things, we are still without a measure of the supremely important thing that spiritual well-being connotes: the capacity to live a life without being knocked off the rails.

It is my suspicion that an exhaustive table of correlations between that and things like the above might contain many surprises and might, incidentally, be quite rebuking to the modern consciousness. Spiritual well-being could, indeed, be the true awareness, the true happiness, the true purposiveness, and the true freedom -- the pearl without price for which all other things can profitably be exchanged. And it might be found that many who are abundantly endowed with other things, even things closely associated with it, know very little of it.

Chapter 4

ELEMENT OF MYSTICISM IN SPIRITUAL HEALTH*

Kuldip Kumar Roy

Awakened man looks not only downward and outward but also upward
and inward. That, probably, is how he chances upon the inner worlds,
supernal powers, and a significant space for his ultimate encounter
and freedom. This leads him to discover for himself the deep and
real affinity in the conceptual understrata of mysticism and spiritual health through the mysterious chambers of his soul and the
spiritual center of the inner being. Traditional and sacred psychology, a science of subjective experience, takes for granted that
life is a means to an end beyond itself. If there are physical
sciences, there no less are metaphysical sciences of which mysticism is an important integral part. To believe the wise, once
man's knowledge of the world has grown, he is impelled to seek
another.

Man is a dweller in many dimensions. This earth alone is not
his nurse and teacher. The powers of all the worlds have their
entrance here. Man's body is a mystery shop. Some time or other,
in unguarded moments or in disciplined plunge, a feeling for the
hidden levels, "other earths," comes to almost all men. As Wordsworth,
the only poet to whom Aurobindo (1949) refers in The Synthesis of
Yoga, said:
        A meditation rose in me that night
        Upon the lofty mountains, and it appear'd to me
        The Perfect image of a Mighty Mind
        Of one that feeds upon Infinity.

Meditation is the mountain path to self-discovery. As is one's
meditation, so will be the man and his culture. Between Rodin's

---

*Besides the resources explicitly cited in this paper, Dr. Roy
calls attention to the references by Ahmed, 1962; Arberry, 1956;
Chisti, 1962; Cole and Sambhi, 1978; James, 1902; Kamali, 1960;
Kohli, 1969; Kuldip, 1971; Venkataraman, 1966, and Weber, 1958.
-- The Editor

Le Penseur and the Sarnath Dhyani Buddha, between Descartes's
Meditations and Pascal's Pensees, Husserl's Fifth Meditation and
Patanjali's Yogasutra lie realms of being, the phenomonologist's
plenty, the existentialist's Eureka.

PRANA OR DIVINE ENERGY

Mysticism is generally traced back to a period three thousand
years before Christ (Possehl, 1977). Its first signs were found
in the Indus Valley Civilization where seals and figurines were
discovered showing men and women in deep meditation, according to
Prof. Ward's Antiquity of Hinduism. These seals and figurines
were attributed to some abnormal or supernormal state of the body
through some divine power which, in effect, is nothing but prana
or divine energy. Prana starts from the base of the spine and,
when awakened, reaches the brain to produce there a higher state
of consciousness called Kundalini. In scientific terms it is the
latent organic energy at the base of the human spine, which lies
dormant until activated either by specific Hatha yoga methods or by
sense control, purification practices, and long meditation, for
which the collective term of mysticism developed over a long span
of time.

Once more interest in yoga, kundalini, transcendental and even
instant meditation has struck a new high, especially in the West,
if not the East, its original home. There is a boom in what one of
the Desert Fathers called "the Science of Sciences and the Art of
Arts." The boom is in keeping with the law of compensations. The
occupational hazards of being modern involve a series of depriva-
tions. As Merleau-Ponty (1967) pointed out, modern man has tended
to jettison the subject and look upon the body as no more than the
sum of its parts with no interior. When the Irish poet spoke of
the "centre" unable to hold, he was not making a political or sociological judgment but describing man's psychological collapse. To
be adjusted to an unjust, unprincipled milieu of nothing but "now"
living -- where "My surface is myself" -- is worse than not to be
adjusted. Can one really belong to a hookup of disvalues, puppets
and pantaloons, masked monsters and naked monomaniacs?

From all this superficiality and showmanship, scientific experiments as carried out in laboratories, particularly at the Research
Foundation for Eastern Wisdom and Western Science in Starnberg,
prove beyond doubt that achievement of a balance and a harmony
within one's own self can be expressed dynamically as a powerful
sexual force. This can result in procreation or, by guiding it up
to the brain center, it can lead to the beatific insight and experience of the mystic. It also can lead to artistic vision and
scientific awareness, regulating the health of the body, controlling the blood pressure, storing up the nervine energy, giving
that strength which enables man to concentrate, and helping the
individual's relationship to society to improve all around. The

main attribute of this state which is visible to others is poise
and dignity, an inner serenity reflected in the outward demeanor.

Prof. C.F. von Weizsaecker's (1977) concept of prana is a moving
potency, spatially extended and vitalizing, which helps one to concentrate. This power of concentration makes it possible to achieve
the psychic state that generates the increase in information,
knowledge, or perception which gives that mental faculty ultimately
leading to God-realization. Various other scientists at the Kundalini
Research Foundation in the University of California and in Germany,
Italy, and Switzerland have conducted studies which concluded that
Kundalini or prana, stimulated by meditation and then drawn inward
and upward into the brain through the spinal canal, can be verified
in medical laboratories because, when prana reaches the brain, it
produces extraordinary illumination and heightened psychic powers.

A Way of Return for such as wish to return, the traditional
lores are full of these road maps showing the way to spiritual
health. Keenly analytic and psychological, Buddhism especially is
replete with these more than Sandow-exercises for the soul. The
four marvelous states (Brahmaviharas) are their major ethical
achievement: Friendliness, Compassion, Joyfulness, Indifference,
maitri, karuna, mudita, upeksa. A passage from ego to superego,
reminding the Ape of his Essence, is the highest common factor of
every mystical programme. Beyond causality, contingency, and conditioning, the scriptures, identifying the world's mind with that of
man, reach out to an unfaltering awareness of the relativity and
non-origination of objects. The state of nirvana, sunya, or samadhi
is the true "dying unto life," the life everlasting.

The height is not without its abyss; behind the stern classical
stance are areas of darkness, morbid, macabre. The contemplation
of the impurities, the skeleton, the Tantric orgies, and the use of
the skull as a drinking goblet come to the mind, romantic agony at
its most rancid. The way down is the way up?

Modern spokesmen are far more moderate. The recent Vedantic
anthology, Meditation (1969) by the Monks of the Ramakrishna Order,
is a model of sobriety. Swami Avyaktananda's Universal Meditation
(1972) offers a simple, rational seven-step practice, from rhythmic
breathing to universal goodwill. In a slightly different key
Thakar's Meditation: A Way of Life (1976) defines mysticism as
"an effortless and choiceless awareness." Self-education by another
name, it underlines Is-ness instead of I-ness. If all men have
not earned the unconditioned enlightenment, that is because, without
an inward turn and a passion for the beyond, the doors of perception
will not open. To fulfill man's being in the world, he has to lift
his eyes beyond it.

Masters (1964) points to an old but neglected truth: Self-
government is a human tendency. One is reminded of Plato's "inward

government of the worse by the naturally better part of us."
To resist conditioning one must learn to be stimulated by "the
other side of the psyche," "the unseen leader in the heart." Non-
response to what is called normal experiences is the way "to starve
the old roots." Love is at once dispassionate and compassionate,
not an easy combination. The less man does ego-wise the more good
happens. To be truly effective for spiritual health, mysticism
should not be a part-time hobby nor an annex to living. Therefore,
"Don't stop being a Mystic."

The introspective bias of the mystic mind and spiritual society
has given rise to different methods of developing the focus of the
mind, among them the familiar Triple Paths of Work, Knowledge, and
Devotion. Common to all the paths is concentration with its three
powers or characteristics. By its help man can know anything he
likes, possess whatever he wishes to, and become what he thinks.
More, he may become what he is. What he should finally strive for
is, of course, the Highest. Advaita's crown jewel is the Absolute,
but   his aim is integral, not excluding that which it transcends.
Not exclusion but integration is the better aim.

MYSTICISM AND SPIRITUAL HEALTH

The mystic path to spiritual health is old, and others have gone
before, along that razor's edge. From these experienced wayfarers
comes the Guide or the Guru. The manuals lay down the marks,
fairly exacting, of the Guru. Essentially, he is a realized soul,
one who also is able to communicate his experience to the disciple.
In spite of the high respect shown to him, he is not arbitrary or
unduly authoritarian. More an elder than a Big Brother, the Guru
comes when the disciple is ready.

Such a Guru alone has the right to initiate. Roughly, there are
three kinds of initiation: shakti, sambhavi, and mantra, working
through the will of the Master, his touch or look, and the sacred
syllable or formula. The idea of mantra -- mananat trayate iti
mantrah, that which saves through contemplation -- is allied to a
sacred science of language. By the Word the world was made, by
another it may be unmade. That the mantra can manifest even now comes
out   convincingly in the case of Sharon Brown, who recently cured
herself of cancer by repeating Om Namah Sivaya.

As the Desert Fathers, the monastic orders, the European mystics
will show, the contemplative life is not unknown there, though
perhaps not so widespread or pervasive. One major distinction
between the Semitic and the Eastern tradition is that one is dualis-
tic, the other non-dualistic. In the West to say, as we in the East
do, "Thou art That (Tatvamasi)" or "I am That (So'ham)," would amount
to anathema. When Meister Eckhart announced, "The eye with which
I see God is the same with which He sees me," the Church looked the

44

other way. The same unorthodox note can be heard in the title and content of another medieval classic, A Book of Contemplation, the Which is Called the Cloud of Unknowing in the Which a Soul is Oned with God.

Two false ideas must be demythologized. First, that mysticism is a gerontic occupation, merely for the old and the exhausted. The truth is the exact opposite: youth is the best time for initiation. What happens in its absence is there for all to see. Second, the life of contemplation is far from being a life of inactivity. In fact, the contemplatives alone have a valid philosophy of action based on principles. One of these is non-attachment. The search for the health, wealth, and happiness of mankind, the quest for freedom, can never succeed through blatantly unpurified motives and methods. The saint alone knows how to defuse the entrenched forces of power and ignorance, whether of tyrants or of technocrats.

How then can one attain the ancestral insights, the racial superconscious? Only through mysticism which expresses the intensity of the soul longing to reach sublime heights in its effort to transcend reality. All here must learn to obey the higher law, what a modern novelist, Saul Bellow, has called "an inadmissible resource, something we all hesitate to mention though we all know it intimately -- the soul." With Sri Ramakrishna Paramahamsa it was the imagery and symbolism which constituted the very texture of his mystical expression, since he firmly believed that Kamini and Kanchan (woman and gold) are the two great impediments to the mystic experience. He believed that in spiritual health through mysticism there are no instant remedies. The purport of his statement is that by Divine Grace, one may have the knowledge of Brahman instantly, but it is like throwing a man on the top of a roof which is bound to hurt him, whereas the gradual and systematic root causes of our mundane troubles through non-attached observation can provide an everlasting cure for psychological illness through meditation. The curve of a rational-individualistic industrial age is bound to lead in this direction, toward a renewed, even enriched, subjectivity.

The Buddha's sermon on the Vulture Peak still reverberates. What the Thunder said can be heard even now, "He who hears the Word sees Me. He who knows the Law knows Me." The world's torn heart cries out for a matching of the two know-hows, old and new. "The Kingdom of God is for none but the thoroughly dead" is more than moonshine mysticism. In Nicholas of Cusa's lovely metaphor, the walls of Paradise are built with paradoxes.

To say that these things are mythical or mystical is not to explain them away but to hit the truth, to enhance their timeless endurance. The presentness of the past proves it to be perennial. Could it not also be the wave of the future? This is at least a high possibility because, as Toynbee has stated, the simple truth,

the art of contemplation, is really another name for the art of
living.

The oldest applied psychology, meditation, is also medicare:
the remedy for the mind diseased, as it also is for false self-
views and essence-blindness. The way to the Self will always be
subjective. Krishnaprem in The Yoga of the Kathopanishad (Prem,
1976) put it beautifully: Here is the universal medicine, that One
Thing in fact which, under one name or another, has been the object
of all sacred quests.

By trying to measure the action of this force scientifically,
medical scientists will sooner or later open up a new field of
investigation conferring validity on spiritual experience which
influences all spheres of human activity. With the successful
arousal of the latent organic energy at the base of his spine, one
can produce a much greater intensification of attention on one's
consciousness; this will accelerate the process of evolution and
produce altered states of consciousness and extraordinary gifts
of the intellect, which may in stages or degrees vary from the
orthodox with a strong spiritual urge toward mysticism to the less
orthodox, so transcending the barriers between sects and creeds
that it can hardly be designated by conventional man-made labels.
It is an accepted fact that, since every altered state of consciousness has a corresponding biological change in the body, mystical
experiences must also be reflected in the body and the brain.

The arousal of prana or Kundalini by long meditation and purification in which the body and the identity are swallowed up by a
single, pointed attention, which might be termed "awareness of
awareness," is nothing other than aiding the individual in his meditation through the six chakras or cycles which the Kundalini must
pierce. These chakras are often thought of as lotuses, with varying
numbers of petals in which the gods and goddesses reside. This
anthropomorphism is merely to show the initiator that there is no
refuge other than the lotuses of the good divine law. Agni, the
fire of aspiration, is "lotus-born."

The concluding lines of a Zen meditation bring the same news.
This very earth is the Lotus Land of Purity, and this body is the
body of the Buddha. It is only our wholeness of being. Bodhicitta,
the Inner sage, heals the many and subtle wounds of separation,
here and hereafter. The chakras help the mystic to think of the
appropriate god or goddess in each chakra, cycle, or lotus to aid
his concentration more fully, using the mental pictures as foci
for pratyahara, dhyana, and eventual samadhi.

I shall now try to present a set of concepts related to the self
through the preponderance of metaphysically secularized ideals. This
will show that medical men and mystics who are conducting their
investigations in spiritual health forms and practices will eventually

46

conclude through empirical observations that not only the spiritual, but also the biological, base of all the phenomena is connected with mystical insight and exceptionally high moral standards.

MYSTICISM AND THE SELF

Among the great potentialities of the self are its inner resources, which are indispensable to attaining sound spiritual health. Although specific Hatha yoga methods are now accepted to awaken Kundalini, the Laya Yoga and Raj Yoga systems differ in their ideas of "inner resources," which is the keynote of retaining or regaining spiritual health through mysticism and constitutes the central philosophy of mysticism. All systems of yoga describe these "inner resources" of mysticism as faith, patience, compassion, love, gratitude, humility, and forbearance. The mystics believe that when these resources are fully utilized by the individual, they tend to have an impact upon his character which protects him against inner afflictions and the impoverishment of self which is detrimental to its growth.

Mysticism considers self-fulfillment as a process of human growth and development in terms of certain spiritual and moral aspects of human character and the realization of the highest possibilities of life. This process of self-fulfillment runs through many stages which are characterized by different states of the psyche. Mystics down through the ages have remarkably shown how these states gradually unfold themselves to the vitalized self. The most desirable state of self-fulfillment is the growth of the Abundant and the Effluent Self.

This state arrives when love, happiness, bliss, freedom, and other self generating experiences become available to the self in abundance and begin to influence directly the person's interactions with the physical and social world. Mysticism shows this as a state of the soul, being one with the Supersoul that leads the self into a realm of greater experiences characterized mainly by happiness and serenity. (The Vedic term of Satchidananda meaning existence, knowledge, and bliss undoubtedly influenced the Hindu, Buddhist, Jain, Sikh, and Sufi mystics.)

Mysticism does not interpret the concepts of freedom and happiness in their abstract philosophical sense, nor in terms of ordinary experiences. Instead mystics derive those concepts' meaning from the specific empirical context relating to the experiences of divine immanence and transcendence. For instance, the concept of freedom implies transcendence from compulsions, strains, and the aimless persuasions of life. If properly pursued, it arms man against failure, against sorrow and calamity, against boredom and discouragement. It perhaps may not prepare for material success, but it will help man to love and share those aims and ideals, the things beyond all price, on which the generality of men who aim at success do not set their hearts.

Happiness is thus regarded by mysticism as an enduring feeling that arises out of a sense of spiritual fullness and abundance. It is also a consequence of relief from agonizing thoughts and feelings. Physical efficiency and intellectual alertness are dangerous if spiritual illiteracy prevails. Civilization is an act of spirit, not of body or mind. Achievements of knowledge and power are not enough for sound spiritual health: acts of spirit and morality are essential. Man must become an active, purposeful force. He must cease to believe in an automatic law of progress which will realize itself irrespective of human ideals and control.

The mystics' concepts of the vitalized and the impoverished self are, in fact, fundamental and necessary for understanding the dynamics of "inner resources." Mysticism refers to this vitalized self in its ability to assimilate, interpret, and evaluate experiences of the phenomenal world and render them productive in life. It also includes the capacity to withstand those experiences that challenge its integrity and existence. It subscribes to the view that the intellect and general level of emotional balance are not enough for responding to the challenge of these experiences in spiritual health because the vital aspects of the self are indispensable to it. Spiritually man becomes impoverished when these resources become unavailable to him for any reason, and symptoms of its poverty emerge in the form of afflictions, including mental illness and the sickness of character.

The worst kind of spiritual affliction, according to mystics, are envy, jealousy, hostility, hatred, pride, greed, dejection, agony, and anxiety. The impoverished self often succumbs to them; thereafter it refuses to grow. They are fatal to human personality. Mysticism in such cases emphasizes the aspect of equanimity -- keeping our cool -- which is perhaps the most vital factor in sound mental and spiritual health. This equanimity is possible only by habitual relaxation through mysticism, by which one has to learn to work and eat in a relaxed way, to do everything with a mental coolness and physical ease. Relaxation is defined as reduction to a minimum of mental and muscular energy, conducive to life. Mystics believe that the "re" in relaxation is to urge man to practice "laxation," loosening or unwinding, again and again. Thus practiced it becomes a tranquilizer and helps to lower the cardio-respiratory rate and elevated blood pressure.

The aim in mysticism is to achieve the maximum possible quietude of the human organism simultaneously with letting oneself go or release. And when we let go we "let God." God takes over when and where man leaves off. Man therefore has to loosen his grip physically, mentally, or emotionally. How very often does man hold on to people, to events, to insults, and to injuries -- and thereby needlessly suffer. Mysticism teaches man to relax his hold. Good memory for bad episodes of life comes in the way of sound spiritual health. Whatever ails modern man, mysticism through meditation is of far greater importance than medication. After all, the power of meditation is tremendous, and mysticism is more than convinced that the power of "choiceless awareness" is much greater than the power of positive thinking, the virtues of which have been convincingly extolled by Dr. Norman Vincent Peale.

There is a well-known prayer: "May God grant me the serenity to accept things which cannot be changed, courage to change what can be changed, and wisdom to know the difference." It may seem strange, but it is true, that all three qualities mentioned herein -- serenity, courage, and wisdom -- are the hallmarks of a spiritually healthy person; these three interdependent qualities also have their genesis in relaxation.

Man's true self is never disturbed or ruffled. It is always serene, as the bottom of the ocean is tranquil though storms may be raging on the surface. This inner true self can be reached through mysticism. By learning to enter the quiet room within, man builds the foundation for the edifice of sound spiritual health because, in the final analysis after all, nothing matters and nobody matters.

There is no implication anywhere in mystic theories that mystic thought has ever by-passed the reality of social influences upon the individual life or that it has failed to realize the importance of the health-fostering social conditions. Mysticism has never regarded self-fulfillment as an isolated process. It only asserts that the best conditions of life would fail to have their growth-fostering effects upon the self which is truly impoverished, and hence, in spite of them, the self would remain infested with afflictions. Spiritual health has no means except its own resources to cope with experiences and to direct them toward the productive solution.

Since mysticism has found through experiences that in the later stages of self-fulfillment these inner resources lead the self to a state of psychic transmutation, it concludes that faith, patience, forbearance, gratitude, humility, etc., are not passive aspects of the self. They are the powers which determine man's reactions to his experiences. Faith is not described, therefore, as a passive belief in destiny but as an inner basis for the positive attitudes through which one asserts the meaningfulness of one's life and individuality and assumes one's responsibility toward it. It is the mainspring of human actions and the power that sustains the inner being of the person.

Love in mysticism, as well as in all spiritual ailments, is regarded as the most vital aspect of human self and character. Its highest expression comes through the unselfish love of the being, and ultimately through the love of God. But the love of man in mystic thought is inseparable from the love of God. It is the master motive, the enduring characteristic of the self-fulfilling person, and the core of his Abundant and Effluent self.

Thus we have at least four different states or conditions of the self which are either attributed to spiritual health or indicative of it. They are (1) the sick self, (2) the impoverished self, (3) the vitalized self, and (4) the Abundant and Effluent Self.

Since mysticism embraces the idea of the intrinsic worth and desirability of attaining the Abundant and Effluent self, it is recommended that the seeker of spiritual health take advantage of the resources which lie within him and direct him to this end. The vitalized self, according to mystic thought, needs guidance to move toward this end, and a sick and impoverished self needs help to overcome its affliction and inner poverty.

Mysticism portrays spiritual sickness in two ways: (1) the sickness of the mind, expressed through such symptoms as anxiety and dejection, and (2) the sickness of character, indicating hatred, envy, greed, pride, etc. It occurs in varying degrees in different characters. Mysticism convincingly argues that the real cure of the psychic and spiritual ailments lies in revitalizing the self. It regards psychological help as a purely human affair and holds that the ultimate aim of psychological help is to enable the individual to become capable of helping himself. Mysticism can render psychic help effective only when the helper is himself possessed of a vitalized self, because what man gives to others through his Effluence he himself must have in abundance. In other words, mysticism shows that such a person must himself act as the growth-fostering agent.

What society needs today is workers devoid of self-seeking and self-aggrandizement, shorn of the maya caused by ego, who can blaze a fresh trail in humanistic thinking by exploring anew the place of subjectivity and inner experiences in human life and relations.

Chapter 5

NEW TESTAMENT CONCEPTS FOR A SOCIOPSYCHOLOGICAL MODEL

OF PERSONALITY DEVELOPMENT

Purnell H. Benson

Personality development can be considered from the practical viewpoint of achieving desirable behavior traits or simply as cause and effect processes to be comprehended by science. From the standpoint of the individual, the end result may be fulfillment of life purposes. For the religious individual, the fulfillment of spiritual aims or of a general sense of inner peace and comfort may be the main result sought from personality growth. The rich spectrum of aims in religious development is displayed in Godin's (1971) overview and elaborated by other contributors to Strommen's (1971) handbook on research in religious development.

VALIDITY OF A RELIGIOUS MODEL OF PERSONALITY DEVELOPMENT

The quest for valid knowledge about the inward side of human development has challenged researchers for a full century. To avoid the reproof of learning little from history, it is worthwhile examining some of the characteristics of valid knowledge about the inner or subjective side of personal behavior. Before describing any model of personality development, it is necessary to discern restrictions inherent in scientific procedures applied to the study of human activity, and before examining a religious model for scientific study, we should realize what the study of models of personality development can accomplish.

Internal and External Sides of Religious Development

Religious attainment may be expressed in subjective conditions achieved by the individual, such as peace of mind, or by the ability to proselytize or provide leadership in the priestly functions of a religious group. Moberg's (1971a) review of surveys of religious practices distinguishes between the internal and external expressions of religion; this distinction sometimes is overlooked by those who are preoccupied with the behavioristic side of ritual or church membership or who, at the opposite pole, concern themselves only

51

with inward experiences of the religious participant. Also acknowledging a clear line between the internal and external, Hoffman
(1971) has analyzed extensively the internalization of moral ideas
in children.

Psychologists a century ago were more circumspect in their distinction between the inner and outer areas of psychology than are
their current successors. In 1890 William James (1950) exemplified
this differentiation and the articulation of methods of inquiry
appropriate to each side of psychology. He and Titchener (1929)
can be regarded as the main advocates in the United States of the
study of inward experience, and especially of introspection as the
technique for searching this inner realm. In sociology Parsons
(1937) has kept alive the tradition of Max Weber with its keen
interest in the inner side of culture and society.

The extremes of internal and external are easily distinguished
as polar concepts. What is visually perceived in space and time,
such as motions of the human body, is patently external. A long
succession of psychologists from Pavlov and Watson to Hull and Skinner
have preoccupied themselves with observing and analyzing these data
of human behavior in its spatial environment. Sociologists have
veered less toward pure objectivism, although Lundberg (1939, 1963)
is remembered for his thorough-going behaviorism.

At the other extreme, an hypnotic trance or the unwinding of a
daydream is palpably an inner, private experience of the individual.
The internal expression of religion consists of what people think
and feel during their religious involvement. The realm of thought,
motivation, and feeling is manifestly the private experience of
individuals, each of whom has his or her own inward world.

The middle ground of perceptual experience is more difficult to
classify. Perceptions are of the external world, yet they are
colored by internal feelings and expectations. They represent a
blend of inner and outer experience.

Personal Equations of Researchers

The topic of the "personal equation" of the observer first came
to the forefront of science in astronomy. It was realized that even.
in the neutral observation of celestial phenomena, the personal
equation of the observer affects reaction times in the recording of
data. Largely eliminated by automatic instrumentation, the personal
equation of the observer is now negligible in most physical sciences,
but it bulks extremely large in the social and psychological sciences.
It is noteworthy that even rats which are experimentally observed
exhibit the cultural traits of their researchers, who project their
cultural biases into their interpretations of animal behavior.

The personal equation of the social or psychological scientist

52

stems from the individual bundle of feelings and motivations in which principles sought are embedded and which yield divergent results. The hallmark of all knowledge worthy of being called scientific is that qualified researchers using the same methods will reach the same conclusions. Such consensus has brought together the vast domain of physical science into a unified discipline of principles. By contrast, psychology and sociology have been fragmented for generations into schools which hold different bodies of theory and which change from decade to decade. These differences frequently stem from divergent personal equations.

Many scientists studying religion hold firmly to the conviction that internal expression of religion, as well as external activities, eventually will yield to the patient efforts of researchers to produce a unified body of scientific truth. They hold this conviction despite the procession of unsuccessful religious scientists through the years. Some psychologists and sociologists   candidly admit never having had a religious experience, yet try to conceptualize the experience of those who do. More problems are involved than inexperience alone. Researchers of religion are divided by methodological impediments in addition to the chasms created by personal equations.

Methodological Circumstances in Studying Internal Aspects of Religion

External data are a matter of public accessibility. Rituals can be observed, membership can be enumerated, statistics can be collected and analyzed. All researchers who choose to observe see the same data at the same time. Verification of data is readily established, since all who are in the locale of observation can point to and communicate the same things at the same time as the others. It can be argued that each external observer has his or her own perceptions. However, their concurrence does produce a world of common objects which are observed.

Observation of internal data does not proceed easily in a public domain, as previously indicated in my scientific study of religion (Benson, 1960: 82-109). Each human being is limited in direct observation to his or her own world of thinking, willing, and feeling. Different observers may experience similar classes of internal data or note similar patterns to which their internal experiences conform. Yet I cannot observe your internal experience, which may be far away in time from mine. I can gain knowledge of your internal experience only if you choose to report your data to me or if I infer the substance of your experience from your behavior or circumstances.

William James (1950) and Titchener (1929) championed introspection as the technique for learning the content of the world of inward experience. James' (1950: 185) description of the role of introspection in psychology in 1890 is classic:

53

Introspective Observation is what we have to rely on first and foremost and always. The word introspection need hardly be defined -- it means, of course, the looking into our own minds and reporting all what we there discover. Everyone agrees that we there discover states of consciousness. So far as I know, the existence of such states has never been doubted by any critic, however skeptical in other respects he may have been. That we have cogitations of some sort is the inconcussum in a world most of whose other facts have at some time tottered in the breath of philosophic doubt. All people unhesitatingly believe that they feel themselves thinking, and that they distinguish the mental state as an inward activity or passion, from all the objects with which it may cognitively deal. I regard this belief as the most fundamental of all the postulates of Psychology, and shall discard all curious inquiries about its certainty as too metaphysical for the scope of this book.

Such advocacy of introspection usually falls on deaf ears in psychology and sociology today. Earlier, introspection led to intense and insoluble disagreements. The scientific requirement that common verification be achieved could not be met, owing to the great difficulty of getting results.

Behaviorists reason that replies to questions about the inner side of experience are admissible as data, since at least the sounds uttered or the marks on questionnaires are matters of common observation. Yet this is akin to saying that the communications of scientists about data are data for analysis, a confusion of data with mere reports of data. Moreover, it can sensibly be argued that, if reports by untrained observers of their inner spiritual experiences are admissible as accounts of data, then reports by those trained in introspection are also admissible.

Indirect observation of the inner world of others, through enlisting them as observers and recording their observations,is a popular technique of sociologists of religion. Participant observation, which combines listening with direct observation of behavior, also is reputable, as in the study of new forms of religion by Glock and Bellah (1976), yet even here wide disagreements separate researchers.

Moberg (1967a: 30) writes:
In other words, the spiritual aspects of man's nature can be studied scientifically only indirectly. When we do so, the logical chain of relationships between our observations and conclusions is apt to be lengthy and weak. The validity of our generalizations therefore will be rather dubious. Yet it is conceivable that concentrated attention to this problem would reveal measuring techniques and instruments of which we cannot even dream at present.

54

In analyzing and interpreting the results of questionnaire studies or of statistics of religious activities, scientific difficulties multiply. The case records or statistical summaries by themselves are pedestrian and cast little light on the meaning of religion to the participants. The inferential leap from external data to the internal meaning is the juncture where the scientific study of religion reaches its real impasse. Different schools of psychology and sociology publish different interpretations, which then fade away as new vocabularies and systems of concepts displace their predecessors.

Since publication of my thorough review of differing scientific views of religion (Benson, 1960), which I hoped would move scientific thinking toward agreement, I have seen little evidence of converging agreement. A leading compilation of readings shows that the disagreements are wide and numerous (Birnbaum and Lenzer, 1969). After nearly a century of effort, it seems evident that researchers are incapable of achieving a science of religious behavior and motivation, if by science we mean a body of knowledge on which there is common agreement.

Those disenchanted with the interpretations by different schools are content to expand upon their statistical analysis of the data. With the aid of automatic data processing, they spin matrixes of correlations, weave factor analyses, and fabricate reams of computer printouts. Such analyses, if uninterpreted, may intrigue those who are fascinated by numbers, but they do not illuminate religion from the standpoint of comprehension, prediction, application, and control. As soon as the tasks of inference and interpretation begin, they fall athwart conflicting schools of sociology and psychology. This is not to say that important scientific tasks are not being accomplished, but their successes fall short of the achievements in the physical sciences.

Disagreement in the Internal Study of Religion

Reference has already been made to the enormous personal equation which infects the scientific work of social and psychological scientists. This is not merely a matter of distorting observations, as in the physical sciences, but much more fundamentally it is a problem of hindering conceptualization by scientists in their analysis of behavior and motivation. In order to press as far toward scientific achievement as possible, it is necessary to pause and examine thoroughly the roots of the personal equation of social and psychological scientists.

The voluminous analysis by Carl Jung (1939, 1958) of the processes of personality development gives us valuable keys to understanding our personal equations. Personality development consists of the gradual unfolding of archetypal forms of thinking and motivation. These are rooted in hereditary structure, yet their development

55

toward fruition is conditioned upon opportunities in the environment. Most critics and many disciples of Jung believe he weights
the scales of development too much in the direction of hereditary
determination of personality characteristics. However, his conceptualization of personality development as the unfolding of the leaves
and flowers of a plant latent in the original seed seems a valuable
construct.

Jung stoutly maintained that the individual cannot become a person different from what one's archetypal potentialities allow. One
cannot be motivated differently from what one's prior development
permits. One is entirely incapable of thinking at levels different
from, or more than a step beyond, prior levels of thought development.

Implications for a social psychology of knowledge are clearly
indicated by these principles of human growth. What one regards as
knowledge is provided by aspects of the individual's intellect by
virtue of the unfolding of the psyche. The individual is bound by
whatever intellectual substance has been conferred by heredity (and
environment). The degree to which book-learning or teaching can
shift the individual into orbits of understanding outside his or her
normal field of gravitation seems highly restricted. In a very real
sense, all human beings are given different mixtures of reality,
and they can know little of what lies outside their personal mixtures. One is reminded of the old Presbyterian view that salvation
is a matter of predestination.

This is not to say that the aspiring student is incapable of
amassing considerable knowledge and insight beyond that afforded by
an alternative route of schooling. What is being said is that
students will cling to some of their prejudices, regardless of the
skill or competence of their teachers. These mentors can close
some of the gaps in learning, but not all of them.

What is characteristic of human beings in general also characterizes them in their vocational role as social and psychological
scientists.
Understanding the nature of the scientific enterprise helps
us to recognize that much "scientific data" about religion
is a product of values, methods, and abstracting processes
of the scientists' own making. The grids for knowledge
which we select from the total web of social life shape our
findings, direct the abstraction process, and as a result
lead to simplified versions of reality which then are
presented as "the truth" (Moberg, 1978a: 8).

For a long time sociologists and psychologists have dialogued
among themselves as to what the nature and reasons for religious
behavior and experience are. We are no more than honest if we
recognize that agreement has not been achieved thereby, despite

efforts by several generations. It seems a reliable forecast that future researchers also will fail to achieve the consensual verification which is the heartstone of scientific knowledge. Side by side we will continue to have sexologists like Kinsey and Freud and religionists like James and Jung. One side insists that uninhibited pleasure-seeking is the key to life fulfillment; the other side insists that an experience of the divine is the supreme value.

The inexorable conclusion to which we are pressed as scientific researchers of religion is that contrasting conclusions cannot be accepted simultaneously as scientific truth. Since common verification of conclusions is the hallmark of scientific achievement, it must be recognized that much so-called knowledge of the internal side of religion or any human activity is beyond the secure domain of science. Scientific inquiry should be pursued as far as possible. The inquiry stops short of yielding scientific knowledge where it is unable to generate scientific agreement.

Nor do these things mean that dependable knowledge is lacking for the religionist. The religionist believes that the truth of religious knowledge is actual, indeed overwhelming, for the devotee who finds this knowledge within the compass of that individual's religious development. The religionist may have strong grounds from historical record or from present experience for accepting principles of faith. Every human being is guided by knowledge which that human being is capable of grasping. Moreover, some are suited by experience and study opportunity to see beyond the limitations of the knowledge to a fuller view of reality disclosed by religious experience and development.

Yinger's (1963: 12-13) statement seems as relevant today as it did sixteen years ago: "What one can say confidently about religion on the basis of present knowledge is not a great deal, and what can be said about religion from nonscientific perspectives may well be more important." This agrees with the viewpoint that social psychologists lack the right either to deny religious models as unscientific or to affirm them as proved by science. These intuitive aspects of knowledge are beyond present scientific verification.

Role of Introspection in Formulating Religious Models

The status of knowledge outside of scientific demonstration by common verification reminds one of the work by Ritschl (1901), a nineteenth century theologian. He denied that the study of religious experience can be a science, but he also claimed that it did not belong to speculative philosophy. It is an internal area where value judgments are revealed, those which are found in Christian doctrine. By implication, introspection is a primary method of Ritschl for disclosing the content of religious experience.

Ritschl's theme was carried further by Macintosh (1919) who

constructed an empirical theology of a personal God, based upon the facts of Christian experience. He describes the method of intro-spection (Macintosh, 1919: 159-160):

As a first method, then, we may begin with our "intuitions" as the reality in question, i.e., with those unreasoned certi-tudes which are firmly rooted in immediate experience, treat-ing them critically and even skeptically, deducing hypo-theses from them, refuting them in the light of experience where this is possible, but otherwise letting them stand for what they still seem to be worth. ...In apprehending the divine, as manifested in the spirit of the historic Jesus and in the truly "Christlike" everywhere, we are identifying the divine with certain qualities....

Since other theologians, not to mention psychologists, have not con-curred with Macintosh's approach, it cannot be considered a science in the sense of commonly verified knowledge.

Manifestly, introspection will not yield the same findings for those who have developed different sets of life experiences. Even within a common religious tradition, individual variations in life development curtail the degree of agreement which is possible from introspective religious experience.

Apart from the individuality of experience, introspection presents formidable difficulties for those who seek insight through its use. Among nineteenth and early twentieth century psychologists, the mapping of dimensions of sensory fields through introspection proved to be a source of disagreement; Titchener (1929), the lone survivor, was finally abandoned by the main stream of psychology. The pro-blem is that searching one's own inner world of experience is an extremely subtle and difficult matter. How many dimensions of intensity of experience are there? Sensory intensity, degree of awareness, amount of attention, vividness, and richness of hue or tone are among the variables suggested. Perceptual mapping through psychometric scaling of questionnaire data provides one answer, but this is not introspection.

Moving from delineating perceptual variables to disentangling the inner processes of thought, motivation, and feeling, we shift from the vivid to the vague and shadowy realm of subconscious or subliminal experience. In response to James' (1936, 1950) challenge to define the variables in the stream of consciousness and to for-mulate their relationships, I (Benson, 1966) have shared the results of an introspective effort which discloses the difficulty of the task and provides a diagrammatic way of presenting results of intro-spection unambiguously. The traditional Christian viewpoint that one cannot find God through one's own efforts is supported by the failure of introspection to yield conclusions on which there is scientific consensus.

Casual self-introspection and sympathetic introspection into the

experience of others through communicating with them play an important part in model building. Hypotheses are stated, theories are
developed, and the parts of a model can be put together for empirical
testing. Such generation of insights has frequently played a useful
role in model building in the social and psychological sciences;
it is basic to the verstehende approach.

In turn, testing models for their consistency with external facts
or for internal consistency with the system they embrace enables
models to be extended and to acquire a more solid base in observed
facts of behavior or in the content of communication, notably through
questionnaire studies. Thus testing the insights of such investigators as Ritschl, Macintosh, or Jung can play a useful role in
constructing models of religious experience and motivation.

The sociopsychological model contained in the New Testament teachings of Jesus Christ and his disciples originated in experiences
revealed nearly two thousand years ago. Christians believe that the
appearance of these experiences through the exceptional personality
of Jesus so far exceeds ordinary statistical expectation that a
unique event in history occurred. Christians infer that this
uniqueness represents intervention by God in human history, and they
expect a similar event will occur again in a second coming of Christ.

The record of details of the experiences at the time of Jesus'
life on earth has been preserved in scripture and is accessible for
consideration. Understanding of the Christian model has been
enriched by the lives and experiences of many followers in the
Christian tradition. Proposing a body of religious doctrines as a
model for study breaks so much with past scientific outlook that
careful review of methodological implications is necessary.

Sociopsychological Models of Religious Experience and Behavior

Typically a sociological or psychological model connects one set
of events in behavior and the environment with another set of similar
events. The behavioral events may consist of verbal or other overt
expressions of behavior. Usually in the theory embraced by the model
are found some propositions dealing with internal processes of motivation and experience. Indeed, the internal propositions give the
model its meaning and significance. They enable a logical interpretation of the external events.

What are the ways in which such a model can be tested? To what
kinds of results does researching the model lead? What practical
applications can be made of the model? The introduction of a model
of personality development constructed from the standpoint of religious considerations is contingent upon answers to these questions.

The model can be examined by data from statistical surveys, which

59

yield averages and dispersions by means of which it can be gauged. The model is tested by its consistency with external events, often in terms of the degree of measurement error or of deviations of the model from observed facts.

Capps (1976) examined 150 empirical studies of religious psychology. He found that 90% of these were correlational studies. Only one (Dittes, 1961) had any semblance to being an experimental study. The desirability of experimentation with test and control groups is that cause and effect relationships can be clearly defined and measured. The difficulty encountered by most questionnaire studies is the "yea-say" effect, the tendency of respondents to exaggerate (or minimize) both religious activity and the joy of fulfillment. Hence spurious correlations may readily arise.

A spiritual model of personality development can be used to examine individual case histories. The sequence of spiritual events in a person's life can be charted and the outcome of spiritual involvement assessed. The adequacy of the model is disclosed by its consistency with observable facts and by the fullness of its interpretation of the data.

One use of sociopsychological models in instructing students or counseling people is to have the model applied by the individual in the ongoing development of his or her own life purposes. In accordance with the model, the person makes decisions and alters activities and opportunities of experience. Then if the desired changes in activity or aptitude result as foreseen by the model, the researcher is assured that the model has worked effectively. In particular, if fulfillment of spiritual aims is experienced, this confirms the end result of the model for development.

It becomes very evident that models in general are not proved by the data, but are merely found to be consistent with the data. From the standpoint of scientific verification, other models might also fit the data. Which model is relevant often becomes a matter of the researcher's preference.

Models of personality development have practical usefulness in educational or clinical work. They guide the instruction or counseling which facilitate intellectual and personality growth. In so doing, their status as knowledge may depend upon the personal or professional convictions of the user. To those inside the religious orientation, the truth of a religious model may appear overwhelming. To those outside, the religious model may appear as a blank area of the unknown.

Jung's (1958: 104-105) comments are pertinent:
Religious experience is absolute; it cannot be disputed.
You can only say that you never had such an experience,
whereupon your opponent will reply: "Sorry, I have."

And then your discussion will come to an end.

Of particular concern is the extent to which testing or using the spiritual model confirms or contests the propositions about internal experience. Since these, from a strict scientific standpoint, are always matters of inference, it must be recognized that scientific proof or disproof of religious experience may fall well outside of scientific purview. This does not mean that the model does not consist of knowledge, but merely that it consists of the knowledge held by the body of believers, but perhaps not by others.

What is of striking significance is that all models of internal personality development are vulnerable to the same inherent limitations as those models which are spiritual in their framework. We necessarily recall again the perennial proliferation of schools of psychology and sociology, each of which has its own leaders and adherents. The same problems of proof arise in all models which introduce principles of internal experience and motivation. Doubtless some researchers would rather not acknowledge this profound impasse in the path of scientific knowledge. Except for models which deal in a trivial way with statistical data, the models of fundamental importance to human beings in their achievement of life purposes and life experiences are very much the product of conceptual schools which do not, and apparently cannot, satisfy the needs of common verification because of inherent problems in the individual attainment of knowledge.

This is not to discourage empirical research into personality or spiritual fulfillment. Rather, even greater effort should be exerted to find domains of common understanding. Even where universal assent is absent, at least for the participants in a particular religious group, the research aids them in applying their model to their own circumstances and problems. They are better able to implement their spiritual goals because of what they learn through researching their spiritual model. Measuring spiritual fulfillment is an important scientific task.

Nor does this sober realization of impediments in the path of socio-scientific knowledge mean that we ought not do everything possible to press the frontiers of common verification as far as possible. What is clear, however, is that knowledge upon which common agreement is lacking still has a valid claim for inclusion in the teaching departments of schools and universities. Thus it is that Jewish, Christian, Islamic, Hindu, Confucianist, and even Marxist models of personality development have a right to consideration in the teaching departments, as long as student interest and teaching competence are available. Detailed models of spiritual fulfillment in religious doctrine have as much right to be explored in teaching and research as the various psychoanalytic, psychological, and sociological models which currently abound in the literature of human knowledge.

61

Following Ritschl (1901) and Macintosh (1919), such knowledge can be designated as intuitive. If a science of intuition is proposed, it will relinquish the claim to common verification as one of its scientific requirements. Verification by a limited group would remain.

Beyond the internal and external aspects of religious systems, the transition from present experience or past history to God beyond experience and life beyond death does not belong within the scientific domain at all. Where beliefs relate to what is immutably beyond experience, no pretense of data to prove such beliefs scientifically can be found, but the beliefs can be subjected to philosophical inquiry and appraisal.

What is the involvement of beliefs in spiritual models of personality development or fulfillment?

First, we need to recognize more clearly than ever before that religious beliefs are important. We have tended to look upon them as dependent variables, assuming that they were consequences of various social factors, thus not needing direct investigation in their own right (Moberg, 1978a: 13).

Beliefs are themselves existent facts, whether or not they are provable or unprovable. It is a fact that certain elements of faith are predominant in Christian life. Whether these principles can be scanned by scientific scrutiny, the beliefs in these principles nevertheless are psychic events in the experience of the individual. The adherence to such beliefs may be of much significance for personality development and fulfillment, so the beliefs, as beliefs, are part of the sociopsychological model.

Investigation into the correctness of beliefs belongs within the social and psychological sciences if the beliefs pertain to verifiable experience. The beliefs may either be confirmed, denied, or left as unproved but possibly true. As for beliefs which have referents outside experience or after death, these cannot be evaluated by science. The body of study and learning which comes to grips with beliefs outside or beyond experience is philosophy. Here the most plausible answers to questions about objects beyond experience are developed. The assumptions involved and the criteria for the reasoning are made explicit in philosophical inquiry. Scientific techniques of observation or analysis may be imported into philosophy for whatever limited applications may be possible. As for the status of the conclusions as knowledge, they have the same potential status as any other results from philosophical reasoning. The exploration and teaching of philosophical methods and results have long been an established part of university curricula. Philosophical inquiry into the likelihood of life after death and of God outside experience is relevant, along with consideration of other objects not directly demonstrated by scientific observation and analysis. The fields of philosophy and social psychology hence overlap when the impact of philosophical thinking upon personality development and fulfillment is examined.

INCLUSION OF STUDY OF RELIGIOUS EXPERIENCE IN SOCIAL PSYCHOLOGY

The spiritual experiences, as well as the beliefs, of religious adherents have strong effects upon their life development. Data concerning these experiences, whether from introspection, questionnaire studies, or case reports, should be admitted into social psychology or whatever branches of learning focus upon personality development. More than this, religious groups take an active interest in shaping the personalities of their children and of new converts. These concerns bring religious experience and religious development into the area of social psychology.

Personality Changes Are Sought by Religious Groups

The advocates of a religious system of belief and behavior usually seek to bring the members into conformity with the aims of the group. The individual is encouraged to give up interests and activities which compete for the time or money that the group seeks or requires. Fundamentalist churches with tithing or even complete appropriation of the individual's resources exemplify this subordination of the individual to the spiritual community.

Beyond continued maintenance of the group, a more basic function is propagation of a new way of life. This way of life may be regarded as prerequisite to gaining the approval of a divine being believed to supply rewards or other benefits to individuals in this life or the next. In Orthodox Judaism, the responsibility of devout Jews to fulfill conditions of the covenant with God is regarded as absolutely vital to the well-being of the group. The individual's observance or disregard of laws imposed by God upon his people is not a matter of individual discretion, but of group survival at the hands of a powerful and jealous God, who may destroy those who are faithless toward him, or at least withold necessities of survival.

Unquestionably the things required of Jews by God have many obvious benefits to the individual, family, or group. The individual gains strength of character and habits of industry which make her or him produce wealth and material things for others. The individual is induced to maintain loyalty to spouse and children. This stability of loyalty and affection assures the family of ongoing fulfillment of the affectional and physical needs of family members. In times of crisis, as in war or famine, when unusual selflessness is required, the subordination of greed, lust, pleasure-seeking, or privilege assures that the individual will provide time, resources, and energetic effort for group welfare.

At one extreme, the weight of requirements to be met by the Orthodox Jew in observing Jewish law and ceremonial can be viewed as a vast proliferation of duties. At the other extreme, the substance of religious law can be summarized in the words of Micah: "What does the Lord require of you? To act justly and to love mercy and to walk humbly with your God" (The Bible, Micah 6: 8, NIV).

God as an Object for Sociopsychological Study

To phrase "walk humbly with your God" implies that the God walked with is a real person or object or at least is believed to be real. Whatever may be alleged concerning the nature of God outside human experience, we are confronted as social psychologists with the object in human experience which is believed by some to be God here on earth. The time is past due when it should be recognized by religious students that theology belongs within the field of psychology insofar as there is an object in inner experience whom followers label as God. The rest of God's nature outside of individual experience is a proper task for philosophy; it starts with data of history or experience, but it proceeds beyond the frontiers of earth-bound science. The task of religious philosophy is to apply the methods of science to the limited data of human experience in endeavoring to reconstruct the likely nature of God beyond experience. Social psychologists, of course, limit themselves to conclusions which are based upon data accessible through experiences.

The affirmation that God is an object in human experience was established more by the work of Carl Jung (1939, 1958) than any other psychologist. Jung regards study of the physical world, and his own work, as not proving the existence of God in the usual manner of scientific proof. Not self-critical about the scientific status of his clinical demonstration of God as an object in human experience, he writes: "God is an obvious psychic and non-physical fact, i.e., a fact which can be established psychically but not physically" (Jung, 1958: 464).

The Hebrew prophet Micah alludes to the pervasive presence of God, with whom the believer walks. Christian writers of scripture declare more emphatically the presence of God in their experience. Referring to God as Christ, Paul writes: "I no longer live, but Christ lives in me" (The Bible, Galatians 2: 20,NIV).

As social psychologists we need not settle the question of whether what believers call God in themselves actually is God according to the criterion of some theologian. The psychological point is that there is something directly apprehended in the personality system which believers call God.

Nor need we as social psychologists to be drawn into the controversy of whether God as experienced by a person is part of the human being or is outside the human being. Rather, we may address ourselves to the question of defining the relationship between God as experienced and the rest of the personality system.

Jung (1958: 7) states the relationship as he observed it from his clinical studies:
[The God-experience is] a dynamic agency or effect not caused by an arbitrary act of will. On the contrary, it seizes and controls the human subject, who is always rather its victim than its creator. The numinosum -- whatever its cause may be -- is an experience of the subject independent of his will.

Jung asserts that human beings cannot readily conceive of God in the abstract, but require a concrete image. The leading interpreter of his religious psychology, Hans Schaer (1950: 139), writes:
The God-image that men make for themselves is not so much a matter of knowledge of some fact external to man as of the expression of a psychic fact, the best possible formulation of some psychic actuality which we have to exteriorize in order to grasp at all.

As Jesus said of himself, "No one comes to the Father except through me" (The Bible, John 14: 6,NIV). So Christians have apprehended God through the personality of Jesus Christ. John further makes clear how knowing God is possible (The Bible, I John 4: 7-8, NIV): "Dear friends, let us love one another, for love comes from God. Everyone who loves has been born of God and knows God. Woever does not love does not know God, because God is love." Sounding like a psychologist, John implies that God is a pattern of ideal love motivating the individual.

We recall William James' (1936) thesis that the higher or ideal self is the ground for apprehending who God is. In explaining religious conversion he writes of the individual experiencing salvation:
He becomes conscious that this higher part is conterminous and continuous with MORE of the same quality, which is operative in the universe outside of him, and which he can keep in working touch with, and in a fashion get on board of and save himself when all his lower being has gone to pieces in the wreck (p. 499).

The significance of admitting an object called God into the empirical domain of psychology cannot be over-estimated. On the one hand, activity of God in the life of the individual becomes an appropriate domain for inquiry along the lines of the case studies analyzed by William James and Carl Jung. On the other hand, claims of believers no longer need be relegated to a never-never land outside psychology where merely dogma holds sway. Christians, as the advocates of a particular psychological framework of theory, are entitled to consideration for a place as a school of psychology in the question for a common ground of scientific truth. That a group of religious devotees may, if they acknowledge the rubrics of psychology, knock at the gates of science is a historical event of far-reaching importance. Other groups besides Christians are also entitled to advance their claims and subject them to scientific scrutiny. This parallels the activity in philosophy which for centuries has examined beliefs concerning life beyond death and God beyond experience.

Having advanced the principle that the human experience of God is a suitable topic for psychological study, we can return to the task of considering Jesus' life and teachings as a model for spiritual growth. We now are able to define spiritual development as personality development in relation to God as experienced in the personality system or as believed to exist outside of human life.

A CHRISTIAN MODEL OF PERSONALITY DEVELOPMENT

In delineating a Christian model of personality development, I try to hold closely to what is set forth in the New Testament. In the actual selection of material, there is room for some latitude of choice. Others might feel that my selection could differ. It is evident especially that some church groups have moved away from traditionally orthodox Christian ideas in developing their own emphases or departures. In this respect, there are doubtless many Christian models of personality development. Nevertheless, what is written in Christian scripture is a firm record. It should not arouse controversy to cite facts of historical record, although interpretation of these historical writings is susceptible to differing viewpoints. My own focuses the concepts of psychology and sociology upon this written record.

Acceptance of Jesus Christ by the Individual

The first step in following Jesus Christ is to receive him into one's life. In psychological terms, this means acknowledging that Jesus is present in one's personality system. Christians believe Jesus is much more than this, but at the least there is a psychological reality. There is also a decision to follow his leading as a guide in one's own life plans and activities. In the parlance of Christians, one receives Jesus as Lord of one's life. This is not simply recalling his image as a historical figure who lives nearly two thousand years ago. Rather, Jesus is regarded as a contemporary who has present-day existence; he is a real, personal being in the experience of the believer. This image is invested with powerful motivation, dominating the individual's personality.

How does Jesus enter the personality system as a psychological force? There are obvious routes for this implantation. Reading the life and teachings of Jesus in the Bible is one way. Hearing another believer tell of what Jesus is doing in his or her life is another. Both of these exposures introduce Jesus simply as an idea of a personal being. Because of the similarity of the idea of Jesus to the motivation of ideal love in the individual, the idea combines with the personality component of ideal love, insofar as this is present in the individual. The altruistic impulse exists at least as a rudimentary impulse in the personality system of the individual. When this fusion occurs, the figure of Jesus ceases to be merely an idea and becomes a motivational system, seeking its own way and making demands upon the person.

According to Cooley (1956a: 139; 1956b: 23-24), altruistic motivation, referred to as "we-feeling," arises in the experience of primary group living. In seeking others face to face, we experience their needs imaginatively and respond to those needs as if they were our own. In this way, their needs become part of our own motivational system. Our ideas of the needs of others become invested with the same motivational force as our ideas of our own needs. Altruistic motivation results from the innate capacity for imagination plus the social experience of group living. Since the biological and social basis for altruism is present in all human beings, all have this motivation, at least to some degree. There is loyalty even among thieves.

According to W. Robertson Smith (1957) and Durkheim (1947), when human beings come to identify altruistic feeling as an influence different from the rest of their nature, the "we-feeling" becomes objectified as a spiritual being. Altruistic motivation becomes spiritual motivation when it is regarded as an object distinct from the rest of the personality system. The object is addressed by communication, as in prayer or other forms of propitiation. This dialogue or interlocution within the lives of individuals has the effect of heightening the experience and influence of the spirit being. This view of prayer is evident in the work of Coe (1916: 302-320) six decades ago.

The implantation of the Jesus figure as a motivational system is facilitated by the internal dialogue of prayer. The believer appeals to Jesus to dominate and direct his or her life. Of course, he or she may hold that the communication reaches a being external to the individual. There is an empirical basis for the conversation between distinct segments of the personality system of the individual. Through prayer, the believer's image of Jesus progresses to the level of a motivational system directing that person's life.

The role of belief in the existence of Jesus as a real being is vital to the seeker's finding Jesus in his or her own life. This is emphasized in the gospel written by John, "For God so loved the world that he gave his one and only Son, that whoever believes in him shall not perish but have eternal life" (The Bible, John 3: 16, NIV).

One can well ask why the figure of Jesus is important to the success of the believer in finding God in one's life. Jesus asserted

67

that no one comes to God the Father except through himself (The
Bible, John 14: 6). This far-reaching statement can be understood
from the insight which Jung (Schaer, 1950: 184) gives into religious
experience:

The living symbol is the formulation of an essentially unconscious fragment, and the more universal this fragment
is, the more universal the effect of the symbol, since it
will touch a chord in each of us.... Only when the symbol
grasps this primitive factor and brings the expression of
it to the highest pitch does it enjoy universal effect.
Therein lies the tremendous and at the same time the saving
power of a living social symbol.

Human beings can poorly apprehend God in the abstract. In the figure
of Jesus as shepherd and teacher, they are able to grasp the nature
of God.

The concrete manner for conveying the abstractions in religious
systems appears in various ways. Ceremonial, sacred objects, religious personages, parables, allegories: these all aid the believer
to apprehend concretely what is otherwise abstract and incomprehen-
sible.

Personality Changes Modeled by the Teaching and Example of Jesus Christ

Reception of Jesus Christ into the individual's personality
system tends to influence his or her motivation and behavior to
conform with that of Jesus Christ. This alternation is accelerated
through learning more of the nature of Jesus' life and studying his
teachings. These teachings become imperatives for reconstructing
the believer's own personality. Fellow-believers urge one to become
more Christ-like. Thomas à Kempis' Imitation of Christ exemplifies
believers' efforts to model their lives after that of Jesus Christ.

What are the characteristics of Jesus' personality? We turn to
the records of the life and teachings of Jesus written down by his
followers from their personal experience, recollection, and oral
tradition. While some researchers raise the question of how closely
these records portray the actual Jesus, this question need not dis-
tract us. Our thrust becomes consideration of the model provided
by the Jesus recorded in the Bible. The close concurrence among the
writers of the gospels adds historical credence in the view of believers. Moreover, Christians believe that the Scriptures were
written by those guided by the highest motivation, that of the Holy
Spirit, so the possibility of error is minimal or non-existent.

What manner of person is revealed by those writing of Jesus' life
and teachings? As to Jesus' early life, almost nothing is written.
The earliest episode which reveals his character is at the age of
12. He ignored his parents' wishes by staying behind in Jerusalem
after they started for home. He did this in order to discourse
with learned men in the Temple (The Bible, Luke 2: 41-50). Else-

where he advises forsaking family ties, if necessary, to follow him (The Bible, Matthew 10: 35-37). Learned in Jewish Scripture, he zealously entered into debate with Jewish leaders about many points of Jewish doctrine (The Bible, Mark 12: 27-34). He sought to place much emphasis upon spiritual living and loving service to others at the expense of ignoring requirements of Jewish law, such as keeping the Sabbath free from any work for others (The Bible, Mark 2: 23-27; 3: 1-6).

Jesus is manifested throughout his ministry as one pursuing a burning mission to disclose to others the nature of God as he understood God. His theological concepts are largely his own discovery; he drew upon Jewish tradition, but he depended primarily upon his own innovation. These concepts are that God loves human beings and requires personal loyalty, rather than adherence to law, as a condition of enjoying the kingdom of God, and that God's nature is revealed in Jesus' own personality of love and service to others (The Bible, John 14: 8-11). Of course, the ethical ideals in Jesus' life and teachings are deep in Jewish tradition, as well as in other world religions. What is distinctive is his regarding God as a being whom people experience directly in their own lives, first in his own person during Jesus' life, and after Jesus' death, as the figure of Jesus and as the Holy Spirit (The Bible, John 14: 16-29). The Jews of Jesus' time did not presume that the Holy Spirit is a daily and familiar companion. The Holy Spirit is God-like motivation, also expressed in other figures and symbols than that of Jesus Christ, such as light, power, and Lord.

Jesus sought to relax the requirements of Jewish law, rather than to dispense with Jewish law altogether. It remained for Paul and other followers of Jesus to dispense with major requirements of Jewish law. Jesus, as explained by Paul, sought to give human beings the spiritual power through the Spirit of Christ to achieve the ethical ideals in Jewish law (The Bible, Romans 8: 3-11). The way of life on which the Christian's life is patterned is that of a personal relationship to an indwelling spiritual being, rather than merely respecting religious customs or religious law. The spiritual being is disclosed by the life-style of Jesus himself.

Besides his teaching, two things seem to stand out in Jesus' own personality. (1) His warm love for human beings is shown by his friendly, tolerant, and genuinely humble relationship to them (The Bible, Luke 10: 23-42; 12: 22-34; 18: 15-17; 19: 1-10). He rejoiced in the fellowship of others. In the simple pastoral life around the Sea of Galilee, where most of Jesus' ministry took place, were found a happy band of followers little worried by the cares of the world, captivated by Jesus' gentle and joyous way of life (The Bible, Matthew 8-9).

(2) Also evident is Jesus' overwhelming commitment to his teaching

mission (The Bible, Matthew 4). This commitment was so strong that it brought him to Jerusalem for a direct confrontation with Jewish authorities (The Bible, Matthew 21-23). The commitment to teaching and converting others has persisted undiminished among Christians down to the present time.

In the turbulent scenes of Jesus' last days in Jerusalem, we find him less warm and friendly, more distant, filled with the foreboding for the ordeal he was about to suffer (The Bible, John 13). He became sharp in his preaching to Jews who did not agree with him (The Bible, Matthew 23) and direct in his reproof of his own followers (The Bible, Matthew 26: 35-56). These things bring out transitory phases of Jesus' character which Christians rarely take as the example for their own lives.

In common with Jews of his time, Jesus advocated frequent communion with God through prayer. He sought to make prayer more a private and personal matter (The Bible, Luke 11: 1-13; Matthew 6: 1-15). He departed from Jewish sensibility in allowing others to regard him as the Son of God (The Bible, Matthew 11: 27; Mark 14: 61-62). Especially among his later followers he was viewed as the first and greatest son of God, but all were called to become sons of God (The Bible, Galatians 3: 26).

The idea of sonship of God means that the follower of Jesus undergoes a second adolescence, this time one of spiritual development, and thus becomes a spiritual offspring of God's Spirit. This second stage of growth under the tutelage of God the Father follows the first stage of growth as the offspring of human parents. All Christian believers are called upon to undergo this second stage of personality growth which makes them offspring of God, as well as the offspring of human parents. For those who grow up in the church community, the first and second phases may develop together.

The final stage in the Christian model of personality development is the fulfillment of spiritual aims. For the devotee, these are not merely some of life's purposes, they are the basic purposes of life. Scriptural references abound in their claims of the joyful life which those who pursue the Christian model of salvation will experience. The Beatitudes (The Bible, Matthew 5: 3-12) exalt a humble spiritual approach to life's circumstances and to the people around one. We have Paul's words concerning the fruits of spiritual living, "But the fruit of the Spirit is love, joy, peace..." (The Bible, Galatians 5: 22, NIV). In the scientific spirit, there is the appeal in the Old Testament, "Taste and see that the Lord is good, blessed is the man who takes refuge in him" (The Bible, Psalm 34: 8, NIV).

CLOSING STATEMENT

We have merely considered Jesus' life and teachings as a model of personality development. The few who achieve really fundamental transformation of their personalities under   Jesus' impact are the exception, rather than the prevailing pattern. Most followers of great spiritual leaders are more conspicuous for their talk than for their deeds. In part this points to the deep roots of personality in biological and social determination. Yet the achievements of those who attain to compelling spiritual vision are a source of joy and leadership to all who are touched by their lives.

The major thrust of this paper is to bring a Christian model of personality development to the attention of social psychologists. Other religious models of personality development also have a claim upon research and teaching in social psychology, just as the extra-experiential principles of religious systems have an intellectual claim upon departments of philosophy in universities.

Bringing religious teaching out of an isolated land of religious dogma into the purview of social psychology should aid those who seek better understanding of themselves and of God, with whom they commune in their experience. Philosophical faith in God beyond experience and in life beyond death raises human hopes, while religious psychology provides the platform on which spiritual living is built.

SPIRITUAL ADVICE TO THE BORN AGAIN

Therefore, rid yourselves of all malice and all deceit, hypocrisy, envy, and slander of every kind. Like newborn babies, crave spiritual milk, so that by it you may grow up in your salvation .... As you come to him, the living Stone, ... you also, like living stones, are being built into a spiritual house to be a holy priesthood, offering spiritual sacrifices acceptable to God through Jesus Christ. -- The Bible, I Peter 2: 1-2, 4-5, NIV.

PART III. SPIRITUAL WELL-BEING AND SOCIOLOGICAL THEORY

Chapter 6

REFERENCE GROUPS AND ROLE STRAINS RELATED TO SPIRITUAL WELL-BEING

William R. Garrett

The interchangeable concepts of spiritual well-being and healthy religion are employed in this discussion as an analogue to somatic health, in much the same manner as mental health serves as a metaphorical construct for conceptualizing psychological stability in relation to physical well-being. Indeed, the physical, social-psychological, and religious realms constitute three dimensions of human existence in which the dynamics of health or illness are relevant evaluative categories. Although these domains mutually interpenetrate each other, they nonetheless remain aspects of individual biographies susceptible to analytical differentiation. The empirical flow of causative influence among the members of this triad evidences a lively reciprocity, since any one variable may function as a triggering mechanism for activating responses in the other sectors of experience.

Identifying a healthy orientation among the complex interactions linking the organic, social-psychological, and spiritual dimensions of life is complicated for social scientists by virtue of the differing criteria indicative of well-being which operate in each sphere. Our intent in this investigation is not to delineate in normative terms the substance of healthy religion, but rather to illuminate the social processes through which actors are able to clarify for themselves the content of appropriate religious roles. Accordingly, this analysis will treat the negotiation process internal to religious communities whereby the notion of legitimate and healthy religion is established. To flesh out the full implications of this line of analysis, some consideration of the impact exerted by secular reference groups would need to be undertaken, but that enterprise falls outside the scope of this project and must be reserved for another occasion.

---

*Reprinted from Sociological Analysis, vol. 40, no. 1, Spring 1979.

73

REFERENCE GROUPS AND THE ESTABLISHMENT OF THE ROLE OF SPIRITUAL
WELL-BEING

Beckford (1975: 7) has recently observed that Americans tend
to favor studies of role behavior in their sociological treatments
of religious phenomena. Our aim is to exploit this theoretical
strength in American religious research by examining the types of
role transactions and strains which emerge out of the process of
fashioning a viable definition of spiritual well-being. The
salient assumption from which this analysis proceeds holds that
religious actors negotiate a view of appropriate role behavior in
relation to several reference groups featured within their total
religious community. Three foci of overriding importance have
been selected for critical evaluation. This selection has been
informed by the seminal explorations of H. Richard Niebuhr, who,
through a series of studies (1945; 1960; 1963), pioneered in the
application of Meadian role theory to the interpretation of religious processes.

The three interaction sequences considered here include (1)
the role reciprocity entered into between a religious actor and
his local church or fellowship; (2) the role interactions linking
a believer and deity, however the Ultimate Being or Power may be
intellectually conceptualized and experientially apprehended,
and (3) the ongoing relationships integrating a religious actor
into that "official model of religion" -- to borrow Luckmann's
(1967) felicitous phrase -- carried by denominational traditions.

Although a rational symmetry normally connects these three
reference groups, conflicts may arise whenever an actor fails to
be properly socialized -- a perpetual possibility, given the fact
that socialization processes are never perfect -- or whenever an
actor discerns substantive discrepancies among the role expectations devolving from one or more of the reference subsystems
to which he is simultaneously oriented. In order to mitigate the
stress created by conflicting role obligations, actors are required to select among those reference groups whose demands they
will heed and those which they will dismiss as inadequate guides
for certain aspects of their total repertoire of appropriate role
behaviors. For instance, on the issue of contraception now current
among Roman Catholics, the official position of the church clearly
affirms that spiritual well-being does not allow for the use of
birth control devices, while at the level of personal conscience
a substantial number of American Catholics arrive at the opposing
conclusion. Furthermore, a majority of priestly leadership
counsels that some types of birth control by artificial means are
appropriate, in contrast to a smaller number of priests who hold
with the official position that artificial means of birth control
are universally wrong (see Greeley, 1977: 156). Clear-cut disagreement on an issue so patently germane to the definition of
spiritual health inevitably thrusts Catholics into a fiercely

74

contested struggle over which practice deserves their loyalty. And when no compromise among reference groups within the religious organization can be attained, only individual role management can successfully extricate adherents from the impasse which competing reference groups foster.

This illustration not only reveals how readily conflicts may emerge amid a cluster of role obligations, but it also serves to underscore the organizational need for maintaining consensus among the divergent reference groups informing individual action. In this regard, definitions of "authentic faith" and "healthy religion" share a common ground, insofar as both rely on attitudinal congruence as a requisite for their operational effectiveness. Moreover, actors who define spiritual well-being in opposition to a related reference group may typically expect censure from that group whose role prescriptions were rejected. Yet, however the conflict over role allocations among religious reference groups achieves resolution, one fact persists as a stubborn reminder of the essential sociality attending the definitional process, namely, that the imprimatur of healthy religion is seldom extended to a specific role-cluster unless consensual agreement as to its basic norms has been recognized by more than one reference group. Hence, we may hypothesize that the construct, "healthy religion," itself represents a negotiated formula whose legitimacy is confirmed for individual actors by some coalition of reference groups operative within the boundaries of their religious institution.

One should not infer from this hypothesis, however, that individual actors behave in pawn-like fashion with their every move predetermined by the reference groups that provide input to their action. Rather, individuals may be understood to retain a measure of voluntarism for facilitating a consensus among functional reference groups, thereby actively contributing to the development of a viable definition of spiritual health. The perspective outlined herein is not theoretically or methodologically wedded to the a priori assertion of a functional dominance of either individual or reference group influences. Our analysis throughout considers each pole in this classic self-community dichotomy as an independent variable. Our focus centers accordingly on those interactive networks connecting individuals and reference groups in the ongoing process of fashioning normative definitions. Before commenting further on the total process, however, we need first to explicate the three interaction sequences already identified as overwhelmingly crucial in framing the rules of religious role performance.

THE REFERENCE FUNCTION OF THE LOCAL FELLOWSHIP

The local church or fellowship constitutes a strategic primary group whose influence is normally the first encountered by the newcomers attaining membership within a religious organization. If we accept as axiomatic Durkheim's (1965: 59) claim that religious beliefs "...are not merely received individually by all the members of (the) group" and view beliefs and religious roles as a property of group life itself, then socialization into the perspective of the local community stands as a _sine qua non_ for admission into group participation.

The religious socialization of most adult adherents normally began at an early age with spiritual nurturance entrusted to the religious community of their parents. Youth who grew to maturity under these circumstances find it difficult to remember when they were not well integrated into the local congregation and when the church's teachings did not form a part of their taken-for-granted world view.

Adult converts record a somewhat different type of social experience. Conversion, in their instance, entails anticipatory socialization (Merton, 1968: 319-25) whereby newcomers acquire familiarity as quickly as possible with the cognitive and behavioral norms of the fellowship. Yet, the end result remains essentially the same: the central teachings of the group relative to healthy faith and practice are assimilated into the personality structure and religious world view of the initiate to form the subjective reality-base which is a requisite for participation in the local congregation. (For a similar theme, see Berger and Luckmann, 1967: 129-163.)

Although it might appear as if religious socialization does not differ decisively from forms operative in other institutional contexts, there is one respect in which this assumption proves misleading. For religious socialization also provides the occasion for apprehending what theologians broadly describe as revelation. That is to say, under the mellow encouragement of the community of faith, religious socialization induces selves to be conditioned from a new point of view which -- following Niebuhr's (1960) useful distinction between observed and lived history -- transforms the events of secular, scientifically understood history into existentially meaning-laden experiences infused with a special parabolic significance for reordering the personal biographies of selves entering the confessional community. Inner history refers to that complex of meanings which superabundantly deepen one's understanding of and relationship to the world as apprehended through the eyes of faith. The appropriation of this internal, lived history necessarily entails a _metanoia_ (Niebuhr, 1960: 83) or conversion, whereby the self through interaction with other selves-in-community undergoes a fundamental reorientation to the historical setting that is perceived simultaneously as an occasion of sacred disclosure.

Furthermore, the indication that _metanoia_ has occurred may be discerned when one is capable of identifying personal being and destiny with the community which transmits the inner history of

76

faith. Religious socialization, then, at once opens up the opportunity for participation in the living memory, tradition, and
celebration of the group, even as it also provides the seasonable
moment for discovering deeper symbolic meanings in events than
can be certified by the canons of historical reason. Moreover,
what is revealed in the personal interactions that move "from
faith to faith" is not only a specific content, but also that this
content has laid a special claim on selves so that hereafter any
rehearsal of the "faith of the fathers" concurrently becomes a
recounting of the "story of our lives" (see Niebuhr, 1960: 43-
90). Within the Christian community, say, this means that the self
would soon come to participate vicariously in those events commemo-
rated by the group as surfeited with intrinsic religious value --
such as the exodus, the preachings of the prophets, the cruci-
fixion of Jesus, the Reformation, and an infinite number more -- for
in these episodes the contemporary self, too, is judged and affirmed,
chastized and redeemed, since God's dealings with the community,
both past and present, are at once God's actions to the person.

Religious socialization is not, of course, the only mode of
revelation, nor do we mean to suggest that all inner history experiences possess the efficacious quality of revelation. Yet,
one salient ramification which does derive from this perspective
concerns the essential role of the community in fostering the sort
of socialization experience which allows for genuine revelatory
occasions. For the base line against which actors measure their
subsequent apprehensions of non-empirical reality is laid through
the interaction with other believers situated in the local fellowship. Herein a self acquires a personal placement amid the structures of existence which subjectively informs his identity,
ethical priorities, and ultimate value commitments. Immured
within this material appropriated by the self stand those normative role prescriptions that constitute spiritual health. Definitions of spiritual health, then, emerge as one dimension of a
larger role-set of proper faith and practice associated with
particular statuses in the local fellowship.

The functional responsibilities of the local reference group
are not completed once the indoctrination process is firmly
launched, however. By an intricate succession of interactions,
feedback to actors conveys evaluations of how closely their performance corresponds to group norms and expectations. In sectarian groups with highly explicit norms, deviance generally
evokes harsh sanctions -- unless actors quickly amend their
behavior. Middle class denominations usually employ more subtle
means of social control. Formal exclusion is rarely invoked,
but there are less drastic methods for dealing with dissident
behavior. Individuals can be alienated from their local fellowships
through such mechanisms as exclusion from committees and leadership positions, subjection of offenders to derisive remarks, ostracism during public gatherings (a functional equivalent to the

sectarian practice of shunning), and, failing all else, overt rebuke by fellowship leaders.

Unsavory treatment of this sort soon convinces wayward members of their persona non grata status in the eyes of their peers, and it leaves open several courses of action. Deviants may reform their action so as to comply with normative expectations; they may switch denominations, searching for a community more consonant with their religious style or they may gradually slip into the status of inactive member. Indeed, the large number of dormant members tabulated by the major religious organizations may not be entirely the result of a gradual waning of faith; many may well have been "pushed" into that status because of their failure to abide by the normative prescriptions laid down by local groups within denominational enclaves.

In addition to socializing newcomers into the perspective of the community, then, the local fellowship also supplies -- in close connection with the belief system of the collectivity -- a lucid definition of moral conduct appropriate to spiritual health. It also acts as a supervising agency for overseeing the conformity of actors to group norms. These operations of indoctrination, role definition, and performance evaluation carried on by the local reference group are counter-balanced, meanwhile, by inputs to the action matrix by other reference groups. Whether ancillary groups confirm or contradict the norms sponsored by the local fellowship decidedly affects the degree of power which it is capable of exerting. Especially critical is the confirmation deriving from the self's encounter with deity, since all questions of legitimate faith and practice ultimately find their source of authority in that notion of the sacred which stands at the vital center of religious life.

THE REFERENCE FUNCTION OF THE DIVINE SIGNIFICANT OTHER

An intellectual territory where social scientists generally fear to tread is broached in this segment of our analysis. The overriding concern, whenever deity is introduced as a variable, is that theological suppositions may insinuate themselves into the warp and woof of the argument, thereby confounding the socio-logical objectivity of the interpretation. Our intent, however, is not to assert a particular conception of deity, but to explore the dynamics of self-God interaction as a basis for comprehending the reference function deity serves for religious actors. For it is our contention that, through a variety of mediums -- mystical, rational, pietistic, ascetic, naturalistic, and so forth -- individual actors apprehend the nature of non-empirical reality and accept its prescribed order for their lives.

Furthermore, it is also our claim that the self-Divine Other encounter may be understood with heightened analytical precision

78

in reference to role theory rubrics. That is to say, self-other interactions with which we are familiar in secular settings can be extended analogically to illuminate the process of self-divine interaction. (This depiction of the interaction process between the self and deity may be troubling to some theorists because it may be viewed as implying that the Other must be perceived as a self in order for role theory rubrics to function effectively. Clearly, the analogy more readily fits the Western concept of God, but Eastern images of sacredness as well as functional alternatives to God, such as Sartre's (1956: 16-45) notion of nothingness, can also be accommodated. For what is crucial is that selves, by encountering non-empirical reality, draw from the experience some behavioral guidelines which are regarded as religiously appropriate. While this response may not satisfy some critics, it should at the very least indicate that the issue has not been overlooked in constructing our argument.)

Proceeding on the above assumptions, the following interpretation may be advanced. In the first instance, some movement through the primary stages of socialization into the perspective of a given faith system constitutes a behavioral requisite for the human actor in the self-God dyad, since such antecedent training is required to establish the cognitive parameters wherein divine-human interactions are rendered intelligible. Although it may be the case -- as Maslow (1970: 30-35) has argued -- that religious organizations strive to control transcendent experiences so as to stave off the potentially disruptive consequences which ecstacy tends to unleash within routinized institutional structures, it also remains true that religious organizations supply a framework of coherent categories for comprehending the meaning of peak-experiences which might otherwise remain so diffuse that they relate only tangentially to the spiritual life of actors.

Yet, previous socialization merely serves as a prelude and referencing point for the subsequent event of divine-human encounter. The moment of contact and illumination carries with it the inherent capacity to overwhelm conventional expectations that are predicated on in-group assumptions. Scholars have introduced various constructs to lend conceptual clarity to the numinal and mystical feelings which believers associate with divine-human interaction, such as Rudolf Otto's (1958: 12-40) experience of the holy, Tillich's (1969: 127-32) notions of ultimate concern and "Kairos," Buber's (1958) I-Thou model, Maslow's (1970) peak-experiences, and a succession of other formulae (see also Wach, 1951; Eliade, 1959, 1963; Van der Leeuw, 1963; Scheler, 1960; Happold, 1967, and Spencer, 1963).

A general pattern common to these accounts is an interactive relationship linking a religious actor to the Absolute. Although the triggering mechanism inducing the experience may run the gamut from ritual action to devotional exercises, moral reflection,

nature experiences (Hood, 1977b), rational contemplation, a burst
of esthetic creativity, or even an intense personal crisis, the
experience itself tends to be recalled as an occasion wherein
the self acknowledges being grasped by a reality whose being is
of unqualified importance for one's existence.

Viewed from the vantage of the human participant, the encounter
may be elucidated as a type of role interaction, wherein role is
understood as
> a sector of the total orientation system of an indivi-
> dual actor which is organized about expectations in
> relation to a particular interaction context, that is
> integrated with a particular set of value-standards
> which govern interaction with one or more alters
> in the appropriate complementary roles (Parsons, 1951:
> 38-39).

We are also proceeding here under the twin assumptions that role
expectations emerge, in part, as a "product of a social interaction
process" itself; hence they are functional for "facilitating interaction between persons" even in those situations where cultural
guidelines for behavior are not fully specified (Miyamoto, 1969:
118). To be sure, appropriate modifications are required to accom-
modate the fact that the Divine Other is not like ordinary alters
encountered in secular experience; but it does logically and empirically follow that an ego, in response to a Divine Alter, feels
constrained to embrace a set of role expectations derived from
his apprehension of the nature of that non-empirical reality with
whom contact has been made. Or, to put the issue somewhat differently, an ego commonly experiences some transformation of his
understanding of reality in the encounter with deity which fosters
the separation of those behavioral patterns that may now be
regarded as religiously sanctioned from those which are clearly
incongruent with the nature of the sacred.

By thus phrasing the issue, we do not mean to suggest that role
patterns for authentic faith are supernaturally disclosed "out
of the blue" -- although some religious visionaries have made such
claims in the past. Rather, what participants more commonly aver
is that the divine encounter becomes the occasion for the growth
of a different sort of knowledge. In an illuminating discussion,
Niebuhr (1960: 152-153) distills the essential meaning of such
events to that sort of disclosure wherein the self knows himself
to be known from beginning to end and discovers himself to be
valued by the activity of the universal valuer. According to
Niebuhr, then, the importance of the revelatory moment inheres
not in the communication of an esoteric, supernatural knowledge,
but in the creation of a new and contemporaneous mode of relatedness
which serves as a fountainhead for the response of faith, a source
of confidence, and the experiential basis for acknowledging the
claim of the moral imperative.

Role theory rubrics provide a particularly useful theoretical infrastructure for analyzing the sort of knowledge derivative from divine-human interaction. For the genius of Meadian role theory -- which Niebuhr (1945, 1960, 1963) adroitly exploited -- held that a social actor linked in an interaction sequence was afforded the opportunity of "taking the role of the other" over against oneself, and of participating in the attitude of the other, even when ego could not in actuality occupy the other's status position. A child, for example, cannot appropriate the roles of mother and father, yet might "take the role of mother and father," particularly in play, in order to understand and accept their attitudes and behavior toward the child (see Mead, 1963: 362-67; 1967: 610-11).

In similar fashion it can be suggested that, in the moment of divine-humane encounter, the self is drawn into sympathetic relationship with deity, whereby it glimpses reality from the perspective of the Divine Other and comprehends the attitude of deity toward the world and the actor's behavior. Thus, the drawing near of the self to the perspective of deity allows an individual to view behavior -- however partially and deficiently, given finite limitations -- as the Other views it, to interpret conduct as the Other might interpret it, and to judge action as the Other might judge it. The meaning unsealed in this event, then, is a relational knowledge of grasping the response of deity toward the world of persons and of comprehending the expectations deity holds out relative to the self's behavior. Despite the qualitative differences distinguishing the finite from the Infinite, the theory of role taking does enable the observer to understand with heightened precision how the attitude of deity is disclosed to the self so as to transform human perceptions of reality and reorder believers' value commitments according to the standards of faith.

As with all arguments from analogy, this interpretation can be banally perverted by pressing the comparison too far. Our claim, it should be underscored, is not that the revelatory encounter empowers the finite self to usurp the viewpoint of deity and behold reality as through the eyes of God. Niebuhr (1960: 59) is entirely correct when he cautions that "...faith cannot escape from partnership with history," so all religious knowledge must be regarded as subject to socio-cultural conditioning. By remaining more modest, our thesis merely advocates that, by being thrust into a radical relationship with deity, persons may be wrested from a self-serving religiosity and forthwith integrated into a transcendent orientation sufficient to disclose to human consciousness an awareness of being known, judged, valued, and redeemed by that Absolute Other responsible for initiating the union.

In one sense, therefore, the moment of divine encounter may be likened to a revolutionary force, by virtue of its capacity for remaking the understanding of the human actor. Doubtless, on the level of belief, this event stands as the beginning of a radical reconstruction of all previously held knowledge and, on the moral level, as the point of embarkation toward a renewed application of moral norms. Accentuating the revolutionary character of this experience, however, does not necessarily imply that old religious beliefs will immediately be disclaimed as erroneous or moral precepts vitiated of their directive power, but rather that the self is henceforth related to them in a context so fundamentally altered that they now acquire a transvalued meaning which is qualitatively different from the signification they carried before. To be sure, the self should not assume that all troublesome questions of faith will have been resolved once and for all in this experience. Yet the remembrance of this encounter's efficacious power can supply that root experience from which the heart reasons in its search for a deeper understanding of the goodness and purpose of spiritual life. Where the pilgrimage of faith leads, meanwhile, depends in large measure on the ability of the self to integrate back into the ebb and flow of social experience the ramifications deriving from participation in the "eternal now."

Consequently, alongside the preparatory stage occasioned by socialization into the perspective of the local reference group and the second stage of encounter with deity, a third movement in this succession of relationships needs also to be reckoned with in order to attain a comprehensive understanding of the reference function of deity in establishing religious role behavior. Specifically, this third movement refers to the sort of denouement process whereby the encounter experience is interpreted, evaluated, and then amalgamated with the testimony of other believers. "Assurance ... we are not mistaken in our ultimate convictions," Niebuhr (1960: 141) avers, "is not to be gained without social corroboration." In part, Niebuhr arrived at this conclusion out of his familiarity with Mead's thesis relative to the sociality surrounding the formation of meaning and the creation of significant symbols. The thrust of Mead's position, it may be recalled, centered in the contention that meaning emerges in a social field when a shared set of symbols is capable of calling out similar, typified responses among interacting selves, so that each is able to participate in the attitude of the other with respect to a given event, verbal gesture, or social experience (Mead, 1963: 75-90; Pfuetze, 1961: 58-75).

When translated into the religious domain and in unpacking the import of the divine-human encounter, this construct proves particularly relevant. For peak-experiences, whatever the level of their intensity, cannot be regarded as self-interpreting. Not only are persons privy to the possibility that their experience may have been nothing more than the wayward imaginations of their own hearts, but they are also motivated by a powerful social concern -- animated in part by the unconditional seriousness of the religious experience itself -- to share their newly acquired insights with

co-religionists. Durkheim (1965: 473) perceptively elucidated
this tendency in the observation that

...a man who has a veritable faith feels an invincible
need of spreading it; therefore he leaves his isolation,
approaches others and seeks to convince them, and it is
the ardour of the convictions which he arouses that
strengthens his own. It would quickly weaken if it
remained alone.

And a final factor impelling selves to share their subjective
experience manifests itself in the concern for enrichment, definition, criticism, and correction which their core-religious experience can enjoy through consultation with others.

For all these reasons, then, selves struggling with the implications of their encounter with deity typically turn to fellow adherents as a source of confirmation and support by testing their
perceptions against the inner historical knowledge possessed by
the community of faith. Moreover, believers are sustained through
this uncertain operation by the stalwart conviction that, if they
have genuinely encountered deity, their experience will coalesce
with the accounts of their fellows who are oriented toward the
same ultimate reality, since presumably the Absolute has revealed
itself to other selves through attributes similar to those disclosed to the individual self.

Predictably, however, validations of a given actor's perceptions are not always forthcoming. At that juncture, the self is
pressed into a difficult situation wherein it must decisively
resolve whether error exists within the narrower reaches of subjective experience or in the collective ruminations of the community.
Some religious virtuosos have been sufficiently confident in the
validity of their personal knowledge to withstand the reproof
of the reference community. Occasionally such self-reliant individuals have become idiosyncratic religionists incapable of hereafter maintaining close bonds with any community of faith, while
others have periodically emerged as the charismatic founders of
new spiritual fellowships. Yet the greater likelihood is that
individuals will, sooner or later, succumb to the tender persuasion
of the nurturing fellowship and distrust the feeble reed of their
own inner light when it illuminates a path tending in a heterodox
direction.

Whichever course is taken, the fact should now be clear that
the ramifications for framing a definition of healthy religion
which derive from the divine-human encounter may take quite ini-
mical directions. Perhaps the more common consequence is that
selves discern in the experience a subjective confirmation of the
role patterns which they have already assimilated through socialization into the community of faith. Hence, the encounter merely
serves to deepen superabundantly the commitment to that role
specification for healthy religion currently informing spiritual

behavior. But the alternative may also accrue: selves may be
inspired to forsake previously established patterns in favor of
a new model yielded, to their minds, in matchless detail by the
overweening quality of the encounter itself. Although a succession
of variables may influence the eventual outcome -- such as the
degree of prior socialization into the local community's perspective, the self's confidence in trusting the veracity of subjective experience, the intensity of the experience, the content
disclosed to the self, and the sensitivity of the local community
in responding to the believer's account of what was disclosed in
glimpsing reality from the divine orientation -- none of these
variables can predict with any reliability the sort of course
likely to be taken in the denouement process.

   In retrospect, therefore, the utility of the analysis just
summarized centers in its capacity to delineate in analytical
terms the social mechanisms by which selves acquire a knowledge of
and loyalty to a specific definition of spiritual health as a
function of their relationship with deity. Throughout this segment of our interpretation and alongside our primary concern with
discerning the processes of establishing notions of healthy
religion, there has flourished an ancillary interest in demon-
strating the need for paying more deliberate attention to the role
reciprocity that links the finite self to the Infinite Other.
Clearly, the cluster of issues arranged around this relationship
represents a neglected subject of theoretical and empirical
research in the scientific study of religion. How widespread is
this pattern of interaction between selves and the Divine Other,
how critical its empirical consequences for defining religious
role patterns, and how intricate its lines of interconnection with
other aspects of the religious institution, are among the questions standing in need of further research clarification.

THE REFERENCE FUNCTION OF DENOMINATIONAL ORGANIZATIONS

   The reference function of denominational organizations operates
at a higher level within the religious institution than the two
agents previously discussed. Denominational life precludes having
as much direct contact between organizational structures and the
believer as the other reference objects. Despite the social distance factor, denominational prescriptions still exert more than a
nominal degree of social constraint by delimiting the range of
beliefs and behavioral options available to small groups and individuals within the church. Indeed, by serving as the repository
for the cultic, intellectual, and administrative resources of the
group qua group, the normative power for defining participant
behavior tends to be concentrated in the higher echelons of the
ecclesiastical structure,even among those denominations formally
committed to a free church polity (see Harrison, 1959: 53-129).
Immediate access to these powerful instruments of social control
places in the hands of denominational leaders not only the means

for establishing authoritative role models for healthy religion, but also the social mechanisms for applying leverage to assure membership conformity to the definitions accorded official status.

In a similar fashion to local reference groups, the function of denominational bodies in sustaining a lively commitment to a sanctioned pattern of healthy religion may be divided between two analytically different social processes. One is concerned with definitional problems and the other with compliance procedures. Both aspects constitute potential problem areas for denominational leaders who are charged with securing operational solidarity among a diverse membership, while simultaneously retaining a sense of continuity between currently accepted role patterns and the church's historical tradition.

The task of formulating the "official model of religiosity" which serves as the basis for behavioral solidarity is somewhat eased by the unique character of the church as a social institution. For the church may be understood -- following Gustafson's (1961) penetrating interpretation -- as a human community of belief, action, memory, and theological understanding, all features which subtly condition that ordering process that eventually culminates in the articulation of appropriate patterns of religious action. Hence, the "official model" ought not to be regarded as a leadership creation for self-serving reasons -- as Luckmann's (1967: 77-106) negative interpretation implies -- but as a property of the life-process of the group itself. Denominational leaders are unable to exclude membership demands in the single-minded pursuit of institutional preservation, for religious elites can no more ride roughshod over the interests of their constituencies than can top management in business over specialist decisions within the technostructure or presidential government over the input of persons who comprise the permanent government. American religious history features countless instances of grass roots revolts against leaders who were perceived as straying too far from the vital center of orthodoxy (see Gaustad, 1973; Garrett, 1973).

Consequently, church leaders must evidence a brisk concern with building a definition of appropriate religious behavior on a consensual foundation which is capable of eliciting a favorable response from a substantial number of those strategic power blocs scattered throughout the communion. Meeting this organizational need will require of the leadership that it allocate ample resources in the forms of monetary support, theological and other forms of expertise, and the opportunity for official recognition. In addition, leadership must also initiate -- within or alongside its bureaucratic channels -- the study groups, task forces,or commissions which commonly function as the instruments for modifying or republishing official policy within the church.

Even under optimum circumstances, however, efforts to maintain solidarity are bound to encounter intractable obstacles. When theological belief systems were more homogeneous within denominations, the task of delineating a uniform model for participant behavior was undoubtedly much easier. Now, however, the relative disassociation between theological systems and denominational enclaves has forced religious collectivities to deal with a wider spectrum of beliefs in the process of fashioning a definition of legitimate role patterns. Yet the limited evidence available also suggests that -- contrary to much conventional wisdom relative to the growing homogenization of beliefs across denominational lines -- theological distinctions of consequences still exist within churches (Hoge, 1976; Glock and Stark, 1965: 86-122), and that it is demonstrably the liberal denominations which incur the greatest difficulties in maintaining belief and behavior cohesion (see Stark and Glock, 1968: 202; Kelley, 1972).

Generally speaking, denominational executives enjoy a somewhat freer hand in the exercise of power when they turn from the definitional process toward the nurturing of compliance to the formula for healthy religion which is worked out in the communal deliberations of the denomination. Again, certain constraints limit the range of administrative controls available to the leadership stratum. Etzioni's (1961) typology of legitimate compliance structures for organizations aptly delineates the sort of leadership dynamics permissible within the context of church administration. Essentially, the model recognizes three types of organizations, namely, coercive institutions which rely on physical force; utilitarian institutions which employ monetary remuneration; and normative organizations, such as churches, which depend on normative power as the mode of social control over participants. With regard to the third type, Etzioni (1961: 40) concludes,

compliance in normative organizations rests principally on the internalization of directives accepted as legitimate. Leadership, rituals, manipulation of social and prestige symbols, and resocializing are among the more important techniques of control used.

Moreover, normative means of fostering compliance are not inherently less potent than coercion or monetary controls. In the hands of a skillful administrator, normative techniques can usually handle all but the most strident opposition by appealing directly to the superiority of the collective wisdom of the group and by overlaying the claims promulgated by the denomination with an aura of legitimacy deriving from the sacred. Rank and file individuals who would dissent from the role norms of the "official model of religiosity" are thrust willy-nilly into the tenuous position of having to demonstrate the heightened cognitive and moral cogency of their viewpoint over against the collective expertise underpinning the institutional perspective. Mounting an effective challenge is an extraordinarily difficult task, especially while dissidents as antagonists remain committed to the same ultimate reality and are a part of that institutional complex whose rubrics are being disputed.

One component of the institutional apparatus, whose latent function obviates in part the probability of dissent arising from the lower ranks, inheres in what Berger (1967: 45-52, 126-157) has described as plausibility structures. These ideational constructs simultaneously function as explanatory and legitimating devices which buttress the reality definitions sponsored by religious groups. Although their manifest purpose is to demonstrate rational linkages between religious values and concrete beliefs and practices, they may also serve as defensive weapons against membership deviance, since any departure from the norms of the church requires the development of alternative plausibility structures by defecting individuals or groups. Only the more sophisticated elements within a denomination are likely to possess the social and intellectual skills for erecting countervailing rationales -- a fact which may well account for the wider diversity evidenced among liberal, higher status denominations.

Accordingly, only relatively infrequently has a full-scale assault been mounted against the role model for appropriate religious behavior fashioned by the deliberative councils of American denominations. This bold conclusion may appear somewhat overdrawn, given the marked individualism rampant in American religiosity from the very beginning (Miller, 1964: 143; Niebuhr, 1957: 80-89). Yet activist individualism has neither proved antithetical to sustained participation in denominational affairs nor sharply productive of antinomian definitions of spiritual health. Indeed, Greeley (1972: 106) rightly underscores the close connection between our individualism and organizational participation with the observation that

we Americans think of ourselves as individualists, but it would seem only as individualists who are almost pathologically eager to join groups. We may decry organizations, but we found them. We may extol the need for individualism, but we quickly seek out others with whom to work.

The pervasive tendency of Americans to manifest their individualism through denominational structures, rather than apart from them, has been partially obscured by the wide diversity of religious symbol systems and the correlative notions of spiritual health available to the general populace. In practical terms, this has meant that radical variance from any one "official model of religiosity" could well bring an actor into line with the orthodox views of another. However, the data do not reveal a serendipitous pattern of individuals skittishly switching from one denomination to the next for capricious reasons. The consumer approach to selecting religious beliefs and normative role patterns so lucidly predicted by Luckmann (1967: 102-106) is a phenomenon whose empirical reality has not yet been confirmed. To the contrary, the pattern of denominational switching now appears to be intimately related to a specifiable set of social variables.

Stark and Glock (1968: 201-203) summarized a long tradition of research when they proposed that a cyclical movement flows through the hierarchical arrangement of American denominations whereby the conservative, lower-status sects draw in members from the unchurched, then lose them to higher status denominations as individuals, and whole generations of members attain upward social mobility. For the majority of church adherents, then, it can be asserted with considerable confidence that movement from one denomination to another correlates significantly with class standing, hence it is not a product, pure and simple, of privatized individual motivation. Rather, religious actors appear to be seeking a denominational system capable of articulating the meaning of their religious experience through cultural categories commensurate with the sophistication level attained in their secular realm.

This fact should not be taken as a signal of thoroughgoing class determinism. All that may reasonably be inferred is that definitions of spiritual health, like other forms of religious expression, cannot escape cultural conditioning from stratification variables, for transcendent faith must always enter into some sort of compromise with historical, ethnic, and other social factors in order to be relevant to human experience.

All of this, of course, holds profound ramifications for the reference function denominational bodies are able to exert over the behavioral patterns of their membership with respect to spiritual well-being. As the most generalized structure of the total institution, denominational organizations serve the necessary role of articulating for the group as a whole the normative criteria for discerning healthy religion and appropriate moral behavior. Out of this complex process wherein top leadership strives to integrate the input of professional experts, the attitudes of the rank and file, and the dogmatic tradition of the church, there eventually emerges an officially sanctioned perspective which we have labeled the "official model of religiosity," along with the supportive apparatus of a rationally developed plausibility structure. Bound up in this "official model" is a relatively precise specification of what constitutes spiritual well-being for the group at large.

Once published, however, leaders are immediately confronted with the ancillary problem of promoting compliance with the institutionalized formula. Since local congregations and individual experience pose an omnipresent source of deviant patterns, the official model inevitably enjoys a somewhat precarious existence. The peculiar strengths of normative controls may mitigate some of the potential for divisiveness among the reference groups integrated under the aegis of the total institutional complex. And, to be sure, top level judicatories regard their specifications of healthy religious role behavior to be superior in quality to any generated at lower positions within the institution. Such an assumption is not merely an exercise in the arrogance of power, but rather it springs from the realization that higher offices enjoy the advantage of serving as the point of consolidation between collective influences -- historical and contemporary -- and the input of religious experts. For these reasons, judicatories jealously guard their normative prerogatives against incursions by those individuals and groups whose representation is less extensive and whose ability to maintain stability and continuity within the institution is markedly attenuated. Thus, denominational leaders must tread a thin red line between controlling dissidents who might undercut the definition of or commitment to established notions of spiritual well-being and nurturing an open system which facilitates the articulation of new insights and applications of the faith with respect to framing models of healthy religion.

CONCLUSION: THE ENDURING TASK OF DEFINING SPIRITUAL WELL-BEING

In one quite profound sense, definitions of spiritual well-being are always in the process of becoming. Just as the meaning of revelation and theological formulations persist as penultimate statements ever subject to revision and renewal, so too must notions of spiritual health endure as provisional standards to be reevaluated and reaffirmed by each new generation. What does remain constant, however, are the social processes by which a negotiated formula achieves formal status as the accepted definition of healthy religion for the total collectivity or for subgroups and individuals within the larger institution.

Reference group theory allows us to delineate with some precision the potential types of influence exerted over individual actors in their interactions with local fellowships, the deity, and denominational organizations. Yet, the variance in the degree of normative control experienced by any single reference group from one historical occasion to the next precludes an a priori determination of their relative strengths. Instead, countervailing and cooperative relationships among the agents in this triad proceed in dialectical fashion to yield a succession of expedient definitions for appropriate role behavior. Knowledge of a church's theological values and institutional goals affords analysts some guidelines for predicting at least where the center of gravity is likely to be for the resulting normative prescriptions, but anything beyond these imperfect and generalized forecasts must necessarily await the deliberative actions of those selves dynamically engaged in interaction with their respective religious reference groups.

NOTHING-BUTTERY REDUCTIONISM

... the 'nothing-buttery' assumption -- that when
you have verified a complete account in one set of
terms you automatically debunk any others -- is simply
mistaken in logic. Often, indeed, it is an example
of wishful thinking (or wishful 'unthinking'). Anyone
who tries to apply this to man, by arguing that a full
explanation of man's brain in mechanistic terms would
debunk man's spiritual nature, is dropping a logical
brick. ... 'Physical', 'mental' and 'spiritual' are
complementary categories, all of which are embraced
by the totality of what it is to be a man. -- Donald
M. MacKay (1974: 72-73), a specialist in brain phy-
siology and Professor of Communications, Keele University, England.

Chapter 7

SOCIOLOGICAL PERSPECTIVES ON PERSONHOOD:

A PRELIMINARY DISCUSSION

Richard D. Christy and David Lyon

Social theory depends not only on a conception of an "ideal,"
but also on an assumption of an "ideal person" (Gouldner 1970: 28).
Over the last twenty years, there has been increasing concern over
what sociology does to the person, often taking the form of opposition to reductionism (Homans, 1964; Wrong, 1961, and Friedrichs,
1970). This concern for the person is also evidenced by the growth
of phenomenological approaches to sociology, such as ethnomethodology, and it has taken more popular form, just as Matson (1964,
1976) noted psychological reductionism had done before it. But
deeper than this has been the feeling that sociology has failed to
cope with the uniqueness of the human person as a "spiritual"
being (Fichter, 1972; Moberg, 1967a). In fact, in his recent book,
Ideal Man in Classical Sociology, De Coppens (1976: 154) suggests
that
    there is a need to investigate the psychological, social
    cultural, philosophical, moral and religious implications
    and consequences of unfolding the conception of an ideal
    man as a spiritual being... .

In Western sociology, the reference point often claimed for the
"ideal person," according to Kolb (1961) and Friedrichs (1961),
has been the Judaic-Christian image of man. Although this has
been rejected by Parsons (1961), who seems to desire a more ecumenical approach, and by others who have been strongly attracted
by Eastern religions (Fletcher, 1975), it is likely that the debate
will continue to center around the Judaic-Christian view of man
for some time to come. But this raises many questions.

Our aim is simply to provide a preliminary discussion on the
person as related to Christian theology and to sociology. It is
an attempt to focus on the issue of the "spiritual" well-being
of the person. This effort at exploring some socio-theological
correlations, as Gill (1975) calls them, is undertaken to highlight the problem and to hint at its possible resolution.

THE THEOLOGICAL PROBLEM

The main difficulty encountered in relating the Judaic-Christian image of the person to social theory, as we see it, is the problem of sin. Some discussions have hedged around this issue, getting no nearer than phrases about "failure to achieve... total orientation" with the resulting "inevitable occurrence of lovelessness among men, the creation of a sense of guilt corresponding to the situation" (Kolb, 1961: 15), or, more vaguely, about "sensitivities nurtured by the Judeo-Christian tradition" (Friedrichs, 1961: 23). Yet others have frankly realized that sociology does not yet seem to be capable of dealing with sin or "evil," as it tends to be termed. Fichter (1972: 117) states boldly: "As far as I can discover, sociologists have no model to explain that man can do evil as well as good." And more recently, Balswick and Ward (1976: 184) have agreed with him: "the model of society which takes into account the fact that man can be motivated by intrinsic selfish interests has not yet been constructed." The latter rightly argue that this is an essential feature of a sociology which takes seriously the Christian view of the person, but they leave the problem there.

It is, of course, ironical that none of those who have claimed the Judeo-Christian heritage in propounding their view of the person have managed to incorporate the understanding which is basic to that view: that people are capable of sin -- "all have sinned" (The Bible, Romans 3: 23). This oversight is reminiscent of the celebrated "Christian-Marxist" dialogue, in which each of the participants seem willing to accept as a starting-point a caricature of their position (MacIntyre, 1969). There too, the concept of sin as being the root of both personal and social alienations and conflicts is conspicuous by its absence or its euphemistic camouflage.

Why is this important? The Judeo-Christian doctrine of personhood sees the person primarily in relation to God, who has created him to occupy a special position in the universe. The person is made in the "image of God" to have dominion over the rest of creation (The Bible, Genesis 1: 26), thus it only makes sense to speak of mankind in terms of the divine referent. The Judeo-Christian view of the person may not be separated from the Judeo-Christian view of God. Notions relating to the "image of God," such as freedom, uprightness, and sociality are openly discussed by socio-theological correlators like Friedrichs (1961) and Fichter (1972). (Even if they may not accept that label, they are at least implicit correlators of social science and theology.) But in the Judeo-Christian view, the person is also seen as a fallen creature, and in this way unlike his Maker. Sin is seen as an aberration from the ideal, an offence against the Maker, something for which people, not God, are personally and socially responsible.

Taken on its own, however, the notion of sin has no immediate explanatory power, as far as sociological theory is concerned, because of another aspect of the Judeo-Christian assumption: that sin is inherent in people, and universal. Nevertheless, as we have suggested, all social theory depends upon a view of the ideal and, by implication, the non-ideal person and society. Thus all social theory has some version of the doctrine of sin: of what is right and what is wrong. Moreover, it is on this notion of a difference between what is right and what is wrong, functional and dysfunctional, or whatever, that sociological explanation rests (Fallding, 1967). Hence there is a strong affinity between the Judeo-Christian and sociological understandings of the social world.

But this is the point: the notion of sin implies a notion of good, and it also implies some standards or criteria of judgment. Therefore, in terms of certain evaluative criteria, one can say whether or not socio-historical tendencies are toward a realization of those ideals. This is why the discussion of sin is so crucial; the notion of "spiritual well-being" must depend upon which criteria are used. The system functionalist, for example, seeking social integration, would say that the criterion for well-being would be economy in the ordering of social experience over time. So in this case a notion like "freedom," which most will agree is associated with spiritual well-being, is reduced to "a subjective feeling of personal well-being which results from the objective fact of living in a functioning society" (Davis, 1953: 443).

In the Christian tradition, spiritual well-being is viewed in a number of ways. At the heart of the notion, we would submit, is the fact of reconciliation with an offended God (The Bible, Romans 5: 9-10); a remade relationship (The Bible, 2 Corinthians 5: 17) which had been severed at the Fall. From this flow all other aspects of spiritual well-being, especially the relationship of the person to the earth, to fellow-creatures, and to self. But this is not "perfection," contrary to what some theorists would argue (Fletcher, 1975). Sin remains, to be overcome in its personal and social dimensions, but this is now undertaken with spiritual power.

Spiritual well-being, in other words, does not depend upon the eradication of sin. Spiritual well-being depends upon establishing a right relationship with God. Paul's desire for the believers at Philippi is that they remain blameless and innocent before God in the midst of a crooked and perverse generation (The Bible, Philippians 2: 14). The process of combatting sin and pursuing the good (theologically, "sanctification;" socially, "social reconstruction") continues until the eschaton.

To sum up: the problem of sin is crucial to a Christian understanding of the person, yet it is an issue which is either avoided, or acknowledged-but-not-dealt-with in existing attempts to relate sociology to theology. On its own, sin cannot explain anything, as all are affected by it, whether they are believers or not. But yoked with a concept of the good, one may begin to establish criteria for the evaluation of social arrangements affecting the person's spiritual well-being ("I would not have come to know sin except through the law," The Bible, Romans 7: 7). However, it is not possible to wrench these ideas from their Judeo-Christian moorings.

The theological argument of sin will not impress many sociologists, except, perhaps, in a suggestive way. One conclusion we have reached, though, is that any attempt at socio-theological correlation relating to the person cannot justifiably ignore the problem of sin.

THE SOCIOLOGICAL PROBLEM

The sociological problem of personhood is a perennial one. The recurring question for the sociologist is whether the person is rightly viewed as object or subject, as actor or reactor, or both? This issue has far better documentation; indeed, it is one of the key issues in contemporary sociology (Rex, 1974; Warshay, 1975; Mollis, 1977). Polarization has taken place between those representing different opinions, and each position is subject to criticism. Douglas (1970) would claim that Durkheim was the founding father of an "as-if" science of social determinism. On the other hand, ethnomethodologists are accused of representing the person as such a slippery subject that "science" stands no chance of capturing him or her alive.

Those engaged in the "sociology and the person" question have, predictably, spent much time on this issue. There has been great concern that the intrinsic humanity of the person has suffered at the hands of sociologists. This, in Christian terms, would be to slight the person as "image of God," and would tend to exclude the 'spiritual,' thus also spiritual well-being. Moberg (1967a), for example, argued that reductionism (of the person to an object) has been one of the main barriers to socio-theological dialogue, while Fichter (1972) concluded his article by proposing that more attention be paid to an adequate understanding of the person. Thus individuals would be seen as creators and producers of culture, not merely as those who have been created and produced by culture.

As we say, the grounds of the argument have been well, though inconclusively, covered. Maintaining Fichter's (1972) position, we would suggest a perspective which is illustrated by Pike's (1971) work in anthropological linguistics. The distinction Pike makes in discussing the structure of language is between the "emic" and "etic" (p. 41). The "etic" is what is initially obser-

94

vable, concerning the regularities which one might first discern in attempting to grasp the structure of a language. The "emic," on the other hand, is that which can be understood only through empathetic involvement in the language: nuances of tone and syntax which escape the notice of the merely "etic" observer forever.

Two points are worth noting. One is that Pike sees language as action, not merely as a vehicle of description. Language is part of, and vital to, everyday social life. (This is itself an important area for social-theological correlation.) The understanding of general social action is related to the extension of the emic/etic approach. The second point is that Pike refuses to divorce the emic/etic approaches. He likens them to lenses, saying that only when one lens is held to each eye will one obtain anything like an image of reality. The emic and the etic are thus complementary.

This distinction is not dissimilar from that of Fichter's (1972) proposal that the person is made by the world and yet makes the world. The etic would correspond to the limiting social-contraint aspect, and the emic to the purposive social action aspect. Yet surely this cannot be considered the whole story. Given that there are constraints of various sorts upon behavior, and given that it is not inappropriate to speak of conscious, undetermined action, there still is the question of what people actually do in given situations. This inevitably relates to the issue previously discussed: that of good and evil. For even if one is fairly satisfied with a view of the person which takes into account both observable regularities and intentional choices, the task of evaluating and understanding these choices is still left open. We shall return to a fuller discussion of this issue in the final section.

We have seen in this section that there are differences of sociological opinion as to how the "person" is to be viewed, there being a particular polarization between the subject and object viewpoints. It was asserted that the dialectic of the person as producing and produced by the world is analogous to Pike's complementarity of emic and etic approaches to lingual social phenomena. But even when one is happier about a choice of perspective, the question of what people have to do and what they choose to do is left open. The notion of spiritual well-being, dependent as it is upon an adequate person-perspective, also involves a judgment by the sociologist of what actually occurs in given situations.

A TENTATIVE SOCIO-THEOLOGICAL MODEL

Everyone knows that he or she can do some things, and may wish to do them (like making music), that he or she must do some things (like seeking order), and that there are some things between which he or she is torn (like revealing the true nature of an illness or

concentrating on encouragement to live). Some things are inevitable
(aging), some things are desirable (music), and some things are contradictory (truthfulness versus tactfulness). (These ideas owe
something of their form, but not their inspiration, to Fletcher,
1975, although we differ from him on many matters.) There are at
least three aspects here; they are related to three major theoretical orientations in sociology.

We feel that many of the existing polarizations, such as order/
conflict, objective/subjective, and radical/conservative, in sociology
are self-destructive to the discipline. Perhaps a trialectical perspective would transcend the present dialectical divisions. The
following diagram therefore is an attempt (1) to outline a trialectical perspective and (2) to propose an integration of the
positions in sociological theories with the theological view of
the person.

A Socio-Theological View of the Person

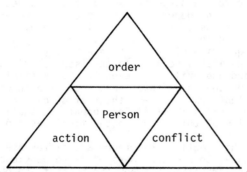

Divine Orientation

order

Person

action   conflict

Responsibility   Human context

Theology
{
Divine Orientation: the person as God's image desires
order
Human Context: the fallen creature knows the reality
of conflict
Responsibility: the person is answerable for action
to God, neighbor, and self
}

Sociology
{
Order: Creating and maintaining social harmony
Conflict: Clashes of interest; power and disruptive
change
Action: Defining the situation; purposive and inten-
tional activity
}

96

First, there is the orderly, integrative view of social relations, which tends to be concerned with regularities in social
activity. This human desire for order is connected to the theological assumption that God has laws for the world. Second, there
is the "conflict" view, which sees human behavior at variance and
devises rules for coping with conflict. This perspective is related to the biblical fall of man. Humans are seen as fallen
creatures with personal and social sins disrupting their lives.
Last, there is the more phenomenological approach to social analysis.
This perspective is interested in purposive and intentional action.
Situations are defined as the cognitive arena of action. This is
related to responsibility in our trialectic. The individual is
responsible above all to God, then to neighbor and to self.

This proposal is, of course, highly tentative. It is suggested
as a stepping-off point, not a finishing post. It is fluid, open
to revision, and not stagnant. But let us consider some implications if we at least initially accept this trialectical perspective
with its socio-theological statement on personhood.

Theological Implications

Sin may be seen as part of the human condition. A conscious or
unconscious recognition of sin may result in a consuming desire
for order. People might seek to satisfy the need for order in a
totalitarian dictatorship. By contrast, the quest for freedom
from restricting order might product an atrophic anarchy. The view
that social life is only a conflict of passions and interests may
result in a destructive pessimism. However, if the problem of sin
is seen as aspects in the life of people who are the image of God
and yet fallen creatures, the social reality of conflict may be
seen realistically. The internally-wrenching questions of the
lesser evil or the greater good may be seen, not as profound deviations from the divine plan, but responsible choices before a just
and loving God. In the socio-historical context, personal action
is closely related to the standards required by God. However, if
sin and good are taken only in their abstraction, those same standards may be tyrannizing and may cause only despair.

Sociological Consequences

Paradigms based on "opposing stereotypes" need not occur. There
is a complementarity between the different styles of social theory.
Any one, taken on its own, tends to be a dehumanizing reduction.
But viewed as a trialectic, the person may be considered in greater
wholeness. If taken on its own, each is shown to be limited. This
position might be interpreted as nothing more than a plea for tolerance among sociologists with differing perspectives of social reality.
But in a fuller sense the trialectical view is proposed out of a
desire for social reality in sociology.

97

Finally, we propose this view of the person to help in understanding the concept of spiritual well-being. First, it is clear that this trialectical view at least allows for the "spiritual" to be taken into account. But it does not equate spiritual well-being with mere law-conformity, mere desire for justice, or mere responsible choice. We have suggested that, in the Christian view, spiritual well-being is fundamentally a right relationship of the person to God and, following that, a right relationship to neighbor and self. Thus, spiritual well-being might be evidenced in society by coming to terms with all three aspects -- the desire for order, the reality of conflict, and the necessity for responsible action. This does not help us with the specifics of a methodology, but it does make one thing plain. If we are to talk of spiritual well-being, there must be a serious attempt at socio-theological correlation. In this paper we have shown that the sociological argument is feeble without the theological, and the theological argument is weak without the sociological. (The complementary argument to this is found in Lyon, 1978.)

Chapter 8

LIFE STAGES AND SPIRITUAL WELL-BEING

Earl D.C. Brewer

The purpose of this paper is to review some work on life stages,
to develop the concept of spiritual well-being, and to interrelate
them.

LIFE STAGES

The folklore of preliterate peoples reflects on life stages.
The Australian Murngin, for example, have a circular view of age-
grading, with the newborn coming as a fish from the totemic water-
hole, moving into higher levels of sacredness with each rite of
passage, and finally at death returning to the sacred well
(Warner, 1937: 16-24). Traditional religions take account of
the changing phases of life (Smith, 1958).

"All the world's a stage," declares Shakespeare in As You Like It.
He delineates seven ages in the acts of man: infant, school-boy,
lover, soldier, justice, retirement in "lean and slipper'd panta-
loon," and the "last scene of all" is "second childishness and
mere oblivion, sans teeth, sans eyes, sans taste, sans everything"
(Clarke and Wright, 1952: 608-9). The recent best seller,
Passages (Sheehy, 1974), attests to the continued popularity of
life cycle material. Diagram 1 shows several efforts at identifying life stages from a variety of viewpoints.

A group of scholars in England took Shakespeare's seven ages as
a starting point for a series of articles appearing during 1964 in
New Society, a weekly journal published in London. This work has
been edited with some new material by Sears and Feldman (1973).
Each stage is treated in terms of biological, psychological, and
competency levels and changes.

Havighurst (1953) works out six developmental stages and relates them to the educational process. Typical tasks are assigned
to each stage. These developmental tasks are thought to arise
from physical maturation, pressures from the sociocultural process,

99

DIAGRAM 1.   APPROXIMATIONS OF FIVE LIFE-STAGE FORMULATIONS

Age	Sears, Feldman (1973)	Havighurst (1953)	Atchley (1976)	Erikson (1963)	Fowler (1976)
70+					
	Old Age	Later Maturity	Retirement	Ego Integrity vs Despair	
60			Phasing Out		Universalizing Faith
50	Middle Age				
40		Middle Adulthood	Maximum Involvement	Generativity vs Stagnation	
	Prime of Life				
30					
20	Young Adult	Early Adulthood	Career Choices and Further Preparation	Intimacy vs Isolation	Paradoxical-Consolidative
	Adolescence	Adolescence		Identity vs Role Confusion	Individuating-Reflexive
10			Early Preparation for Occupations	Industry vs Inferiority	Synthetic-Conventional
	Childhood	Middle Childhood		Initiative vs Guilt	Mythic-Literal
5				Autonomy vs Shame	
	Infancy	Early Childhood		Trust vs Mistrust	Intuitive-Projective
0					

100

and the changing desires, aspirations, and values of the personality. He defines a developmental task as
a task which arises at or about a certain period in the
life of the individual, successful achievement of which
leads to his happiness and to success with later tasks,
while failure leads to unhappiness in the individual,
disapproval by the society, and difficulty with later
tasks (Havighurst, 1953: 2).
This developmental concept is used by Duvall (1957) in her family
life cycle structured around the ages of the children. The two
major stages for individuals are the family of orientation in
which one is a child and the family of procreation in which one
is a parent. Her eight stages start with a couple in the formation of a beginning family at marriage and end with the dissolution of the family upon the death of one or both of the spouses.

Atchley (1976: xi) develops an occupational cycle to support
his work on retirement. With the massive pressure toward work,
especially in industrial societies, a person's life stages may be
seen as preparation for, choices of, engagement in, and withdrawal
from jobs. This tends to become a dominant element in all other
aspects of personal growth and development.

Erikson's (1963) psychosocial stages focus on the younger
years and flow out of his psychoanalytic theories. These stages
represent not only an approximate passage of time but also a
dialectical formulation of tasks. The crises confronted by persons at various stages may not be resolved satisfactorily and
may be carried forward into later years. Erikson rejects the
notion of progressive achievement or development from stage to
stage but rather sees the issues of earlier years reappearing
later. What begins in infancy as a struggle between basic trust
and mistrust may be involved in mature years in ego integrity
versus despair. This positive-negative, life-death dialectic
characterizes all his stages.

Fowler's (1976) faith stages build on the work of Piaget
(Piaget and Inhelder, 1969) and, especially, Kohlberg (1974).
The later uses six stages of moral development based upon changing
orientations to moral authority. These move from an obedience
and punishment orientation of the first stage to moral choices
based on conscience or principles in the last stage. These moral
stages take on something of the character of developmental tasks,
in that later ones build on earlier ones, and also something of
the dialectic of Erikson in that problems of earlier stages may
reappear in later ones. Kohlberg has verified his theory not
only in studies in the United States but on a cross-cultural
basis as well.

Fowler (1976) depicts six stages of faith development. Like
Kohlberg (1974), he adapts many of the presuppositions of develop-

101

mentalism as well as the polar tensions of Erikson (1963).
Fowler has tested his stages in interviews with persons of all
ages. His stages are defined in terms of increasing complexity
and differentiation from the intuitive-projective faith of early
childhood to the universaling faith of middle or mature years.
The latter stage is seen as occurring only rarely, although it
is the ultimate goal of faith development.

Obviously, this review of some of the literature of life stages
has touched only a few highlights. It is sufficient, perhaps,
to indicate scholarly interest in the formulation of life stages
or periods roughly in relation to age chronology. The differences
in the stages of Diagram 1 depend on the theoretical orientations
and practical purposes of the authors. In most cases, only a
loose fit, if any at all, is intended between the stages and the
chronological years between birth and death. With the exception
of Atchley (1976), the authors devote much more attention to the
earlier than the later years. This imbalance is being corrected
by studies in the mature years and aging (Lowenthal et al., 1975;
Binstock and Shanas, 1976) and in death and dying (Sudnow, 1967).

Age-grading and life-staging are, obviously, more complicated
in complex than in simple societies. The changing number and
complexity of social roles in which a person may be involved
vary from a few in infancy to many in the middle years to a few
again in older age (Bates and Harvey, 1975: 265). Theoretically,
the quantity and content of life cycles may be expanded to cover
a wide range of interests and to cope with life struggles in various
settings (Neugarten and Hagestad, 1976). Even the constants of
birth and death have become more malleable through birth control
and increasing life span.

This discussion of Diagram 1 is adequate to indicate that the
life course is marked by an increasing number of critical events.
Between birth and death come such events as toilet training,
learning to talk and walk, first day at school, early sexual
experimentation, license to drive a car, leaving home, going to
college, first job, marriage, first child, changing jobs and/or
marriage partners, serious illness, retirement, death of a spouse
or close friend. Many of these events may be identified with
life stages and defined in terms of responses of persons, cultural
meanings, and social structures surrounding them. In between such
high points or transitional events, persons organize and carry
on their everyday life in relationship to their stage and station.
The adequacy of everyday life within stages and at the transition
points between them may be thought of as spiritual well-being.
This leads to an exploration of this concept.

SPIRITUAL WELL-BEING

The concept of spiritual well-being, in the present context, seems to have arisen in connection with the 1971 White House Conference on Aging. Given the sensitivity of the United States Government, it was a way of avoiding the use of the word "religion." A voluntary association subsequently formed pursued this concept. The group came up with the following definition: "Spiritual well-being is the affirmation of life in a relationship with God, self, community and environment that nurtures and celebrates wholeness" (Cook, 1977: A67). This serves their practical interests in relating traditional religious agencies to the welfare of the aged population.

The purpose here is theoretical and involves an effort to define spiritual well-being within sociological traditions and to relate the idea to life-stages studies in well-being or quality of life. (These terms are used interchangeably here, although there is a tendency in some literature to use "well-being" for the more personal and "quality of life" for the more societal aspects of life.)

Indicators of well-being or quality of life tend to deal with either the adequacy of institutional arrangements which constitute "objective" measures, such as the number of hospital beds in the population (Bauer, 1966; U.S. Department of Health, Education and Welfare, 1969), or with individual responses to daily life situations which provide "subjective" measures, such as satisfaction or happiness scales (Campbell and Converse, 1972; Strumpel, 1974). In both cases, such indicators deal with the ordinary, stereotypical, everyday aspects of life. The addition of the word "spiritual" to the concept may be viewed as negative, confusing, and unnecessary, or it may be seen as leading to a more complete and holistic perspective of everyday life. The latter view is taken here.

The Mandala

A theoretical model of what might be involved in the concept of spiritual well-being is illustrated in Daigram 2 which, perhaps appropriately, follows the style of the mandala, an ancient religious art form (Tucci, 1961; Jung, 1968; Arguelles, 1972). The development of the model involves comments on aspects of this diagram. The focus, as seen in the center circle, is upon everyday life situations, specimens of everybody's everyday, everywhere (Douglas, 1970). Borrowed from phenomenological philosophy (Schutz, 1967; Berger and Luckmann, 1967; Schutz and Luckmann, 1973), everyday life refers to the taken-for-granted existence which is shaped by tacit assumptions, conventional wisdom, and customary practices. Persons and groups create and maintain life-worlds as cultural webs of daily existence. These daily realities

DIAGRAM 2.   A MODEL OF SPIRITUAL WELL-BEING

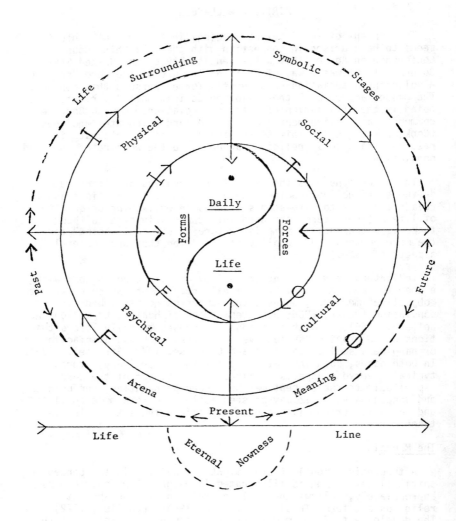

emerge from the yin-yang interplay of forms and forces, of entities and energies, of constancy and change (Capra, 1975).

Circle 2 of the diagram points to four significant aspects of everyday life: psychical, physical, social, and cultural.

It may be, as Teilhard de Chardin (1961) proposed, that life-forms, from the most simple to the most complex, exhibit higher and higher levels of consciousness. Certainly, the psychical dimension of human life points to the highest levels known to us. "I as a center of conscious awareness together with whatever I call mine" describes this aspect of everyday life situations. (Words such as I are underlined when used in a special sense.) I, the self viewed subjectively, flows into different forms based on different relationships and roles claimed as mine. The psychic I denotes the I-me self as the center of conscious awareness. It is through this psychic self that all else is experienced or known. Indicators of mental well-being and emotional health apply to this aspect of life.

The physical dimension of daily life refers to the physical environment as well as the bodies of people and their inter-relationships. The physical I derives from these I-it (natural environment) and I-my body interactions. Here lie the surface understandings and measures of the quality of the natural worlds of air, water, soil, life-forms, and the human-made worlds of technology, materials, structures, agriculture, and so on. The human being as a physical organism interacts directly with various aspects of the surrounding ecological environment. Measures of physical health and well-being focus here. Also, due to massive pollution (air, water, soil, and life-forms, as well as noise, ugliness, congestion, and other forms of human pollution), environmental studies and actions are directly related to the quality of life.

The social aspect of everyday life is based on I-You relationships with You being the self viewed objectively. The social I or self emerges from these group involvements. These I-You interactions pluralize into We-Them groups of various types and sizes in the society. Everyday life situations involve families and groups at work, play, government, education, health, religion, and so on. Such groups and institutional arrangements make up the social resources available in daily life. Measures of the adequacy of such resources are related to the levels of the quality of life.

The meaning systems and behavior patterns are cultural dimensions of everyday life. Tacit assumptions, stereotypes, and taken-for-granted attitudes, expectations, values, symbol systems, goals, and beliefs inform daily existence. Habitual and customary patterns of activities provide much of the content of daily life.

Here the cultural self is formed out of I-my meanings and patterns of actions. Little work has been done on measures of cultural adequacy.

These four aspects of everyday life should not be seen in separation but in holism, not in rigid placement within the quadrants of the diagram but in flowing and fluid energies around, up and down, below and above, within and beyond the circles, as if in cross sections of spherical and global designs. These mandalic movements provide pulsating yin-yang energies with and between the forms and forces of changing human situations. In the diagram, these may be visualized as a dynamic whole system (Weinberg, 1975) in terms of an ITOF cybernetics model (Parsegian, 1973). Here the energies, entities, and events together with the meanings, intentionalities, and relationships may be seen in circular flux as inputs, transformations (thruputs), outputs, and feedback into the next cycle of inputs. This process of moving within and through everyday life situations does not run around in circles as the fixed diagram indicates. Rather it spirals (Purce, 1974) forward in ever new space-time frames. Like the drive chain of a moving bicycle, it never turns around twice on the same ground.

This brief review of a way of conceptualizing everyday life needs elaboration at several points. Yet it may serve as the core around which to think about ordinary indicators of quality of life. Obviously, measures of lower or higher levels of well-being, whether subjectively felt or objectively determined, may relate to the adequacy of each of the four dimensions, their dynamic interrelationships with each other and with the life stages. The present literature on indicators of quality of life or well-being deals largely with this range of human circumstances (Moberg and Brusek, 1978). It hardly takes account of the transcendent dimension of human existence. This seems to await theoretical development which takes seriously the spiritual aspect of daily well-being.

The Transcending Process

Human beings, in the model being developed here, have the capacity and necessity to transcend themselves reflectively in the process of developing and maintaining personhood and grouphood. This transcending process is a normal part of ordinary behavior, as in memories of the past or anticipations of the future. This reflective quality of human consciousness separates homo sapiens from lower forms of animal life. The need of persons and groups to transcend themselves is considered the foundation of the spiritual or religious dimension of life. Within the past decade or so, there has been a resurgence of efforts to recover the transcendent aspects of human life in the midst of the unidimensional and flat existence in modern industrial society (Maslow, 1971;

106

Johnson, 1974; Brewer, 1975). To religion is to participate in this search for transcendence, and spiritual well-being is a measure of the adequacy of the quest. ("Religion" is sometimes used as a verb in this paper to indicate its dynamic qualities. The words "spiritual," "religious," and "religioning" are used synonymously here.)

This transcending process is shown in the model by four lines that divide the circles into quadrants and illustrate some modes of transcendence which serve to interrelate ordinary life and its extraordinary beyondness arenas. They may be thought of as "Jacob's Ladders" up and down which the traffic of transcendence flows. When serious questions arise in everyday life, individuals and groups begin processes of searching for answers. They move beyond the immediacies of the ordinary in quests for confirmation or condemnation or in search for new visions or insights. One end of this religioning process is grounded in the ordinariness of everyday life, the other in the outer reaches of mystery.

The ladders interrelate meaning and mystery, the factual and the imaginary, the known and the unknown. They represent the transcending movements from the immediacies and trivia of everyday life toward the most ultimate considerations available to persons or groups. The ultimating process may provide the criteria for goals and directions as well as for issues of personal and societal morality. This transcending process moves reciprocally from order to disorder, from routinization to imagination, from tradition to change, from the expected to the unexpected, from the secular to the sacred, from the profane to the holy, from the ugly to the beautiful, and from the conscious to the unconscious. The process begins in the low emotionality of the taken-for-granted character of everyday life, but it may rise to high levels of transcendent proportions. Emotions may explode whenever and wherever there are sensitive breaks in the ordinary round of life. Peak experiences (Maslow, 1970) often involve intense feelings. High emotions of hate, fear, awe, reverence, and love frequently characterize transcendent experiences.

These are some examples of areas of human experience which interrelate everyday life situations and the resources of beyondness symbolic areas. The transcending process is much more complex than indicated; it has mixtures of ascendence-descendence along pluralistic dimensions. These energies of reflective transcendence not only move up and down individual ladders but are mixed holistically through the cyclical ITOF cybernetics system mentioned above. Together these comprise a unique field force within which the yin-yang entities and energies of human experiences and actions flow and form, reflow and reform.

Symbolic Realism

In the spaces beyond the outer circle, persons and groups with various cultural contents and symbolic meanings landscape the arenas which surround their everyday life situations. This process of symbolic realism interrelates ordinary existence with ultimate significance (Bellah, 1970). These symbolic reality systems consist of "over-beliefs" (James, 1902: 503) in various entities, events, energies, relationships, and meanings which are assumed to possess ultimate significance for the persons or groups involved. In this way, the collective representations of Durkheim (1965) and the idealized forms of society of Fallding (1974) become symbolic contents related to ordinary existence through transcendence. Such symbolic contents may arise from traditional religions (Judaism, Christianity, Islam, Hinduism, Buddhism, Confucianism, and so on) or nontraditional religions (over-beliefs in civil religions, such as nationalism, economism, schoolism, scientism, or in personal religions, such as individualism, groupism, workism, hedonism). Other ancient and modern "altars" include racism, classism, sexism, and ageism. These "gods" may have negative or positive impacts on everyday life. Obviously, in a pluralistic society these symbolic meanings arise from a variety of sources. They may reinforce each other, as in the case of the Protestant ethic and capitalism, or be in conflict (hedonism and workism). They comprise a complex of very important symbols, myths, beliefs, attitudes, feelings, rituals, and customs which are used to answer questions raised in ordinary existence. In the religioning process, persons or groups sort out, or have sorted out for them, such cultural contents or "gods" in some hierarchical order as ultimate sources of transcendence.

The Temporal Dimension

The remaining features of the model of everyday life situations concern the past-present-future and "eternal now" time lines in the diagram. Here persons or groups within the present transcend time both toward the past and the future. In doing so, memories of the past and anticipations of the future feed back to inform the present. These "double dialectic" or twin reciprocal feedback loops shape and reshape the living moment as well as the past and future. The ultimate transcendent quality of this temporal dimension is the extension of the time lines, both at the bottom and top of the diagram. These extended lines are curved around the outer circles so that the past-present-future line is joined with the life-stage line. This conception of curved time is absorbed into the "eternal nowness" of human experience. The mandalic diagram potentially joins the eternity of time with the infinity of space into a mystical experience of a new level of space-time. It provides the farther reaches of measures of spiritual well-being.

The central idea of the model, then, is that ordinary existence is surrounded by extraordinary ranges of symbolic possibilities for human beings. The religioning or transcending processes between the inner and the outer circles of the diagram and along the temporal lines provide the multiple, depth, and holistic dimensions of the model within which to add measures of "spiritual" to indicators of well-being or the quality of life. For present purposes, the temporal dimensions provide the bridge between this model and life stages.

LIFE STAGES AND SPIRITUAL WELL-BEING

The remaining task is to bring together the concepts of life stages and spiritual well-being. A summary discussion of each idea may serve as a bridge between them. Life stages, within any theoretical approach, are related in one way or another to chronological ages. Each stage is, among other things, a slice or a part of a person's daily life-line. As such, it has a beginning, a middle, and an ending. The beginning of one stage is related to the ending of another, while the middle represents a period of relatively stable everyday life within that stage. The ending-beginning aspects of stages are transition points, whether experienced as events of crises, of public notice (positive or negative), or as gradual and private shifts.

Becoming a licensed automobile driver in the United States, retiring from the labor force, and marriage are usually public events, while struggles with ego identity and moral or faith issues may be largely private. In any case, such stages shape the life course in terms of transition points and stage periods. The changes may take on the characteristics of the rites of passage (separation, transition, incorporation) of van Gennep (1960: 10-11) or the structure/anti-structure dynamics of Turner (1969) through liminality and communitas to new stages or structures.

Spiritual well-being deals with the adequacy with which persons or groups reflectively transcend the structures of everyday existence and appropriate the meanings, values, and symbolic resources available to them. This transcending process or religioning performs two seemingly contradictory functions: it endows with ultimacy or divinity the status quo of everyday life, and it provides a push beyond the present situation. The first is the gravity or holding-in-place function: the second is the breakthrough dynamic (Weber, 1963). Historically, these have been designated the priestly and the prophetic aspects of religion, respectively. This ambiguity of religion (Baum, 1975) in the transcending process provides a connection between the concepts under consideration.

Spiritual well-being at the "stable" middle portions of life stages involves transcendent appropriation of symbolic meanings which make valuable and worthwhile a particular "domesticated" slice of daily living. The "nowness" of this phase of age-grading is transcended to become a part of the "eternal now." The ordinary is endowed with the extraordinary, the usual with unusual significance. The dull, taken-for-granted routines (a low level of spiritual well-being) are quickened and given trans-cendent meaning, endowed with divinity (high level of spiritual well-being). The transcending process provides the symbolic basis for order and importance in ordinary living.

Yet the old order changes! No matter how much a child may enjoy the latency period (Erikson, 1963), he or she is conscious that puberty (physical and social) is just beyond. The retired older person may be reaping the full benefits of a long work life, yet he or she knows that death, the ultimate transition, is nearer than ever before. The transcending process within the model developed above is a guiding light through these transition points or rites of passage. Here, there is a separation or break with the past as the old stage is left behind, a transition to the new, an incorporation into the next stage. This breakup of old structures and the creation of new ones, this time of disorder prior to a new ordering, is characterized by Turner (1969: 95) as liminality and by Havighurst (1953: 5) as the teachable moment. The level of spiritual well-being at these transition points in life stages is critical. Often it is low due to the lack of transcending experiences in utilizing symbolic resources in such ending-beginning phases. High levels of spiritual well-being would be measured by the ability, adequacy, and meaningfulness of giving up the old and moving with confidence and joy into the new. This breakthrough function of religion would apply to any of the transition points in life stages from birth to death.

CONCLUSION

Much work remains on this model of spiritual well-being and life stages. Erikson (1963) with his dialectical psychic pressures and Fowler (1976) with his stress on the content and dynamics of faith provide help along the way. Further theoretical work is needed on the nature of life stages as such and on the ambiguous role of religion as transcending process. Work on indicators of well-being which take account of the spiritual dimension and the dynamics of life stages is urgently needed. Primordial questions about human life and living should be raised and empirical re-search quests mounted to deal with them. Until such work is done, much research on indicators of quality of life or well-being will remain on a unidimensional, nontranscendent level (Land and Spilerman, 1975).

A concluding remark may take a modern myth to compare with the ancient Murngin one used in opening this paper. It comes from Carl Jung's (1960) discussion of the stages of life. He compares the life course to the course of the sun during a day's time. Infancy emerges from the collective unconsciousness and moves through various stages of ascending development and expansion until reaching the zenith. From that point, descendence sets in with a final return to the collective unconscious. Yet this descending mode of transcendence in the second half of life may involve, as among the Murngin people, continued ascendence in the symbolic life, in mysticism and wisdom, in sacredness and holiness.

The level of spiritual well-being of older persons as they face death, the ultimate transition point, need not decline along with the level of physical well-being. The modern world with its emphasis on the ascendent modes of the morning of life is ill prepared to cope with the cultural and psychic risks and riches available in the evening of existence. Relating the concepts of spiritual well-being and life stages to each other should serve to ennoble both the ascending the descending phases of life.

THE HEALING POWER OF SPIRITUAL WELL-BEING

Spiritual change apparently has an effect on rheumatoid arthritis similar to that of ACTH and cortisone, although the response is not so immediate. But while these hormones bring relief only while being taken, spiritual change removes some basic disturbing factor that has upset the entire body, and the improvement is lasting (Swain, 1962: 129).

Chapter 9

THE DIALECTIC OF SPIRITUAL EXPERIENCE AND SOCIAL STRUCTURE

Edwin Dowdy

This paper represents an attempt to develop the concept of "spiritual experience" within the sociology of religion and to set up a provisional framework for its analysis. The term "dialectic" will be used here to convey the notion of something more than a simple relationship between supposedly disparate entities. If we need to compare such concepts as individual religiosity and church, or church and society, or individual and society, we must be aware that it is not a matter of dealing with pairs of mutually exclusive opposites. We shall investigate some ways in which the components of each pair merge into each other, develop out of each other, hold a "dialogue" of self-recognition and mutual recognition, and presumably emerge into new social possibilities.

WHAT IS SPIRITUAL EXPERIENCE?

Spiritual experience is that aspect of religious behavior in which the individual attempts to contemplate, comprehend, or become something quite different from what is given in normal daily routine; it is in a way self-transcendence, a search for the altogether other.

In what Sorokin (1947) would call a sensate civilization one naturally meets the objection that no such other "reality" exists, that it is a figment of the imagination or an idealistic mystification. This aspect of religious behavior is largely ignored in sociological literature, partly no doubt because it is not amenable to our tools of analysis. Max Weber desisted altogether from defining religion. The functional line from Durkheim (1947) to Geertz (1960) provides helpful operational descriptions, but these seem to remain on the level of behavioral and social psychology. Luhmann's (1977; and Dahm, Luhmann, and Stoodt, 1972) cognitive approach, of the meaningful reduction of the complexity of its environment for a system, also tends to ignore this aspect, although his conceptual width and degree of abstraction might include it formally.

Two examples of definition may help to clarify the meaning of the term spiritual experience. Julian Huxley's (1948) suggestion is on a cosmic level; in his account there are discontinuous stages of evolution: inanimate nature, life, mind, and possibly a dawning "spirit" or spiritual life. Each succeeding stage is contingent on, potential in, and in part contradictory to, the previous one, and each opens up a vast new spectrum of possibilities. At the other extreme of definition there is the entirely individual approach of Weizsaecker (1977: 161). Here we find "five objective principles" arranged in a progression: the useful, the righteous, the true, the beautiful, and the holy. Each of these principles

> describes an experiential quality which can scarcely be anticipated from the previous qualities, which penetrates ...into the previous, seemingly closed world. In each transition there is a reversal of values, a death of the gods.

Thus in the useful, the self overcomes instinct and is able to plan its own self-directed future; in the righteous, the self finds a challenge to transcend itself radically, and so on.

It is this sort of transition to a new level of experience, regardless of any culturally-induced perception of stages, which is represented here by the expression "spiritual experience." It is a matter of transcendence in that the self is no longer content to remain in the same state; however, it does not necessarily involve the postulation of any supernatural state or supernatural being.

It may seem a matter of some embarrassment that Gehlen (1940) makes no use of such a concept. His definition of religion (the obersten-geistigen-Fuehrungssysteme) includes only (a) cognitive orientation to the world, (b) directives for human interaction, and (c) comfort and the conferring of meaningfulness in situations of individual need and suffering. However, this definition clearly refers to functions of religion rather than to religious experience.

Relevant in this connection are the attempts of philosophical anthropologists to answer the question: Which is the unique property that makes man different from the other animals? Perhaps the bestknown answer is that of ekstasis, the argument that man can observe himself and his actions, being able not only to lead his own life according to self-imposed goals, but furthermore to examine his performance critically in the light of those goals. This approach meets some approval in theological circles. It is perhaps not as extreme as the notion of spiritual experience proposed in this paper.

SOCIAL STRUCTURE AND INDIVIDUAL EXPERIENCE

Some examples of spiritual experience will be discussed and compared below, but first there should be a brief outline of two aspects of social structure, called here "advanced capitalist society" and "religious organizations." The latter term may be explained quite simply as the presently-given churches, sects, and religious movements.

The concept of advanced capitalist society is borrowed from Habermas (1976).[1] One has in mind the sort of contemporary Western society of which the Federal Republic of Germany is perhaps the most developed example. The greater proportion of industrial activity and of the appropriation of profit is in private hands, but taxation provides a "welfare state"; strategic decisions are affected by government policy or made by government agencies, and the state continually reconstitutes market conditions. Indeed, after an era of liberal capitalism, the economy and state have become recoupled. Through taxes the state supports the market by such means as organizing supranational economic blocs, unproductive consumption as in the case of armaments, guiding capital into sectors unprofitable to the market, improvement of the infrastructure (health, education, transportation, housing, etc.), investment in research and development, heightening productivity by vocational schools, providing welfare, and repairing some of the ecological damage resulting from productive processes. Even general wage levels are subject to political negotiation. In this model the "steering problems" and "legitimation crises" of the system adopt a distinctive form, and traditional forces of motivation are weakened. The following analysis presupposes such a type of political-economic environment.

In an attempt to set up guidelines for a discussion of this topic questions such as the following arise: Is spiritual experience to be thought of as something given or not given, or does it lie on a range of degrees? If the latter, where is the cut-off point? Where do we locate the parameters of relationship between the individual and society? Between church and society? Between individual and church or sect?

The Individual and Society

The first question might be approached by analogy with the philosophy of perception. (Thus, "I perceive an object which is colored red; red is defined as occurring within a certain range of the spectrum.") It seems more appropriate, however, to work with an extreme case as the "ideal type" in the Weberian sense. In the readily available literature perhaps the most convenient example for an ideal type is that of "Zen" practice. The fascinating contradiction here is that the individual exerts himself, strives for something, makes "attempts" (to quote a word from the preliminary definition

---

1. The justification for adopting this model involves the problem of the non-arbitrary selection of social theories generally, which cannot be treated satisfactorily here. Another point which also can be alluded to only in passing is that this sort of systemic approach tends to conceal processes of the exercise of power; there seems, however, to be no reason why complementary analysis should not be able to repair this deficiency.

at the beginning of this paper); yet the entire project is vitiated
if there is any thought of self, of striving, or of something to be
achieved. The individual tries to escape from normal ways of thinking and desiring. "We root out the emotionally and intellectually
habituated mode of consciousness, and then find that a pure state
of consciousness appears" (Sekida, 1975: 101). But this happens
only as the individual self is dissolved by "seeing into the non-
existence of a thingish ego-substance" (Suzuki in a dialogue with
Thomas Merton, 1968: 109).

The familiar contention that this sort of experience is not
necessarily limited to Asian cultures can, I think, be substantiated
by consulting the works of certain Christian mystics, such as Eckhart
(1956-1963) and John of the Cross (Juan de la Cruz, 1940-1952).
This dialectic of being and becoming does not make sense in terms
of ordinary experience or scientific description. It is not simply
a cognitive construct. We are in the quandary of not being able to
"handle" it and yet not daring to ignore it.

The relationship between individual and society, in so far as it
touches on spiritual or any relatively autonomous form of experience,
tends to be depicted one-sidedly in either a pessimistic or optimistic fashion. We have the later work of Marcuse (1967a, 1967b),
which proposes that man is programmed by society to want, to see,
and to hate in specific ways. On the other hand, the proponents of
"pluralistic society" maintain that we "have never had it so good,"
that alternatives abound, that, for instance, the paperback market
provides an educational break-through of readily available information and intellectual stimuli. While there no doubt is some truth
on both sides, it may be more productive to consider an intermediate
line of argument, that of "character formation" within a system
of advanced capitalism. Here the names of C. Wright Mills (Gerth
and Mills 1953), Peter Berger (1977; Berger, Berger and Kellner, 1974),
and Juergen Habermas (1969) come readily to mind.

In Berger's analysis, modern consciousness has two key facets of
"functional rationality" and "pluralism." Functional rationality
refers to the domination of a technocratic ethos in which, among
other things, it is supposed that human affairs can be reduced to
problems soluble by some form of social engineering. The term
"pluralism" has the connotation of simultaneous provinces of meaning,
often in conflict, which must be tolerated. It is linked to a value
concept: the "right to meaning." In a modern society this implies
"the right of the individual to choose his own meanings. In pre-
modern societies it implies his right to abide by tradition" (Berger,
1974: 195-196). All this, of course, is subject to an examination
of the processes of ideological control in any given society.

According to the analysis of Habermas (1969), the social system
develops its own steering exigencies. Decisions are made in terms
of administrative convenience and crisis-avoidance; the system

cannot respond to questions of value. This crucial finding is rather congruent with Weizsaecker's (1977) remark to the effect that politics is concerned with only the first two of his "objective principles," the useful and the moral-righteous, and furthermore operates by means of power and domination. In this scenario consciousness is focused on material progress and contemporary crises, such as environmental pollution. It is taken for granted that the state can and should provide for most human needs -- in principle, for all but those of the private and privatized sphere, if we omit the ambiguous situation of the economy.

The Church and the Individual

The relationship of church and society has shifted in recent times. Previously a "world church" claimed to be, and was seen to be, something particularly distinct from society. It claimed the exclusive possession of truth and grace; in the extreme case it was a hierocracy, to use Weber's term. Such claims are now increasingly perceived as not merely absurd but even meaningless. There is ever greater criticism of the historical use of power by churches. (A recent popularization of such criticism may be found in Deschner, 1972, 1974.) There is greater recognition, as in the work of O'Dea (1966), of the dilemmas of churches organized as bureaucratic institutions. Moreover, much research in North America has shown that the local church tends not to provide religious leadership; it tends rather to reflect local societal norms, for instance racist norms. The overall trend seems to be a delegitimization and loss of relevance of national and world churches and an increased merging of local churches with the surrounding community.

The relationship of individual and church or sect has also been the subject of intensive research in recent decades. In traditional Western society the figure of the risen Christ has been the sole legitimized exemplar of a transcendental life. The presentation of this figure has usually been authoritative; counter-images have characteristically led to excommunications, schisms, persecutions, and further dogmatism. Jesus has been represented as redeemer in at least two senses, concerning one's helplessness and one's guilt, but there is an occlusion of both senses in modern society, where it is thought our helplessness may be repaired by other agencies, and our feelings of guilt are traced to social determinants.

The long-term trend seems to be a weakening of the larger churches. increasing numbers of people turn to smaller religious groups, seeking a "tailor-made" solution to their perceived personal problems; they "shop around" until they find some group which seems satisfactory for the time being. Some influential proponents of religious experience, such as Krishnamurti (1953), resolutely refuse to form sects. In the Roman Catholic Church the practice of confession, traditionally held to be of vital importance, has fallen away drastically. The new, not officially sanctioned, forms of Beichtandacht and <u>Beichtgespraech</u> seem to provide functions for significantly changed norms, especially regarding personal guilt.[2]

QUESTIONS FOR INVESTIGATION

Obviously, the notion of spiritual experience entails profound conceptual difficulties. How does one ascertain what spiritual experience might be available in a North American fundamentalist church which offers salvation after death as a sort of insurance policy, which opposes social reform or even the teaching of evolution as individually debilitating, and which defends "law and order" to protect the privileges of the flock? How can a dialectic be supposed if spiritual experience sometimes involves a withdrawal from, or indifference to, society?

Whatever the difficulties, one feels that it is worth while to investigate the aspects of society and churches which tend to facilitate or to hinder spiritual experience. The rationality of Western society fosters frenetic and carefully structured mental activity; the wisdom of the East says, "Be still." Can we have both? Perhaps the churches will ultimately fail, not because of their historical "errors" of intolerance, suppression of women, repression of sex, falsification of documents, and so on, but because of their failure to nurture a religious need.

2. I am grateful to Gregor Siefer of Hamburg University for this information.

Chapter 10

RELIGION AS SUBJECTIVE EXPERIENCE AND SOCIAL REALITY

Demosthenes Savramis

Recently sociologists, especially the so-called new sociologists of religion, as well as journalists, critics of culture,
pessimists, and "Death of God" theologians, have predicted the
slow death of religion and the demise of Christianity. The
communistic and bourgeois observers agreed about this diagnosis.
Meanwhile, however, a revival of religions of all kinds has occurred
in the communistic as well as the capitalistic world. "The state
is dying out -- religion is blossoming" wrote the illustrated
Belgrade army magazine Front (Kroll, 1971: 39) in a recent issue,
and one of the Beatles, who in 1966 asserted that they would become
more popular than Jesus, today sings about Jesus as "My Sweet
Lord."

One of the most bewildering manifestations in the realm of the
spiritual life of contemporary humanity is the fact that, as Ernst
Benz (1971: 7) says, "in most parts of the world new religions
spring up and make a permanent impression." To be sure, the
appearance of these new religions and their generally surprising
expansion is scarcely noticed by the European mass media and most
sociologists of religion, but this does not alter the fact that
these new religions exceed the scope of power of all the older
religions. This, indeed, applies even in Buddhist, Hindu, and
Islamic areas as well as in the hitherto predominantly Christian
lands (Benz, 1971; Lanczkowski, 1974).

Furthermore, it is noteworthy that modern man has a strong
desire for ecstasy and for becoming one with the transrational.
On the occasion of the presentation of a film about the Pentecostals
by the Jesuit Father, Reinhold Iblacker of Munich, which was trans-
mitted in December 1973 by the Third Program of the NDR/WDR, the
German public learned that over 25,000,000 Christians of all confessions belonged to the charismatic movement. For the first time
in Europe, the charismatics or Pentecostals demonstrated the "gifts
of grace" of the Holy Spirit in front of television cameras; they
spoke in tongues, prophesied, and healed the sick through the
laying on of hands. Suddenly we realized that there are men and

119

women in our "secularized" society who accept the promise of Jesus
that he would send the Holy Spirit to his disciples, who share
the pentecostal experience of the Apostles, and who acknowledge
the Pauline teaching that every Christian can receive the gifts
of the Holy Spirit.

Illustrations which support the thesis that religion is flour-
ishing are not lacking. One which may be singled out is the religiosity of youth (Hoellinger, 1972) who show a special interest in
the non-scientific forms of the meaning of life. Many seek their
salvation in Buddhism, in astrology, in other Eastern religions,
in drugs, in the psychedelic movement, or in gurus, all of which
promise them a solution for their troubled condition.[1] Although
many sociologists speak of "the end of metaphysics," it is empirically evident that a quest for the metaphysical is characteristic
of today's youth.

The implications of this for Christianity are that today's
youth do not resonate with the ecclesiastical value system, but
the Christian value system speaks constantly more to them. Even
in Russia, where atheistic propaganda tries to convince youth
that religion is nothing more than magic and where the religious
person is discriminated against and persecuted, youth show an unusual interest in religion, particularly in the Christian sects which
are willing to sacrifice and refuse to compromise.

SECULARIZATION AND "THE END OF RELIGION"

In spite of the numerous facts which illustrate the thesis that
religion is blossoming, there continues to be discussion in the
circles of the newer sociologists of religion, culture pessimists
and critics, and theologians of "The End of Religion" concerning
the alleged disappearance of the holy in industrial society, of the
deChristianization of contemporary society, and similar topics.
(See, e.g., Acquaviva, 1964, and Savramis, 1967, 1969.) How can
this phenomenon be explained?

We shall consider first the popularization of the conception
of those Marxists who, from the perspective of a vulgar Marxism,
view religion and religiosity as closely connected with the powerlessness of people and their desire to overcome their problems.
Since these spring from their natural social environment, religion
dies the moment that socialism is victorious. To be sure, one
does not speak in civic circles of a victory of socialism which

---

1. Unheilssituation, a concept which can be translated as calamity,
damnation, depravity, disaster, evil, harm, hurt, mischief, spiritual
decay, spiritual illness, trouble, unwholesomeness, etc. The context
determines our English translation of this word, which appears frequently in the German manuscript. -- Translator and Editor

makes religion superfluous, but rather one means that modern man
no longer needs religion because man himself is in the position
of being like a god ruling over his environment.

During a conference on the theme of "Secularization," a professor of systematic theology in a Catholic theological faculty
of a German university affirmed that people previously needed
religion because they experienced fear (Angst) of many things
(such as natural catastrophes) which could not be explained and
therefore were considered to be the work of supernatural powers.
Modern man has an explanation for these things. He knows that
neither God nor demons cause them. Whenever possible, he applies
remedies which set him free from all powers that threaten his
existence. In other words, because modern man can shape his
environment as he wishes, the function of religion in contemporary
society can be replaced by innerworldly social and political power
and movements, as well as by the rational organization of life.

Reference to "The End of Religion" is often supported in part
by opinions of this kind, which are expressed by many academics
in a code that is difficult to understand, as in the case of the
theologian cited above. A very important and decisive role in
the extension of the thesis of the end of religion and the demise
of the holy in contemporary society has been played by the newer
sociologists of religion and those who have been impressed by
the secularization thesis (see Savramis, 1967, 1969, 1973a).
Because they justified their exclusive concern with ecclesiastical
sociology through the conscious or unconscious equation of religion
with Christianity and of Christianity with organized religion,
secularization was identified not only with the decline of the
institutionalized church but also with the alleged deChristianization
of contemporary society and with "The End of Religion." The
few who did not concern themselves exclusively with practical
problems of the church are overwhelmingly general sociologists
who understand little or nothing about religion and religiosity
and who therefore ignore the important fact that it is possible
to understand that which we name religion apart from the accumu-
lation of data or the help of mathematical social science analysis.

Only those who empirically grasp the experience of reality in
its broadest sense and, in spite of overpowering practical materialism, are in a position to distinguish between two forms of
experience, namely, the empirically experienced incident and the
objective event, are able to grasp and interpet phenomena like
religion and religiosity. For religion is a multidimensional
phenomenon. Every definition of religion is useless if it does
not take into account the fact that the moment of the experience,
the encounter, and the answer which is manifested in behavior
belong to the phenomenon of religion. Religion hence is simultaneously a personal experience and an objective social reality.

121

FOLK RELIGION AND UNIVERSAL RELIGION

Through his definition of faith as the experience of being captured or grasped by that which is one's ultimate concern, Tillich (1961: 9) has created a very broad basis for the comprehension of both simple religion and special religious experiences. On the one hand, this definition eludes the reduction of religion to society as well as the equation of religion with theism; on the other hand, the faith experience is elevated to become the essential nucleus or core of religion. If we combine this definition with the possibility that religion can be understood as a historic form of the question about comprehending the overall purpose of being, then we obtain a good formula of that which is contained in the subjective, personal, religious experience. I would define it as the experiential apprehending (Ergriffensein) of that which can give our lives an absolute, unifying, and valid sense of meaning. The decision as to what can give our lives an absolute, all-binding, and unifying sense of meaning is closely connected with the answer we give to the question, How can I be delivered from the evil which arises out of the dark side of human existence?

Although every religion answers this question in various ways, a close connection between religion and spiritual well-being, salvation, or wholeness (Heil)[2] may be observed in all religions. Moreover, for this understanding as well as for the forms of deliverance from what is known and experienced as the evil situation of mankind, there exist differences between particular meanings of folk religion and universal religion.

The principal characteristic of folk religion is that the carrier of religion is collective, so salvation is a collective matter. Sociologically, the individual is basically secondary. All of the thoughts, feelings, and behavior of the individual are collectively controlled, for the group does not recognize the personal life of the individual. Life in the group demands that the individual fit himself into the group and be subordinate to it, so he does not attain self-consciousness; ideas of an independent existence and personal responsibility are foreign to him. If a person develops such a strong feeling of his own accountability that he

---

2. Heil is a concept which can be translated as happiness, luck, prosperity, redemption, safety, salvation, welfare, and well-being, to mention but a few of the major possibilities. As a verb, heilen means to heal, cure, restore, or make well. The overall significance of the word is closely related to spiritual well-being or wholistic health. The context has been used as a clue in our choice of English equivalents for this term, which the author uses frequently. -- Translator and Editor

must separate himself from his group, he ceases to find himself in the situation of a folk religion. Because his existence is meaningful only in the context of his exclusive group, salvation can never be attained as an individual but only as a member of the group, which is alleged to be the exclusive bearer of religion.

Even as the group, on the one hand, extinguishes individual religious practice, it also, on the other hand, gives the person all things. It provides him with the possibility of life itself and of participating in all of the qualities that it possesses. The group surrounds him, and he can live in the primordial social bond. In this relationship he can pass over into the religious sphere, and salvation flows to him from it. As a member of the clan or tribe, he has access to the godly reality; better stated, the reality of the godly essence locks him in as soon as he becomes a member of his group. The ancient germanic religions are an example of this; in them the solidarity of kinship partners with each other was astonishingly strong, and life as a mysterious conception found everybody together.

One must not overlook the definition of "life" here; it does not mean the being of the individual but that of the entire kinship group. Since the group can function only as a unit, every deed of the individual is not his personal responsibility but rather that of the entire group. The fortune or misfortune of the individual is similarly abstracted from the person; the entire kinship group must carry it. If the behavior of an individual is identified as evil, the entire tribe is damaged, and its life is poisoned. The iniquitous member is cast out, and it is certain that no self-existence can begin outside of the group. The exclusion means nothing other than that he has been cut off from life and advanced toward death. The concept of death is not linked here with dying physically; rather, it is equivalent to alienation from tribal life.

The structure of the folk religion has two characteristics. First, the people in the broad sense (e.g., Romans, Germans, etc.) are the bearers of the religion, not a particular social class, and second, salvation is found through group affiliation. In contrast, universal religion (Mensching, 1959: 51ff.) is basically a religion of the individual; in other words, the individual is the bearer of the religion.

Universal religion has other important characteristics. It presupposes damnation rather than salvation. It assumes that the world is an object for rational knowledge and conscious design. In its frame of reference a new collectivism can arise, so one must speak of a continuing process in which the schema of collectivism-individualism-collectivism is reproduced and shows us that man has been detached from the old collectivism of the folk religion in order eventually to settle again into a collectivity. The final distinction from the primordial collectivity is that we encounter a narrowing of the concept of the folk; in contrast to the primordial collectivism of the folk religion, the scope of the collectivity arising from the universal religion pertains to popular beliefs, the beliefs of the people (Volksglauben; see especially Mensching, 1957: 58-76; 1959: 138-139).

In the folk religion the entire people (Greeks, Romans, Germans, etc.) are carriers of the religion; they have a vital, organized unity with a sacred character. In the universal religion the carrier of the faith is the beliefs of the people, just as a specific social class is within a high culture. In the case of popular beliefs we observe a religiosity of the masses, the carrier of which is always an unorganized majority whose chief characteristic is the primitive structuring of religious thought and feelings.

The individual in the folk religion receives the benefits of the group which guarantees him salvation. The religion of the masses can see the person only as a number in the multitude. Authority and worth as designated by his religion stand over against him; they do not reside in him. The individual in the folk religion is without consciousness of his own existence because he is enclosed in the group once and for all for his well-being and redemption. Just because he is a member of his religious group, his behavior is religious. In contrast, the individual in the mass religion, who is conscious of his damnation, is offered no possibility to take part in either a collectively provided salvation or to attain a personal salvation through a direct encounter with the Holy.

The worth of the individual in the folk religion resides in the group's need for him because the group's productivity is accomplished through its individual members. In mass religiosity the individual does not possess this worth because he belongs to an unproductive multitude, which often produces destructive and dysfunctional consequences. The great chance which the individual has in the mass religion is that he can easily be disentangled from the collectivity. He can depart from his traditional milieu and, if necessary, start a new process of the above-mentioned schema of collectivism-individualism-collectivism in the strength of his personal charisma.

THREE MODELS OF SALVATION

From the description of the differences between folk religion and universal religion, it follows that in the universal religion the content and form of the spiritual illness of the individual are determined independently of the group, and that all the more so because each person experiences and recognizes this situation differently. This also means that the decision concerning that which

124

can give one's life an absolute, binding, and valid meaning is personal; it supersedes the experience which the individual deems to be decisive for abolishing his trouble.

Between experience and decision, or perhaps even earlier, an encounter with strong personalities occurs, those who appear as charismatic leaders or teachers and who establish religions or world views as a materialization of the experience and knowledge of salvation by the founder. They exert the function of release; i.e., they provide a decision-making orientation for the individual which provides a form of relief from his damnation.

In spite of countless systems which promise salvation, there are basically but three important models (Savramis, 1970). The first seeks well-being in absolute spiritualism, mysticism, contemplation, etc.; in it the world and the value system bound up with it are totally negated or ignored. The second elevates the world as an object of rational knowledge and conscious formation in the conviction that, alongside the work of the gods, one's own deeds are essential for redemption. The third sees the conquest of the spiritual illness of the individual in materialism.

If the world and matter, be it one's own body or merely material things, are looked upon as the source of ill-being, it naturally follows that there is only one possibility for abandoning it, namely, total opposition to all material values and needs which one can designate as mental or spiritual. People who think thus decide for that which is entirely different; at the cost of all that is perishable or temporal, they adjust themselves to an irrational world in which they are elevated into another form of existence and promote the spread of a religiosity of feeling at the expense of a rational religiosity.

The decision concerning that which can give our lives an absolute and binding sense of meaning is called here "for heaven -- against the earthly," that is, against the worldly and the rational. Consequently, this decision is at the same time a renunciation of every claim to power, authority, and leadership. People who make this decision become followers of religions which promote mysticism, as well as that attitude or position which Max Scheler (1963: 111-112) describes as the holy irony of superiority:
Poor, dear human being -- how difficult God has made it for you, that you must rule over me, that you must have a greater part in the systemic evil of this world than I.

That person who chooses the worldly and the rational in answer to the question of what can give an absolute, binding, and valid meaning to life thinks differently. This certainly is not because he is against heaven but because he believes that God desires social action by the faithful in order to shape social conditions in conformity with His commandments. The ideal type image of this man is the ascetic Protestant (Weber, 1920), who gave back to the Greek word askesis the positive sense of practice involving positive attitudes toward attaining positive goals which are promoted in a religious as well as economic and societal manner. (See especially Weber, 1920.)

Alongside the conviction that God desires human social action, which the inner worldly asceticism promotes at the cost of the external, a still more important factor must be mentioned. That which convinces the person to consider the rationalization of his conduct in the world as an important religious duty is the recognition that salvation, or the release from the unwholesome human situation, can neither be sold away nor negotiated. One must accomplish it oneself. This insight carries with it the distinction that the domains of culture, the economy, the state, and the society can each be recognized independently. One result is the autonomy of these areas over against the claim of religion to be absolute. In its institutionalized form, for example as a church, it wishes to subjugate these domains under its single system of values and organizational arrangements.

MARXIST MATERIALISM

The conviction that salvation, in contrast to the lost situation of man, can neither be sold nor negotiated and that consequently one must work it out for oneself offers the best prerequisite for materialism that one could set forth, for it makes a person accept material things as the only given reality. In this case, one sees salvation or release from an evil situation as a logical consequence of the satisfaction of one's material needs. All values which stand in the way of this liberation must be overcome and destroyed. People who thus decide the question of what can give life an absolute and unifying purpose decide for the earthly and against heaven.

In this connection we must distinguish between two forms of materialism. The one is a common or vulgar practical orientation, and the other is a theoretical or philosophical materialism which combines redemption from the evil situation of man with awaiting a paradisical condition of eternal happiness in which a system of beliefs and values will reign. This consists of principles and hopes which can be designated as religious.

Because theoretical materialism, such as that of the Marxist imprint, concerns itself with the purpose of life, it has developed a belief system out of a conviction which can be described as at least the functional equivalent of religious convictions, i.e., convictions which cannot be looked upon directly as religion but which nevertheless intrinsically exhibit sociologically significant characteristics of the religious perspective. After all, it is not an accident that Marxism has developed into a variety of

religion which strongly reminds us of the Christian religion with
its teaching of paradise (primitive Communism), of sin (possessing
and ruling over people, which reaches its climax in capitalism),
and of redemption and particularly eschatology (the classless
society). It also has its prophets and martyrs.

Finally, we must not forget that the "atheism" and "materialism"
of Karl Marx did not originate primarily in an intent to fight
against God (Post, 1969). Marx wanted to humanize man, to free
him from all constraints which dehumanize him. This decision <u>for</u>
man compelled him to struggle against the religion he knew,
namely, institutionalized Christianity, because this religion had
deteriorated into a dangerous ideology which legitimized the
exploitation and oppression of man by his fellowmen, thereby
metaphysically dehumanizing humanity. Marx was rightly convinced
that a successful critical analysis of socioeconomic reality
presupposes the critique of religion.

Marx's greatest mistake lies in the fact that he was not in a
position to distinguish between the Christian value system and
the ecclesiastical or churchly value system. Because he identified
religion, God, and Jesus with the "men of God" and the institu-
tionized Christendom of his day, he condemned religion absolutely
as the ideological cause and effect of all cruelty which was
imposed by the economic, political, and social reality. He
viewed religion as causally correlated with facts in the society
in which he undertook a critical analysis, including the societal
and ecclesiastical value systems, both of which had been totally
removed from the Christian value system.

POPULAR PRACTICAL MATERIALISM

In the case of historical or philosophical materialism we can
speak of a hidden God who operates in the anthropology of this
materialism. In the case of vulgar and practical materialism,
however, a situation occurs in which it is no longer God but
idols that impress human existence. As one expects, this is not
conceded by the person who has fallen prey to vulgar materialism;
he insists that he is continually in a situation in which he, like
a god, is shaping his environment and ruling over it, and that is
certainly so because neither gods nor idols exist in this environment. In other words, this person is characterized by that manner
of thinking mentioned earlier which claims that the function of
religion in contemporary society can be replaced by innerworldly
material values.

In the case of the increasing scientific perspectives in the
world and the rationalization of everyday life, modern man notices
somewhat suddenly that the world which he has formed, to use the
words of Max Weber (1920: vol. 1, 204-205) has produced "specialists
without spirit" and "epicureans without hearts" who can accomplish

127

nothing but evil. The result is a total societal problem of purpose or meaning which precipates psychic illnesses, depression,
suicide, and other maladies.

Modern man tries to counteract his evil situation with the
help of psychoanalysts and psychotherapists who have taken over
the function of "secular priests." Psychoanalyst Hirsch (1972)
has correctly proclaimed that little can be expected from the
psychotherapeutic method. It can produce a sense of well-being
(Wohl) but not the wholistic salvation (Heil) of the person.
    And that makes the psychotherapist make his judgments
    on the basis of his medical practice. He has the task
    of healing the acute and chronic diseases of his patients.
    He should not, however, imagine that he can free them
    from existential predispositions like fear, purposeless-
    ness, and guilt to which every person, sick or well, is
    subject. Healing in the sense of salvation therefore is
    the conclusive liberation from the existential predis-
    positions and with it from the dark side of human exis-
    tence; it is the concern of religion (Hirsch, 1972: 9).

This truth was discovered by the youth movement; as mentioned
earlier, contemporary youth have a peculiar interest in the non-
scientific forms of the meaning of life and are characterized by
their desire for metaphysics. Certain important socially conditioned symptoms of today's youth may be perceived as social illnesses. These include growing uncertainty, which results from the
loss of their own identity; the lack of orientation, which as both
cause and effect of uncertainty leads them to hectic efforts to
find an answer to the question of purpose in life, as well as to
discover a more beautiful world; the social aspects of their evil
situation, which are caused by the "grownups" in the material
realm of life, and, above all, the vulgar practical materialism
which characterizes everyday life in industrial society. For
this reason, the refusal of youth to become unconditionally a part
of contemporary society, together with the symptoms correlated
with this refusal, can be interpreted as attempts to understand
and to cast off their evil situation.

RELIGION AS A SOCIAL REALITY

It is evident, therefore, that religion is not and cannot
become a private matter. The subjective, personal religious
experience, that is, the comprehension of that which can give
one's life an absolute and unifying purpose, compels the person to
specific social conduct which objectifies his faith experience.
Thus religion becomes a social reality which the person takes
seriously in his social, political, and moral actions because they
are given a meaningful arrangement that can deliver him from his
evil situation.

Our description of the sociological and religious situation of the individual in the realm of both the folk and the universal religion suggests the following important starting points for the understanding of religion as a societal reality. The types of societies which are strongly oriented to the tradition of a folk religion consider the local group to be higher than the individual person with the result that the individual is compelled to conform to the will of the group. This leaves very little room for independent thought and conduct. Obedience and dependence are important values; violation of them can wreck disaster.

Since the highest value is the salvation which is given through the group and especially its tradition, individuals are not oriented toward change. On the contrary, they consider any recent changes to be a form of concurrence with the established arrangements which the local group, and thus the person himself, explicitly guarantee to support. Therefore they carefully guard the familiar. Religion and its sanctioned arrangements also belong to the category of that which emanates from the sentiment that it was always thus and can never be otherwise. It is therefore almost impossible to have a renewal of religion in the domain of a folk religion because even a criticism of religion is out of the question.

In contrast, societies which are oriented toward the tradition of a universal religion carry within themselves the germ of dynamic change. This does not mean that the germ will inevitably develop, that change is unavoidable, or that change will be indisputably positive or constructive. What is important is that the individual's salvation is no longer presupposed, for in the universal religion, as we saw, the person does not stand in a position of salvation, but rather in one of damnation. Salvation must be sought and found individually. The constant search for it and its attendant release from the evil situation creates the prerequisites for tension between and reciprocal action by religion and society, both of which can be changed and renewed.

In the face of his unwholesome situation, the individual begins to think and act independently. Consequently, he will either become a member of an alternative group that promises him the wholeness which he seeks, or else he will himself establish a group which promises that wholeness to others which he himself has discovered (or believes he has discovered) through revelation, faith, reflection, and so forth. Between these two alternatives of aligning himself with an existing group and establishing a new group are, of course, other possibilities. One might, for example, join a group in order to renew and reform it.

In every instance it is evident that the individual is enabled to think and act independently. This includes questioning the tradition, should he perceive it to be unwholesome. If he is charismatic and gathers a following of persons who accept him as

such, he may even refuse to accept the tradition and instigate more
or less revolutionary changes. The stronger the feeling that
traditional arrangements are cursed, the greater will be the
pressure to bring about dynamic and revolutionary change in the
current social and religious order.

Under these circumstances a variety of situations may develop
which can be the starting point of new value systems that carry
their own norms. Their stability in terms of capacity for change
depends upon whether the action of individuals promotes or prohibits
casting off the evil that is experienced. In the final analysis,
the forms of redemption from evil and of the conduct conditioned
to respond to them constitute the most important factors for over-
throwing either a sacred or a profane social order and deciding to
establish a new one.

In this connection the Reformation of Christendom led by
Martin Luther offers an ideal type of a revolutionary reorganization
and renewal of the prevailing sacred order which depended upon
the conviction of a single person. He was convinced that God
will not and cannot allow anyone to reign over the souls of men,
and he therefore wanted to bring about revolutionary change and
renewal of the prevailing profane social, political, and cultural
order. In other words, the Reformation produced a previously non-
existent revolutionizing of the societal value system through
which it freed the Christian value system from the clutches of the
ecclesiastical value system (see Savramis, 1971: 78-104).

RELIGIOUS PLURALISM

Religious legitimation was given to individualism through the
Reformation. This opened new opportunities to seek salvation
independently of the collectivity. Through autonomous thought
and action a person can seek, find, and implement his own redemption. As a result, he also soon discovers that his unwholesome
situation is identical with his self-imposed immaturity. Henceforth he hopes to correct this situation because he has declared
his freedom from dependence to be the highest value.

The sociological consequences of the religiously conditioned
efforts of man to free himself from all constraints are especially
evident in the reduction of the chances of survival of the traditional value systems. Their validity has been derived from sharing
the political, economic, and social world from top to bottom with
their inequality, force, suppression, uncertainty, and accompanying
fear (Angst). This is particularly observable in western industrial societies, whose development is causally connected with the
Reformation and in which monopolization of salvation through a
specified institution is impossible. In place of such a monopoly
value pluralism prevails. It asks for respect for all values that
have meaning to an individual for his redemption from his evil

130

situation.

The existence of a large supply and a strong demand in the market of values which is implied by value pluralism and, above all, the negative concomitant symptoms of this phenomenon are the price that the individual must pay in order to be delivered from his spiritual illness by the means he considers proper according to his personal faith. They also offer the guarantee that a continuous revaluation of worth is possible, according to which the absolute and binding meaning of life may be sought in the difficult manner which they have made available. This can be facilitated only by those religions which have taken seriously the emancipation interests of humanity.

Finally, value pluralism, which shows respect for all values that can be important for redemption from evil, brought two very important modern manifestations to the forefront, namely, the dialogue between the world religions and tolerance. Behind this phenomenon is the recognition, supported by modern religious research, that

The organizational forms and unique spirit of all historical religions are determined by humane, psychic, and spiritual presuppositions. Therefore there is in the depths of all religions both a unity and kinship to each other and a historical differentiation and variation. This diversity rests also upon the divergence of the structuring of the soul in the Orient and Occident, as well as in their individual mental and spiritual differences (Mensching, 1967: 598).

It therefore is appropriate to say with Rabindranath Tagore (as cited by Mensching, 1974: 182) that the different religions should let their diverse lights shine for the diversified world of souls which need them.

-- Translated from the German by
Helen H. Moberg

(In addition to the references cited in the text, the author recommends the following resources: Berger, 1973; Fuerstenberg, 1964; Gardavsky, 1969; Otto, 1936; Post, 1969; Schlette, 1971, and several of the publications of Mensching and Savramis.--The Editor)

THE NATURAL AND SPIRITUAL BODY

So will it be with the resurrection of the dead. The body that is sown is perishable, it is raised imperishable; it is sown in dishonor, it is raised in glory; it is sown in weakness, it is raised in power; it is sown a natural body, it is raised a spiritual body. If there is a natural body, there is also a spiritual body. -- The Bible, I Corinthians 15: 42-44, NIV.

PART IV. QUALITATIVE RESEARCH ON SPIRITUAL WELL-BEING

Chapter 11

LOCATING SELF AND GIVING MEANING TO EXISTENCE:

A Typology of Paths to Spiritual Well-Being Based
on New Religious Movements in Australia

Norman W.H. Blaikie and G. Paul Kelsen

While the concept of spiritual well-being is a relative new-
comer to the sociology of religion, much of what it seems to imply
has been the concern of sociologists for half a century or more
who have dealt with such topics as the problem of meaning or the
various functions religion performs for the individual. Nevertheless, given that the pursuit of well-being of some kind is fundamental to the human condition, there appears to be ample scope
for further exploration of what constitutes spiritual well-being
in our contemporary world.

How can an understanding of this issue best be achieved?
Instead of engaging in a literature review or a theoretical discussion, we have chosen to explore the everyday conceptions of
spiritual well-being with the aim of producing a typology of paths
to it. This typology will form the basis of a theoretical account
of the religious seeking of young people since the early seventies. In particular, we shall explore the notion of spiritual well-
being as it relates to the processes of joining and maintaining
membership in new religious movements in Melbourne.

THEORETICAL BACKGROUND

In order to place the issues of concern in this paper in their
socio-historical context and within a theoretical framework, it
will be necessary to develop two themes: to discuss the problem
of maintaining the plausibility of a world view and of achieving
and sustaining a satisfactory identity in a pluralistic society,
and to trace the socio-political developments which led to the
rise of the various new religious movements.

A major premise on which this paper is based is that, due to
the fact that complex societies are characterized by a highly

segmented plurality of life worlds, both private and public, which
lack any adequate overarching system of meaning to integrate these
various spheres of individual experience, members of such societies are forced to find or construct a "home-world" which will provide a secure and meaningful social base. These "home-worlds" may
range from marriage through to membership in a religious sect,
each differing to some degree in its precariousness and in the problems associated with its maintenance (Berger et al., 1974: 63-66).
The pluralistic situation contains the potential for an individual
to experience a relativizing of all life worlds, especially in times
of rapid social change, such that it becomes extremely difficult to
maintain the plausibility of any ultimate beliefs or values. Given
the anthropological necessity for finding some way to make life
meaningful (Weber, 1963; Schutz, 1963; Berger,1967), including having
some sense of identity, it is clear that modern pluralistic societies
place their members in circumstances of potential meaninglessness and
permanent identity crisis (Berger et al., 1974: 76-82). Not only do
members have to somehow reconcile the sub-worlds in which segments
of their lives and their various identities are located and between
which they are constantly required to move, but the biographies of
some members are also likely to be characterized by changing allegiances to different and competing ultimate definitions of reality;
the modern individual is peculiarly "conversion-prone" (Berger et
al., 1974: 77, 81).

    In spite of these potentials, however, many individuals manage
or choose to maintain a reasonably consistent world view and
identity. Musgrove (1977: 13) has suggested that while "adults
are capable of more fundamental change than many psychologists
will admit..., 'consciousness', 'identity' and 'the self' are far
more resilient and resistant to change than important contemporary
schools of sociology and social psychology will concede." Individuals differ in the extent to which they are likely to experience
circumstances which might result in their finding themselves in
a liminal or "homeless" state. Based on the evidence from a
number of case studies, Musgrove has argued that liminality is a
prelude to change or conversion, but he goes on to suggest that
the direction of change is age related. "Change which is towards
society's centre may occur at any age; but change which is away
from the centre is largely age-based, occurring most easily and
commonly between the early twenties and thirties" (Musgrove,
1977: 221).

    Significant cultural transformations have occurred in the last
decade and a half, particularly in the U.S.A., but also in a less
dramatic manner in Australia. The social activism of the late
1960s and the various movements of the counter culture which
developed out of it were accompanied by a decline in the plausibility of traditional religion. Bellah (1976) has argued that in
the U.S., up until the sixties, two world views had been successful in providing meaning and generating loyalty, utilitarian
individualism and biblical religion. The former with its view of

human beings in control and attempting to maximize their self-
interest, and the latter with its view of God being in control
and with its other-worldly concerns, managed to coexist throughout
American history because the latter essentially supported the
social arrangements of the former. However, both were inherently
incompatible and were subsequently undermined by the advent of
the scientific world view, particularly the social sciences
(Glock, 1976: 357-359). Hence, at a macro level, societies
such as the U.S.A. and Australia have been pluralistic since
their settlement. Religious divisions and the advent of secular
world views have compounded the pluralism.

There is some evidence from the U.S.A. to suggest that there
has been a shift in dominant meaning systems. Wuthnow (1976: 172)
has demonstrated that
        ...theistic and individualistic understandings have
    witnessed a noticeable decline in the past several decades
    while social-scientific and mystical ideas have shown
    an equal increase in importance. Thus, during the same
    period in which various forms of social unrest and ex-
    perimentation have increased, there has apparently been
    at least a gradual shift in the systems of meaning by
    which Americans make sense of their lives.

While the accounts of Bellah (1976) and Glock (1976) are consistent with the pluralistic thesis, the latter is more concerned
with problems which individuals face as they move between sub-
worlds in which the various segments of their everyday lives are
located. In spite of the incompatibilities which an observer
may want to identify in either the competing macro world views
or the micro meaning systems associated with these sub-worlds,
it is possible for groups to construct and maintain for themselves a world view which does not recognize such incompatibilities
or which compartmentalizes or rationalizes them. Pluralism
does not necessarily produce plausibility problems, but when it
is combined with social instability and/or a sense of uncertainty
about the future, a high level of precariousness is likely to be
experienced. Instability and uncertainty are likely to be produced by events which expose the incompatibilities between, or
the contradictions within, world views and meaning systems.

The 1960s was such a period. Many young people in both Australia
and the U.S.A. became not only disillusioned with traditional
religion as a source of meaning and purpose, but they also began
to reject affluence and education as being able to provide happiness and fulfilment (Bellah, 1976: 339). Cock (1977) has argued
that in Australia in the sixties the children of middle class
professional parents had been socialized with high expectations
for life in families which provided intellectual stimulation and
training in personal competence. This and their extensive education, frequently in the humanities and the social sciences, had

produced a critical awareness. They began to reject as dehumanizing the future offered by their society, a future of working for the corporate state in order to consume the goods and services it offers. They experienced a widening gap between their expectations and what they experienced or felt able to achieve (Cock, 1977: 118).

With the VietNam war as a catalyst, many turned their attention, in varying degrees, to social and political issues. In time, with some successful outcomes on more minor issues, but with a growing sense of frustration and hopelessness on the major issues of stopping the war and producing fundamental changes in the structure of society, it became increasingly popular to withdraw into some counter-cultural activity and life-style, to create an alternative society.

Australian youth lacked the other major catalyst in the U.S.A., the civil rights movement, but they had American youth as an inspiration and their activities as models. However, the racial issue followed as part of the political protest, for example, against the visit of a South African rugby team and in support of Aboriginal rights.

It is not possible to mark clearly the beginnings of this search for alternatives in Australia, but by 1971 various forms of it were in evidence. Many of the communal alternatives were short lived, leaving their members with little option but to return to the society they had rejected. Some of them, particularly those who had become part of the drug subculture, eventually found the resulting precariousness led them to seek the order, security, and direction of various successor movements which were invariably deeply influenced by some Asian religious tradition. Of the American situation Bellah (1976: 341) has argued that:
 In many ways Asian spirituality provided a more thorough
 contrast to the rejected utilitarian individualism than
 did biblical religion. To external achievement, it posed
 inner experience; to the exploitation of nature, harmony
 with nature; to impersonal organization, an intense ·
 relation to a guru.

An important aspect of this shift from political activism to religious alternatives was a tendency to adopt a different philosophy of social change, or to abandon any interest in it. Those political activists who became religious evangelicals of some kind inevitably shifted from a philosophy of changing structures to one of changing individuals. Others, who from the beginning or as a significant transitory phase had been involved with drugs, became more interested in their own religious experience and inner reality rather than proselytizing some belief system. Some of these continued a commitment to social change which was frequently expressed as a generalized concern for world unity.

136

Both of these alternatives were combined in the counter culture and became the focus of disputes between rival movements; they continue to divide the members of contemporary movements. The alternatives might be typified as a concern with the well-being of the world as against a concern for the well-being of the self. Movements differ in the extent to which they emphasize one to the exclusion of the other or in the relative priority they give to both.

We are not suggesting that these stages represent distinct, even if rather short, historical periods; if anything, they overlap and merge into each other. Nevertheless, they appear to be typical of the biographical experiences of numerous young people over the past ten years. The remainder of this paper is concerned with developing an adequate account of what it was that this generation was seeking in these new religious movements. If they were looking for some kind of spiritual well-being, what was it? Was more than one type of spiritual well-being sought? If so, what were the characteristics of each, and what predisposed an individual to seek a particular type?

SPIRITUAL WELL-BEING

Space does not allow, nor does the methodology used require, a definitive discussion of the concept of spiritual well-being at this point. However, a sensitizing or working definition is necessary.

We shall leave aside the area of material well-being, which entails the satisfaction of such basic needs as food, shelter, and perhaps economic security, and concentrate on what might be called existential well-being. In terms of available theoretical concepts, existential well-being could be regarded as combining a sense of meaning and purpose, a secure and stable identity, and a feeling of belonging. To have a sense of well-being it is suggested that individuals need to know what to do and why, who they are, and where they belong. In situations where an individual lives in a relatively unchanging, socially stable, and taken-for-granted world, beliefs are usually regarded as absolutes, meaning and purpose are obvious, identity is given and is usually accepted, and belonging is natural and inevitable. As we have seen, a pluralistic situation, combined with some disrupting events, has the potential for making all these aspects of existential well-being precarious.

Spiritual well-being might be regarded as that type of existential well-being which incorporates some reference to the supernatural, the sacred, or the transcendental. To define spiritual well-being this way is, of course, to buy into the longstanding debate over what distinguishes a religious world view from other world views. Insofar as this paper is concerned with social

137

movements which clearly include a "religious" characteristic defined in terms of the supernatural, sacred, or transcendental, this proposed working definition seems to be appropriate.

By combining and elaborating the analyses of religion of both Weber (1963) and Durkheim (1965), later sociologists have argued that religions, and particularly the various traditions of biblical religion, provide their members and adherents with meaning and belonging. (See, for example, Greeley, 1972: 69). These theories imply a conception of spiritual well-being. As we shall see later, the concepts of meaning and belonging require much clearer theoretical specification in order to provide an adequate account of membership in either new religious movements or traditional religious groups.

THE TWO RELIGIOUS MOVEMENTS

Two religious movements provide the major source of our data, the Divine Light Mission and two branches of Buddhism. However, over the course of the past two years participation in and interviews with members of other movements was undertaken: Hare Krishna, the Unification Church, Baba Muktananda, Transcendental Meditation, and sections of the Christian charismatic movement. The association with the Divine Light Mission (DLM) extends back to 1974, two years after it was established in Melbourne. Contact was first established with the Buddhist groups in 1976, some form of Buddhism having existed in Melbourne for about 25 years. While the Hare Krishna movement has been the most conspicuous of all those mentioned, at its peak the DLM probably had the largest following of any new religious movement with a membership of around 700.

The DLM had its origins in India. It was founded in the West, initially in the U.S.A., in the early 1970s. Guru Maharaj Ji was only a boy when he took over the leadership of the movement in India at the time of his father's death. His mother and his brother were also significant figures during the early period. (Messer, 1976, gives a detailed description of the early period of the movement in the U.S.A.)

The Divine Light Mission in Melbourne has gone through three distinct phases. In the initial phase from early 1972 to the end of 1973 the movement was very much an extension of the counter culture, having a distinctly Eastern character. The teachings of its leader, Guru Maharaj Ji, consisted simply in "giving Knowledge," a set of four sensory experiences achieved through certain meditation techniques, rather than a set of beliefs or moral principles. Devotees, or premies, initially "received Knowledge" from a mahatma, one of the Guru's itinerant representatives. They were then expected to attend Sat Sang regularly

138

(nightly meetings for devotional activities and informal discussions, including personal testimonies) and to do "service" for Maharaj Ji. "Service" was not clearly specified, but it included proselytizing, doing the daily chores in the communal households, being involved in administration, and fund raising, such as running a used goods shop. Premies were not supposed to eat meat, eggs, or fish, or to drink alcohol or smoke. They lived either in ashrams (households of celibate premies who devoted all their time and possessions to "service"), "premie centres" (communal households closely linked with an ashram, which included married, noncelibate couples and children), or a "premie house" (a household consisting of a family or a few premies which was less clearly linked with, or regulated by, an ashram). The Sat Sang centres, which were usually incorporated in the ashram, were decorated to look like an Indian temple. The premies wore white robes around the ashram and premie centres. Candles and incense were burned, and Indian jargon was regularly used. The movement incorporated a distinctly anti-establishment orientation and was treated suspiciously by members of traditional religious groups. By the end of this period Maharaj Ji was regarded by many premies as the "Messiah returned."

The second phase extended from the beginning of 1974 to the end of 1976. The movement became more Westernized, increasingly bureaucratized, and accommodated to middle class values. Indian sayings were used less frequently, premies were less likely to prostrate themselves before a photograph of the Guru, and he became less significant than the "knowledge" itself. This may have been due in part to the considerable public criticism he received for his outward display of material possessions. In order to reduce cognitive dissonance among the members and to facilitate proselytizing activities, his place in the movement had to be played down. By early 1975 meetings were being arranged in a public building in one of Melbourne's wealthier suburbs. These were designed to attract a very different section of the population, predominantly middle class housewives, by presenting meditation and "knowledge" essentially as a means of coping better with their existing daily activities.

By the end of 1976, two of the features of this second phase had been reversed. Much of the international and local bureaucracy had been dismantled. Ashrams were abandoned, and the new style of proselytizing was discontinued. Premies tended to live more as couples with their growing number of children, or in small households. Meditation came to be seen more as a way of communicating with, or being with, Maharaj Ji.

Some of these changes follow the well documented developmental trends in all sectarian religious groups, but the later reversal of some of these appears to have been influenced both by top level policy decisions overseas and the life cycle changes of the

members. While the movement experienced a considerable turnover
in its membership over these years, the predominant age of the
premies had moved from the late teens and early twenties to
the middle and late twenties because a core group of about 150
has remained in the movement from its beginning.

While the view premies had of Maharaj Ji changed over this
period and was never uniform at any time, the underlying philosophy
of the movement remained relatively stable. It was centered on
the notions of "peace, love and happiness" as being the universal
human needs which the movement was designed to satisfy. On the
surface at least, this constituted spiritual well-being, and
the path to it was to overcome the distractions of false pleasures
by gaining knowledge through meditation. As we shall see, however,
members' conceptions of spiritual well-being and the paths which
they followed did not necessarily follow these prescriptions.

The Buddhist movement in Melbourne is composed of two classical
orders, the Hinayana (the "narrow" way) and the Mahayana (the
"broad" way). The Hinayana order is the smaller of the two. It
places more emphasis on meditation, is more demanding in terms
of the denial of ego and materialism, and has an older membership,
mainly over 35 years of age. It has a basic membership of about
100 but an average of only about 10 persons attend the weekly
meditation group. The active members vary in the style of their
commitment, some being concerned mainly with administration, some
with the teaching of the dharma, and others mainly with meditation.
It has no monks of its own in permanent residence, so it is
compelled to rely on visiting monks from overseas.

The Mahayana order has a much younger membership (18-25 years)
and has experienced a considerable growth over the last 10 years.
While this growth has the appearance of being just a fad, the
movement represents yet another context in which the younger
generation has been seeking some kind of "home."

The movement is concerned with the achievement of enlightenment
and self-realization through the nihilation of ego. It espouses
a rejection of material things and particularly a sense of self
that is derived from what one possesses or the roles one plays.
Buddhist practice in Melbourne takes three forms: following a
particular monk as a charismatic figure; knowing the dharma and
honouring the Buddha in ceremony and rites, and practicing meditation. While most individuals concentrate on one form, some
engage in all three.

In spite of the fact that these two movements have strong
links with Eastern religious traditions, they differ in a number
of important ways. The DLM is a new sect of Hindu origin; Buddhism
is an ancient religion. The DLM has a living charismatic leader
whose decisions and pronouncements determine the "shape" of the

140

movement and guide the followers; they rely largely on the spoken word. Buddhists have to rely on interpretations of the ancient texts, and while the learning of meditation requires a competent teacher, usually a monk, and Buddha is the focus of much attention, the movement lacks charismatic leadership. The DLM has received considerable attention from the media and has actively proselytized, while the Buddhist groups have been left alone by the media and have maintained a low profile. These differences provide a broad range of possible paths to spiritual well-being for investigation.

METHODOLOGY

The issues discussed in this paper are only one aspects of a study which has been concerned essentially with continuity and change in an individual's conception of self and world view. The central focus has been on the processes of conversion to new religious movements. The research has extended over a period of five years and has included the use of participant observation and unstructured, focussed, and structured interviews at various stages.

The method of theory construction is derived from that suggested by Schutz (1963) and Glaser and Strauss (1967) and stands in the dialectical or hermeneutic tradition (see Blaikie, 1974, 1978). In contrast to the positivistic tradition, particularly its hypothetico-deductive branch, theory is viewed as the product of a process which involves an ongoing movement between the actors' typifications and meanings and the technical concepts and theories invented by the sociologist. It involves what Giddens (1976: 79) has referred to as a double hermeneutic, "relating both to entering and grasping the frames of meaning involved in the production of social life by lay actors, and reconstructing these within the new frames of meaning involved in technical conceptual schemes."

This process can be illustrated by tracing the theoretical developments in the research. During 1973 and early 1974 both authors had a number of conversations with members of the DLM and other new religious movements. Later in 1974 participant observation was undertaken in a DLM ashram and some premie houses, and unstructured interviews were conducted with some of the members. This was followed with semi-structured interviews with a random sample of 50 DLM members. At this stage the concern was with access and motivation to join the movement. Two dominant interpretations of self and the world were established, "religious" and "secular." A high degree of continuity was found, i.e., those members who had had a religious upbringing joined the DLM in search of God or meaningful religious experience, while those members who lacked a religious upbringing looked for a secure and stable social environment (see Kelsen, 1975).

When contact with other movements was established in 1976, with the view of testing this continuity hypothesis, the religious/ secular dichotomy began to collapse. Theoretical attention shifted from the effects of primary socialization to the influence of significant others, and the notion of world view became pro- blematical; it became difficult to specify what this meant in each movement. In addition, while continuity could be explained, discontinuity or conversion could not. Hence a further 50 inter- views were conducted with members of other movements mentioned above, and the responses, particularly to the open-ended questions, from the 50 DLM interviews were reexamined to look for evidence on the source of authority and the influence of significant others. The problem of relating the notions of world view and self remained. At this stage various ideas in the literature were explored, and a tentative typology linking the concepts of authority and significant others was developed from the work of Riesman (1971) and Hampden-Turner (1970).

During the second half of 1976 and early 1977 interviews with a further 50 DLM members and 27 from the Buddhist groups were conducted using some tentative hypotheses derived from the earlier research. A number of theoretical developments followed. The most important of these was a shift in the notion of world view from one concerned with the content of beliefs to the taken-for- granted meanings and assumptions that provide a frame of meaning within which social action occurs and in which the self is ex- pressed. (Among other things, a world view in this sense provides typical recipes for typical problems.) A model of the conversion process was developed in which change was identified with this revised conception of world view, and a completely revised typology was developed.

While it was not an original concern of this study, it is possible to translate this new typology into one that identifies three paths to spiritual well-being. Before discussing them, it is important to note that they have been derived from, and are intended to represent at a more abstract level, the meanings which social actors give to their quest. Existing sociological concepts have been used only as either sensitizing concepts in the early stages of the research or as a way of ordering and generalizing from descriptions of the social actors' world. Following the impli- cations of Schutz's (1963) postulate of adequacy, at the end of each interview the typology was presented to the respondent, and the interviewer indicated which one he considered applied. The respondent was asked for comments. In almost every case the respondent understood the three types, confirmed the interviewer's judgment, and was able to place others within the types.

PATHS TO SPIRITUAL WELL-BEING

Three paths emerged, each of which represents a mode of locating

self and giving meaning to existence. In the <u>Ritualistic</u> path,
self is located in, and meaning is achieved through, the fulfillment of particular roles in response to taken-for-granted expectations. Ritualists see themselves in what they do and/or what
they possess, belonging is achieved by being part of the institution in which these roles are located, and peace and happiness
are achieved by successfully fulfilling the "right" role. Recipes
to problems, and ultimate concerns, are contained within these
roles. The audience which judges success constitutes the source
of authority. Answers to such questions as "Who am I?" or "What
is the purpose of Life?," if asked at all, will be answered,
respectively, in terms of roles occupied and what constitutes
successful role performance. Ritualists are concerned solely
with externals, not with the meaning of the content of what is
said or done; justifications for any role are likely to be given
in terms of other roles rather than ultimate meanings. For
example, the role of church goer might be justified in terms of
the role of being a Christian; "A good Christian goes to church."

In the <u>Charismatic</u> path, self is located in the central relationship with a charismatic figure, living or dead, and is usually
supported by a close association with other devotees. Meaning is
gained from "the master's" word and from doing his will. Everyday life is characterized by a degree of detachment from whatever
roles have to be performed. Personal imperfection is accepted;
salvation is sought through complete surrender, and unity with
"the master" is achieved through meditation or prayer. Experience
is likely to be used as a justification and is regarded as superior
to any form of logical reasoning. For example, whereas the Ritualist
might say, "I believe in God because I am a Christian," the
Charismatic might say, "I believe in God because I have experienced
Him through prayer."

In the <u>Mystical</u> path, there is a detachment from the physical-
temporal world and there is a surrender to the experience of
Being. Self is seen to be more fully realized through this
experience, and peace and happiness are achieved by being at one
with the universe; experience and meaning become as one. Mysticists
attempt to see themselves as being independent both from what they
do and from a "stronger one." They live for the experience of
the present, having neither expectations nor goals for themselves
or others, and they see neither success nor failure in terms of
how others react to what they do. To be a Ritualist is to act
in terms of what is "right;" to be a Charismatic is to believe
what is right through the experience of God (or Jesus, etc.);
to be a Mysticist is to deny being such a person while at the same
time denying not being such a person.

An important component of the world view associated with each
type is the conception of time, which, together with space and
causality, are the three components specifically identified by

Luckmann (1967: 53) in his definition of world view. For Ritualists, the present is seen to be mainly a means to some end; they tend to be future oriented, but their future is somewhat insecure and dependent on their own efforts and the approval of others. Charismatics are oriented to the present; concern for the future is unnecessary, as it will be taken care of by the "stronger one." Mysticists are also present oriented but differ from the Charismatics in that they let go all attachments to either roles or others. Time is also related to ideas about where spiritual well-being will or can be achieved, i.e., in this life or the next.

It is clear that each path entails an identifiable conception of spiritual well-being. While some individuals may follow a mixture of paths, there is a strong tendency to remain mainly within one path at a time. However, the changes of path are of particular interest, for, we would argue, it is only in these cases that conversion can be said to have occurred. Hence, shifts between religious groups in which an individual continues to follow the same type of path to spiritual well-being involve only changes in content, not in world view or frame of meaning. This typology, then, provides a theoretical framework for an analysis of religious conversion, and, while this does not specifically concern us here, some discussion of movement between the types will facilitate a more detailed understanding of spiritual well-being.

Table 1. Paths to Spiritual Well-Being, Past and Present, by Movement

Movement		Path to Spiritual Well-Being							
		Ritualistic		Charismatic		Mysticist		Total	
		%	N	%	N	%	N	%	N
D.L.M.	Past	64	(32)	32	(16)	4	(2)	100	(50)
	Present	8	(4)	84	(42)	8	(4)	100	(50)
Buddhist	Past	81	(22)	4	(1)	15	(4)	100	(27)
	Present	30	(8)	11	(3)	59	(16)	100	(27)
Total	Past	70	(54)	22	(17)	8	(6)	100	(77)
	Present	16	(12)	58	(45)	26	(20)	100	(77)

Of the 77 members of the two movements who were interviewed during 1976 and 1977, 70% (N = 54) had previously been Ritualists (64% or N = 32 from the DLM and 81% or N = 22 of the Buddhists). (See Table 1.) In fact, the Ritualistic type was derived essentially from the paths which members of both movements followed

prior to joining one of the movements, rather than from their
present conception of spiritual well-being. It has both religious
and secular forms, including the world views discussed by Glock
and Bellah (1976). Some members had simply followed a secular-
materialist life style; others had been involved in traditional
religious groups in which the Ritualistic path is dominant. A
few (8%) from the DLM, but nearly a third of the Buddhists
(30%), have continued to be Ritualists within these movements.
The DLM not only attracted a considerable number of former
Charismatics (32% were in the past), some of whom were members of
political movements, but the movement is now made up mainly of
individuals who follow this path (84%). In contrast, only one
Buddhist was formerly a Charismatic, and a majority (59%)
are now Mysticists; only four (15%) were formerly Mysticists.
Hence, each movement appears to have drawn its membership mainly
from individuals who were formerly Ritualists of some kind, but
now, not surprisingly, is composed of persons who tend to follow
a particular path, Charismatic in the DLM and Mysticist in the
Buddhist groups. However, the other paths are also represented
in both movements, particularly the Ritualistic path among the
Buddhists.

Given the limitations of this study, it seems reasonable to
conclude that these movements have provided an opportunity for
young people who have become disillusioned with traditional religion and capitalism (both of which are dominated by ritualist
modes of locating self and finding meaning) or with radical political movements (dominated by a charismatic mode of locating
self and finding meaning) to find an alternative path to spiritual
well-being. A few case studies will help to illustrate this.

CASE STUDIES

The following six persons illustrate not only the characteristics
of each path but also the changes of path associated with movement
membership. Three are drawn from each movement.

DLM 1. Tom was formerly a secular Ritualist. His world began to
fall apart when his girlfriend left him and he was conscripted
for military service. His expectations about who he was going to
be (job, marriage, etc.) collapsed; the future could no longer be
taken for granted.

"I went to a Divine Light Mission concert. Maharaj Ji said give
your devotion and I will give you the experience of God. After
the Festival I began to ask what am I doing here (why am I living?).
Till then I was just happy; I didn't think about anything. Now
I felt lonely and withdrawn. I got into drugs for a while --
acid and dope -- but that didn't help. The world seemed like a
stage with no reality. Then a friend took me to Sat Sang, and
later I took Knowledge. Now I live in a premie household -- there

145

is an incredible sense of love. Guru Maharaj Ji is stability and a beautiful person, the Holy name, or who I meditate upon -- the guiding light. I just want to be a little child and let Guru Maharaj Ji make decisions for me."

Events did not allow Tom to continue to locate himself in a Ritualistic world. The resulting seeking produced a change to a Charismatic path, a shift from roles and role performances to a reliance on a "stronger one." In this way the original problem was not so much solved as trivialized. Unexpected role changes could now be coped with as they would no longer threaten his sense of who he was or his source of meaning.

DLM 2. Pauline rejected any kind of Ritualistic path at an early age and had been a Charismatic seeker, looking for a stable sense of self in a "stronger one." This is not surprising, as she had been brought up in an orphanage, felt the need of "real" parents, and had a strong belief in Jesus. She married at 19 but failed to find the "stronger one" in her husband. The marriage lasted only a year.

"I was a searcher from a young age. People didn't seem genuine -- just playing games, roles. ...I got into dope and drink. I couldn't face this or that. I always looked to others because I felt that they were stable, but I got let down. I met a couple of premies by chance -- I had found it. I took Knowledge two months later. When I saw Guru Maharaj Ji, it was Jesus. I always wanted something constant -- everything in this world was continually changing. No longer can marriage be a source of security for me -- it is Maharaj Ji."

Pauline has remained a Charismatic. In joining the DLM she simply found a satisfactory charismatic figure who, for the present, provides her with a sense of spiritual well-being.

DLM 3. Jan had been a seeker for many years but out of curiosity rather than in response to a crisis. She had become bored with "straight" society. She was, nevertheless a Ritualist; when seeking change or spiritual fulfillment, she merely chose to do something different.

"I went to North Queensland ... had a good time. I lived in communes, knew hippies, and went to meetings of the Ananda Marga, Buddhists, T.M., and Baba Muktananda." Jan took Knowledge "because a friend did" and there was little urgency in doing so. "It seemed a peaceful experience. It was a new experience, a source of stability. But I had found these in such externals as a job and commune life-style. I am thankful to Guru Maharaj Ji."

This last comment is not typical of a Charismatic and would be unusual for a premie. Jan's view of life "as a flow," and the

lightheartedness with which she has sought spiritual well-being
in neither a particular role nor a "stronger one," suggests she
has a tendency toward a Mystical path.

Buddhist 1. Les was not introduced to the movement by a
friend, nor was he driven to it by some crisis. He simply came
across Buddhism in a book and became curious. Les was a Mysticist
before joining the movement. "I've always strongly rejected
blind faith and a personality God. I've always believed that all
religions are valid when practiced purely."

Les is clearly a Mysticist now. "Freedom is the freedom within. ..." This is opposed to the Ritualistic notion of freedom,
which is the ability to move at will in the external, material
world. "What you see (in Buddhist roles and rituals) may appear
as non-freedom, but it lies within." Les meditates to experience
nothingness.

Buddhist 2. John has always been a Ritualist and still is.
His sense of self has always been bound up with the role of
"intellectual," and being a Buddhist is an extension of this.
He is good at quoting the "do's" and "don'ts" of Buddhism and is
skeptical about the value of experience for its own sake.

"At university I became interested in philosophy. I have read
widely in Buddhist literature. I do not meditate. I think it is
only self-hypnosis -- it seems irrational. I find Buddhism
intellectually interesting ..., but I do drink and I go to parties.
If I took on Buddhism too deeply, what would my friends think?
I would be considered absolutely eccentric. I am seeking something that would be more than what I have found in life. I never
had a really good role in life. People should know more about
what Buddha said. I can tell them."

Since his roles are his source of identity, John shows the
characteristic concern for the reactions of his significant others;
he expresses a need for social recognition. This and the fact
that he views Buddhism essentially as a philosophy or even an
ethical system clearly make him a Ritualist.

Buddhist 3. Andrew was formerly a Ritualist and is now a
Mysticist. The change was brought about by a crisis in his life.

"I was a weight lifter. I got ill and bombed out. I gave up.
...I was very unhappy. I didn't know what I wanted to do for
about a year. When I was at school, I was told that I was ugly.
I had an inferiority complex. I went to the Buddhist society
and learnt to meditate. I really enjoyed myself. Now I understand why I was suffering -- it was the nature of attachment to
the material world. God I now see as a state of mind."

147

Andrew has found the solution to his problems in detaching himself from the "success" or "failure" in what he does, as judged by others. Now he is concerned with the experience of Being.

THEORETICAL IMPLICATIONS

Without further research, it is difficult to know whether these three types will adequately account for the paths to spiritual well-being adopted in all religions and their various branches. However, by studying people who have been brought up on occidental religion and are now members of groups which derive from two of the major oriental religions, we would seem to have some guarantee that they at least represent the major paths.

There are some obvious links between our types and Troeltsch's (1931) typology of church, sect, and mysticism, but our typology is concerned with an individual's search for a location of self and a source of meaning, i.e., solutions to the individual-society of dilemma, whereas Troeltsch was concerned with forms of religious organization based on solutions to the church-world dilemma. We would expect church-type religious organizations to be populated by Ritualists and sect-type religious organizations mainly by Charismatics. However, the variety of sect types that can be identified, in terms of their particular solution to the church-world dilemma (Wilson, 1969), makes any attempt at simply integrating these two typologies not only pointless, but a detraction from the value of each. In any case, Troeltsch's typology may not have much relevance to the modern situation (Steeman, 1975: 203).

Again, there is a strong association between our typology and Weber's (1963: 151) paths to salvation. Both deal with alternative solutions to the problem of meaning, but whereas Weber couched this in terms of the discrepancy between expectations and experiences, we have couched it in terms of looking for a "home" in a world that has collapsed. Weber's scheme assumes the acceptance of some expectations; ours suggests that it is the destruction of the taken-for-granted attitude toward expectations, especially for Ritualists, which has been the common source of homelessness or anomie in our contemporary world. In his discussion of the ritualistic path to salvation, Weber was concerned with specifically "religious" activity rather than our more general interest in the location of self and the source of meaning. Both approaches, however, imply rule-following to achieve some end. Weber (1963: 152) suggested that devotion induced by ritual can escalate into a piety which can take on a mystical character; it leads to the possession of a subjective state. Insofar as the achievement of this state is an individual's prime goal, we suggest that they are following the Mysticist path; our Ritualist performs roles, even the role of worshiper, in order to meet

148

external expectations and to achieve some "state or grace."
The Ritualistic path is the most rational in Weber's terms.
The Charismatic path obviously has a very close affinity with
Weber's (1947: 361) discussion of charisma in that rule-
following is rejected.

Troeltsch's third type, mysticism, has been largely neglected,
particularly by those theorists concerned with applying his
typology to American society (e.g., Niebuhr, 1929). In any case,
both Troeltsch and Weber had difficulty with it because they
believed that mysticism leads only indirectly to particular organizational forms, but Troeltsch (1931: 994) at least recognized
its importance within Christianity, seeing it as "a welcome
complement to the Church and the Sects." Weber's conceptualization of mysticism, however, led him to view it rather negatively
because of its tendency to be indifferent to the condition of
the world (see Garrett, 1975, and Robertson, 1975).

It is possible that our types need to be subdivided, not only
to provide a more detailed account of the orientation of the members of the movements under investigation, but also to be able
to apply them in other contexts. For example, in applying the
Mysticist type to traditional religion it may be useful to differentiate between the two forms discussed by Troeltsch (wider
mysticism, which provides legitimation and support for established
ecclesiastical structures, and narrower technical mysticism,
which undercuts the form and structure of organized religion).
Some clearer distinctions need to be made between "secular" and
"religious" versions of each path, particularly in the case of
the Ritualistic path. However, one of the major values of the
typology is that it need not be tied specifically to "religious"
or "spiritual" paths to well-being. It provides a framework
for discussing conversion not only between religious paths, but
also from secular to religious paths, or vice versa. To be
consistent with the methodology being adopted in this research,
such elaborations should emerge from further research using the
hermeneutic approach, not from "the literature" or armchair
theorizing.

We hope that our types provide for a more detailed theoretical
specification of the concepts of meaning and belonging. Belonging is viewed differently within each type: the Ritualist normally
belongs to an organization or institution through fulfilling particular roles; the Charismatic "belongs" to a charismatic figure
through surrender and discipleship; the Mysticist belongs to the
universe through merging his Being with it. Hence, an individual
lodges or locates his self through some form of belonging and,
out of this, meaning is achieved. Not only is meaning intimately
linked with belonging (Robertson, 1975: 243; Curle, 1972), but
it also has its source in more than the specific beliefs or theo-
dicies which a movement provides. It derives largely from what is

149

taken-for-granted, from the frame of meaning within which a sense of belonging is achieved.

CONCLUSION

We have attempted to provide an understanding of some aspects of religion in contemporary society by focusing on the discontents and searchings of young people and others who have experienced some disenchantment with dominant life styles and established religion. By means of a dialectic/hermeneutic methodology, we have developed a typology of paths to spiritual well-being, based on a conception of world view as the frame of meaning, or taken-for-granted assumptions, within which social actors not only conduct their everyday lives but also locate themselves and find meaning.

In our sample, some respondents have remained within the same type of path or world view but may have changed some of the content. For example, they may have previously pursued a Charismatic path as Christians but are now followers of Guru Maharaj Ji. Others have changed paths, mainly from either a secular or religious Ritualistic path to either a Charismatic or Mysticist path. This kind of shift is normally related to some crisis in which the taken-for-granted expectations about the future are threatened or collapse. Pluralism and events of the 1960s have substantially contributed to this.

While the methodology adopted does not preclude the "intrusion" of available theoretical ideas, it is clear that our typology, in spite of its apparent affinity with that of Troeltsch, confronts a different problematic. It is concerned with meaning structures rather than organizational structures, and it demonstrates that within even small organizations a diversity of orientations is possible. For example, whereas some religious groups may be founded on a mystical orientation, the Mysticist path can be found in various contexts. The plausibility structure for such a path may be just a small sub-group within an organization.

While our study might be seen as offering some support for the revival of interest in Troeltsch's third type, we do not consider that it offers support for his prediction (1931: 381) or lament that mysticism would very likely become the predominant form of religious life. Mysticism offers a path to those who have nothing to lose or who can afford to relinquish both a commitment to the pursuit of "Ritualistic" goals and to a concern for the approval of others. It could be that Weber was correct when he suggested that mysticism emerges when something has gone wrong in a society (see Robertson, 1975: 249-250). However, the Charismatic path offers another alternative for those who need a secure "home," and this is likely to be the case for some individuals during any period of social or political unrest. During periods of social stability it is possible that Ritualistic paths may be more attractive.

SPIRITUAL CONCERN IN WHOLISTIC HEALTH CARE

It is unwise to divide the patient into various parts and areas, since he is a unity and must be cared for always as a whole being. ...The doctor or nurse who ignores spiritual involvement with his patient is actually not avoiding the issue. Lack of spiritual care and concern are negativistic and destructive to the patient at a time when this aspect of his care becomes all-important and physical and psychological methods become meaningless and fruitless. ...Medicine of the Whole Person ...is extremely salutary and productive of healing (Reed, 1969: 135-136, 116).

Chapter 12

WHOSE SERVICE IS PERFECT FREEDOM: THE CONCEPT

OF SPIRITUAL WELL-BEING IN RELATION TO THE

REVEREND MOON'S UNIFICATION CHURCH*

Eileen Barker

This is an essay in caricatures. It is an exercise in which
I draw a series of pictures, of Ideal Type visions, with which I
try to illustrate how members of a particular religious group
can, despite incredulity from outsiders, believe that through
their membership in the group they can achieve a greater degree
of spiritual well-being than they could otherwise achieve in
contemporary Western society. The group is the Reverend Moon's
Unification Church.

The caricatures start with a somewhat mystical picture of
spiritual well-being as self-realization through self-transcendence;
this is followed by a more down-to-earth sociologist's comment.
Then there come five pictures of modern western society: the
achievement-oriented world of the materialistic rat-race; the
antinomian world of the amorphous counterculture; the mystified
world of the alienated cogs; the disenchanted world of the rationalized cogs, and the secularized world of the spiritually inarti-
culate. Next follow two pictures of life inside the Unification
Church: the brainwashed world of the Moonie Robot and the Family
world of spiritual well-being. Finally the essay characterizes five
aspects of the Unification Church which, taken in conjunction,
could contribute toward the creation of the second (rather than
the first) picture of the Unification Church in its opposition
to the pictures of the outside world. The five aspects are the
sharing religious community, the charismatic messiah, the

---

*This study is being supported by a grant from the Social
Science Research Council of Great Britain, to which the author
is most grateful. She is also grateful for discussions with
Earl I. Hopper, whose forthcoming book (1979) covers much that
is relevant to this essay.

articulated theology, the structured nomos, and the mundane challenge.

In none of the pictures is there any metaphysical claim to represent a Platonic reality. The pictures are merely meant to indicate ways in which social realities can be viewed, not to pronounce on what reality itself might be. They are, however, drawn from pictures presented to me during a study of the Unification Church. They are also painted in terms which will, I hope, be recognizably familiar to those acquainted with classical sociology and its concern with the relationship between the individual and society and the ways in which the development of man's "true potential" can be promoted or impeded by the social context within which he finds himself.

SPIRITUAL WELL-BEING AND SOCIOLOGY

The first caricature is a somewhat mystical picture of spiritual well-being as self-realization through self-transcendence. At once it must be admitted that, beyond saying that the spiritual is a non-material aspect of man, it would be difficult to proceed further without denying or including what someone else would undoubtedly insist on or exclude. Nonetheless, let us start by denying that the spiritual includes all non-material aspects of man. It is not merely consciousness, feelings, or emotions.

I want to suggest a picture in which the essence of spiritual well-being is to be found in an expression, a discovery, or a fulfillment of self through transcendence of self. Spiritual well-being will thus be realized when, free from immediate material concerns, there is an unimpeded flow of reciprocity between that which embedded in one's innermost self and that which goes beyond and is greater than oneself.

A man must look for the spiritual within himself, but at the same time it is that which connects him to something beyond himself. It grows through, and is nurtured by, relationships -- relationships of love, of exploration, of recognition, of belonging, of being part of, and of being a whole only through being a part.

Spiritual well-being is to be in communication, in communion, with that which goes beyond oneself in order to be whole in oneself. It is to be able to give as one receives and to receive as one gives. It is to feel satisfied and hungry at the same time; satisfied that the beyond to which one is attuned is good; satisfied that satisfaction can never lead to satiation. Realization can only lead to expectation.

The experience of spiritual well-being is a present. There can be the memory of a past and the hope of a future, but these belong

to a different plane of consciousness, for, once the realization
is recognized, there comes the reduction to cognitive or emotional
reflection which threatens to relapse into awareness of self
rather than transcendental realization. The "I" then contemplates
the "me" in the celebration of self, rather than losing and finding the self in discovering itself beyond selfhood. It is not
that one cannot achieve spiritual well-being while reflecting in
cognitive or emotional vein, but rather that the reflection has to
be in some way other than directed toward the self; it has to be
open to exchange from beyond the self rather than mere examination
or reorganization of that which already exists within the self.

For while it is a present, spiritual well-being is not a static
present; it is a process, a verb; it is being, and becoming through
being. One cannot achieve spiritual well-being and "be" without
"becoming." It is a relationship that offers an unchanging promise
of infinite variety. It is a relationship that cannot be captured
or encapsulated beyond its moment of life. It is a living flow
of energy -- the spirit floweth -- it is not clogged up but free,
free to be subordinated to the greater spirit in whose service is
perfect freedom.

A More Down-to-Earth Sociologist's Comment

All this is of course nothing but paradoxical rubbish to any
sensible behaviorist. What on earth can it mean to talk about
loss and discovery of selfhood, of realization through the transcendence of the partial whole to the whole part? And, of course,
in behaviorist language it does mean nothing. But could the sort
of spiritual well-being that I have tried to suggest, to indicate
(to say "describe" would, almost by definition, be self-defeating)
-- could such a concept mean anything in sociological language?

We are immediately beset with difficulties. On the one hand,
what I have been talking about concerns private subjective experience, and, on the other hand, it allows for the existence of
some phenomenon or phenomena that transcend the self and through
which the self can in some way grow or develop a potential. In
other words, we are faced with both the methodological problem
of lack of access to the subjective experience of others and the
metaphysical problem of assessing the status of not only a transcendent reality, but of its relationship to the individual.

There is at certain frontiers a very slender line between the
practice of theology and that of sociology. This in itself is
not necessarily "a bad thing," but it is a dangerous one which
threatens those of us who believe that one should distinguish
between (1) those areas of discourse where we believe that our
acceptance of the "facts" is constrained by objective "out-there"
realities which are accessible to all through the five senses
and (2) those areas in which facts can be accepted only as the

155

result of some existential choice (more or less determined by social factors). In other words, I would want to claim that, in principle at least, there are certain phenomena, statements about which can be discussed with reference to a sharable empirical epistemology, and there are other phenomena, statements about which cannot be justified or refuted by reference to empirically sharable observations. That said, however, it must also be accepted that, on the one hand, many, if not most, of the phenomena which sociologists study cannot be "seen" in any straightforward manner, and, on the other hand, there are undoubtedly many reported cases in history in which groups of people have shared what can only be described as common non-empirical experiences.

The next point to be made is that sociologists have always assumed certain philosophical anthropologies -- more or less explicit positions about the essential nature of man and his potential "true self." From some of the classical assumptions of this nature of man there have issued critiques of modern society insofar as it creates barriers which prevent the realization of men's true selves. If such theories have any truth in them, then it is possible that those situations which purportedly stunt men's true development might well give rise to difficulties in experiencing spiritual well-being.

Already it can be seen that the exercise is going to entail a reductionist translation of my picture of spiritual well-being. It is reductionist in that it will look for man's transcendence of himself arising out of relationships with other people. It is also reductionist in that it is limited to a monistic world view rather than a dualist world view as I accept, indeed insist, that it is beyond the competence of the sociologist to introduce into his work a world of spirits, or indeed any Eternal Spirit, which could act as an independent variable for the sociologist, though not of course, for the believer.

The reductionism can be defended insofar as spiritual well-being is being approached negatively by looking at factors which might inhibit it rather than those which would promote it. One can well argue that it is safer (both epistemologically and ethically) to assume we know more about what spiritual well-being (or "the Good") is not, rather than what it actually is. Be that as it may, we can still say that if we accept that man is a social animal, it is not altogether implausible that one of the paths to being able to experience spiritual well-being is to experience growth and transcendence at the level of human relationships.

The exercise is not, however, reductionist in that it certainly allows for the emergence of the spirit of man with properties independent of its material origin. The sociologist may be unable either to assert or to deny the ontological existence of an independent transcendental reality, but he would have to be foolishly

156

skeptical to deny that men have subjectively experienced a relationship with what they genuinely believe to be such a reality
and, through such a relationship, have realized what can only be
described as spiritual well-being.

FIVE CARICATURES OF SOCIETY

With this perspective in mind, let us turn now to five pictures
which constitute thumbnail sketches of society as it can be
experienced by young people today. Perhaps only one aspect of
these pictures will have been experienced as reality by some of
the young people, but for the majority of those joining the Unification Church there is, at least in their presently reported
statements, an indication that most, if not all, of the pictures
have in some way impinged upon their consciousness. Either implicitly or explicitly, the members have articulated dissatisfaction
and frustration with their erstwhile inability to achieve their
self-perceived potential or to experience what we are now calling
spiritual well-being. (A report on some relevant findings from
my study of the Unification Church can be found in the Appendix
of this paper.)

The Achievement-Oriented World of the Materialistic Rat Race

In the first picture we find young people facing an achievement-
oriented society where a rat race competition demands academic
success at an early age. There is little hope of climbing up the
ladder by other than educational means. All are given equal opportunity to succeed, the conventional wisdom goes, or at least all
from the comfortable, well-off achievement-oriented middle classes
which comprise a considerable proportion of the followers of the
so called New Religions. Others will be intelligent lower class
youths who may patently not have been given equality of opportunity.
For all but the very bright (and perhaps lucky) there must be
failure. They will not reach the top because both status and
economic achievement work on a zero-sum calculus: if Tom is first,
Dick can only hope to be second, while Harry will be a failure in
third place. The goal that is offered is first. To achieve less
is to be less. There is only one first in the rat race. How
can one transcend oneself when one is demonstrably inferior? With
what or whom can one expect to communicate if one is defined as,
at best, second class?

The Antinomian World of the Amorphous Counterculture

Perhaps the reaction was predictable. As a counter culture
it could be seen racing through the youth of the "sixties." If
there were to be no firsts, if achievements were not to be measured by any standards, then all could be equal, all could achieve
everything -- or nothing. In the creation of the second picture
rules, standards, and criteria of comparison were rejected in

157

order to allow for the fulfillment of each person as an individual at his own level. Each was to do his own thing unencumbered by the standards and criteria of others. But now, of course, he had no means of knowing he had achieved anything. He became lost by himself. We cannot transcend ourselves to a greater standard when all standards are denied. Normlessness, lack of direction in a life without goals or purpose, is the inevitable result. The individual becomes bogged down in the vast expanses of anything or nothing which face him as his sole existential choices. He is alone. He cannot plug into anything to pull his lonely, unattached spirit up by its sagging bootstraps.

This second picture describes the social situation encapsulated in Durkheim's concept of anomie. Here the underlying philosophical anthropology rests on the supposition that man needs some sort of moral authority. He needs his goals to be limited so that they can plausibly be achieved by the means available at a particular time and place. An anomic society is one in which individuals flounder because infinity is offered and therefore nothing is obtainable. There is a lack of adequate moral control by the community in which the individual finds himself. There is no "full stop," as it were, which allows him to feel something has been achieved; reality is not anchored in a realist setting; pathogenic goal orientation, as Earl Hopper (1979) calls it, is rife.

It is not difficult to describe the situation of much of modern youth in these terms. Young people find themselves in a permissive society where, in theory, anything goes. The world is their oyster. But only a few can pry the oyster open and find a pearl waiting inside.

The Mystified World of the Alienated Cogs

The third picture rests on Marxian philosophical anthropologies of Homo Faber and Zoon Politikon (Marx, 1970: 42, 125). Man is essentially, by nature, a creative animal and essentially, by nature, a political animal. Man creates himself through interaction with the environment and his fellow men. He creates tools as means of producing his (in time created) needs, and he becomes human as he lives with others. But the artifacts and relationships that he has created become separated from him and face him as things in their own right and over which he has no control. He becomes alienated from the product and the process of his work, from his fellow human beings, and from himself. Transcendence or realization of his true self as a creative creature is cut off as he experiences the reified object of his creation as an alien thing rather than as his own product. His relationship with others, too, becomes constricted and constricting. He becomes an object of exchange rather than an agent of exchange. He feels that he is powerless to contribute; that he cannot give of himself or to others (Tiger and Fox, 1972; see Chapter 5, "Give and Take," for a Marxist perspective on this point). Those who believe they are living their lives fully and creatively are suffering from an induced false consciousness or, to invoke a more existentialist perspective, are guilty of mauvaise foi.

The Disenchanted World of the Rationalized Cogs

The fourth picture overlaps in many ways with the first and third, but it focuses on a Weberian concern with the process of rationalization. Zweckrational action (Weber, 1947: 115), having become the typical mode of action, has produced a generation banging at the bars of its self-created iron cage. Formalization of goals and relationships is carefully mediated by rules laid down with the goal of furthering the efficiency of yet more rational means to yet more distant and unquestioned rational goals. The individual becomes a cog in the mechanical, clockwork society. He is certainly part of a whole, but he plays his part as a wholly uncreative entity, interchangeable with other cogs and restrained from imaginative and transcendent explorations of self or from potential growth beyond the dictates of technological and bureaucratic necessity.

In such a world only the charismatic leader can offer promise of relief; he provides a revelation of a great "beyond" and a bridge whereby the individual might attain that which has been revealed. Through his revelation and example there is the glimpse of hope, of expectation of something better, something which allows the individual to break free of the iron cage.

The Secularized World of the Spiritually Inarticulate

The fifth picture draws on a cultural rather than a structural dimension of the disenchanted world. It is a negative picture in that it merely points to the relative absence of a social milieu or language within which the spiritual can be fully explored.

In order to transcend oneself -- to go beyond oneself -- it is necessary to have the language with which to form the bridge of communication with the "other," whether it be the language of love or of sublimation. It is not, of course, that relationships of transcendence cannot be experienced through non-verbal language or communication, but such experiences must be limited. The scope for further exploration that socially shared myth and common symbolic concepts can offer is enormous. Modern secular society does, on the whole, deny the individual the full range of such relevant tools for self-transcendence which have been available in other times. (This is very apparent from the work being done by The Religious Experience Research Unit under the direction of Edward Robinson at Manchester College, Oxford and by David Hays at Nottingham University.) To talk about sex is no longer taboo, but one has to be very careful with whom one confides and with whom one dares to explore the existence of a super-empirical world. In this picture it is not always socially acceptable to admit to deep spiritual experiences or to recognize and foster these socially.

Where established religious institutions flourish, or at least survive, the tendency is to frown on direct personal experience. There one finds an emphasis on a purely cognitive relationship with the Creator, or else a jealous priesthood of mediators. Seeking a hot line to God or the world of the spirit through personal exploration and relationships is declared to be a dangerous or narcissistic overstepping of the self by a religious elite which is seen to be more concerned to maintain a hypocritical hold over man than a true communication with God.

TWO CARICATURES OF THE UNIFICATION CHURCH

So much for some pictures of the world in which a young man or woman might perceive himself or herself to be. What about the social reality of the Unification Church? There is, of course, no one reality, there are many. But let me briefly sketch two further pictures in caricature.

The Brain-Washed World of the Moonie Robot

Opponents of the Unification Church are certain that its members are quite unable to realize their true potentials. The young people with all their lives before them have left a good job or university to spend long, exhausting hours toiling without reward, selling tracts or candles in the street, on doorsteps, or in pubs for an exploitative and heretical charismatic who gathers up all the surplus value of their labor for himself. They have become brainwashed zombies with no minds of their own. They have abrogated to an authoritarian organization all responsibility for personal decisions at all levels of importance. They have pledged themselves to degrading bondage. Their future has no security. They can have no hope of self fulfillment. They lead a life of blind, sub-human slavery. Spiritual well-being cannot possibly enter into such a picture. A "Moonie" has no selfhood to realize, let alone to transcend.

The Family World of Spiritual Well-Being

But life in "the Family" (as members call their Church) can be seen in a very different light. The believing members feel that they are contributing to the creation of something far greater than themselves and that they are, moreover, highly privileged to be doing so. Outside they see the material world of capitalism or the atheistic world of communism as the external prisons of the soul. The Unification Church offers a way out of such cramping environments. They are the ones who are really

160

working to fulfill the purpose of God's creation of man. They can be real men in God's image -- the truly human members of the Heavenly Family on earth. Whether or not the world considers them to be suffering from false consciousness, the members themselves lead what they believe is a creative existence in which they relate to their fellow men on a deep and sacrificial level, growing through the experience of giving and taking as part of a community in which they each play an important and recognized role.

What are some of the ways in which this last picture can be effected? How is it possible that Unification members have come to feel that they have increased their control over their own lives and over what is to happen in society; that they are more happy and secure; that their life now has direction, purpose, meaning, and unprecedented value; that they have been offered an opportunity of fulfilling and transcending themselves? And how have they come to believe that they can now achieve a standard of spiritual well-being which is higher than ever before and far above that of the average man in the outside society?

FIVE FUNCTIONAL ASPECTS OF THE UNIFICATION CHURCH

This final section outlines five general aspects of life in the Unification Church and tries to indicate how these could to-gether function to militate against the blockages to spiritual well-being as experienced in the five pictures of the outside world which have been sketched above. None of these functions is in itself peculiar to the Unification Church, but taken in conjunction with one another as institutionalized practices and beliefs, they contribute toward the particular recipe for spiritual well-being that the Unification Church offers.

The sharing religious community

Members of the Unification Church live together in a community of like-minded believers. The Church as a whole is known as the Family; members refer to each other as brothers and sisters; the Rev. and Mrs. Moon are known as Father and Mother or True Parents. Members take their meals together. They usually sleep together in single sex dormitories, and many, though not all, of their personal possessions are regarded as communal property. Former friends and relatives will be invited to visit the centers and perhaps to attend courses or a parents' week-end. Occasionally visits are made to non-members' homes, but on the whole contact with outsiders is confined to specific economic or proselytizing activities.

One's identity is primarily defined by whether or not one is a member of the Church. It is a situation which Mary Douglas (1970) would describe as one with high group and low grid control. In such an organization the achievement-oriented, individualistic

161

rat-race becomes irrelevant. One can of course fail by spiritual or Family standards, but if one does fail, it is not because of someone else's success. In the Kingdom of Heaven all can be saved. Some, of course, will be more saved than others, but there is no zero-sum status hierarchy operating in the spiritual community. Achievement is oriented toward God and one's personal relationship with Him as an individual, but at the same time it is as a member of the community rather than as an individual that one is the vessel for the salvation of the world. So long as each individual plays the role allocated to him, however humble that role may be, he is an integral part of the group's success (or failure).

Despite various suggestions that have been made to the contrary, there can be no doubt that for the vast majority of its members the Unification Church is, by any definition, a religious community. For none but a few of the leaders can there be any material gain; a few, a very few, of the members are in the Church for political reasons; the community spirit and the Happy Family atmosphere admittedly provide a strong drawing point for many initiates, but to be committed to life in the Unification Church, certainly as it is lived in the United Kingdom, without accepting most, if not all, of the religious motivation and raison d'etre behind the movement would be well nigh impossible for all but a tiny minority of people.

Membership of a believing community has frequently been recognized, most notably of course by Durkheim (1915), to have positive cohesive functions for the individual as well as for the group. The believer is anchored; he has direction given to him by an authority which transcends his own and yet of which he is an integral, essential part. This can be seen quite clearly in the case of the Unification Church. There are, of course, attendant difficulties, but the Family member can share, explore, and witness to the spiritual in communal affirmations of the transcendent. From a Durkheimian perspective he is surrendering himself to that whole of which he himself is a living part; from the member's perspective he is supported and guided by the community in a relationship with God that had often seemed impossible in the outside world.

The Charismatic Messiah

Members in England rarely become converted to the Unification Church under the spell of any personal charisma on the part of Sun Myung Moon. There is, however, what might be termed a "growth charisma of office," and this develops over time into gratitude, respect, and filial love for the man. This happens to fit quite well with the members' own view of the Messiahship, which is seen as an office to be held by a man who comes to perform certain deeds and to offer a revelation that will lay the foundation for the restoration of the Kingdom of Heaven on earth.

162

That Reverend Moon is the occupier of this office is the
strongly held belief of most members. For them the presence of
the Lord of the Second Advent on earth has re-enchanted the disenchanted world. The expectation of the millenium offers not only
promise for the future but a direction and an urgency which dispels
hopeless drift and loss of purpose for the present. Reverend
Moon has already laid an important foundation for the restoration
of the world through his marriage in 1960, and it was through
him that the Church's theology, the Divine Principle, was revealed.

The Articulated Theology

The Divine Principle is arguably the most coherent and all-
embracing theology to have emerged in the twentieth century
(Bryant and Richardson, 1978). Unlike most of the other "New
Religions," Unification theology provides a clearly worked-out
literature which answers an enormously wide range of theological,
spiritual, and personal questions and also paints an extraordinarily
detailed picture of the properties and meanings of this world and
the next.

I have described elsewhere some of the ways in which acceptance
of the particular beliefs of Unification Theology to be found in
the Divine Principle can contribute toward a situation in which
the life style of the members makes understandable sense (Barker,
1978). Here all that need concern us is that through the Divine
Principle the Unification Church offers its followers a language,
a myth, and a world view. The theodicy explains and offers a way
of overcoming the existence of evil and suffering; the eschatology
offers the hope and expectation of the restoration of the world and
the bringing about of the New Age within the foreseeable future;
the cosmology offers a reconciliation between scientific materialism
and the values of the spirit and offers a divinely inspired framework for relationships at all levels -- relationships of exploratory reciprocity, or sublimation, and of transcendence. Believers
are offered purpose, direction, and meaning in sacrificial dedication and devotion.

The sacred language of the Divine Principle is reflected in
the shared day-to-day language of its followers. The member's
spiritual brothers and sisters allow, indeed expect, him to have
personal experience of a transcendental relationship. The interpretation of such experiences, whether they be dreams, visions,
or just "feelings," is certainly monitored and controlled by those
with spiritual expertise, but the experiences themselves are direct
and unmediated by church or priest. The member no longer has to
suppress but can acknowledge publicly,articulate, and develop,
with specialist help, a personal relationship with Someone beyond
himself, Someone who both nurtures and refreshes his spiritual
being. He belongs to a spiritual community.

The Structured Nomos

The Unification Church is organized on strongly hierarchical
lines; relationships at all levels tend to be defined as those
between leader and follower (though it is perfectly possible that
the leader in one situation will be the follower in another, and
it is stressed that those in leadership roles are in the position
which must contribute the most love). To unite behind the leader
is a necessary prerequisite for the bringing about of the Kingdom
of Heaven on Earth. While discussion is allowed and even, in
theory, encouraged, one must still, in the end, follow one's
leader, even if he is wrong on certain occasions -- and it is
freely admitted that this can happen. The reason for this is that
if all were to decide individually on the correct course of action,
then God would have no opportunity of showing the leader where he
had been mistaken and letting him correct his error before proceeding to utilize fully the strength of the group as a united
body. The individual must be prepared to accept decisions on where
he is to live, what work he is to do and what his future role is
is to be. It is Rev. Moon, acting as the agent of God, who will
suggest who his marriage partner is to be.

But what the outside world sees as exploitative manipulation
can in fact be experienced as liberating opportunity. The Church
member will certainly face the hardships of authority, but he will
also enjoy tests and challenges to be overcome within the security
of a clearly defined context. The minutely hierarchical structure
of relationships results in practically every member finding
himself at some time or other in a position of leadership or
accepting special responsibility for a particular undertaking.
Normlessness is replaced by carefully delineated boundaries of
prescribed and proscribed behavior. Standards and rules based on
the Divine Principle are regulated and affirmed by the sharing
community and dispel the angst of existential choice demanded by
the permissive, antinomian counterculture.

The Mundane Challenge

If the Kingdom of Heaven is to be realized on Earth, then not
only spiritual but also earthly means must be employed to ensure
its immanent and imminent arrival. To fight materialism with
weapons which it can understand, one needs to organize, to publicize,
to involve oneself in the worlds of business, communication,
entertainment, politics, science, and academia. And, of course,
one needs money.

The Catch 22 of alternatives that the outside world posed was
the choice between a world with a vaguely specified goal of self-
realization but unspecified or immeasurable means of achieving it
on the one hand, and a world of specified and measurable means to
either the empty achievements of materialism or the despair of

failure on the other hand. One could opt out of conventional society into the self-indulgence of undirectional hippiedom with its opiates of the chemical trip and indiscriminate sex, or one could become a cog mechanically performing in the rationalized and disenchanted iron cage of economic bureaucracy with its opiates of alcohol, television, a new car, or spectatorship either at the local football club or at the alienating and impersonal ritual of institutionalized religion. How, in such situations, can one aspire to spiritual well-being?

But what if one's life is focused around achievements which are monitored at a simple mundane level and yet are part and parcel of creating the Kingdom of Heaven on Earth? The goal is to start up a new centre, to organize a workshop, to collect five hundred or even a thousand pounds in a week. These are not easy goals. They present a challenge, but it is a challenge that demonstrably can be met. One stretches oneself. Trust in God is vindicated by achievement. Occasional -- and it is remarkably occasional -- failure, can be accounted for by Satanic intervention. Each individual knows what he has to do, and usually he can do it. Members of the Unification Church may have broken away from a world dominated by Zweckrational action, but their behavior cannot then be characterized as haphazard, traditional, or affectual. Rather, it can be typified as Wertrational action, action which applies a rational orientation to an absolute value (Weber, 1947).

The mundane challenge offers measurable and achievable means to a sacred goal. It offers the opportunity for growth, initiative, and development of self within carefully circumscribed boundaries. And it offers Church members a chance to give, to see themselves as being of use, to contribute to not only the sharing community, but to society as a whole and, most importantly, to God.

While the materialistic world might grudgingly or patronizingly allow its youth to receive from the community, it rarely allows the satisfaction of reciprocal donation. Today no one is interested in those who wish to sacrifice themselves for the greater glory of God or country; those who wish to help the poor, the weak, and the oppressed are constantly thwarted by the institutional barriers which society has seemingly erected for the greater rebuttal of the young and eager idealist.

In the Unification Church the burning desire of a frustrated youth to contribute is allowed creative and measurable expression. In place of the powerlessness experienced in a crazy world run by a "them" of faceless bureaucrats, Godless politicians, grasping businessmen, self-centered "Christians," and an apathetic mass of gutless voters, the Unification Church member now finds he can play his part in controlling the future of the world. Despair gives way to hope. By uniting together behind their leader, the

165

members can overcome where, as individuals, they were helpless. United they have the strength and power to transcend all obstacles and to lead the world back to sanity and to God's original purpose.

CONCLUSION

This essay has contained only caricature sketches of life inside and outside the Unification Church. It does not pretend to have included the many qualifications that a complete or detailed picture would demand. It has sought merely to try to indicate some clues as to why members of the Church could claim to experience a state of enhanced spiritual well-being. While remaining methodologically agnostic as to the truth or falsity of any particular belief, it has defined spiritual well-being in terms of a transcendent relationship and then reduced this to an exploration of the transcendent as it might be experienced firstly through relationships of reciprocity with others, including the abstraction called "society," and secondly through belief held by church members in a transcendent reality of a sacred kind. The pictures of modern society were drawn from the experiences of the members, but they were also couched in terms reminiscent of some of the classical critiques of sociological theory with their underlying assumptions about the way in which certain social situations can prevent the individual from realizing his "true potential."

In conclusion, the essay has tried to indicate ways in which certain aspects of the Unification Church function to deal with some of the classically recognized problems of modern industrial society so that its members, by living a God-centered life, are taken out of themselves in their relationships with others at both primary and secondary levels. They can hope to become themselves through giving of themselves as part of a united team which is working to realize the spiritual renaissance of mankind for the first time since the original sin was committed in the Garden of Eden. The resolution of an existential angst of choice is achieved by submitting to a greater authority which has the moral legitimation of a religious revelation and the Second Coming. Creative exploration of reciprocal relationships in a community of like-minded believers allows for the transcendence of alienation; clearly defined rules and achievable goals overcome anomie; the messianic leader and millennial hope offer an opportunity to escape from the disenchantment of rationalization; the security of the community and the concepts and myths of the theology provide a context and language for the expression, recognition, and exploration of transcendence.

The individual member of the Unification Church can identify himself as part of a greater whole; a whole in which he experiences himself as an organic, contributing cell, not a mechanical clockwork cog, nor yet a cut-off directionless unit; a whole in which

166

he can experience both the loss and discovery of himself; a whole in whose service he seeks to find perfect freedom.

APPENDIX

All 450 English-speaking members of the Unification Church in the United Kingdom and about a hundred members in the USA (most of whom are seminarians) have been asked to fill in a 41-page questionnaire. At the time of writing this paper, the collection and coding of these was not complete, but the following data were obtained from a random sample of fifty questionnaires completed by British members.

Respondents were asked to assess their spiritual well-being during five stages in their lives: (a) up to the age of 10; (b) from the ages of 11-16; (c) from the age of 17 up to 6 months before meeting the Unification Church; (d) during the 6 months before meeting the Unification Church; (e) now. They could classify their spiritual well-being as: (1) much better than average, (2) better than average, (3) about average, (4) below average, (5) much worse than average.

The answers hence reflect the respondent's subjective experience of his own spiritual well-being as he perceives it now compared to (a) how he now sees his own spiritual well-being at different periods in his personal history and (b) how he perceives the spiritual well-being of other people in general. Any validity that the answers have is thus not of an absolute objective or even an absolute subjective status but of a relative one stemming from the respondent's subjective feelings at the time of filling in the questionnaire. There is, of course, also the ever present problem that respondents may wish to make a particular impression on the researcher. I fully acknowledge this as a difficulty. However, from my experience of Church members through interviews and participant observation I am prepared to believe that the majority of respondents filling in the questionnaire are trying to tell the truth, as they (at the time) see it, as honestly as possible. While the data should be seen in the light of these possible restrictions, I believe they still provide interesting and illuminating information.

I. Spiritual Well-Being

Three-quarters (78%) of the members reported that they were now enjoying "much better than average" spiritual well-being, two-thirds of these not having assessed their spiritual well-being that highly for previous periods; 14% said their spiritual well-being was now "better than average," and 8% said "average." If one compares the difference between the present standard of spiritual well-being and that reported during the six months before joining the Church, none said their spiritual well-being was worse than then; for 14% it stayed the same; for 36% it rose one class (e.g., from "better than average" to "much better than average"), 22% went up two classes, 16% up 3, and 12% up 4 classes.

Of the 78% who now reported being in the "much better than average" class, 15% had never dropped below "above average," and 26% not below "average," 33% had at some time dropped to "below average," and 26% to "much worse than average." Those now in the "average" and "above average" classes had a roughly similar distribution in ranges of spiritual well-being.

Only 4% said their spiritual well-being had ever been higher than it was now; 60% were now higher than they had ever been, and the remaining 36% were at a level they had reached but not surpassed during some previous period.

If one were to draw a graph with spiritual well-being on the Y axis and time on the X axis, most of the members (70%) would produce some sort of U-curve or, more commonly, a J-curve; only one respondent would show a straight line (at "average"), and all the remaining 28% a curve that slopes more or less sharply and more or less steadily upwards (i.e., the variation shows both sharpness and steadiness).

II. Material Well-Being

The patterns described above contrasted quite markedly with the replies given to a similar set of questions on material well-being. Twenty percent of these answers gave straight lines at "much better than," "better than," and (mostly) "average." Fourteen percent sloped upwards, another 14% downwards; 12% had a U-curve and 36% an inverted U (the remaining 4% produced more complicated patterns).

Although most of the respondents in the sample live under roughly similar material circumstances, their subjective descriptions varied considerably. Twelve percent considered their material well-being now to be "well above average," for 16% it was "just above average;" 44% said "average," 12% "just below average," and 10% "well below average" (6% did not reply).

III. Happiness

In assessing their happiness, half the respondents said they were now "very happy;" just over a third were "happy," and the rest (10%) said they were "alright." Most of them were evenly divided between either being happier than ever before or else saying they were at least as happy as they had ever been before. Ten percent, however, did say that they had been happier during previous periods of their lives.

Almost half would give a U-curve on a happiness graph, and nearly a third an upward slope; the rest would either show a downward curve (10%), no change (2%), or a zig-zag ending with an upward sweep (10%).

If one looks at their assessment of their early childhood up to the age of 10, one sees that 31% remember being "very happy," then 33% "happy," 20% "alright," 10% "just bearable," and 6% "miserable." It is interesting to note that all of those who said that their spiritual well-being now was only "average" said they were either "happy" or "very happy" during this early childhood period.

IV. Health

As spiritual well-being is sometimes thought to be related to physical well-being, it is of interest to note that over three-quarters of the sample reported that they now enjoy either "excellent" (30%) or "good" (46%) physical health. Eight percent said their health was now good except for a particular acute illness, and 12% reported their health as "fair." None reported having "poor" health now, although several said that they had had poor health in the past. It is not infrequently claimed that illnesses from which members had been suffering for several years disappeared when they joined the Unification Church. Eighteen percent said they now had better health than they had during the six months before they joined the Church; 10% said their health was worse, and the rest did not show any change.

Sixteen percent mentioned histories of bronchitis, asthma, or related afflictions; explanations for these varied between contracting tuberculosis, having allergies, and having nervous dispositions. Eighteen percent admitted to having had fairly serious nervous disorders (including attempted suicide); here the explanations ranged from social (e.g., being subjected to sexual assaults by a stepfather), to physical (e.g., brain injury), to general psycho-somatic complaints.

V. Power to Control

Another relevant dimension concerns the degree to which members have felt, now and during the six months before they met the Church, that they had power (a) over their own lives, (b) over other people they knew, and (c) to alter the state of the world.

(a)   Forty percent stated that they felt that they had more control over their lives since joining the Church, and 42% thought they had as much as before. Of the 18% who said they had less control over their own lives than before joining, nearly half were from the small group who scored lowest on the spiritual well-being scale. Two-fifths (38%) of the sample said they felt they now had complete control over their lives, 55% "quite a lot," 8% "some but not much," and one person replied "very little." No one reported feeling that they had "no power to control their own life to do what they want now."

(b)   A roughly similar pattern emerged on the question about the amount of power the member felt he or she had over others, except that only 4% said they felt they had "complete control" and they added the rider that this was only in their role as God's instrument. Over half said they felt they now had "quite a lot" of control. About half felt they had increased their powers to control others, and just under half reported that they did not experience any change.

(c)   The most spectacular reports of changes in feelings of power were recorded in response to the question as to how much power members felt they had to alter the state of the world. Eighty percent said they felt they now had "quite a lot" of control, the rest (apart from one member who said he never had had and still had none) having either "complete control" (11%) or "some but not much" (7%). Only a few (12%) thought their power in this area had not changed, and nearly half of these came from that small proportion of the sample not reporting "well above average" spiritual well-being. All the rest believed their power to alter the world had increased -- and increased to a very considerable extent, most of them having believed they had either "very little" or "no control" over the state of the world until they joined the Unification Church.

VI. Self Assessments

    Members were asked to describe themselves by giving six key words or phrases for each of the five periods. Obviously the range of answers that such a question elicited prohibits much in the way of quantitative analysis, but the following patterns can be seen.

(a)   About half the members described themselves at some point up to the age of 16 as having been: intellectual, clever, brainy, scholarly, bright, academic, or ambitious; roughly half of these indicated withdrawal from the academic scene over the age of 17 with entries like these: lazy, disillusioned with school, or looking for something deeper in life. Some blamed society for the educational system; some blamed themselves, and with others it was not clear where the fault lay, but there was a clear recognition that an early orientation and potential to achieve academically had in some way become thwarted.

(b)   For the six months before meeting the Unification Church common entries were these: purposeless, searching for a goal in life, looking for meaning, did not know what to do, frustrated, insecure, uncertain, lost.

170

(c) This was in marked contrast to entries for "now," which repeatedly stated that the member is happy, hopeful, goal oriented, secure, optimistic, purposeful, strong, clear, intelligent, and creative.

(d) One factor which may surprise sociologists is that very few roles were offered in the self-descriptions. Nearly all the entries were about personal characteristics.

(e) Absence of data on control groups at this point means that there is no way of assessing just how representative the entries are. For purposes of this essay, what is of moment is that the members certainly state that they have endured frustrations in the past and that these are now alleviated.

VII. Educational Achievement

As a possibly more objective underpinning to the subjective experiences of the members, it could be seen from questions about educational achievement that a considerable number of the members did quite well in their examinations and then achieved slightly disappointing results at a later stage. However, there were also those who had never had a very good performance and yet others who continued to do well throughout their educational career, achieving good second class honours degrees.

DECISIONS AS SPIRITUAL ACTS

...the direction taken by an instinct is determined ... by the mental and spiritual directives of the person in question. It is hardly more than an excuse when someone says that they have been led astray by this or that autonomous impulse, in place of assuming personal responsibility. The choice of direction is a mental and spiritual act, even if this act takes place in the subconscious (von Gagern, 1954: 38).

Chapter 13

THREE PATHS TO SPIRITUAL WELL-BEING AMONG THE MORMONS:

CONVERSION, OBEDIENCE, AND REPENTANCE

James T. Duke and D. Wayne Brown, Jr.

Spiritual well-being is a topic which has occupied the minds of people in many nations since the beginning of recorded history. Nevertheless, sociologists continue to find the topic difficult both to conceptualize and to measure.

The attempt to develop one or more over-all social indicators of the well-being of a given society (Bradburn, 1969; Campbell et al., 1976; Andrews and Withey, 1976), associated with the quality of life movement, has likewise found the concept of spiritual well-being an elusive one. Research in the United States generally has found that a relatively small percentage of people consider religion as an essential aspect of their feeling of well-being (Campbell et al., 1976: 349-374. But see the chapter by McNamara and St. George in this book -- Editor). However, there are both theoretical and practical reasons for supposing that spiritual well-being should be a significant component of any indicator of social well-being in most populations (Moberg and Brusek, 1978).

One of the most difficult challenges in the development of an indicator of spiritual well-being is that there are numerous religious bodies with a great diversity of religious beliefs and practices. What may serve as a social indicator of spiritual well-being for one religious group may be inappropriate for another. Case studies of specific religious bodies may help us to identify essential elements which ought to be included in measures of spiritual well-being. It is with this intent that we turn our attention to spiritual well-being as it is conceptualized and practiced in one religious organization, The Church of Jesus Christ of Latter-day Saints, commonly called "The Mormons" (Green, 1970).

173

STATEMENT OF PURPOSE AND METHOD

In this paper we shall first examine some of the fundamental principles of Mormon theological teachings as they relate to the beliefs and practices concerning spiritual well-being of members of the Mormon church. We shall direct our attention specifically to three "paths" by which Mormon people seek spiritual well-being: (1) conversion to or memberships in the Church, (2) obedience to the commandments of God, and (3) repentance.

We shall draw upon a diverse set of sociological data, gathered by application of several different sociological methods. The primary method has been participant observation by the senior author both as a lay member of a number of Mormon congregations and as a Priesthood leader of one congregation for five years. This report also uses several unpublished surveys, one undertaken by the Mormon Church's Missionary Department and the other by one of the Church's missions. A number of case studies and depth interviews have also been conducted, which help to flesh out and give substance to the authors' conclusions. This work, however, is tentative in many respects; it needs to be followed by more extensive research studies.

THE MORMON PERSPECTIVE ON SPIRITUAL WELL-BEING

Mormon theological teachings[1] begin with the belief in the Godhead, composed of three personages: God the Father, his son Jesus Christ, and the Holy Ghost. Mormons believe God the Father is a glorious, resurrected person who has previously lived a mortal life and who now reigns over this world and many others as an omnipotent, omniscient, perfectly loving, and perfectly righteous person. His work and his glory is to bring to pass the immortality, perfection, and happiness of mortal men and women who are his children (Talmage, 1913: Chapter 2). The second member of the Godhead, Jesus Christ, is the son of God the Father. He is the Firstborn of the Father as a spiritual offspring. He served as the Jehovah of the Old Testament, was made flesh and lived a mortal existence on this earth, and then served as the saviour of the world by overcoming death (through the resurrection) and hell or sin (by taking upon himself the sins of all persons,

---

1. In addition to the Bible, Mormons also accept three other works as scripture, or as the word of God (Church of Jesus Christ of LDS, 1830, 1833, 1858). These three are The Book of Mormon, The Doctrine and Covenants, and The Pearl of Great Price, hereafter listed only by their titles and the conventional references to specific parts. Readers who would like an introduction to Mormon theological teachings are encouraged to read these scriptures, or any one of the following works: Talmage, 1913, 1915; Richards, 1950.

thereby enabling each person to become clean again through repentance and to return to live with God eternally after death) (Talmage, 1915). The third member of the Godhead, the Holy Ghost, is a personage of spirit who serves as a messenger from the Father to mankind, inspiring them to righteous living (Doctrine and Covenants 130: 22-23).

According to Mormon teachings, all persons were created spiritually by God and lived with him in a pre-mortal spiritual existence. God then created this world. Humans come to this world to experience mortality, to gain physical bodies, to prove themselves, and to learn to utilize their free agency by making choices between good and evil. God has created a mortal environment in which each person may choose between the enticings of God or of the Devil, but each individual must ultimately be responsible for these choices and experience the consequences of them.

God gives commandments to his mortal children through living prophets and through continuing inspiration and revelation by the Holy Ghost. Persons who have received these laws are then accountable for their obedience to them. Persons who have not been taught the laws of God or who are not accountable by reason of age, physical or mental handicap, or other reasons, are judged according to the light which they have received (Book of Mormon, Alma 12: 31-32).

After each person's mortal life is ended, he goes to the spirit world again; there his progress and learning continue. Eventually, each person must stand before God and give an account of his mortal actions. Those who have lived righteously will be resurrected into the highest of three degrees of glory, called the Celestial Kingdom. Those who have been partially righteous but not valiant will live in the Terrestrial Kingdom, and those who are unrighteous will live eternally in the Telestial Kingdom. Each is a kingdom of glory, but they differ as the sun differs from the moon, and as the moon differs from the stars in glory (Doctrine and Covenants, 76: 50-109).

We come now to the essence of the question of spiritual well-being according to Mormon theology. A person is in a state of spiritual well-being if he is currently living as righteously as he is capable of living, if he is choosing to obey the commandments of God as fully as he can, given whatever limitations of knowledge and ability are present. Spiritual well-being is ultimately determined after one's mortal death. Each person will be judged by God and rewarded with that degree of glory which he has earned during his mortal probation. A person is spiritually healthy to the extent to which he is obedient to the commandments and inspiration of God.

Mormons believe that the individual himself is responsible to evaluate his own righteousness and worthiness, although ultimately God will be the final judge. The individual may deceive himself about his own worthiness, but the promptings of the Spirit and the individual's own conscience help him to avoid rationalization and come to an accurate assessment of his spiritual well-being if he sincerely desires to know his standing with God. Fasting, prayer, scripture reading, meditation, and service to others are aids to put the individual into communication with God so that he may understand God's commandments and how they should be applied in the individual's life. Mormon Bishops who hold a priesthood calling as "judges in Israel" are also able to discern an individual's spiritual well-being and to counsel the individual as to the manner in which he may improve his life.

The good life, Mormons believe, is found by trying to live in accordance with the "mind and will of God." This brings ultimate happiness in the Celestial Kingdom, but it is not coextensive with what is normally called happiness or pleasure in this life. Righteousness is achieved by constant effort, by diligent striving to find the will of God and do it, by patience, longsuffering, gentleness, and meekness (Doctrine and Covenants, 121: 41-46).

Mormons are known as a happy people, but they are also reputed for their hard work, their commitment to the Protestant Ethic, their leadership skills, and their adaptability to group and institutional settings (O'Dea, 1957: 150-151). Mormons are also generally characterized by their high needs for achievement, their strong emphasis on family and education, their health code, their advocacy of chastity and marital fidelity, and their missionary zeal (O'Dea, 1957: 141-154).

Having high standards of morality and achievement, Mormons tend to experience some guilt and frustration when their efforts do not enable them to reach their goals (Bahr, 1978). Some people, both converts and those born into the Church, find the standards too high, the expectations too rigorous. But an increasingly high number of Mormons find that they are able to live such standards and find happiness therein.

THE ROLE OF TRIALS AND TRIBULATIONS

Mormons believe that this mortal world is a place to experience both tribulations and happiness. God presents problems and difficulties to people to strengthen them and help them to learn to overcome their weaknesses (Doctrine and Covenants 121: 7; 122: 7). God allows Satan to introduce sin in order that people may have the experience of learning to choose good from evil, thereby learning how to use their God-given "free agency." Mormons believe that "opposition in all things" is a precondition to learning to make choices and to the development of free agency (Duke, 1976). The ultimate tribulation is sin, but individuals can overcome the

176

effects of sin by (1) not sinning themselves and (2) accepting
and loving others who commit sins even if these sins are hurtful
to oneself or one's loved ones. Many persons in religious history
are noted for overcoming great difficulties, including Moses and
Paul the Apostle. In Mormon history, Joseph Smith, Brigham Young,
and the present Mormon prophet, Spencer W. Kimball, are notable
for having faced impressive tribulations and having overcome them
(Kimball and Kimball, 1977).

ARE MORMONS HAPPY?

We have as yet no definitive answer to the question, "Are
Mormons happy?" But we interviewed a random sample of 92 Mormons
in Provo, Utah, to inquire as to their happiness. In this preliminary study we asked respondents to place themselves in one of
three categories of happiness and in one of three categories of
religious activity.

Table 1. The Relationship of Religious Activity to
Happiness Among Mormons in Provo, Utah (in percentages)

	Very Active	Moderately Active	Seldom/Never Active
Very Happy	43	11	33
Moderately Happy	50	89	59
Unhappy	7	0	7
Total	100	100	99
(N)	(56)	(9)	(27)

As Table 1 shows, the majority (61%) of the Mormons interviewed
said that they were very active in their church. Of these persons,
43% were very happy, and 50% were moderately happy. But the majority of persons who are seldom or never active were also either
very happy or moderately happy, so   the correlation between
religious activity and happiness is low (Gamma = .184). This
compares with a comparable survey conducted by the Gallup Poll in
the United States in 1975 which also used three categories each
for happiness and religiosity (Gallup, 1975: 30). In this study,
very few persons reported themselves to be unhappy, and a very
modest correlation was found between religiosity and happiness.
In the Gallup data, however, a much lower percentage (26%) reported themselves to be "very religious," but among these fully 76%

177

said they were very happy.

In our data, females were both more likely to report themselves as active in the church and to say that they were happy. The correlation between activity and happiness was stronger for females (Gamma = .32) than for males (Gamma = .00). About equal numbers of old and young persons reported themselves as inactive (36%), but old persons were more likely to be moderately active (19%). Young people tended to be more polarized (either very happy or unhappy, either very active or inactive) in their behavior, whereas older people tended to be more moderate in their responses.

Our tentative conclusion, therefore, is that spiritual well-being and self reports of happiness are very different phenomena, so reports of happiness cannot be used validly as indicators of spiritual well-being among Mormons. Many Mormons feel a sense of spiritual well-being while being modest in their reports concerning their personal happiness. Happiness is a reflection of many other life situations besides religious behavior.

For Mormons, an adequate measurement of spiritual well-being would begin with questions about obedience to various specific commandments of God, as taught by the Mormon Church, concluding with questions concerning whether the individual felt that he was living in accordance with the will of God. We hypothesize that Mormons can make fairly accurate self-judgments concerning the heavenly kingdom they are presently worthy to enter and that they can place themselves into one of these three kingdoms without undue difficulty. At least our preliminary interviews show this to be true.

We may take as typical an interview with a 30 year old married woman living in fairly prosperous circumstances in a small Utah community. When asked what things gave her the greatest sense of well-being, she answered: her church and her family. She mentioned that her church taught that she and her family could attain eternal life and be a family together through eternity. Her husband was a companion and friend, and her children were well and healthy. Her greatest worries were the community environment, including drug problems among the youth, and the school environment. She characterized herself as both very active in her church and very happy, but probing revealed that she felt that there were many areas of her life that needed improving, such as greater service in the Mormon temple and more time spent with her children. She felt that she needed to improve herself intellectually and to be more sociable and outgoing in her social relationships. When asked specifically about her standing with God, she responded that "most of the time" she felt accepted by God and worthy to live with him again in the Celestial Kingdom.

SOCIOLOGICAL THEORY AND RIGHTEOUS LIVING

From both an interactionist and a functionalist point of view, it can be expected that those persons who give meaning to religion, who say that it occupies an important place in their lives, and who believe that they are following the teachings of their moral order will be well integrated into their social group, will feel accepted by others, and will feel a sense of spiritual well-being. A Durkheimian perspective leads us to suppose that those persons who conform to the moral order of their social group will feel a sense of social and of spiritual well-being.

Theoretically, this would be true no matter what the content of the moral system of the group may be, as long as the individual feels that he or she is conforming to group standards of morality. However, Mormons believe that the promptings of the Spirit will help the individual to follow God's moral principles and, conversely, make it difficult for an individual who was following a moral code contrary to the laws of God to find happiness or a sense of well-being in such behavior. Mormons recognize that self-deception is prevalent in this area of social behavior, that many people who are not living righteous lives may be lulled into feeling a sense of well-being in the short run. Ultimately, however, these people experience the natural consequences of their behavior. For Mormons, the principle is summarized in an epigram from the Book of Mormon: "Wickedness never was happiness" (Alma 41: 10).

In summary, Mormons believe that "righteous living" and obedience to God's commandments is the major path to spiritual well-being, and that only those who live in accordance with the moral principles given by God will experience eternal spiritual well-being in the presence of God in the Celestial Kingdom.

CONVERSION AS A PATH TO SPIRITUAL WELL-BEING

The Mormon Church is a proselyting church which sends missionaries to many parts of the world. It believes that it is the only true church in the world today, although Mormon theology teaches that there are many righteous people who are not Mormons and that most churches possess extensive if incomplete truths. The marks of the one true Church of Jesus Christ, according to Mormons, include a living prophet, continuous revelation, the Priesthood of God (authority given by God to act in His name to perform ordinances and blessings), and a correct knowledge of the Godhead and of the Atonement. Ultimate happiness comes to individuals only through the true Church of Christ, and everyone will eventually have the opportunity, either in the mortal life or in the spirit world which follows mortality, to choose whether or not to accept membership in the church.

179

CONVERSION AS A SOCIAL AND PERSONAL CHANGE

Individuals who are unhappy with their present lives might be expected to be more likely to seek a change in their lives which will restore to them some sense of happiness. Studies of conversion to the Church of Jesus Christ of Latter-day Saints show that this is generally true, although it is difficult to aggregate all converts into one type and to generalize about all of them. For the most part, however, converts who leave another church to join the Mormon Church are persons who have experienced a sense of religious or spiritual malaise and who are either actively or passively seeking some resolution to this sense of malaise. As one convert put it,

From the period of my first recollection I had an almost insatiable desire to know the "truth". . . . The desire to know the truth was intensified as I studied and prayed and as I attended first one church and then another, but there was something missing in all of them for me. I formulated my own hodge-podge of a philosophy about life and death as I read numerous books and articles and listened to assorted sermons. But as I pondered the New Testament I found much that I could not understand. I decided that all religions were "man-made" and that therefore mine could be as valid as any other (Rector and Rector, 1971: #1, 4).

This sense of something missing was put to rest with his conversion to the Mormon Church:
No sooner did I start to read the Book of Mormon than I knew that at last I had found that for which I had been searching (Rector and Rector, 1971: 7).

A study conducted by the Mormon Church's Missionary Department (Anderson, 1977), a mail questionnaire of 226 converts baptized in July 1975, concluded that before conversion the individual tended to be prepared for conversion by a host of experiences, "a myriad of small influences and personal moments of decision." Persons who later joined the Mormon Church were characterized before their conversion as discontented. Many had joined other churches seeking for spiritual fulfillment, although very few were "very active" in their previous church. Most said that they were dissatisfied, with fully 50% of them characterizing themselves as "very restless" before conversion. Only a few of them experienced a personal crisis before conversion, such as the death of a loved one, a divorce, or other personal tragedy.

Concerning their personal needs and feelings, the respondents in this survey tended to desire changes in their lives in four important areas, namely,
(1) a closer relationship with the Lord, (2) being a

180

happier person, (3) being a better person, and (4) being more at peace with themselves (Anderson, 1977: 74).

While these converts tended not to be active in their previous church, they tended to place special importance upon personal prayer. They tended to be religious people without a strong commitment to any particular religious body.

But most important of all, persons who joined the Mormon Church mentioned the influence of a member of the Church: "I knew a Mormon." Persons who had a close friendship with a person who belonged to the Church were much more likely to have a favorable impression of the Church and to investigate its teachings. "Fellowshipping" is regarded as an integral part of the process of conversion by Mormons. Converts who were introduced to the Church by a personal friend or family member were more likely to remain active after their baptism.

CHARACTERISTICS OF CONVERTS

The Mormon Church sends missionaries to virtually every nation in which its missionaries are welcome. In 1975 approximately 95,000 converts were made worldwide, with 42,000 in the U.S.A. and 53,000 in other nations. Over 19,000 converts were made in Mexico, where the Mormon Church is experiencing phenomenal growth. High rates of conversion were reported in Brazil, Chile, England, Japan, and the Philippines, and moderate rates in Canada, Argentina, Colombia, Ecuador, Korea, Australia, and West Germany.

Relatively low rates of conversion were found in Africa, the Middle East, and Central Asia, where the Church has few missionaries, and in the nations of Austria, Finland, Norway, Portugal, and Sweden (where there were 105 converts in 1975).

World-wide, about 54% of converts are females and 46% are males. An unpublished study of converts in a Canadian province showed that converts to the Mormon Church there tended to be young (average age 22.9 years), from the middle socio-economic strata, and of average education. Almost 50% were single.

The socio-economic status of converts seems to vary significantly from area to area. In Korea, where one of the first converts was a person of high position who did graduate work in the United States, many of the converts have been of above average status. In other places, such as some communities in Mexico, the majority of converts are very poor. It is not unusual to find only one or two persons in a local ward in Latin America who can read well, or who can play the piano to accompany the congregation in their singing.

THE PROCESS OF CONVERSION

Persons who are introduced to the Church by friends or family members are more likely to join the Church than those who are first contacted by missionaries, who often go door to door presenting their message to interested persons. One surprising finding of the Canadian study was that persons who were introduced to the Church by friends were more likely to remain active in the Church after baptism than those who were introduced to the Church by family members.

Almost all converts (91%) reported having had to make significant changes in their lives upon conversion, and, again surprisingly, those who made the most significant changes remained the most active converts. Persons who later fell into inactivity were more likely to report that they had to make few changes upon conversion to the Mormon Church.

After having the teachings of the Church presented to them, converts approach the crisis of decision. The three factors that seem to be most significant in leading these converts to make the decision to be baptized, according to the studies reported, are (1) personal prayer, (2) study of the Book of Mormon, and (3) actively trying to live the principles of the Gospel.

> The evidence is that the doing of the word becomes more important to a person's decision to be baptized than hearing a profusion of words at this point. The statistics indicate that very seldom does any one feature of our beliefs or a single doctrinal point do the job of conversion by itself (Anderson, 1977: 76).

SPIRITUAL EXPERIENCES AND CONVERSION

Frequently, but not universally, the decision to be baptized is made after a spiritual experience, almost always as a result of prayer. Three published conversion stories have been selected as illustrative.

A young, black, single male reported that his conversion was preceded by giving up marijuana, cigarettes, and drinking and by becoming chaste. Then,

> I tried studying the philosophers . . . . admittedly I didn't give them years, just minutes, but none could tell me by their works where truth was. . . . The only name that came to my thoughts at this time whom I hadn't tried was Jesus Christ. So I bought a Bible, realizing I hadn't given him a chance. I had judged the Bible by the people I knew to be Christians and rejected it because of their conduct

182

and their own confusion concerning Christian scripture. I read the New Testament first, wanting to see if I could pick up its spirit; and if I could, then I would be willing to follow Christ's teachings for the rest of my life.

After reading a portion of Matthew, I was convinced that it was true. Every time I would read a verse that was potent, it would just leap out at me, while the parables all seemed to vibrate within me with new meaning. I tried to absorb so much that I couldn't go beyond a few verses without stopping to marvel at its truth (Rector and Rector, 1971: 92-93).

A young, single, Christian minister in India reported that he had gone to the mountains to a tourist resort for a vacation. He borrowed a book from the local library which discussed Christian heresies. An article entitled "Is Mormonism Christianity?" was so unfavorable to the Church of Jesus Christ of Latter-day Saints, which he had never heard of before, that he wondered about it.

While he pondered and wondered, his mind was illuminated and he received certain knowledge that the Church he was reading about was the true Church and that it taught the true doctrine. Astounded at the experience, and not knowing what to do next, (he) prayed that he might know where to find this Church (Rector and Rector, 1971: 141).

Another young man, a married Orthodox Jew from New York City with a professional education, reported this experience:

As we arrived at about this point in the Old Testament, it seemed to me that a brilliant light started to come into the room where we were. I am not able to explain how it happened; all I know is that it did happen. And with this light came the Rauch Elohim, or the Spirit of God. Something leaped inside of me, causing me to jump up, and I shouted to my friend, Junius, "I've got it! I've got it!"

He asked, "What have you got?"

"I know now that Jesus is the Messiah."

I found myself sobbing with joy and relief, and for a few minutes we were silent (Rector and Rector, 1971: 62).

One who reads many of these conversion stories is struck with the diversity of experiences which accompany conversion. Often there are several experiences, usually different from each other.

183

What seems consistent is that the individual recognizes the experience as a spiritual one, as a communication to him from God.

The experience of the young man in India, quoted above, is rare in that the spiritual experience <u>preceded</u> his investigation of the Church and came without being sought. Usually such experiences come only after a degree of knowledge and information is acquired and while the individual is seeking to judge the significance and truth of that information. Again, prayer and prayerful attitudes are important ingredients of a spiritual manifestation.

Such spiritual manifestations do not cause conversion, however, since some converts report having received spiritual experiences which they did not act upon. Miraculous and mystical experiences lead to conversion only if such other factors as prayer, study, and trying to live the teachings accompany them. Fellowshipping is a social aid which gives support and encouragement in the process of making the decision and in the social adjustment which follows the decision to be baptized.

DOES CONVERSION MAKE THE CONVERT HAPPY?

The overwhelming conclusion derived from case studies of Mormon converts is that conversion results in a number of personal changes which give the individual a heightened sense of spiritual well-being and happiness. One must be careful with these data, however, since persons who report such changes are almost invariably those who have been integrated into the Church, who maintain a high level of activity, and who are verbal in their reports of the conversion process. It is more difficult to obtain case studies of persons who were converted and baptized and then "fell away" and became inactive.

Case studies of converts are full of expressions of happiness and personal growth. Several excerpts will illustrate this. A 60 year old single Welch woman, who formerly had been a Catholic nun, expressed herself this way:

> Oh, how happy I was that night of my baptism! I
> have never experienced such joy and peace I
> really felt Christ calling me to come to him . . ..
> I felt so clean, and I knew that the Holy Ghost really
> had taken up residence in my soul (Rector and Rector,
> 1971: 167).

A single female physician summarized her life changes thus:

> Now, eight years later, I look back on my experience with
> a continued sense of awe and wonderment. It is a source
> of strength to me that I, of all people, should be so
> fortunate as to find this gospel, this pearl beyond price....

My profession and all other concerns pale into insignificance beside the effect of the Church in my life. The gospel has been an enormous help to me not only in my personal life but in my profession. It gives me a feeling of confidence and peace and allows me to tolerate high stress levels emotionally and physically. ...the gospel puts life and death, pleasure and pain, in perspective (Rector and Rector, 1971: 39-40).

REPENTANCE AS A PATH TO SPIRITUAL WELL-BEING

Mormon theology, like that of most Christian denominations, teaches that all persons have sinned and that no individual by himself can return to the presence of God. Mormons have a different view of the Atonement of Christ, however, than most Christian denominations. They believe that Christ took upon himself the sins of every person, paying the penalty for each sin ever committed in the mortal world (Book of Mormon, 2 Nephi 9: 20). This enables Christ to extend mercy to sinners and forgive sins. But such mercy is extended only to those who repent of their sins and diligently seek forgiveness. Forgiveness wipes the record clean, so to speak, and enables the individual again to be free from sin and clean in the sight of God, thereby enabling him to return to the presence of God after his mortal death.

Mormons believe strongly in repentance and forgiveness; it is an essential step in the ultimate goal of returning to the presence of God in the Celestial Kingdom. Repentance is a continual process, since the typical person sins everyday in some way.

Many sins can be repented of by the efforts of the individual himself, in communion with his Father in Heaven. However, serious sins (e.g., murder, sexual sin, theft, etc.) need to be confessed to the Bishop, who presides over the local Mormon congregation called a Ward (with typically about 500 members), and who holds the Priesthood keys as a "judge in Israel."

The senior author served as Bishop for five years and had many opportunities during that time to participate intimately in the repentance process. The following discussion, therefore, is informed by participant observation as a Mormon Priesthood leader with a specific calling to counsel with persons during their repentance and help them to receive forgiveness of sins from God.

Individuals who have a strong social attachment to their social group, but who have broken one or more of the norms of the group, will feel some pressure to refrain from their non-conformist behavior and to return to conformity. If the group has a strong moral code, as does the Mormon Church, the self-image of members of the group becomes entwined in their conformity, and non-conformist behavior often injures one's self-respect and self-

185

image. A consciousness of sin thus leads to tension and guilt; it provides a social-psychological condition necessary for a change of behavior. If such change does not take place, or if the individual does not have a strong commitment to the group, then the probability is high that the individual will withdraw from the group and break his ties with it.

Mormons who are committed to the church and who desire to remain in good standing in the Church usually seek to be obedient to its teachings; when disobedient, they often seek through repentance to return to good standing.

STEPS TO REPENTANCE

Repentance in the Mormon Church normally consists of a number of steps, each of which is essential in the repentance process. These are: (1) remorse, (2) confession to God, and to the Bishop if the sin is a serious one, (3) a change of behavior and a forsaking of the sin, (4) forgiveness of others, (5) penalties or loss of privileges, (6) restitution to those who have been injured, where appropriate, (7) a sufficient period of time in which to demonstrate renewed conformity, (8) diligent service to others, and (9) the receipt of forgiveness from God. There is no implication here that steps must be taken in the order listed, but it has been observed that people who successfully accomplish repentance take some account of all nine steps. We shall discuss each of these steps briefly.

1. Remorse. Ironically, remorse and faith are closely related, for only if the person has faith in the moral code he has broken does he feel a heightened sense of remorse at having broken it. Remorse is the motivating power which leads the individual to attempt to rectify his mistake and to put his life in order again. For some people, the remorse is immediate, and they therefore begin the process of repentance immediately. For others, the sense of remorse grows slowly as the individual gradually builds up his commitment to the Church. Sometimes confession does not come until years after the commission of the sin, following a long period of remorse as well as of strengthening of faith.

2. Confession to the Bishop. This is often the most difficult step in the repentance process; it is required only if the sin is a major sin (although the definition of just what sins need be confessed to a bishop is not always clear). Bishops normally interview persons at certain times of their lives, such as the ordination of a young man in the Priesthood (which is normally bestowed upon all males at the age of twelve), marriage in the temple, and the annual renewal of a "temple recommend," which enables a worthy adult to attend special services in Mormon temples, which are regarded as extremely sacred places. Such interviews by the Bishop include questions as to worthiness and whether the

individual is free from serious sins. Confession may take place during such interviews, but it is more likely to be initiated by the individual who desires to talk to the Bishop for the purpose of confession. The Bishop listens to the person's confession, counsels with the individual about the steps necessary for repentance, gives encouragement, and otherwise offers help to the individual. Such confessions are treated as strictly confidential; the Bishop is under an obligation not to speak of them to anyone else.

The social psychological impact of confession is often remarkable. The individual frequently feels a great sense of release. While he knows the repentance process is not complete, he feels that he has taken the major step necessary for forgiveness, and he feels a renewed confidence that he can accomplish the process. Such a sense of release is followed by a more long-lasting sense of peace when the other steps are completed.

3. Forsaking the Sin. To Mormons, repentance means change. The most significant indicator that the person is truly sorry for his sin and desires to repent is that he refrains from the sin and changes his pattern of behavior. If the sin is one of adultery, for example, then the adultery must cease, and the individual must become chaste again. Continuing in sin is regarded as a sign of lack of repentance and leads to condemnation by God.

4. Forgiveness of others. Often another person is involved in the sin or has served in some way as an instigator or accomplice. Mormons believe that one must forgive others if one seeks to be forgiven himself. Such forgiveness of others may take the form of approaching the other person and discussing the sin with him, asking him for forgiveness, and expressing one's forgiveness of the other person. Or such forgiveness of others may be inward, a change of attitude toward the other, an attempt to refrain from condemnation of others by word or thought.

5. Penalties. If the sin is a serious one, the individual will normally suffer loss of certain church privileges for a period of time. For example, a person who has committed adultery may not be admitted to a Mormon temple for a period of at least a year following such a sin. Occasionally the individual may be excommunicated from the Church for his sin, but this usually comes only if the individual is unrepentant or if the sin has been repeated numerous times. Forgiveness is still possible, and the individual may be rebaptized after sufficient repentance. However, the penalty of the loss of privileges (release from a church position, denial of attendance at the temple, etc.) is much more common than excommunication.

6. Restitution. If the individual has injured another person, full repentance requires that he make restitution. If a person

has stolen money from another person, he must return the amount stolen. If he has injured another person's reputation through gossip, he must seek to remedy this through appropriate actions. The principle of restitution requires that conditions be restored, as nearly as possible, to those existing before the sin took place. Often this is difficult or impossible to accomplish, but the repentant person must seek to make restitution as far as possible.

7. Period of Time. Minor sins can be forsaken and forgiven almost immediately, but major sins require time, both for a change of attitude to take place and for a demonstration that the individual has truly forsaken the sin. The Bishop will normally counsel with the sinner concerning the period of probation during which privileges are lost. The period of time may run from only a few days to a year or even more. Such periods are normally flexible and depend upon the change which has taken place in the person repenting.

8. Service to Others. The individual demonstrates his repentance not only by refraining from the sin committed, but by attempting to obey every commandment of the Gospel. He seeks opportunities to demonstrate his love of God and his fellowmen through service to others.

9. Receipt of Forgiveness. Only God can forgive, according to Mormon teachings. Such forgiveness is communicated from God to man through the medium of the Holy Spirit. Individuals can know if they have been forgiven if they approach God through diligent prayer (Book of Mormon, Enos 4-5). The Bishop is called upon to make a judgement as to the receipt of such forgiveness, especially when the individual seeks ordination in the Priesthood, temple marriage, or renewal of a temple recommend. But the Bishop does not forgive. He does recognize and legitimize the repentance process through extending the blessings of the Church and through the removal of the loss of privileges.

THE RESULT OF REPENTANCE

The normal result of this repentance process is an often amazing sense of renewal within the individual. The individual experiences a cleansing. He feels pure again in the sight of God. His self-image is restored, and he feels that he is worthy again to live with God in the Celestial Kingdom. Inner changes are more remarkable than outward changes, but the external behavior of the individual often changes markedly too. While most repentance leads the individual to behave in a different way than he previously did, for some individuals repentance leads to a totally new direction, a totally new way of life.

THE CAUSES OF SIN: THE MORMON THEORY OF SPIRITUAL WELL-BEING

While external circumstances and environmental forces are recognized by Mormons as contributing to sin, Mormon theology teaches that individuals normally have freedom to choose between good and evil. Ill health, poverty, inadequacy in social relations, death of loved ones, or other crises are more likely to be followed by sin and a deterioration of a sense of spiritual well-being. However, Mormons believe that such problems and difficulties are obstacles to be overcome. Some persons with severe disabilities remain happy, righteous, and retaining a sense of spiritual well-being, while others become bitter and spiritually unhealthy. The difference lies not so much in the external circumstances as in the individual's response to these circumstances.

Conversely, success in one area of life can lead the individual to greater conformity and a greater sense of spiritual well-being. However, again, success and righteousness are not universally correlated, and many people who are successful are not committed to religion.

Mormons therefore believe that an individual's righteousness is normally separate from his environmental circumstances and that individuals have the freedom to make choices concerning their spiritual behavior and attitudes.

Spiritual well-being may have a multiplicity of components, such as those normally included in studies of religiosity, e.g., cognitive, experiential, belief, activity, etc. Mormon theology, however, would conclude that spiritual well-being comes to the individual as a result of (1) accepting Christ and his teachings and joining Christ's Church (which Mormons believe is the Church of Jesus Christ of Latter-day Saints), (2) obeying the commandments of God to the best of one's ability, and (3) repenting of one's sins in an attempt to remain clean in the sight of God. Persons who have done these   things, in the Mormon view, may be said to be in a state of spiritual well-being: that is, they are acceptable to God, who is the ultimate judge of all mankind.

SPIRITUAL INTUITION NEEDS RESEARCH

Experienced ministers oftentimes report a cultivated sense for identifying signs of spiritual health. In the presence of an individual or group, they have a "feeling" of the situation. ...There is every reason to believe that such practiced intuition and experienced judgment is genuine. ... The basic weakness of identification by intuition is that it relies on distortable inner processes which operate outside our conscious knowledge and control. ...Without the possibility of comparing cultivated intuition with reliable bench marks, there is little hope for arresting or detecting cumulative errors in judgment. ...

To establish a person's degree of Christian maturity ... may seem a bit risky. ...The "negative argument" ... implies the somewhat disconcerting conclusion that it is easier to tell who is not a mature Christian than who is a mature Christian. ...Protestant theology must be understood behaviorally before it is adequately understood theoretically (Duncombe, 1969: 18-19, 21, 178).

Chapter 14

THE DEVOTION TO ST. ANTHONY IN THE SANCTUARY OF PADUA

(PILOT RESEARCH)

Paolo Giuriati

The subject of this communication (popular devotion to St.
Anthony of Padua) belongs to the much broader and more complex
context of the Anthonian phenomenon, that is, the whole of demon-
strations derived from, centered on, and/or associated with Anthony
of Padua. By the words popular devotion to St. Anthony we mean, as
an initial working approach, the whole of either devotion, attachment, or veneration toward St. Anthony of Padua, or of the acts
and practices of worship, or of attitudes and behaviors which are
shared and lived by a certain number of individuals who are not a
part of the establishment or of the intelligentsia of organized
society or of intermediate social bodies, including the religious
institution, but who form the basis of an inclusive society as
its common constituents.

There are numerous dimensions of the Anthonian phenomenon
(AA.VV., 1977), including the image of St. Anthony, the colleagues
of the saint, the pastoral operators who follow and appeal to him,
the worshipers, and the works of St. Anthony (Scapin, 1977).
We have chosen for the first stage of research the image of St.
Anthony and the devotees or worshipers as the foci or poles for
our system of socio-cultural analysis.

Only in some sectors of the phenomenon and on the part of some
other disciplines -- history and art, for example -- has the study
been systematically pursued, despite the complexity and the rather
remarkable quantitative dimension of the phenomenon itself. In
order to assess this dimension better, it will suffice to consider
official sources (see Scapin, 1977) which indicate between 1960
and 1970 the arrival of 49,681 pilgrimages at the Basilica of
Padua, of which 27,261 originated in Italy and 22,420 in foreign
countries. During the same period 263,950 masses were celebrated
in the same basilica, and hosts were distributed for 6,255,900
communions. Research carried out by the author during the month
of June 1975 (see Giuriati, 1977d: 330-335) confirmed similar

quantitative dimensions of this phenomenon, which also extends far back in time and has a world wide influence. St. Anthony died in 1231 and was canonized (i.e., declared a saint by the Pope) in the following year, 1232.

Only for the last few years has the Anthonian phenomenon become the object of systematic sociological research. Besides, the quantitative dimension of the phenomenon is such that the scholar as well as the curious amateur may wonder what the average worshiper asks of St. Anthony. How does he imagine him? What place and what role does St. Anthony hold in the religious life and sacred universe of the believer? What are the motivations that quicken their devotion to St. Anthony?

Of course, in order to understand the present we must also understand the past without forgetting that such a phenomenon by its articulations of both quantitative and qualitative features seems to represent an ideal domain for interdisciplinary research. At present, an interdisciplinary research project is under consideration, a project sponsored by the Center for Anthonian Studies in Padua. As a preliminary step, a first colloquium has already taken place (AA.VV., 1977). In this context, an effort was made to work out a synthesis of all that could be considered certain or almost certain, as in the domain of history and art, for example and, with respect to other fields including sociology, to formulate the first working hypotheses emerging from the exploratory survey and to make extrapolations from other research or from other theoretical deductions. From this foundation of research, we give here some of the most significant results for sociology and the other human sciences. We must emphasize that this is not a definitive product, but only one that is still in the hypothetical stage. (In the Colloquium, three contributions related especially to the psychological aspect of the phenomenon: Vergote, 1977; Riva, 1977; and Mattellini 1977. The sociology of knowledge was the basis for Delooz, 1977.)

Concerning the social sciences, the results of our own multidimensional survey on devotion to St. Anthony (Giuriati, 1977d) will be integrated with the findings of complementary research by others.

INITIAL QUESTIONS

The main questions asked by the promoters of the project, the organizers, and the participants at the first interdisciplinary colloquium on the Anthonian phenomenon are essentially the following (Scapin, 1975: 220-223; 1977: 76-79):
What are the dimensions, the components, and the variables intervening in or accompanying the Anthonian phenomenon yesterday and today?
On the whole, is it a unique phenomenon? If yes, to what extent

does it present itself as atypical in relation to the manifestations belonging to the same or similar domains of popular
religious life?
What is its current vitality and possible future evolution, given
the conditions of mobility and change of religious life in
contemporary society?
What is its past and present connection with religion in general
and, in particular, with the religion of the Church in which
the person of St. Anthony is considered to be both a member
and a model for others; an official examplar or paragon of
both its social and cultural aspects?
What is the most adequate theoretical-conceptual-methodological
apparatus for systematic analysis in this research?

The preceeding questions have concentrated attention on a few
points in particular, such as the following:
The historical identity of St. Anthony and the historical evolution
of the Anthonian phenomenon.
Types or models of worshipers of St. Anthony.
The styles of and features in devotion to St. Anthony.
The relationship between devotion to St. Anthony and Christian
faith.

The social and cultural analysis was placed into the above
context. It aimed above all at elaborating the current pattern of
devotion to St. Anthony and the styles of and factors in that devotion. We shall report some information about the results obtained
(Giuriati, 1977d: 321-323, 347-348, 384-385). Other aspects of
the phenomenon were incidentally or indirectly considered, but
the immediate site of this research was the Basilica of the Saint
of Padua.

CONTRIBUTIONS TO KNOWLEDGE OF THE PHENOMENON

The Socio-Cultural Point of View

First of all, let us turn our attention to the methods and
sources which have been at the sociologist's disposal. (1) Recording the numbers of pilgrims and pilgrimages, of masses celebrated,
of communions, and of confessions which took place during the month
of June 1975 (Giuriati, 1977d: 326-340). (2) Observing the cultural behavior of the worshipers during the visit to the sanctuary
of Padua (Giuriati, 1977d: 340-341). (3) A casual sample of 100
persons, exploring their overall religiosity in relation to their
devotion to St. Anthony (see Giuriati, 1977d: 348-384). (4)
Exploration, even in other European countries, which aims to determine certain traits in the devotion to St. Anthony in a non-
Italian context (see Giuriati, 1977a: 202-210). (5) Supplementary comparative analysis (see Giuriati 1977b: 227-241). We
have compared the requests addressed to St. Anthony by worshipers
in the sanctuary of Padua with the invocations of the French

193

pilgrims analyzed by Bonnet (1976), who collected and copied them during the summer of 1975 in the "Notebooks of the Pilgrims" in eleven sanctuaries in France. (See also Giuriati 1977c, with respect to the devotion to St. Anthony of Padua and to St. Anthony of Thebaides in two regions of Italy, Abruzzi and Veneto.)

Concerning the requests made by the average worshipper, our research revealed several things. St. Anthony is a thaumaturgical or miracle-working saint; he specializes in granting graces. The favors that are requested of him are as much generic as specific: to retrieve lost objects, to find a life companion, to be exempt from accidents or illnesses, to be protected against dangers of body and of soul.

There exists a common basis for the requests addressed to all the miracle working saints, but St. Anthony seems to be one of the most popular, especially in the psychological, socio-cultural, and economic domains. He also receives strictly "spiritual" requests, such as petitions for salvation of the soul, the love of God, and love for their neighbors.

The data permit us to search further into the universe of the worshipers. In regard to the dimension pertaining to worship, a first finding pertains to the constant, imposing, and cosmopolitan flux of pilgrims and pilgrimages to the Basilica of Padua. In the month of June 1975 we counted 270 pilgrimages (3/5 from Italy and 2/5 from foreign countries on five continents), 14,700 organized pilgrims, 1,800 masses celebrated and 85,000 communion hosts distributed at the Basilica, and 21,000 confessions heard (Giuriati, 1977d: 328-339). (We must note, however, that the Festival of St. Anthony is celebrated during the month of June.)

Furthermore, through participant observation, the general pattern of worship and behavior by the typical pilgrim is revealed to be generally rather weak in folkloric manifestations. This pattern revolves around five elements: confession, participation in the mass with communion, a visit to the Saint's tomb, devotional prayer of supplication, and petition imploring help. In regard to a good portion of the worshipers, everything is reduced to the two attitudes of supplication and petition. In the past, traditional forms of individual devotion included such widely diffused customs as the pilgrimage on foot or the habit of clothing one's child like a little friar for a short time. These practices seem to have disappeared (Giuriati, 1977d: 340-345).

The survey relating to the models of religious life if the worshiper (Giuriati, 1977d: 347-384) drops a hint of a largely spontaneous and ecclesiastical religiosity of the common people. They are solidly bound to their families, to their work, to the future of their children, to remembering their neighbor, and to asking God, through the intermediary of St. Anthony, for help to avoid the dangers of life and even to become better persons. The average worshiper appears neither informed nor interested in the historical identity and devotional biography of St. Anthony. The attraction toward St. Anthony does not seem to depend on his actual personality but rather renown for his reputation for past miracles, the hope for future miraculous events, and the traditional habit of personal or family devotion to St. Anthony, as well as on the hope for concrete interventions in the needs of daily life and existence.

In any case, for the greatest number of devotees St. Anthony is not the only star in the sacred cosmos. He is associated with God, Christ, the Virgin Mary, and other saints. In the same way for the greatest number of worshipers devotion to St. Anthony is linked with a more or less profound and/or routine and traditional feeling of belonging to the Church. Only rarely is the Church refused, treated polemically, or totally ignored; however, the religious practice is most often normal, or it may even be fervent.

The phenomenon seems to find its unity in a stable and often supplicative religiosity in which prayer is above all a petition with a view to an exchange: it is the request of the faithful to his sacred intercessor, who will give to him the grace requested. This is connected with the traditional family circumstances, with the rites of entry into and progression in the Church (baptism, first communion, marriage, death, funerals), with individual piety (the personal prayers are generally said with a regular rythm, even daily, and/or during moments of need, of despair, of depression, of exaltation, with the difficulties and vicissitudes of life centered on three key points: work, home, and family.

Several indices (Giuriati, 1977d: 381-383) permit us to conclude that the characteristics of the religious life of the worshipers vary as functions of such factors as age, sex, occupation, school attendance, geographic origin, and rural or urban background. For example, young people are found to be more "theocentric" in their personal piety, more sensitive to ethical and spiritual requests and to altruism in their prayers, more dynamic, and more open to attitudes of oblation and of solidarity in the general configuration of religious life.

Among those who come from Southern Italy, there is more frequent evidence on the indices of an autonomous religiosity independent of the church with less fidelity to the practice of the sacraments and more readiness to address onself to the saint mainly in moments of danger.

On the other hand, among the women from Northeast Italy, particularly those who are aged or middle-aged, whether married or not, we ascertain an ecclesiastical piety, nourished through the

195

practice of the sacraments, the catechism, and "the surrender to God." All of that does but one thing alone with the personal devotions and the expectation of "an encounter with the Christ," once the hour has come.

The Socio-Historical Point of View

The results of the sociological analysis can be appreciated better when one takes into consideration the conclusions of the historical and artistic research presented at the first colloquium of Anthonian studies. The Anthonian phenomenon and the devotion to St. Anthony have, naturally, a permanent point of reference in St. Anthony himself. As happens to many other personalities and saints (see Delooz, 1977: 421-426), there exists a remarkable amount of shifting between the historical identity of Anthony -- insofar as it is possible to know it critically from the rare sources available -- and the "constructed" images emerging from the popular devotion to the Saint, those of hero worship, of the devotional hagiography, of art, of tradition, and of literature. During his lifetime Anthony was a particularly competent scholar in the domains of theology and the Holy Scriptures, an organizer of studies, an effective preacher, a polemicist, a defender of orthodoxy, a promoter of the spiritual, penitential, and ascetic renewal of the believing masses, a reliever of the poor and the simple by practical interventions which were not always crowned with success. This man, little by little and day by day after his death, simultaneously became the Saint of pilgrims and of the suffering, the miracle-worker, the effective protector-intercessor, the "defensor civitatis," the hammer to the heretics, etc. (see in AA.VV., 1977, especially Vecchi, Gamboso, and Marangon).

Evidence of this evolution includes some eloquent testimonies to the successive levels, attributions, and variations of the manner in which and iconographic symbols by which St. Anthony is represented: a brother in good health with a book or a flame, very young, ecstatic, beardless, with a lily in his hand and the infant Jesus in his arms (Delooz, 1977: 423; Giuriati, 1977a: 202-203).

At the root of the several current images of Anthony, there should be a progressive and stratified development which during the first centuries is only local, generated at Padua, in the Franciscan order, and in a few other places (see Gamboso, 1977: 88-90). Gradually a kind of devotion and worship with a cohesion of many factors is assimilated through a dynamic and reciprocal osmosis:
The specificity and complexity of the man Anthony and the roles
    played by him during his life.
The slow formation of an ecclesial and Franciscan hagiography
    aiming at presenting him as the Catholic apostolic champion,
    the promoter of "mirabilia Dei," the exemplary religious,

196

the father of "the simple" and of the poor, the man-servant of
God, and the "vanquisher of the devil."
The partial dependence of his hero worship cult on the antecedent
    forms of devotion toward more ancient saints.
The social and cultural context in which he had concluded his
    earthly life, that is to say, Padua and its contemporary and
    past vicissitudes. The social and class dynamics between the
    population which inhabited the area in that era and afterwards,
    the cultural and worship traditions which were inspired by
    Anthony and which developped in the folkloric forms of the
    Anthonian festivals and in the construction of his basilica,
    expressing in its grandiosity and in its basilical dome struc-
    ture the supreme glorification of a personality who was no
    longer merely the "numen urbis," a patron saint of but one
    city.
The internal vicissitudes and the work of diffusing Anthonian
    devotion on the part of the Franciscan order.
The spiritual, ethical, social, and cultural climate of the
    Reformation and Counter-Reformation era and the pastoral
    strategies put into play by "the ecclesiastical system."
The expectations, motivations, and reactions of simple believers,
    which represent one of the most important links of the entire
    chain.

    The questions of knowing whether the historic identity of the
Saint and of the role played by him during his lifetime were and
and still are the primary or secondary causes, or indeed if both
are coincidental occasions in regard to the evolution and per-
manence of his constructed images, remain unanswered. Likewise,
the question of knowing if there exists a direct or simply incidental relationship between the devotion to St. Anthony of Padua
and that toward St. Anthony of Thebaides, protector of animals,
is unsolved. The questions await responses even if, from what
we know at present, one could indeed give an affirmative response,
at least from certain points of view (Giuriati, 1977a: 207-208;
1977c: 323-333).

    At the bottom of the different constructed images of St.Anthony,
especially the devotional images, one can ascertain a remarkable
uniformity in the representations, roles, and functions which
worshipers attribute to him. They view him as a miracle worker-
protecter-intercessor because of a series of extraordinary interventions. These include retrieval of lost objects, provision of
material prosperity, protection against physical and moral harm,
protection against accidents while traveling, conveyance of salvation of the soul, assurance of health of the body, defense against
evil forces, assistance in a good choice of partner and a happy
marriage, etc. (Giuriati, 1977a: 203; 1977c: 323-333; 1977d:
357-362). One cannot deny that several of these services (prestations)
are commonly attributed to other saints, but it is also curious
that certain of them are considered to be Anthonian specializations,

such as intervention in regard to lost objects, and, in rather large measure, the "affairs of the heart" and travel accidents.

Two aspects deserve particular attention: the convergence between what is expressed by the traditional iconographic symbols, the devotional invocations, the invocations of sacred and profane literature, and the individual invocations of today's pilgrims in regard to the expectations of graces from St. Anthony, and the clear subdivision in the domain of competences attributed by their respective worshipers to the two homonymous saints, Anthony of La Thebaides and Anthony of Padua. To the first seems entrusted the sylvan, pastoral, and rural domain (protector of livestock, flocks, harvests, etc.), and to the second, the power of intervention in the domain of human life, of even the existence of the worshipers and the events of existence which can happen even beyond the peasant life (Giuriati, 1977c). It is this, perhaps, that explains the larger "hold" of the devotion to St. Anthony of Padua in a society which is passing from traditional to contemporary orientations.

The Socio-Psychological Point of View

Socio-psychological analysis with the goal of illuminating the process and motivational mechanisms, both individual and collective, which are at the origin and basis of the persistent devotional image of St. Anthony has resulted in diverse interpretations: (1) as a self-response to existential and class requirements (see Cipriani, 1977: 436-437;   Elio, 1977: 230-233, 454-455) in the search for significance, justification, and compensation for privations, frustrations, and conditions of an "alienated" life, which is the fate of the subordinate classes; and (2) as the product of an idealization (see Riva, 1977: 258-261; Mattellini, 1977: 283-289) which perceives St. Anthony as an object and the objective of which is not to imitate him as a model but rather to see him as a powerful protecter, a distributer of divine power (a role which is related to a form of primitive religious life, not necessarily Christian). This aspect, which is diversely elaborated, assumed, and integrated by the ordinary devotee in a Christian-ecclesial frame of reference, would produce in the one who lives it a simple and spontaneous attitude of confidence, which precedes the moral-ecclesial implications, even if not in opposition to them.

In this perspective, even the pilgrimage to the sanctuary of the Saint should be understood as a search for physical contact with an available and beneficent numinous being (numineux) in order to lay hold of his power, often in a festive, ethically unexciting frame of reference which sometimes remains marginal to or polemic toward the official worship. To that, it must be added that these people know very little about St. Anthony. Because of the lack of knowledge about the life of the Saint,

198

moreover, the unusual aspects of his life have functionally
replaced the fact that his was a very normal life (Riva, 1977:
258-261; Mattellini, 1977: 283-289). The duties performed by
him during his life would have helped to give him the privilege,
after his death, of being the distributor of prodigies rather than
that of the model for one's life and the "mirror of Christian
virtues" for people to be inspired by and imitate, according to
the rules of Theology and of Catholic spirituality (Riva 1977:
251-252; Visentin, 1977: 466-473; Panteghini, 1977: 482-483).

MARGINAL CONSIDERATIONS ON CONTRIBUTIONS TO THE KNOWLEDGE OF THE ANTHONIAN PHENOMENON

The phenomenon of and the devotion to St. Anthony present themselves, in their entirety, as a very complex reality which could
easily be falsified if it were forced by partial and unilateral
explanations. The different types of interpretations (the expression of "natural" religious life, present in all of the historic
religions; the expression of subordinated classes parallel to or
as an alternative for the official religion, managed by the dominant classes; or other interpretations) are important interpre-
tative keys, but none could explain the phenomenon if it alone
were used. Explanation of it requires a vast, complex, and refined
series of instruments and conceptual methodological models to bring
to light certain trails that one finds in all forms of devotion,
inseparable from the big questions which are peculiar to each
religious experience: the problem of moral and physical evil,
the meaning of life and of death, the beyond.

An interesting framework for the study of the Anthonian phenomenon could be the one represented by the conceptual model of
social communication. The historic identity and the writings of
St. Anthony, the different constructed images of the Saint, his
devotees, the numerous cultural and worship expressions, the
Anthonian promoters and works, could all represent the elements
of a circuit or of a transmitter-receptor system in which the
components, with their reciprocal effects, could be studied
directly by multiple and simultaneous methodologies (textual criticism and content analysis of written documents, participant
observation, and other methods relevant to the current events).

One point that must still be clarified relates to the interdisciplinary orientation. The question is whether this form of
research must limit itself to a series of autonomous, successive,
and juxtaposed focuses upon a particular object by all investigators, the results of which then can be compared and integrated
only when trying to draw conclusions, as was done at the first
Colloquium (AA. VV., 1977). The alternative is for the interdisciplinary approach to attempt to express itself in truly cooperative projects which relate to defining the object, specifying the
concepts, and selecting models and methods of analysis for the

investigation and interpretation of data. Discussion of the results
and comparison of findings then could follow. That is the goal
of the Second Colloquium of Anthonian Studies in Padua, April 9-11,
1979, which will be centered around the theme, "The Image of St.
Anthony."

-- Translated from the French by
Charles F. Potts, Jr.

Chapter 15

A SOCIOANALYTICAL NOTE ON

PSYCHOPATHOLOGICAL TRENDS AMONG THE CATHOLIC CLERGY

Otto Maduro

Continual contact with Catholic clergymen during the last eighteen years, alongside of studies in the sociology and psychology of religion, have made me notice phenomena which could be regarded as psychopathological trends among the contemporary Catholic clergy. Among these phenomena I should underline (a) the increase of psychical disorders among Catholic clergy, and (b) the decrease of the capacity for many to remain as clergy for their entire lives. It seems to me -- although empirical research is yet to be done in order to support this hypothesis -- that (c) both these phenomena are more frequent among the clergy who are engaged in a radical criticism of traditions than among the conformist kind of clergymen.

Some recent approaches of psychopathological phenomena have stressed the need to overcome the merely biological or psychological views on psychic disorders. They set forth the usefulness (both for research and for treatment) of a sociological perspective linked to the biological and psychological ones. Among these approaches, that of Bateson (1956) and Laing (1961, 1965), on the one hand, and that of Mendel (1972), on the other, seem to me particularly interesting, fertile, and useful in order to explain the psychopathological trends among contemporary Catholic clergy.

In doing research on psychopathology, Bateson (1956) and Laing (1961, 1965) arrived at the conclusion that there are schizophrenogenic families and outlined the "double bind" theory of the origins of schizophrenia. As Sedgwick (1972: 23) puts it,
the expression 'double bind' refers to a specific pattern of disturbed communication, detectable within pathological families, in which one member is subjected to a pair of conflicting injunctions or 'binds', both of them highly unsettling or traumatic; a third injunction, implicit in the situation, may prevent the threatened party from leaving the field and so avoiding the conflict.
The result of this "double bind" -- in the long run -- is schizophrenia,

unless the concerned party becomes able to leave the field.

I suggest that an increasing number of clergy are placed in a "double bind" situation. The first injunction: a clergyman is supposed to keep the lay people attached to the Church (e.g., through inculcating the official Catholic doctrines on politics and sexuality); second injunction: the laity are increasingly disposed to abandon the Church if it does not make its doctrines on politics and sexuality flexible (e.g., allowing lay people to vote left or to use contraceptive devices), thus placing the clergy in a conflicting situation; but, third injunction: tradition and official procedures, as well as microsocial attitudes within religious orders, create psychosociological conditions which prevent the clergy from leaving the religious field.

Gerard Mendel (1972), on the other hand, has suggested that many a psychological disorder is both the expression and the displacement of a microsocial conflict. As he puts it in French,
When the conflict cannot be expressed at the political level, then it expresses itself through the materials and elements of the immediately underlying level, that is, the psychological level. And, if the latter is damaged, then it (the conflict) will be expressed through the underlying level, the physiological one (p. 18).
Otherwise stated, a social conflict without the possibility of overtly expressing and developing itself at the political level will tend to express and develop itself as a psychological conflict (at the individual level); similarly, an affective conflict which cannot be expressed and solved at the psychological level, will tend to develop into a physiological symptom.

In this sense, I would elaborate on the "double bind" of the clergy by saying that the Catholic Church has traditionally prohibited (more implicitly than explicitly) the open expression and development of internal conflicts at any other level than the private, individual level (mainly through confession). Thus, if it is true that the contemporary situation of the Catholic Church increasingly places its clergy in a social "double bind" (a conflict between the rules that they should inculcate and the attitudes of the lay people toward these traditional rules), then, Mendel's (1972) hypothesis would lead us to think that this "double bind" tends to express and develop itself as a psychological conflict.

To conclude these hypotheses, I would simply suggest that there are psychopathological trends of a specific nature among the contemporary Catholic clergy; that these trends arise from a "double bind" situation in which the Catholic clergy are placed, as the Church's traditional rules and the lay people's modern demands are increasingly in conflict and cannot be simultaneously satisfied; that this "double bind" situation leads to individual psychological conflicts among the clergy because the open expression of such a social conflict is not institutionally allowed within the Church, and that a socioanalytical approach to such trends could be useful not only for their explanation, but also for their clinical treatment, as Bateson (1956), Laing (1961, 1965), and Mendel (1972) have proposed for similar situations in contexts other than the religious field.

THE BIBLE ON SPIRITUAL TRUTHS

We have not received the spirit of the world but the Spirit who is from God, that we may understand what God has freely given us. This is what we speak, not in words taught us by human wisdom but in words taught by the Spirit, expressing spiritual truths in spiritual words. The man without the Spirit does not accept the things that come from the Spirit of God, for they are foolishness to him, and he cannot understand them, because they are spiritually discerned. -- The Bible, I Corinthians 2: 12-14, NIV.

Chapter 16

MUSIC AND HEALTH WITH A KEY TO HARMONY:

THE ENGLISH EXPERIENCE

David A. Martin

I begin with a rather crabbed quotation from a review by George
Steiner of Jacques Attali's "Bruits," published in the Times
Literary Supplement, May 6, 1977. He puts forward an argument,
which he has made familiar, concerning the shift from the library
to the shelf of records. He says that
     the reasons for this musicalization of sensibility lie
     very deep: in the hunger for substitute forms of reli-
     giosity or "metaecstasy", in the insight that unlike
     books, which are read alone, which cut one off in their
     imperative of attention, music can be listened to so-
     cially, that it offers the attractions of simultaneous
     intimate and familial or collective emotion.

In this paper I want to pick up the kind of issue raised in that
quotation with particular reference to England and the history
of English musical culture. My general theme is the way serious
music has moved into some of the open spaces evacuated by institutional religion. In the course of the discussion I will make a
comparison with the way experience of Nature has also acted as a
modern substitute for religion.

THE CAUTIOUS MARRIAGE OF MUSIC AND RELIGION

     The role of music is clearly connected with the theme of "Religion
and Spiritual Well-Being." Music has been anciently associated,
like religion, with taming the savage breast and healing the dis-
tempered soul. "Art thou troubled? Music will calm thee." Men
have apostrophized music as "Du heilig Kunst." They have sought
in it images of order and ecstasy. The power of harmony can make
men whole, either by "ordering their affections aright" or by
releasing pent-up energies which might otherwise be destructive.
The very idea of harmony is used as a general paradigm of right
relationship and appropriate ordering.

Up to the onset of the modern era music has usually been conceived (in Luther's phrase) as "the handmaid of religion," though
it has also been regarded as dangerous and demonic. The association of dancing with sexuality has made ethical religions in the
monotheistic mould quite suspicious of the powers of music and
intent on regulating them. So while music has been welcomed as
a subordinate power, subject to a greater, it has also been sus-
pected. A man may be taken out of himself, but it does not always
follow that he is thereby taken into God.

All the same, music has been allowed to play the role of handmaid to religion on conditions and subject to regulations. Byzantine
tradition enshrined certain tunes as perfect icons of the divine,
and so it froze them into a timeless heaven. Medieval theory
accorded a good moral character to some modes, a sinister character to others, thus providing a musical analogue to the four humors.
The Council of Trent set out norms of propriety, disallowing
certain kinds of sensuousness and display and insisting on the
primacy of the word and the rite. As is too well known, Calvinism
was suspicious of music in church and prevented any musical expression outside the four-square psalm tune. This attitude, however,
did not apply to music outside church, unless of course it was also
inside a theatre. Lutheranism had a few reservations about music.
It was only with the simultaneous advent of secular operatic
intrusions and of pietism that a serious tension developed. A
late instance of this tension is the "Leeds Organ" controversy in
early nineteenth century Methodism.

I give these varied instances simply to underline the special
relationship between music and religion throughout the whole history of the church, and the intermittent sense of rivalry that has
led to the banning of an instrument or of a mode or a style of
music.

FROM THE MUSIC OF THE SPHERES TO AMIABLE ENTERTAINMENT

The Renaissance view of music drew more straightforwardly on
just those Platonic and Neo-Platonic traditions which had lain
behind the attitudes of the Byzantine and Catholic Churches. There
was less moralistic suspicion and a more direct incorporation of
music into philosophic systems. Music was part of that same underlying "natural" harmony of relations which informed architecture.
The mathematical coordinates of perfect spatial relationships
also informed perfect aural relationships. Milton and Shakespeare
both give eloquent expression to this view, as for example in the
"Ode on Christ's Nativity" or in Lorenzo's speech in "The Merchant
of Venice":
There's not the smallest orb which thou behold'st
But in his motion like an angel sings
Still quiring to the young-eyed cherubim.
In most Renaissance conceptions music is not grudgingly admitted

206

as handmaid to religion; it is itself one of the divine powers.
But it is not yet a fully autonomous power, merely an element in
the Pantheon, one mode of the divine activity.
From harmony, from heavenly harmony
This universal frame began.
From harmony to harmony
Through all the compass of the notes it ran,
The diapason ending full in man.
   ("A Song for St. Cecilia's Day," 1687)
Dryden writes at the point where new conceptions of music are
beginning to make their way alongside the ecclesiastical and Renaissance view. The late seventeenth century is the great period for
odes to Saint Cecilia, patroness of music. Some of these embody
a semi-classical view of music as capable of evoking all the human
emotions from love to madness to bellicosity. But the late seventeenth century is also the period when music emerges as entertainment. So we have a shift from the idea of music as a wand, evoking
first this mood and then that, exciting the mad and quieting the
beasts, to the notion of incidental pleasures provided by sounds.
In Vauxhall Gardens or Dorset Gardens the casual quality met to
parade and talk, and music provided an accompaniment to a polite
saunter. Similarly, of course, with attendance at the opera:
lords and ladies visited the theatre to be seen as much as to listen.
Opera provided a spectacle just as music provided an entertainment.

   This same period is notable for other changes which may be
connected in complicated ways with the shift in the approach to
music. The most important change is secularization: a slackening
of faith into unobtrusive piety, a rejection of all enthusiasm,
the revelation of a cold mechanical universe in which the spheres
make no music. The modality of thought moves from the theological
to the philosophical. A man might be -- almost -- openly atheistic.
Prose becomes measured, elegant, observational. The mystical inti-
mations of Browne, Traherne, Vaughan, and Herbert about the natural
world go underground. Music and nature simultaneously lose their
numinous gleam. They cease to shadow the infinite world.

   These changes are very familiar but the link between them and a
new conception of music is little explored. It may be that music
lost its place in the sphere of the divine even as the divine
spheres themselves disappeared into outer space. It may be that
even as a man openly avowed his atheism, he also admitted his lack
of musicality. Musical and religious deafness are now allowed
options. Dr. Samuel Johnson, for example, is a man of exemplary
piety but appears to have no developed musical sensibility. His
is all verbal sense and no musical sensibility. It may even be
that "measure" defined a modulation from certain kinds of musical
intensity and tension which might evoke visions and ecstasies to
a more precisely ordered time, to a controlled sensibility con-
templating this or that within discrete boundaries. For example,
Purcell's divine songs in the "Harmonia Sacra" are the last examples

of an intense religious sensibility. Handel's Chandos Anthems
only one generation later are grand and eloquent, but the intensity has been elided and the emotion smoothed out.

This is not to say that all these changes happened everywhere
and at once or that they were not contradicted quite quickly by
very different tendencies. Christian reservations about music,
especially about music in the theatre, continued to be expressed.
Opera was not allowed in Lent, and this made a social space for
oratorio. And John Newton, evangelical Rector of St. Mary Woolnoth,
exclaimed against the "Messiah" in a long series of sermons on the
ground that it distracted attention from the Redeemer. Composers
themselves maintained a religious attitude toward music throughout
the eighteenth century, not only Bach, who lived in a largely
pre-Enlightenment atmosphere, but also Handel and Haydn. Handel
represented a massive shift from church to theatre, but there is
no doubt about his piety or his Christian charity. "Messiah"
was performed again and again, as a contemporary remarked, to set
at liberty the captive and to relieve the orphan and the fatherless.

HOW THE ENGLISH COLONY DIFFERED FROM THE CONTINENTAL EMPIRE

All these preliminary observations are necessary to make sense
of more recent conceptions of music, especially as none of the
ancient traditions has been entirely superseded. However, the
next stage in my argument is complicated by the fact that it is
impossible any longer to treat England as a useful instance of
general European tendencies. Indeed, there is some difficulty
doing so even from the time of Purcell (1656-1691). The modest
civic style and the Palladian decorum of early eighteenth century
England contrasted strongly with the grandiose conceptions of enlightened despotism, and it is sometimes argued, for example by
Wilfred Mellers, that the death of English opera is all of a piece
with a preference for Palladianism rather than the Baroque (or
Classic) and with a settled distaste for unlimited monarchy. But
whatever the problems of keeping within an English context in the
late seventeenth and eighteenth centuries, they are immediately
compounded when we arrive at the period of the French Revolution.
In any case, from Purcell onwards England is a musical colony,
invaded by Handel, J.C. Bach, and Haydn; it becomes increasingly
odd to treat the colony as a primary instance of the broader
musical empire. Hence any focus on England must include some
comparisons with Europe.

The years 1790-1810 are the time when the musician emerges as
a prophet, writing music to accompany the march of revolution or
of nationalism. On the whole, music has been and has remained the
least political and revolutionary of the arts, but "Fidelio,"
the "Eroica," and Choral Symphonies are self-consciously prophetic
documents. They embody the hopes and despairs of the revolutionary
ferment. At the same time the musician also acquires the status

208

of virtuoso and minor entrepreneur. He is released from a secure role among the service personnel of Kings, Electors, and Archbishops and enters the service of the market. He depends more on the market and less on patronage. And he adds the character of "star" to the office of prophet. As "star" he appears before the audience and inaugurates the era of the public concert, appealing to wider and wider sectors of society. Insofar as he takes on the office of prophet, he composes music which exemplifies a new kind of seriousness. His music expresses the new romantic awareness of nature, as well as "absolute" music.

All these changes took time to acquire a secure root, and the "serious" character of music was not fully grasped till the mid-nineteenth century. Three decades after Beethoven's death people were more likely to know his symphonies in Liszt's piano transcriptions than in orchestral form. Liszt himself lives two lives: as entertainer-virtuoso and as serious musician, extending the language of music and inventing the symphonic poem. All the same, what "Fidelio" and the "Eroica" proclaimed at the onset of the century was established by the 1850's.

Most of these changes were exported from the German Empire to the English colony, but in a highly dilute form. When we see how England appropriated these major changes on the mainland, we become more aware of what is distinctive about the Channel. First of all, of course, the revolutionary trumpet was muted. Just as Britain evaded enlightened absolutism, so it bypassed revolutionary absolutism. So just as Britain lacked opera, so it lacked the revolutionary and nationalistic overtones which from time to time infiltrated operatic composition. Second, the shift to "absolute" serious music was less pronounced. To put that point in another way, the new seriousness was expressed in the democratic choral tradition rather than in orchestral music, and there was a less marked divorce between music and institutional religion.

The last point must be expanded. Even on the continent music maintained strong links with religion and some kind of connection with the Church. Beethoven wrote the Ninth Symphony, but that nevertheless invoked a free humanity standing united before God. He also wrote a supreme invocation of the Deity in the Missa Solemnis. Similarly Berlioz, who followed Beethoven in panegyrics for Napoleon, also composed the "Te Deum" and "The Childhood of Christ," in spite of being an atheist. Even in France, the most secularist of cultures, there was an institutional link with the Church in the French organ school and among composers like Fauré. All the same, the weight of serious performance and composition lay in opera, orchestral, and chamber music, each of which marked transitions away from the church. Opera was a shift to the theatre, orchestral music to the civic concert hall, chamber music to the salon and the drawing room.

ENGLISH MUSIC AS DEMOCRATIC PARTICIPATION: CHOIR AND BAND

The transitions in England were much less dramatic. Opera in any case barely existed, and orchestral music was much less developed than in Austria and Germany. The major transition was from the old elite style of the cathedrals and the royal chapel to the democratic choral society. This was the natural course of change, given that the long traditions of stable (if limited) political liberty were established in partial alliance with democratic dissenting religion. This culture was not likely to foster profound artistic creativity, but it could encourage democratic musical participation. Since the theatre and the opera belonged to the devil and the upper class, "participating democracy" might express itself in the hymn, the brass band, and the choral society. Choirs and bands sprang up all over the north of England in the wake of dissent and the industrial revolution. A perfect illustration of this is provided by the artisans of Lancashire, mainly weavers and Methodists, who sang Handel and even composed their own music. They also performed Haydn in Cross Street Chapel. But the weight of the tradition lay in singing. One weaver walked twenty miles to Manchester simply to look on the score of Handel's "Solomon." Handel was persuaded to compose three tunes to hymns by Wesley. So there developed a culture of singing dissent, outside the scope of the cathedrals, colleges, and chapels of the elite, but firmly attached to religion. Indeed the pious artisan might contrast the religiosity of dissent with the indifferentism of the elite.

This is how music retained a peculiar link with religion in Britain and how musical seriousness was channelled through the democratic choral society. Moreover, this same tradition of brass band and choir simultaneously expressed political dissent and contained it. Brass band and choir carried the impulses of moderate liberal reform and checked revolutionary ideology; in so doing, they played a role analogous to chapel culture in general. The "Sacred Harmonic Society" of London, for example, was identified as a vehicle of this liberalism; it was, however, much less revolutionary and much more religious than its French analogue, the Orpheon, or the subversive choral societies of Vienna. Being less revolutionary, it was eventually accepted; the Sacred Harmonic Society sang at the Great Exhibition of 1851.

THE SPECIAL LINK: MUSIC, CIVIC SENTIMENT, RELIGION, AND NATURE

Given these crucial differences between Britain and the continent, it is now possible to suggest how and why music was part of the nexus that also linked religion to national civic sentiment and to feeling about nature. In England it became uniquely possible to link together musicality, the worship of nature, and civic and national pride. This is the matrix out of which the special sensibility of modern English musical culture has sprung.

But how did these themes interweave over time? Let me take first the special English version of romantic feeling about nature and the intense nostalgia for the countryside occasioned by the industrial revolution. Then I will go on to the theme of civic and national pride as realized first in the form of "pork and beef" and then as a brooding evocation of the "sweet especial rural scene." The two themes are, of course, interwoven; even in the eighteenth century, Britain and its countryside was heir to Rome and took on the lineaments of a favored Israel. (The Virgilian strain in Englishry is nicely documented in John Chalker's "The English Georgic.")

For the eighteenth century the natural world was a vista and a prospect. Nature was a landscape with figures, carefully ordered or set in nice disorder. God was displayed in the steady movements of the heavens and the great chain of being. He had designed his creations with exquisite care, and Nature was the book in which men might read the purposes of God. Every delicate natural mechanism illustrated his infinite intelligence.

Then gradually Nature emerged as a power in its own right. The book of natural phenomena opened up a mystical union with God and conveyed a spontaneous moral impulse. The awesomeness of divinity was translated into human awe before the mighty universe. The world had the aspect of the sublime and might attract men's free worship and communion. So Nature became a domain where man discovered the religious impulse and acknowledged religious feelings: awe, communion, admiration, worship, renewal, healing, consolation.

This theme requires emphasis here because it was so strongly related to the emotions engendered by music and by ecclesiastical religion. Music, nature, and religion were all sides of the same pyramid, reaching up to the same apex. Perhaps in no European culture was there such a union of feeling, allowing natural creation, revealed religion, and inspired music to work together for moral and religious good. Indeed, the poetic images used to describe the religion of nature borrowed freely from Christian associations and musical metaphors. Thus Wordsworth in "Tintern Abbey": "So with an eye made quiet by the power of harmony, and the deep power of joy, we see into the life of things."

When Wordsworth watched a sunset, it awoke in him reflections on immortality. He also saw Britain as a land of liberty in which democracy had implanted itself more firmly than elsewhere. Indeed. Wordsworth illustrates all the themes that run together in the course of the nineteenth century: the inspiration of scripture, the power of music, the divine influence of nature, and the special role of England in blazing the path of liberty and democracy. In

other cultures all these varied themes might be distinct or
jarring, but in the special circumstances of England, they could
be seen as uniquely conjoined.

THE REUNION OF CATHOLIC NOSTALGIA WITH WHIG AND TUDOR MYTH

There is no space here to fill in all the complex interrelations
which built up in the course of the Victorian era, except to refer
to one marked disjunction which in the end became a conjunction.
The disjunction was the revival of medievalism and of enthusiasm
for Catholic culture, including the guild. This was bound to
clash with the Tudor myth, with the Whig interpretation of history,
and with Protestant individualism. Yet in the end it did not; the
two sides eventually moved closer to each other and emphasized
elements they held in common. Thus the choral societies were
initially repelled by the "oratory verse" of Elgar's "Dream of
Gerontius" but were in the end captivated by the mighty chorus,
"Praise to the Holiest in the height." The revival of mumming
and mysteries and of the great sixteenth century masters could
be seen as easily as a part of Tudor sentiment as a part of a
Catholic revival. The carol appeared alongside the hymn, and the
folk song alongside the ballad and the patriotic ditty. The
school provided the Bible on the one hand and the Nativity Play
on the other, and they soon came to appear one common inheritance.

Musical culture took its roots in this potent amalgam: Catholic
and Tudor nostalgia, Protestant hymnody and folk song, cantata
and mass. Benjamin Britten raised this stock to the level of
genius. The consequent union of feeling brought together the
church and the countryside, the pacifism of dissent and patriotic
pride. The result is clear. As institutional religion has faltered,
the union of sensibility has remained. Music and nature and
worship were indissolubly joined in the nineteenth century and
have not been separated since. Rather, Englishmen have thought
that they performed their religious duty by going for a walk in
the country or by listening to Purcell or Handel or Vaughan
Williams. Their Catholic and Protestant past is somehow united
in a mythic present for which the institutional church is a background tapestry, an architectural reminder.

MASS TO PICNIC, SERVICE TO CONCERT, WORD TO SOUND

I have tried to suggest why Englishmen enjoy a special association of sensibility. The countryside can be their confessional,
the concert their mass. The sacred rites of Catholicism and the
psychic seriousness of Puritanism have together been channelled
into the meal in the country and serious listening in the concert
hall. A man begins as a Methodist and ends in the Bach choir.
Music has become a kind of theophany, replacing the Word and even
-- if George Steiner is correct -- replacing words. The universal
church of sound is now a channel for feelings of exaltation,

212

release, consolation. And in England, for reasons I have suggested, uniquely so.

SOCIAL ASPECTS OF SPIRITUAL WELL-BEING

...the quality of our spiritual life as we perceive it is often associated with the quality of our involvements with people. When a friend turns cold, when we feel left out and forgotten, we may experience all of the emotional dynamics of a religious crisis. ...Paradoxically it is precisely our faith in God which may sustain us when our friends reject us (Hulme, 1978: 84).

Chapter 17

THE FOURTH DIMENSION: APPLICATIONS TO THE SOCIAL SERVICES*

Larry Renetzky, ACSW

It is well recognized by both professional and lay people that there are three dimensions in life: the biological, psychological, and sociological. Today we have a tendency to specialize in one of these with numerous in-depth specialties within each. To be sure, some have sought to understand the interrelatedness of these three dimensions, but as information expands in each, it becomes increasingly difficult.

To compound matters, the more studious religious community adds to the three dimensions the theological. Even fewer people attempt to understand the interrelations of the theological to the others. Because of the tendency to specialize, to become enveloped in one dimension, and not to see the whole person and the way in which all four dimensions come to bear in a person's life, I am suggesting a new concept, the Fourth Dimension. The new term could better have been called "spiritual," but since "spiritual" has different meanings for different people, I have chosen to define the Fourth Dimension as follows:

The Fourth Dimension is best described through three component parts, each of which is essential: (1) It is the power within a person's life that gives meaning, purpose, and fulfillment; (2) It is a person's will to live; (3) It is the belief/faith that the person has in self, in others, and in a power beyond self. For most Christians this power beyond self is centered in God the Father, the Son, and the Holy Spirit. Whether one is a Christian or not, I maintain that the Fourth Dimension as defined is innate and inherent in the lives of everyone, regardless of the presence or absence of theological or religious beliefs. Just because a person is not fully, or partially, aware of this "power beyond self" does not for a minute minimize the actual existence

*Reprinted with minor revisions from The Paraclete: Journal of the National Association of Christians in Social Work, 4(2): 104-118, Winter 1977.

of this power in his/her life and in the universe. However, the more a person is tuned in to this "power within/beyond self," the greater is his/her spiritual, physical, psychological, and social well-being. This will become more apparent as the three component parts are further delineated.

The Fourth Dimension is the basis or foundation for the other three dimensions. Just as a house needs a good foundation to withstand the weather, so do the other three dimensions need a good foundation so a person can meet all of the adversities and challenges of life. The Bible tells us that we were created in the likeness and image of God and that God is a Spirit. It follows that God has built His Spirit into us. Perhaps we are not aware of this spiritual dimension until we have a personal encounter with God or recognize in some degree a power beyond self. I have found in my clinical practice that as a person plugs into and grows in this Fourth Dimension, she/he discovers Christ, and the dormant Fourth Dimension becomes alive within. For example, the born again Christian can know personally this spiritual power beyond and within self much as God intended when He created us in his likeness and image. A person need not be estranged from this God power and rendered spiritually impotent. She/he can know the abundant life in a personal way through actualization of the Fourth Dimension.

The relationship between the three components of the Fourth Dimension to the other three dimensions will now be explained in more detail.

THE POWER WITHIN: MPF

Meaning, Purpose, and Fulfillment (MPF) can best be demonstrated through the roles that make up our lives. In this way, the psychological and sociological dimensions are embraced and undergirded.

Diagram 1. The Personal Well-Being X-Ray

MALE ROLES*	MPF:	Meaning	Purpose	Fulfillment
		Past MPF	Present MPF	Future MPF

1. Husband
   Divorcee
   Widower
   Sweetheart

2. Father

3. Job (Breadwinner)

Diagram 1. (Continued)

4. Son

5. Brother

6. Uncle

7. Grandfather

8. Self

9. Friend

10. Religion

11. Student

12. Maintenance Man

13. Others: (Playboy, Cousin,
Doormat, Dishrag, Bookkeeper,
etc.)

14. Void

100%	100%	100%

*The corresponding FEMALE ROLES are these:

1. Wife	5. Sister	13. Others:
Divorcee	6. Aunt	(Playgirl,
Widow	7. Grandmother	Cousin, Doormat
Sweetheart	8. Self	Dishrag, Mis-
2. Mother	9. Friend	tress, Bookkeeper,
3. Job	10. Religion	etc.)
(Breadwinner)	11. Student	14. Void
4. Daughter	12. Homemaker	

Furthermore, there is a practical application to the social services. This application can be seen through what I call the Personal Well-Being X-Ray and the Self Wheel.

The Personal Well-Being X-Ray (Diagram 1) is generally applied by asking the client to list the various roles, in any order, that make up his/her life. Then the client thinks about the degree of meaning, purpose, and fulfillment (MPF) that he/she would assign to each role. This is all predicated on the fact that each person needs to have a "purpose in life," "meaning out of life," and

217

"fulfillment or satisfaction from life." Frequently during this exercise a person will discover that a large part of his/her 100% MPF out of life is a void.

The therapist/instructor explains that the sum of all the percentages given to each role cannot exceed 100%. The client is then encouraged to ask, "How much of my 100% of meaning, purpose, and fulfillment out of life do I get from my role right now as mother/father, husband/wife, job/homemaker, etc.?" Usually the client needs some examples of a percentage that might be assigned to different roles. For example, if a male assigns 90% of his MPF to his job, then he has only 10% remaining for all of his other roles, such as husband, father, etc. It is usually best to start with the present first and reflect only later on the past and the future. (More on this later.) As the client continues to assign a certain percentage to each role, it must be stressed that all of the roles together amount to no more than 100%.

Even though the MPF concept is a fairly simple one, it can be easily misunderstood. Therefore, before the client starts to assess certain percentages of MPF for each role, two misconceptions need to be explained: (1) Many energetic people say, "I give 100% in each role." Energy is not the same thing as MPF. Such people may well be giving 100% energy in each role, but this is not the same as MPF. Some roles, no matter how energetically they are exercised, may have very little MPF for that individual. (2) Another common misconception is that the amount of time spent in a role is the same as MPF. This does not necessarily follow, as one may spend a lot of time in a role and receive very little MPF. The following example will show the contrast between the amount of MPF derived and the time and energy spent in a role.

While counseling with a couple I discovered through use of the Well-Being X-Ray that the husband had only 5% MPF in his job role, although he spent much time, approximately 75% of his waking hours, at work. He also expended much energy in this role, as he had one full-time job and two part-time jobs. It is also significant to note that 45% of his 100% MPF was a void, which he was trying to fill up with his drinking. He was on the way to becoming an alcoholic. When his wife heard this and saw it demonstrated through the Personal Well-Being X-Ray, it helped to clarify for her how her husband was hurting. It helped to establish a dialogue between them that cleared up many fears and misunderstandings for both of them. Their relationship improved significantly within just a few months, and their MPF as husband and wife went from 0 - 5% to 15-20%. This was primarily due to dispelling the wife's fear of "another woman" and recognizing that her husband's total MPF was low due to the void in his life.

The use of this Personal Well-Being X-Ray created a dialogue which identified some critical events and results: The wife recalled that she had become pregnant while they were engaged. Her husband quit his senior year in college. They were married, and he started to work. He never realized his vocational dream because three children came early in their marriage, and he just worked harder than ever to provide for his family. This resulted in three jobs and led to a void in his life. The wife noted the cause for this void and extended herself by going to work. This freed up her husband to quit one of his jobs and proceed to complete his BA, thereby realizing his vocational dream. Within two years, their life was much more in order: their marital and family relationships improved (more loving and caring), the husband obtained a teaching position, his drinking greatly subsided, his void went from 45% to around 5%, and there was a steady increase from 1% to 15% in the MPF of their religious role.

Out of this example another important point to be understood is the contrast between the PAST, PRESENT, and FUTURE. This contrast can help people understand where they are now in relationship to the past and where they want to go in the future with their lives. Through this process a person can vividly gain new perspectives and goals for life. It is quite significant when one suddenly sees oneself through the process of this Personal Well-Being X-Ray. It is as if the "horse blinders" have fallen off; the individuals can now more fully see and understand where they have been and where they want to go with life, rather than just trotting blindly ahead.

In approximately one thousand Personal Well-Being X-Rays, I have found that as the MPF increased in most roles, the religious role increased significantly as well, and the void decreased substantially. Overall, the MPF increased only in those cases where the following well-known Christian principles were exercised: "The measure that you give is the measure that you get" (The Bible, Luke 6: 38); "You reap what you sow" (The Bible, Galatians 6: 7); "You may give without loving, but you cannot love without giving" (Petty, 1962: 10). The third principle distinguishes between selfish and unselfish giving. I have found a strong correlation between unselfish giving and what I will call "spiritual well-being:" the greater the unselfish giving, the greater the spiritual well-being within each individual. This spiritual well-being was not always manifested through a person's corporate worship, although it usually increased in time. Frequently a person began to draw closer to God through prayer, Bible reading, a quiet time, more loving relationships, communing with nature, and a healthier self-love.

Now, let's look more closely at the relationship between MPF, spiritual well-being, and a healthy self love as illustrated by the Self-Wheel.

The Self-Wheel

Jesus said, "Love your neighbor as you love yourself" (The Bible,

Matthew 22: 39). In essence, if one does not have a healthy self-love, it is impossible to love one's neighbor, spouse, children, friends, etc. One may give with the attitude, if I do this for you, what are you going to do for me? This is a selfish attitude, rather than a loving attitude. Scriptures tell us (The Bible, I John 3: 3) that "God is love." Since love is of the spiritual realm, then one cannot give love unless he or she has the treasure of love within. Therefore, spiritual well-being is expressed in a person through a healthy self-love that in turn can be manifested in one's various roles through relationships with others. This can be demonstrated through the "Self-Wheel" (Diagram 2).

Diagram 2. The Self-Wheel

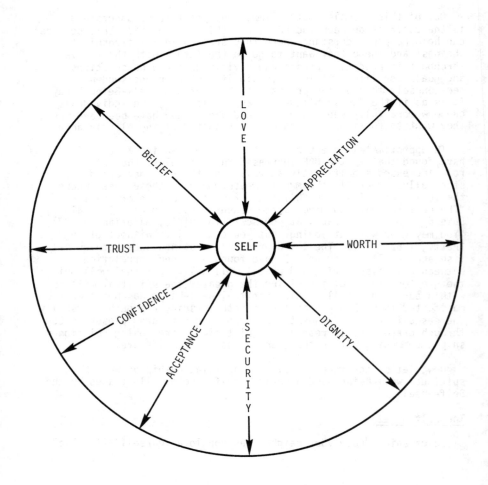

220

The Self-Wheel can be understood best in this way: a wheel that has spokes is strong and supportive as long as the spokes are strong and sturdy. "Self" can be healthy and giving if the spokes of love, appreciation, worth, etc. are vital, alive, and feeding into and out of "self." To put it another way, think of self as the heart, and the arteries of the heart as love, appreciation, worth, etc. The healthier the arteries, the healthier the heart. If the arteries have any blockage or start to become hardened, this adversely affects the heart. In the same way, the healthier the arteries of love, appreciation, worth, etc., the healthier is "self." It works like this: As people develop a healthier self love, they can more spontaneously love or appreciate another person. Furthermore, if people feel they are worth something, then they have something to give in all of the roles that make up their Personal Well-Being X-Ray.

The following is a means to measure the healthiness of each spoke or artery of the Self-Wheel: Take each spoke of an individual's Self-Wheel, and determine whether it is closer to 1 or 10.

Unhealthy   Healthy

1   2   3   4   5   6   7   8   9 10

SPOKE OR ARTERY OF THE SELF-WHEEL

The closer a person is to 10, the healthier is that artery of love, etc., and in turn the healthier is the "self." The closer a person's artery is to 1, the more unhealthy is that artery of love, etc., and thereby the more unhealthy is "self."

I have found that the correlation between a healthy self and MPF in a person's role is very high. In fact, as the arteries become healthier in a person's Self-Wheel, then the MPF in various roles also increases and little or no MPF void is evident. I have found in my clinical practice that a healthy self and MPF in a person's life as revealed in the Personal Well-Being X-Ray go together like a hand and glove, or like a Christian and love. It is also true that as an individual's MPF increases in the respective roles, she or he develops a healthier self as reflected by a number closer to 10 in the various arteries of love, appreciation, worth, etc.

Which comes first, a healthy self, or an adequate MPF in a person's life? That, in a way, is trying to answer whether the chicken or the egg comes first, yet, if I had to choose one, I would probably say the healthy self. Of course, the relatedness of the two is quite strong and obvious.

I have also discovered that as people develop a healthier self and their MPF increases in their life's roles, their spiritual well-being also improves. They have less need to escape through religion or to present an image that all is well spiritually. Rather, they are able to "go on into perfection" and to be really honest and forthright in their spiritual relationship with God, His Son Jesus Christ, self, and other people. There is more recognition of the importance of the power of the Holy Spirit in their lives and less need to prove that they can do it all by themselves. Once individuals do not have to prove themselves so much, they can and usually do give more time to improving their spiritual well-being, unless they get lazy and careless and just coast along.

I am able to use the above exercises to determine the components and level of MPF and how healthy the self is in a very direct way in my counseling with people. Through the exercises, I am also able to get insight regarding their spiritual well-being. Furthermore, I am able to see how the Fourth Dimension directly involves the sociological and psychological dimensions, as implied through the above material. It has a direct application to the social services.

THE WILL TO LIVE

The biological comes into play much more in the Second part of the Fourth Dimension, which I define as "a person's will to live." In an in-depth study on "faith healing," I discovered that the greater a person's will to live, the greater the chances of making it through all kinds of illnesses and other adversities of life. The reverse was also true -- that the less a person willed to live, the more apt he or she were to die. It is well documented that many people die from the lack of a will to live; their deaths cannot be attributed to an illness, heart attack, or other organic dysfunction.

I will not elaborate further on the relatedness of the Fourth Dimension to the biological dimension. I am primarily interested here in the impact that the Fourth Dimension has on the other two dimensions and in their relationship to the social services.

BELIEF/FAITH IN SELF, OTHERS, AND BEYOND SELF

Also affecting the "will to live" is the intensity of belief that a person has in self, others, and a power beyond self. The person who really "believes and has faith in self" strongly usually is more vibrant and alive and has a stronger will to live. The person's "will to live" is further reinforced by the belief/faith that the person has in others, which very definitely affects the MPF derived from life. The greater the belief and faith a person has in others, as well as in self, usually the greater is the MPF in the various roles that make up that person's life. Of course, the greater the MPF in life, the less a void is present. The less void present, the greater is a person's will to live. It all works together.

Important as are the above demonstrated points about the Fourth Dimension, its final component is probably the most important, "the belief/faith that a person has in a power beyond self." Many factors in life can and do have a profound negative impact and effect on a person's MPF, will to live, and belief/faith in self and others. When faced with these negative and adverse happenings in life, one must have a belief and faith in a "power beyond self" to carry oneself through. The Christian realizes this power through God the Father, Son, and Holy Spirit. In his introduction to Your God is Too Small Phillips (1961: ii) says,

> There are undoubtedly professing Christians with child-
> ish conceptions of God which could not stand up to the
> winds of real life for five minutes. But Christians are
> by no means always unintelligent, naive, or immature.
> Many of them hold a faith in God that has been both purged
> and developed by the strains and perplexities of modern
> times, as well as by a small but by no means negligible
> direct experience of God Himself. They have seen enough
> to know that God is immeasurably "bigger" than our fore-
> fathers imagined, and modern scientific discovery only
> confirms their belief that man has only just begun to
> comprehend the incredibly complex Being who is behind
> what we call "life."

I have noted over a thirty-year period of working with people that the "bigger" a person's God (power beyond self) the less apt he or she is to panic, and the more capable she or he is to cope with the adversities and trials of life. My experience has shown me that a person's "bigness of God" concept is directly related to the "belief/faith" a person has in this power beyond self. Jesus Christ (The Bible, Matthew 17: 20) tells us that a person who has an actualized faith no bigger than a grain of mustard seed can move mountains of personal problems and adversities. Furthermore, I would like to suggest that such a person can more significantly touch the life of another person mentally, emotionally, physically, socially, and spiritually. "Nothing shall be impossible unto you."

TA and The Triune

Transactional Analysis (TA) has given us a model that helps us to see how we behave and touch the lives of others. For the Chris-tian, the power beyond self may be further understood in light of TA. I will briefly demonstrate how this model in part can relate to and embrace the Godhead -- the Father, Son, and Holy Spirit. (I thank a Christian brother, Dennis Gibson, Ph.D., for the following illustration on the relatedness of TA to the Triune.)

223

Diagram 3. TA: Two People Interacting

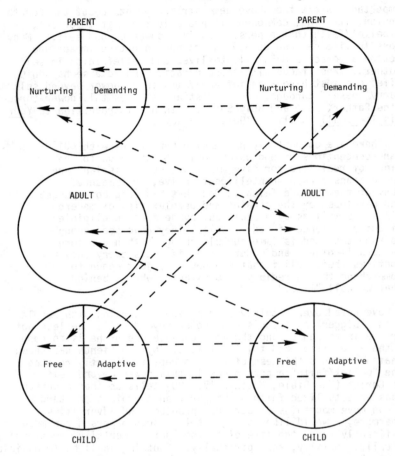

We all have within our makeup elements of parent, adult, and child, as defined by TA. The interaction between these three parts can either make for more MPF within our lives or greatly hinder our relationships. For example, Diagram 3 illustrates several possibilities:
1. As two persons interact Demanding to Demanding, this brings fighting, confusion, and breakdown of relationships.
2. As two persons interact Demanding to Adaptive, this brings momentary peace, but since the interaction feeds on fear, it is a destructive force in positive relationship building.
   The same goes for Adaptive to Adaptive, but they can usually

224

Diagram 4. TA: Father, Son, Holy Spirit

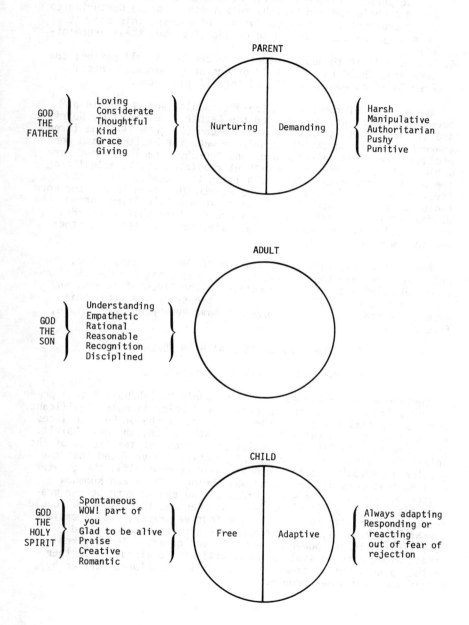

PARENT

GOD
THE
FATHER
}
Loving
Considerate
Thoughtful
Kind
Grace
Giving
}

Nurturing | Demanding

{
Harsh
Manipulative
Authoritarian
Pushy
Punitive

ADULT

GOD
THE
SON
}
Understanding
Empathetic
Rational
Reasonable
Recognition
Disciplined
}

CHILD

GOD
THE
HOLY
SPIRIT
}
Spontaneous
WOW! part of
  you
Glad to be alive
Praise
Creative
Romantic
}

Free | Adaptive

{
Always adapting
Responding or
reacting
out of fear of
rejection

225

survive longer on this interaction than on Demanding to Adaptive.
3. As two persons interact Nurturing to Nurturing, this helps to
build a wholesome and healthy relationship, as do Nurturing to
Adult and Nurturing to Free Child. Of course, this doesn't
mean they are never demanding or adaptive, but these are mini-
mized.
4. Too much Adult to Adult interaction creates a dull person; too
much Free Child to Free child brings about permissiveness;
Free Child to Adult is like mixing oil and water.

The balance of these three (parent, adult, and child) in a
person is important, just as God the Father, Son, and Holy Spirit
are all important and make up the Godhead (Diagram 4). The three
(parent, adult, and child) in balance make for healthier and more
wholesome personal relationships and thereby a healthier and more
whole person, one who, maybe without realizing it, is actualizing
the Godhead within the life and helping to actualize it in the
lives of others. In this way, the Fourth Dimension is all the more
consummated and brought into fruition in people's lives through the
Godhead as they actualize (1) this power within that gives MPF,
(2) the will to live, and (3) the belief/faith in self and others
and in power beyond self.

For Christians, this actualization of God the Father, Son, and
Holy Spirit within their lives is fully realizing the Fourth Dimension and helping to set it in motion in the lives of others, and
in the world as a whole. Then people can truly say with their
lives, "In God, we live and move and have our being" (The Bible,
Acts 17: 24).

RELATEDNESS OF BELIEF/FAITH IN POWER

BEYOND SELF TO SPIRITUAL WELL-BEING

Certainly, the relatedness of a person's "faith/belief in a power
beyond self" to his or her spiritual well-being is most significant.
This is especially true for the Christian, as she or he actualizes
personal belief and faith in God the Father, Son, and Holy Spirit.
The Bible in Galatians 5: 22 tells us that one of the fruits of the
Spirit is "faith." In my clinical practice I have found that the
greater a person's "faith" in God (power beyond self), the greater
will be that person's spiritual well-being. If we can somehow
better measure a person's belief/faith, we can in turn better measure his or her spiritual well-being. Perhaps this "somehow" could
relate specifically to a person's effective prayer, Bible reading,
worship experiences, etc. and how they affect the actualized
belief/faith in the power beyond self and others. These three
areas, along with possibly others, will not be discussed further
in this paper, but in time hopefully will be explored further by
myself and many other people.

226

I have found that a person's spiritual well-being is directly proportional to her or his actualized faith in God (power beyond self). Yet in 25 years of counseling, I have not always found a similar correlation between spiritual well-being and actualized belief/faith in self and others.

The correlation between a person's spiritual well-being and belief/faith in God may be much higher than the correlation between his or her spiritual well-being and the belief/faith in self and others. Some of the reasons for this are directly related to one's negative and ill experiences as a child and adult, which have a profound impact on how one sees and accepts self and others, thereby affecting the belief/faith that he or she has in self and others. This embodies much of the counseling that is done within the social service field, but, unfortunately, many counselors do not relate this in any way to the Fourth Dimension. They deal with it as if it were strictly in the realm of the psychological.

CONCLUSION

Much more could be said and explored regarding belief and faith in God (power beyond self), in self, and in others, as well as about MPF in life and the will to live. It is my intention to press on to explore more ways to measure the relevance of the Fourth Dimension to one's life, thereby reflecting upon one's spiritual well-being. I believe that the application of the Fourth Dimension to the social services is most relevant and profound, especially for Christians, whose Lord said, "Inasmuch as you have done it unto one of the least of these my brethren, you have done it unto me" (The Bible, Matthew 25: 40). Of course, this relates to many areas of social services, but I have not discussed these areas here directly, except as they relate to counseling with people. Suffice it to say, "If someone who is supposed to be a Christian has money enough to live well and sees a brother in need -- and won't help him -- how can God's love be within him?" (The Bible, I John 3: 17 LB).

I believe that the Fourth Dimension embodies, and even directs, much of the successful counseling that is done. Certainly, the application of this Fourth Dimension to the social services needs to be explored and developed much more, especially in direct correlation with spiritual well-being. Together, we must strive to find better ways to measure a person's spiritual well-being so that individuals can be helped to understand and accept more fully the importance that spiritual well-being can and does have in their lives. I maintain that one's spiritual well-being directly or indirectly affects all of his or her life, as well as the lives of others, flowing through all of life with a rippling effect.

Applying the Fourth Dimension practically and soundly within the social services, as well as within churches and other institutions, will mean that we view people and life more clearly in a wholistic framework and approach. We will demonstrate that life is more than just three dimensions -- the biological, psychological, and sociological -- but is also the spiritual which I have defined the Fourth Dimension.

(In addition to the references cited in the text, the author has referred to Appel and Strecker, 1958; Frankl, 1963, 1965; Frost, 1965; Harris, 1973; Heynen, 1973; Hutschnecker, 1974; Keyes, 1972; Nee, 1965, 1977; Osborne, 1973; Oyle, 1975; Peale, 1974, 1978; Schuller, 1969; Solomon, 1977; Tournier, 1962, 1964, 1968, 1973.-- The Editor)

PART V. QUANTITATIVE RESEARCH ON SPIRITUAL WELL-BEING

Chapter 18

MEASURES OF RELIGIOSITY AND THE QUALITY OF LIFE:

A CRITICAL ANALYSIS*

Patrick H. McNamara and Arthur St. George

The past few years have seen the publication of two ambitious
efforts to survey subjective evaluations of the quality of life
in America. Campbell, Converse, and Rodgers (1976; hereafter
referred to as CCR) analyzed results of personal interviews with
2,164 persons eighteen years of age or older living in the United
States during July and August 1971. Andrews and Withey (1976)
based their analysis on five national surveys of American adults
conducted between May 1972 and October 1973 (N=5200) and a local
survey in Toledo conducted in July 1973 (N=222).

Both studies, we feel, deserve attention from sociologists of
religion. Both include religiosity items correlated with measures
of "well-being" and life satisfaction, but we focus on CCR because
it contains more numerous and diverse measures of religiosity.
Its availability on data tapes through the University of Michigan's
Inter-University Consortium for Political and Social Research make
possible exploration of the role of religious indicators beyond
that undertaken by the study's authors. (The Andrews and Withey
data were made available by the ICPSR after this paper was written;
we intend also to analyze them along the lines suggested by this
paper.) It is thus possible to test the strength and independence
of various measures of religiosity with regard to dependent variables
salient in the study, e.g., the summary measures of "well-being"
developed by the authors. We shall reflect at the paper's conclusion upon methodological and theoretical issues suggested by
our analysis.

Previous researchers (Hadaway and Roof, 1978; Hadaway, 1978)
have taken note of problems in CCR's analysis of the relationship

---

*The data used in this chapter were made available through the
Inter-University Consortium for Social and Political Research. The
authors are solely responsible for analysis and interpretation.

between religiosity measures of indicators of quality of life. Hadaway, for example, in a reanalysis of CCR's data, discovered that, due to a coding error, Campbell et al. reached incorrect conclusions concerning the religiosity-well-being relationship. Whereas the CCR found this relationship to be negative, Hadaway's reanalysis shows that the relationship between religious-mindedness and well-being is actually positive (as is the case with religious-mindedness and personal competence).

As our own analysis will show, these problems are only symptomatic of a broader conceptual difficulty contained within fundamental assumptions the study makes concerning religiosity and its relationship with personal well-being indicators. We also believe the study's findings, when subjected to a more refined analysis, have implications for assumptions basic to functional theory in the sociology of religion. We have elsewhere, for example, examined the implications for deprivation-compensation theory inherent in a reanalysis of CCR's data (McNamara and St. George, 1978).

THE RELIGIOUS FACTOR IN CCR

CCR's questionnaire contained the following eight religiosity items:
1. Importance of having a strong religious faith (as one of several "domain satisfactions").
2. Religion as an area of life yielding satisfaction or dissatisfaction (each measured by a 7-point scale).
3. Religious preference: Protestant, Roman Catholic, Jewish, or something else (and, if Protestant, what church or denomination).
4. Frequency of attendance at religious services over the past year.
5. How religious-minded respondent is (from very to not at all on a 5-point scale).
6. Frequency of attendance, when growing up, at Sunday school or religious instruction classes (regularly to never on a 4-point scale).
7. Membership in a church or synagogue.
8. Membership in a church (synagogue)-connected group.

The authors point out that the first item in the above list (importance of having a strong religious faith) ranks fourth among the eighteen domains of life experience in the proportion of persons naming it as one of the two most important domains (a happy marriage, good family life, and good health outrank it, in that order). (The eighteen domains they included were marriage, family life, health, neighborhood, friendships, housework, job, life in the United States, city or county, nonwork, housing, usefulness of education, standard of living, amount of education, savings, religion, our national government, and organizations you belong to. The respondent was asked for both importance of and

satisfaction/dissatisfaction with each.) In predicting life-
satisfaction (an overall summary measure), the importance of religious faith ranks ninth after health, marriage, family life,
national government, friendship, housing, job, and community
(Campbell et al., 1976: Tables 3-4 and 3-5, pp. 84-85, contain
complete listings of these domains, which are central concepts in
CCR's research). Shades of the familiar "deprivation theory"
arise when the authors tell us that
    "having a strong religious faith" is more important to
    women than men, to older people rather than younger, to
    those with less rather than more formal education, and by
    those with low incomes rather than those better off
    financially (p. 88).

    Religion receives little attention subsequently until Chapter
10, Marriage and Family Life. Only how often the respondent
attended religious services as a child is entered along with three
other "early circumstances" (size of home town, whether one grew
up in a "broken home," and father's education) in predicting
satisfaction with marriage. None of these four related "in a
very significant way to satisfaction with marriage" (pp. 324-325).

    The following chapter, Personal Resources and Personal Compe-
tence, gives religiosity more consideration. The authors conceptualize personal competence as depending upon one's command of a
battery of "personal resources." These are divided into three
categories: (1) ascribed resources, which include intelligence,
health, attractiveness (intelligence and attractiveness as assessed
by the interviewer); (2) achieved resources, embracing family
income, respondent's income, and education; (3) other current
resources, that is, time, number of friends, and religious faith.
Religious faith is indicated by the item, "In general, how religious-
minded would you say you are?" (p. 355)

    Here, in our opinion, the authors candidly let the cat out of
the bag. They admit that "our investment in the domain of personal
religiosity was cursory;" then, after noting that this variable
shows some correlation "in the expected direction with other items
like childhood religious instruction" and religious service attendance, they affirm that religious-mindedness "seems to strike
closest to what one would think of as religious faith" (p. 355).
Therefore, they employ it as the sole indicator of religiosity
as a personal resource. Its performance is less than impressive.
It has little impact on the sense of personal competence; in fact,
what small association appears is in a negative direction (though
compare Hadaway's 1978 correction noted previously). The authors'
comment rings once again the bell of deprivation theory:
    It seems most probable that people whose life situa-
    tions are, for other reasons, relatively unfortunate,
    and who lack therefore even average feelings of well-
    being, may be more disposed to cling to religious

231

values as a compensatory resource (p. 370).

RELIGIOSITY AND LIFE SATISFACTION

Entertaining the bias of the sociologist of religion that religiosity deserves better treatment than CCR accorded it, we focused on ways of discovering whether religious-mindedness and one's attendance at religious instructions as a child were indeed the best predictors of the quality of life index scores.

We devised the following analytical strategies: first, we ran zero-order correlations of each of the eight religiosity indicators against the principal dependent variables utilized in the study. Perhaps the most important finding is that, with regard to CCR's central dependent variable, the Index of Well-Being, satisfaction from religion ranks first. Table 1 ranks religiosity indicators according to their zero-order strength on several dependent variables central to the study. In three of the five variables listed, satisfaction from religion ranks first among the eight. In two of the five variables, satisfaction with family life and the index of general affect, the correlations (.27 and .24) are substantial relative to the others expressed. Religious-mindedness makes a relatively poor showing. It ranks among the top four in only one of the five dependent variables; in fact, it exhibits a sharp contrast in strength (.14 vs. .27) with the satisfaction from religion variable. Controlling for other relevant variables, such as SES, age, and marital status, diminishes the zero-order correlations slightly, but the rank-order remains unchanged. (We have chosen to omit these partial correlations because of space considerations and our judgment that their presentation would add little to the substantive conclusions of our research.)

Having seen that satisfaction from religion is a more important predictor than the CCR authors allow, we then explored the possibility that satisfaction from religion is part of a set of religiosity variables and that this set correlates highly with two sets of principal dependent variables, the Index of Well-Being and Index of Personal Competence. These two sets form a major focus of CCR's study. The procedure of canonical correlation is designed to facilitate such analysis and to determine further whether or not religious satisfaction is relatively independent of other religiosity indicators as a predictor of the dependent variables in question. Table 2 presents these results.

Considering first the Index of Well-Being, we see that one factor was extracted which explains six percent of the variance in the relationship of the independent and dependent variables. Although this figure is relatively low (accepting a correlation of .30 as a minimum level of significance), the important feature is the pattern of loadings between the two sets of variables. Here we clearly see that, with regard to the independent variable set,

TABLE 1

ZERO-ORDER RANKINGS OF RELIGIOSITY MEASURES ACCORDING TO SELECTED
INDEPENDENT VARIABLES

Dependent Variable	Relig. Item[1]	Ranked Zero-Order Correlations
Life-Satisfaction Index	(4)	.18
	(3)	.17
	(5)	.17
	(2)	-.15
Index of Satisfaction with Marriage	(1)	.15
	(4)	.13
	(3)	.13
	(5)	.13
Satisfaction with Family Life	(1)	.27
	(3)	.21
	(7)	.14
	(4)	.14
Index of Personal Competence	(6)	.10
	(4)	.08
	(5)	.08
	(2)	.07
Index of General Affect	(1)	.24
	(5)	.22
	(3)	.20
	(4)	.19

1 Religiosity Items:
   (1) Satisfaction from religion
   (2) Dissatisfaction from religion
   (3) Importance of Strong Religious Faith
   (4) Frequency of Church Attendance
   (5) Church Membership
   (6) Church Group Membership
   (7) Religious-mindedness of R
   (8) Frequency of Religious Instruction in Years Growing Up

233

TABLE 2

CANONICAL CORRELATIONS

1. Religiosity Measures with Index of Well-Being

Independent Variable List	Loadings: Factor I
Belong to a church....................................	.10
Belong to a church group.............................	.23
Frequency of church attendance	.11
How religious-minded are you	.12
Frequency of religious instruction	.13
How important religious faith is	.11
Satisfaction from religion...........................	.89

Dependent Variable List (components of Index of Well-Being)

Life interesting/boring	.06
Enjoyable/miserable	.07
Worthwhile/useless	.22
Friendly/lonely.....................................	.23
Full/empty	.04
Hopeful/discouraging	.01
Rewarding/disappointing	.43
Challenging/frustrating	.28
Satisfaction with life as a whole	.10

Canonical Correlation: .27 sig. .001

2. Religiosity Measures with Index of Personal Competence

Independent Variable List	Loadings: Factor I
Belong to a church	.72
Belong to a church group	.29
Frequency of church attendance	.07
How religious-minded is R	.12
Frequency of religious instruction..................	.19
How important is religious faith	.02
Satisfaction with religion	.04

Dependent Variable List (components of Personal Competence Index)

Confidence in Life...................................	.41
Plan Life/Leave to Luck	.88
Can Carry out Plans	.03
Can R Run own Life	.28

Canonical Correlation=   .17 sig. .000

234

only satisfaction from religion has a significantly high loading (.89) and that this is paired with the only variable in the dependent set with a comparatively high loading, i.e., whether life is rewarding or disappointing (.43). No other factors were extracted in the canonical analysis; that is, no other unique sets of independent and dependent variables could be found that explained any but an insignificant amount of variance. Therefore, once the independent influence of religious satisfaction and rewarding/ disappointing is partialed out, no other unique sets of independent-dependent variables could be extracted.

We conclude, at this point, that even our strongest indicator, satisfaction from religion, relates to only one component of the Index of Well-Being and not very strongly at that. We note in passing that CCR's favored indicator, how religious-minded are you, is not salient by itself nor in combination with other religiosity variables. We are at a loss to explain why only this particular dependent variable (life as rewarding/disappointing) correlates with satisfaction from religion.

If we turn our attention to personal competence as the dependent variable, we see that only one canonical factor was extracted which explains a mere three percent of the variance. We cannot, then, place much confidence in the canonical loadings of this factor. With this caveat in mind, we observe that the unique set which emerges consists of the independent variable, belonging to a church, and the dependent variable, "plan life or leave it to luck"(Table 2). Here neither satisfaction from religion nor religious-mindedness has significant loadings.

The analysis thus far opens wide the possibility that satisfaction from religion is part of a larger set of satisfaction measures. When these are taken into account, satisfaction from religion may diminish in predictive power. To test this, we performed a multiple classification analysis using personal competence as the dependent variable and all of CCR's measures of domain satisfaction as independent variables. We found, first, that no one satisfaction measure stands out above the rest in predictive power. The beta weights of the various domain satisfaction measures ranged from .04 to .17. Satisfaction from religion ranks in the lower one-third of domain satisfactions. Given the fact that the various domain satisfaction items taken together explain only seven percent of the variance in predicting personal competence, the strong possibility of interaction effects remains. The next analytical step (beyond the scope of this paper) is a systematic search for such interaction effects with satisfaction from religion as the central variable.

LIMITATIONS OF THE CCR RESEARCH

To return to our earlier point, does religion function as a

235

compensatory resource in the respondents' sense of well-being? We feel that CCR has not thoroughly explored this issue with the data at hand. Religiosity, we recall, received "cursory treatment." As stated above, we have elsewhere (McNamara and St. George, 1978) pointed out that religiosity, as measured in CCR, seems to function as a "value-added" phenomenon in the sense that it enhances the subjective well-being of those who already are status-advantaged, i.e., the married, the financially secure, or, in relationships such as that between satisfaction and family income where the "deprived" seem "helped" by religion, the non-deprived are "comforted even more." Those who are "deprived" according to traditional measures remain so independently of how much they esteem or practice their religion.

Other critics of social indicators and quality of life research (e.g., Phillips, 1978) have questioned the validity of the findings from the standpoint of possible interviewer-respondent interaction effects. We are inclined, however, to examine other aspects of the validity issue. We have two main concerns: First, the gross imprecision of the empirical referents used to define quality of life. For instance, asking respondents whether their lives are full, empty, or somewhere in between, asked in conjunction with other similarly ambiguous and event-(or mood-) dependent questions seems to beg for one of two outcomes: (a) a mood/event response set, such as "everything is enjoyable, worthwhile, friendly, full, and hopeful;" or (b) a tendency to check the "neutral" category for all items.

Second, including religiosity with other quality of life measures that are qualitatively different but quantitatively measured on the same scale seriously jeopardizes the validity of the findings. For example, Andrews and Withey's (1976) "delightful-terrible" scale, a seven-point scale used to measure affective evaluations of an individual's quality of life, is a good example of this problem. Under this one scale, respondents are asked to evaluate how they feel about their religious faith immediately after being asked about their housework, the weather, their car, and how safe they feel in their neighborhood. They are subsequently asked about their job, pay and fringe benefits, how much fun they are having, schools in the area, and the entertainment they get from television and other media. This juxtaposition relegates religion to one more everyday problem or concern, and, in effect, trivializes it by inferring that the respondent can as readily rate his/her religion as the family car. The very format of the question is tantamount to invalidating religiosity (as measured) as an indicator of spiritual well-being. In neither CCR nor Andrews and Withey (1976) is the respondent invited to reflect in any depth on how central his or her religious practices and beliefs are to life as a whole.

Chapter 19

SOCIAL CORRELATES OF SPIRITUAL MATURITY AMONG

AMONG NORTH AMERICAN MENNONITES*

J. Howard Kauffman

The purpose of this paper is (1) to report on the development
and use of a "Religious Life Scale" as a composite measure of religiosity or, more particularly, "spiritual maturity," (2) to examine
the relationships between spiritual maturity and a number of independent and dependent variables potentially related to it, and (3)
to note whether such relationships discovered within a Mennonite
population differ in significant ways from reported findings on
other populations.

CONCEPTUALIZATION

A considerable variety of concepts has been introduced by social
scientists in their studies of the social and cultural aspects of
religion. Without arguing the merits of one definition rather than
another, it may be helpful to clarify how concepts are defined for
use in this study.

"Religion" is viewed as those beliefs and behaviors which pertain
to supernatural (Vernon, 1962). In the sociological literature,
"religion" refers to a particular set of beliefs and practices which
identifies a faith (Catholic, Protestant, Jewish) or denomination
(Roman Catholic, Baptist, Mormon). A person's religion is, therefore, normally identified in terms of his denominational affiliation.

"Religiosity," now widely used in the sociology of religion,
refers to the degree to which religious beliefs, attitudes, and
behaviors permeate the life of an individual (Finner, 1970;
Himmelfarb, 1975). It implies "religiousness," but the latter is
awkward and seldom appears in sociological literature. The obvious

---

*This paper is reprinted with minor adaptations from Sociological
Analysis, vol. 40, no. 1, Spring 1979.

assumption is that some persons are more religious than others. Therefore, by using an appropriate measure, persons can be ordered along a scale or continuum of religiosity. Such measurement is necessary, of course, if we are to discover what factors are related to religiosity as the dependent variable; that is, to discover answers to the question of what kinds of persons are more religious than others. It also permits the study of religiosity as the independent variable; that is, to observe how differences in religiosity affect variations in other aspects of life and thought. The utilization of a valid measure of religiosity thus becomes an essential ingredient in any attempt to discover the life situations that affect people's religiosity or to observe how religiosity affects their attitudes and behavior in other areas of life.

A variety of parallel terms have been used to refer to religiosity, each suggesting a slightly different orientation to the concepts of religion or religiosity. Lenski (1961) spoke of "religious orientations" and (1953) "religious interests." Stark and Glock (1968) and several others prefer "religious commitment." Still others use "religious involvement" (Faulkner and DeJong, 1966; Himmelfarb, 1975) and "religious intensity" (Campbell and Magill, 1968). King and Hunt (1969, 1975a) get along merely with "religion" and "religious dimensions." Moberg and Brusek (1978) introduced "spiritual well-being" as a related concept. The concept of "spiritual maturity" introduced later in this paper is close to this.

THE DIMENSIONS OF RELIGIOSITY

It is generally agreed that religiosity contains a number of aspects or "dimensions." Lenski operationalized two dimensions of religious group involvement: (1) associational involvement, measured in terms of church attendance, and (2) communal involvement, measured in terms of the degree to which the primary relationships of an individual are limited to persons of his own religious group. He also derived scales to measure two religious orientations: (1) doctrinal orthodoxy, that is, assent to the prescribed doctrines of the respondent's church, and (2) devotionalism, which is the individual's pattern of relationship to God, particularly through the practice of prayer.

The dimensions of religious commitment offered by Stark and Glock (1968) have been widely utilized by other investigators. Their five primary dimensions are:
(1) Belief -- adherence to the church's doctrines.
(2) Religious Practices -- acts of worship and devotion, subdivided into:
   (a) Ritual -- church attendance and table grace.
   (b) Devotional -- private prayer and Bible study.
(3) Religious experiences -- feelings or sensations of being in relationship with God or supernatural beings.

(4) Religious knowledge -- information about the Bible, church history, and church rites and traditions.
(5) Consequences -- the effects of religious belief, practice, experience, and knowledge in persons' day-to-day lives.

In regard to the "consequences" dimensions, Stark and Glock (1968: 16) indicate that "it is not entirely clear the extent to which religious consequences are a part of religious commitment or simply follow from it." They, therefore, do not include it in their further analyses of data.

Their analysis also includes four secondary dimensions:
(1) Particularism -- belief that one's own religion is the only right one.
(2) Ethicalism -- belief in certain ethical principles.
(3) Communal involvement -- percentage of the respondent's organizational memberships that are religious.
(4) Friendship dimension -- percentage of close friendships that are within the same congregation.

Nine of the above dimensions were measured by scales which, when intercorrelated, revealed that ethicalism was unrelated to the other dimensions.

The number of dimensions that can validly be included in a measure of religiosity has been a matter of much debate. Most investigators accept the validity of the belief, ritual, devotional, and experience dimensions and have produced data which empirically support such conclusions. Beyond this there is much disagreement.

The religious knowledge dimension has been called into serious question. Stark and Glock (1968) report that intercorrelation coefficients were lower for knowledge than for the other primary dimensions. They point out that knowledge and belief can be expected to be positively associated, but that is not necessarily so. One can have knowledge with little belief, or belief with little knowledge (Nudelman, 1971). Himmelfarb's (1975) results led him to reject knowledge as a dimension of religious involvement. Weigert and Thomas (1974) found the knowledge dimension to have little relationship to the other dimensions. Faulkner and DeJong (1966) obtained a significant correlation between their "intellectual" (knowledge) scale and the other four scales making up their "5-D" religiosity scales. Others who have used the 5-D scales have obtained similar results (Clayton and Gladden, 1974; Ruppel, 1969). However, the validity of the intellectual dimension of the 5-D scales has been questioned (Weigert and Thomas, 1969; Gibbs and Crader, 1970).

Actually, only one of the four items comprising the intellectual scale used by Faulkner and DeJong (1966) appears to measure knowledge.

The item asked the respondent to identify the names of the four Gospels. The other three items asked for the respondent's belief about the story of creation, about miracles, and about "religious truth." It is interesting to note that in Clayton and Gladden's (1974) use of this subscale, no significant relationship was obtained between the "Books of the Bible" item and the other religiosity items, but significant loadings on the religiosity factors were obtained for these three "belief" items.

Reporting on more recent research, DeJong, Faulkner, and Warland (1976) find that religious knowledge and social consequences appear to be totally separate dimensions that are essentially unrelated to the other dimensions investigated. They conclude that the remaining dimensions (beliefs, experience, and religious practices) constitute a "generic religiosity factor" of which these can be considered sub-dimensions.

There is even less support for including the "consequence" dimension as a component of religiosity. The consequences or effects of religiosity on other dimensions of people's lives have usually been operationalized in terms of political participation, social activism, social prejudice, and other ethical concerns. Results have been mixed, but generally very low correlations have been produced between these consequences and the other measures of religiosity (Finner and Gamache, 1969; Clayton and Gladden, 1974).

Several attempts have been made (Hoge, 1972; King, 1967) to operationalize Gordon Allport's concepts of "intrinsic religion" and "extrinsic religion." As Hoge points out, the results have been "troubled by conceptual diffuseness and questionable scale validity." King and Hunt (1969) did not succeed in factoring out a useable intrinsic-extrinsic dimension and concluded that the extrinsic dimension (which correlated positively with other religiosity dimensions) is doubtful as a measure of religiosity.

"Salience" -- the importance which persons attach to their church membership and participation -- has been investigated as a variable intervening between orthodoxy (as well as other dimensions of religiosity) and consequential variables (Bahr et al., 1971; Gibbs, Mueller and Wood, 1973; Roof and Perkins, 1975). The findings indicate that the relationship between religiosity and various dependent consequential variables may hold only for those who attach high importance to their church involvement and not for those who see their church participation as of less importance.

SOURCE OF DATA

In 1972 the writer and his colleague, Leland Harder, were employed to conduct a survey of the membership of five Mennonite and Brethren in Christ denominations. Data were collected by use of a lengthy questionnaire completed by 3,591 members of 174 congregations. The two-stage systematic random sample was drawn from all congregations in the United States and Canada affiliated with the five cooperating churches. Approximately 70% of the target sample members in the 174 participating congregations returned a completed questionnaire. The findings reported in this paper are for the entire sample and include certain analyses not in the published monograph (Kauffman and Harder, 1975; see its appendix for relevant details of methodology). The five cooperating denominations, together with their total U.S.A. and Canadian membership and the number of respondents in the sample for each, as are follows:

Denomination	Membership	Sample
Mennonite Church	89,273	1,202
General Conference Mennonite Church	55,623	614
Mennonite Brethren Church	31,327	712
Brethren in Christ Church	10,589	619
Evangelical Mennonite Church	2,950	444

Several scales measuring dimensions of religiosity were constructed, but no composite scale was introduced in the earlier report. This paper introduces a new composite scale and presents the results on the Mennonite population for purposes of comparison with the findings of other investigators referred to in the previous section.

Scales designed to measure the following dimensions of religiosity were constructed (see Kauffman and Harder, 1975, for information on the construction and testing of each):
(1) General Orthodoxy: Belief in God, Jesus as Son of God, Jesus' resurrection, Biblical miracles, life beyond death, Christ's return to earth, and Satan as a personal devil.
(2) Devotionalism: Practice of private Bible reading and prayer, participation in family worship, feeling of closeness to God.
(3) Associationalism (church participation): Attendance at Sunday services, Sunday School, and week-day services; importance of church participation, and holding leadership positions.
(4) Bible Knowledge: A test on eight Bible characters and events.
(5) Religious Experience: A 14-item measure of the extent to which the respondent feels he has experienced the presence and ministrations of God, Jesus and the Holy Spirit; has had other holy experiences, and has been influenced by the devil.
(6) Communalism: The respondent has always been a member of the same denomination, his close friends and parents are of the same denomination, he favors marriage within the same church, and has a sense of belonging, loyalty, and satisfaction with his own church.

This dimension may actually be peripheral rather than central to
religiosity.
(7) Evangelism (witness): Speaking to others about the Christian
faith and inviting non-Christians to worship services.

Several scales measuring attitudes toward social and ethical
issues were also derived, but we view these "consequences" as
dependent variables in relation to religiosity rather than components of religiosity.

Table 1. Intercorrelations of Religiosity Scales

| Scales | Scales as at left | | | | | | | | |
	2	3	4	5	6	7	Sum	$\bar{X}$	Rank
1. Devotionalism	.534	.553	.434	.376	.291	.265	2.453	.409	1
2. Associationalism		.461	.310	.280	.277	.331	2.193	.365	2
3. Evangelism			.458	.284	.189	.191	2.136	.356	3
4. Religious Experience				.375	.180	.070	1.827	.304	4
5. General Orthodoxy					.153	.068	1.536	.256	5
6. Communalism						.114	1.204	.201	6
7. Bible Knowledge							1.039	.173	7

A test of the interrelationship of these dimensions of religiosity
is given in Table 1. All of the Pearsonian coefficients of correlation are positive and statistically significant, although several
of the Bible Knowledge coefficients are barely significant. The
seven scales are listed in the order of the size of the average of
the coefficients. The Devotionalism scale appears to be the strongest measure of religiosity for this population, with Associationalism second. The Bible Knowledge scale is weakest, and several
of its coefficients are so small as to suggest that knowledge is
an independent variable and, therefore, not a valid measure of
religiosity. This conclusion corroborates the findings of other
studies reported earlier.

The fact that the belief dimension (Orthodoxy) ranked fifth may
reflect the tendency of Mennonites to place church participation and
personal piety ahead of a creedal or doctrinal emphasis. There may
also be a statistical factor operating; since over 90% of the respondents took the most orthodox position on most of the orthodoxy
items, the distribution is skewed to one end of the scale, resulting
in a minimum of variance in scale scores. This may cause the

Orthodoxy scale to discriminate less than if the scores were more widely dispersed.

DIMENSIONALITY

There has been much debate on the question of whether religiosity is unidimensional or multidimensional. Some investigators (Stark and Glock, 1968; Morton King, 1967; Campbell and Magill, 1968; Weigert and Thomas, 1974) have stressed the independence among the several dimensions of religiosity, hence viewing religiosity as multidimensional. Others (Gibbs and Crader, 1970; Clayton and Gladden, 1974) have obtained higher correlations among the dimensional scales and therefore question the assumption of multidimensionality. When factor analysis has been applied to a large number of religiosity items, the tendency is for at least two factors to emerge, thus suggesting multidimensionality. When primary dimensional scales are intercorrelated, rarely have any coefficients as large as .7 been obtained. Most coefficients range from .2 to .5, thus indicating that the dimensions are not all measuring the same thing, that is, religiosity is unidimensional. On the other hand, independence cannot be claimed if coefficients of this size are obtained, since some interrelatedness or interdependence must be inferred. Indeed, if the intercorrelations among the dimensional scales were quite low, suggesting strong independence, then their validity as components of religiosity would have to be called into question. Too much independence means no relatedness.

We are, therefore, left with a dilemma in respect to the question of dimensionality. Our empirical measures of the logical dimensions of religiosity do not indicate sufficiently high relatedness to affirm unidimensionality, and if they show some relatedness, as they should to be valid dimensions, we cannot claim strong multidimensionality. A good measure of religiosity will not be either strongly multidimensional nor strongly unidimensional. It will include items representing several of the stronger dimensions and will exclude items representing dimensions that are only weakly related to the stronger dimensions.

The purpose of measuring religiosity, of course, is to study its relationship to the various dependent and independent variables which are of interest to the investigator. The particular measure or measures to be used will be determined by the nature of the research problem and the inclinations of the researcher. There are at least three possibilities: (1) Use several scales, each measuring a valid dimension of religiosity. This recognizes the dimensions as partially unique and, therefore, likely to yield different coefficients of correlation with the respective dependent and independent variables. The disadvantage is that the data analysis becomes more complicated due to the larger volume of statistics, and it is more difficult to arrive at conclusions about religiosity as a unitary concept. (2) Use a single-dimension scale, the one that measures that dimension of religiosity which is most valid for the research purpose at hand. This simplifies the analysis, but it leaves open the question of whether a single dimension, however good, is an adequate measure of religiosity. (3) Use a composite scale made up of items representing each of several valid dimensions of religiosity. This simplifies the data analysis, especially if a large number of dependent or independent variables are to be included. Although the separate contribution of each of the several dimensions is lost, as a single measure of religiosity it should be better than any one of the dimensional scales used alone.

A RELIGIOUS LIFE SCALE

For purposes of this study, it seemed advantageous to use a composite scale. Consequently fourteen items representing the four dimensions of religiosity that rated highest in Table 1 were combined into one scale. The items and responses are listed in the Appendix.

Calling this Religious Life Scale a measure of "spiritual maturity" requires some explanation. Perhaps "Religiosity Scale" would have sufficed. However, the components of the scale express a considerable emphasis on the spiritual aspect of life. The scale is heavy on personal piety and on a sense of the transcendent as contrasted with the more social dimensions of religious expression. Moberg (1967a) stressed the spiritual component of religiousness as the very essence of the religious life, and urged sociologists of religion to give more attention to this element in efforts to operationalize religiosity. He also noted that the Biblical view of man stresses his spiritual nature. Likewise Gordon Zahn (1970) stressed the importance of the depth and intensity of the "inner religious commitment" in identifying religiosity. The Religious Life Scale is an attempt to incorporate more of these ideas.

It should be clear that the scale, which is here called a measure of "spiritual maturity," is only one measure of religiosity among others that have been constructed by researchers. The content of each measure differs somewhat from the others. In this case a "belief" dimension is not included, and certain new items are introduced. It should also be noted that "spiritual maturity" is not to be equated with "spiritual well-being" as set forth by Moberg and Brusek (1978), although the scale is, both conceptually and operationally, probably closer to a measure of spiritual well-being than other measures reported in the literature.

A number of things are implicit in the content of the Religious Life Scale. Most religious bodies have certain expectations of their members. They are admonished from pulpit and printed page to "bring forth the fruits of the Spirit" in their daily lives.

244

Christian denominations expect their members to pray, study the
Bible, attend services, contribute to offerings, provide leadership
in church programs in line with their abilities, witness to their
faith, look to God for help, and achieve some sense of spiritual
growth as the years go by. In addition, a church member should
not be ridden with doubts with respect to the tenets of his faith,
and he should be guided by some spiritual goal or purpose in life.
It is not intended here to argue the validity of these churchly
expectations, but rather to assert that they are commonly proclaimed
by those who represent the values and teachings of the churches.
The rigor with which these elements of spiritual growth and maturity
are proclaimed will vary, of course, from one religious body to
another.

The Religious Life Scale stresses doing and feeling more than
believing or knowing. That is, it is a measure of the more manifest
aspects of religion -- how one expresses his religion (by praying,
attending, serving, giving, witnessing), as contrasted with the more
covert belief dimension. No belief (Orthodoxy) items are included
in the scale. This may appear to be a weakness to those investigators who have found the belief dimension to rate high among the
dimensions of religiosity. For Mennonites, who stress discipleship
and religious practices rather than creed, this is a less serious
omission. It also recognizes the relatively low variance on the
Orthodoxy scale that was obtained from the Mennonite population.
(Gaede, 1976, has constructed and tested a causal model for belief-
orthodoxy on the Mennonite data set on which this paper is based.
He included several variables which are not introduced in this
paper.)

Table 2 contains the results of a factor analysis of the Religious
Life Scale. The analysis yielded three factors with eigenvalues
over 1.00. The table gives the factor loadings for the three
factors before and after rotation. The termination of the ortho-
gonal factor rotation indicates that Factor 1 has its principal
loadings on the devotional items, the witness item, and several of
the religious experience items.Factor 2 loads principally on the
associationalism items and the group worship item (which is really
a form of association). Factor 3 loads most heavily on the religious experience items. Several items appear to be "complex
variables," that is, they tend to have substantial loadings on
two or more factors. This suggests an interrelatedness between
the dimensions (factors) that comprise the scale.

Table 2. Factor Loadings for Unrotated and Varimax Rotated Matrices of Items in the Religious Life Scale

Scale Items*	Unrotated Factors**			Rotated Factors***		
	1	2	3	1	2	3
Devotionalism:						
1. Bible study	.74	-.15	.05	.55	.49	
2. Private prayer	.69	-.18	-.13	.64	.34	
3. Group worship	.58	-.12	.22	.33	.53	
4. Prayer re temptation	.65	-.21	-.28	.71		
5. Prayer re decisions	.73	-.09	-.27	.73		
Associationalism:						
6. Attendance	.55	-.18	.46		.71	
7. Giving	.44	.06	.09	.25	.29	
8. Readiness to serve	.63	-.10	.28	.32	.59	
Evangelism:						
9. Witness	.62	.05	-.10	.51	.25	.27
Religious Experiences:						
10. Closeness to God	.76	.15	-.16	.62	.25	.41
11. Discouragement	.30	.58	.05			.65
12. Doubts	.48	.41	.10			.57
13. Progress	.66	.08	-.01	.48	.33	.32
14. Purpose in life	.61	.12	-.05	.45	.26	.34

*Listed in the order they appear in the Appendix.
**Principal factor with iterations.
***To highlight the principal loadings, only loadings of .25 and over are shown.

SPIRITUAL MATURITY AS THE DEPENDENT VARIABLE

For the 3,350 respondents who answered all the scale items, the scores on the Religious Life Scale ranged from a low of four to a high of 58 within possible limits of zero and 59. The mean score was 39.2. The correlations between spiritual maturity and several independent variables are given in Table 3. For the sake of comparison, the correlations for the separate dimensions of religiosity are also given. Since the Pearsonian coefficients are based on assumptions of linearity in the related variables, it was necessary to check for non-linearity by examining cross-tabulations of the respective variables.

In respect to the age of respondents, religiosity increases with increasing age. To check for non-linearity, the respondents

Table 3. Correlations Between Religiosity Scales and Independent Variables

Independent variables	Religiosity Scales					
	Religious Life	Devotion-alism	Associa-tionalism	Evang-elism	Religious Exper'nce	General Orthodoxy
1. Age	.37	.34	.16	.39	.12	.19
2. Sex (females higher)	.06**	.08	-.03	-.04	-.04	.09
3. Residence (urban higher)	-.05	-.06	-.10	.03	-.05	-.15
4. Socio-economic status	.06	-.01*	.17	.08	-.07	-.20
5. Education	.01*	-.04	.11	.04	-.05	-.20
6. Income	-.06	-.11	.03*	-.06	-.04	-.06
7. Occupation (ranked)	.15	.08	.21	.16	-.02*	-.11

*Not significant at the .05 level.
**Coefficients for sex are Tau C. All others are Pearsonian r.

were classed into four age groups: 13-19, 20-29, 30-49, and 50 years and over. The oldest group scored highest on all scales except Associationalism, where the 30-49 group was highest. The teenagers were lowest on Religious Life, Devotionalism, and Associationalism, and the 20-29 group was lowest on the other dimensions. The differences between the two younger age groups were quite small on most items and dimensions. In general, the relationship between age and religiosity measures is strongly positive. Various studies (Allport, 1961; Argyle, 1959; Glock, Ringer, and Babbie, 1967) have concluded that religious interests and commitment tend to be lowest among persons between the late teens and middle 20's, after which there is a gradual rise throughout the life span. Our findings corroborate these conclusions on most dimensions, but not all. As indicated in the Lutheran study (Strommen et al., 1972), the low points on religiosity scales do not all appear in the same age group. This points up the need for looking at a variety of religiosity items and dimensions to test the impact of age on religious commitment.

A composite scale will not reveal the variety of ways in which age is related to different dimensions of religiosity.

Mennonite males and females differed very little on spiritual maturity. On the composite scale and the Devotionalism and Orthodoxy dimensions, the females rated higher. On the other three dimensions, the males scored very slightly higher as indicated by the negative coefficients, which were just barely large enough to be statistically significant. A number of studies have demonstrated that women score slightly higher than men on measures of religiosity (Glock, Ringer, and Babbie, 1967; Kersten, 1970; Campbell and Magill, 1968). Where significant differences appear, women almost always rate highest. Exceptions were noted by Campbell and Fukuyama (1970), who found in a sample of United Church of Christ members that men tended in larger proportions to get into positions of leadership in the churches, and by Campolo (1971), studying American Baptists, who found larger proportions of men than women attending worship services and other church services or meetings. Mennonites apparently also conform to these exceptions.

The findings on residence indicate that, with reference to the linear correlations in Table 3, urban respondents score slightly lower than rural respondents on all scales except Evangelism. This supports (albeit rather weakly) the hypothesis that urbanization results in secularization or a decline in religious commitment and involvement. A look at the cross-tabulations, however, provides a slightly different interpretation. The respondents were ranked in four classes of increasing urbanity and decreasing rurality: rural farm, rural nonfarm, small city, and large city. Those living in the large cities scored lowest on the composite scale and the Devotionalism, Associationalism, and Orthodoxy scales. However, the rural farm respondents rated lowest on the Religious Experience and Evangelism scales. The rural farm group scored highest only on the Orthodoxy scale and shared highest scores with the rural nonfarm group on the Devotionalism scale. The middle groups achieved the highest scores on four of the six measures. Thus a curvilinear distribution on the residence variable is most evident. We conclude that the gradual shift of the Mennonite population from rural farm to rural nonfarm and small city residence does not result in loss of religiosity. Only the 20% who live in the larger cities evidence a slight decline in religiosity.

Demerath's (1965) summary of research on the relation between social class and religiosity indicates that positive and linear relationships have been observed between social class and church membership, attendance, and involvement in religious organizations. Only in large cities does it appear that there is a slight dropoff in religiosity, as measured by these variables, in the upper class. Otherwise, the higher the class, the higher the religious involvement. But Demerath points out that these are measures of "Churchlike Religiosity" and that certain other "Sectlike Religiosity" measures might show quite a different picture. Indeed, sectlike religiosity was found to be negatively related to social class. Therefore, the relation between socio-economic status and religiosity depends considerably on what measures are being used by the investigator.

The Mennonite data indicate that socio-economic status (a scale derived by combining the variables of education, income, and occupational rank) has a slight positive correlation (.06) with the composite Religious Life scale. But a review of the separate dimensions tells a fuller story. Socio-economic status (SES) is related to Associationalism by a coefficient of .17 but to Orthodoxy by -.20. This confirms other findings that the lower class tends to retain more conservative beliefs but to be less involved in the organizational activities of the church as an institution. From the linear correlation (-.01), it would appear that social class bears no relation to devotional practices.

However, a scrutiny of the cross-tabulations of SES and religiosity indicates a non-linear pattern. The respondents were placed into four status categories: upper, upper middle, lower middle, and lower. The upper class scored highest on none of the scales and was lowest on Devotionalism, Orthodoxy, and Religious Experience. The upper middle group was highest on Associationalism (in line with Demerath's observations), Evangelism, and the composite Religious Life scale; it was lowest on none of the scales. The lower middle group was highest on none of the scales and was lowest on the composite and Evangelism scales. The lower class was highest on Devotionalism, Orthodoxy, and Religious Experience scales (corroborating Demerath's theory); it was lowest on Associationalism. These findings further underscore the necessity of looking for non-linearity in connection with variable intercorrelations, particularly when religiosity is being analyzed as the dependent variable.

The last three rows of coefficients in Table 3 permit a separate examination of the three components of SES: education, income, and occupation. Income has the most consistent relationship to religiosity measures, low negative coefficients emerging for nearly all scales. Both education and occupation appear to affect different religiosity dimensions in different ways. Both are substantially related negatively to orthodoxy and positively to associationalism. Of the three variables, education appears to produce the most variation in religiosity scores.

The relation of spiritual maturity to several other background variables was also investigated. No significant relationship was observed between spiritual maturity scores and the age of conversion and of baptism. (The median age at conversion was 13.8 years and at baptism, 14.9.) Likewise, the scores did not differ significantly when respondents were classified according to the rank order of their birth. Those respondents who came into the Mennonite churches from other denominational backgrounds did not differ significantly from those who were never members of another denomination. The clergy scored significantly higher on spiritual maturity than laymen. When type-of-leadership categories of clergy, lay leaders, and non-leaders were observed, a coefficient of association (Tau C) of .29 was obtained. Non-resident members of congregations scored lower than resident members (Tau C = .11). Members of congregations with less than 200 members scored slightly higher than those belonging to congregations with over 200 members.

SPIRITUAL MATURITY AS THE INDEPENDENT VARIABLE

It is not appropriate here to analyze in detail the relationship of spiritual maturity to a large number of dependent variables. Attention will be limited primarily to those dependent variables that have received the attention of other investigators. A further limitation we will impose is to utilize only the composite Religious Life scale in reviewing the relationship of religiosity to the dependent variables.

A number of studies from Kinsey et al. (1948) onward have demonstrated a positive relationship between religiosity and restrictive attitudes toward sexual relations outside of marriage. Unfortunately, most of these did not go beyond the use of church membership and/or attendance as measures of religiosity. Using a composite religiosity scale, Clayton (1971) found that sexual permissiveness was negatively correlated with his composite religiosity scale and three subscales. Cardwell (1969) obtained similar results. For the Mennonite data, a coefficient of association (Tau C = .21) indicated a positive relationship between spiritual maturity and opposition to sexual relationships outside of marriage.

Two recent studies of attitudes toward abortion found low but significant positive relationships between religiosity and opposition to liberalized abortion (Clayton and Tolone, 1973; Finner and Gamache, 1969). A positive coefficient of association (Tau B = .18) between spiritual maturity and opposition to non-therapeutic abortion was obtained for the Mennonite sample.

Cygnar et al. (1977) studied the relationship between religiosity and prejudice toward minority groups, finding that the ritual, knowledge, and orthodoxy dimensions were not related to prejudice. Roof and Perkins (1975) found orthodoxy to be positively related to political conservatism, racism, and anti-Semitic, anti-Catholic and anti-Black social distance scales. Results for Mennonites were similar. The orthodoxy scores were negatively related (r = -.15) to scores on a scale representing favorable attitudes towards other races. Orthodoxy scores were also positively related by a coefficient of .20 to scales measuring anti-Semitic and anti-Catholic attitudes. On the basis of the broader Religious Life composite scale, however, there was no significant relationship between spiritual maturity and racial attitudes. The coefficients of correlation between spiritual maturity scores and the anti-Semitic and anti-Catholic scales were .12 and .13, respectively. It is concluded that religiosity among Mennonites is slightly associated with prejudiced attitudes.

No significant correlation was observed between Mennonite religiosity and degree of political participation, nor did religiosity make any significant differences in church members' attitudes toward government welfare programs to aid the poor. If it is assumed that increased religiosity should make church members more concerned for and favorable toward the poor and minorities, the results of this study are disappointing. The fact that attitudes on these ethical issues are relatively independent of religiosity is further evidence that such attitudes should not be regarded as a dimension of religiosity.

CONCLUSIONS

The results of this investigation point to the following general conclusions:

(1) Religiosity is a broad concept; any attempt to measure it must recognize that it is composed of a number of interrelated dimensions. Only those dimensions should be included whose measures show substantial correlations with other valid dimensions.

(2) A single composite measure of religiosity can be efficient as a device for relating general religiosity to a variety of dependent variables that might be of interest to investigators. However, a composite measure will tend to hide the differential effects of the several separate components of religiosity.

(3) A composite measure of religiosity should certainly include items representing the dimensions of devotionalism, associational-ism (church participation), and religious experience. Probably the dimension of belief-orthodoxy should be included, especially for populations representing the "creedal" churches. This appears to be less necessary for Mennonites and other groups which put less emphasis on creed.

(4) Religious knowledge and ethical consequences do not appear to be valid dimensions of religiosity.

(5) The Mennonite data suggest that "communalism" is weakly related to religiosity and should probably not be used in a composite scale. However, a dimension of "witness" is validated.

(6) The relationships between religiosity and other variables are greatly affected by the particular items included in the com-

251

posite measure of religiosity. A scale including an item on involvement in church organizations will favor middle-aged persons who tend to be more involved than other age groups, probably for reasons of skills and social status. Items on orthodoxy, devotionalism, and religious experience tend to favor lower class persons,while items on associationalism favor high status persons.

(7) The religiosity of individuals varies according to certain background variables. The findings on Mennonites indicate that age exerts the most significant influence on religiosity, with education second when dimensions are observed separately. Socioeconomic status, rural-urban residence, and sex come next in order, but their correlations with religiosity are very low. A correlational model would predict that the most religious Mennonite would be an elderly female with a professional occupation, residing in a rural nonfarm area, and having a low to moderate income. It would not matter how much education she has.

(8) The relation of religiosity to social and ethical "consequences" yields somewhat disappointing results when one takes the subjective position that a religious person should show concern and compassion for the downtrodden, the poor, and the minorities. The apparently independent relationship of religiosity to attitudes favoring these groups continues to be one of the enigmas produced by research on religiosity. Should not those who are more spiritually mature and religiously committed show a greater love and compassion for the ones for whom Christ came to minister?

APPENDIX: THE RELIGIOUS LIFE SCALE

Following each item and its responses are given in order in parentheses (1) the "discriminative power" score of the Item Analysis Test, and (2) the Pearsonian correlation coefficient for the item-to-scale correlations.

A. Devotionalism:

1. How often do you study the Bible privately, seeking to understand it and letting it speak to you? Never, seldom, occasionally, frequently (at least once a week but not daily), daily. (2.0) (.75)

2. Other than at mealtime, how often do you pray to God privately on the average? Several times per day, daily, occasionally, seldom, never. (1.9) (.68)

3. How often do you experience a family, private, or cell group devotional period in which the Bible or other religious literature is read? Never; seldom; occasionally, perhaps once a month; once a week, more or less; several times a week; daily; more than once

a day. (3.2) (.66)

4. When you are tempted to do something wrong, how often do you ask God for strength to do the right? Very often, often, sometimes, seldom, never. (1.5) (.63)

5. When you have decisions to make in your everyday life,how often do you ask yourself what God would want you to do? Very often, often, sometimes, seldom, never. (1.7) (.71)

B. Associationalism (church participation):

6. On the average, how often have you attended church worship services (on Sunday morning, evening, and/or other days) during the past two years? Never, a few times per year, once or twice a month, almost every week, once a week, more than once a week. (1.5) (.58)

7. In line with the world's needs and your resources, how frequently do you give in offerings the amount of money you feel you should give? Always, usually, sometimes, seldom, never. (1.3) (.50)

8. To what extent are you interested in serving your home congregation in Sunday School teaching, church project leadership,or other responsibilities for which you have abilities? Strongly interested, interested, some interest, a little interest, no interest. (1.9) (.66)

C. Evangelism (witness):

9. How frequently do you take the opportunity to witness orally about the Christian faith to persons at work, in the neighborhood, or elsewhere? Very often, often, sometimes, seldom, never. (1.4) (.64)

D. Religious Experiences:

10. In general, how close do you describe your present relationship to God? Quite unrelated, rather distant, between distant and close, fairly close, close, very close. (2.4) (.75)

11. How often do you feel discouraged in your efforts to live a Christian life? Very often, often, sometimes, seldom, never. (0.9) (.35)

12. How often do you have doubts about your own salvation? Very often, often, sometimes, seldom, never. (0.8) (.53)

13. In regard to the quality of your spiritual life, which of the following best describes your progress during the past couple of years? I am making definite progress, I am making a little progress, I am staying about the same, I have lost ground a little, I have

definitely lost ground. (1.6) (.67)

14. To what extent are you conscious of some spiritual goal or purpose in life which serves to give direction to your life? I am not aware of such a goal or purpose, I have a rather vague feeling of purpose, I am somewhat conscious of such a goal or purpose, I definitely feel guided by a spiritual life goal. (1.6) (.63)

(In addition to references cited in the text, the author has referred to Nelson and Dynes, 1976, and Tapp, 1971.--The Editor)

Chapter 20

SUPER-SAINTS AND MINI-SAINTS

Being a Comparison of the Most Spiritual with the Least Spiritual
among Recovering Alcoholic Clergy

Joseph H. Fichter

It is now part of the conventional wisdom in the field of alcohol
treatment and rehabilitation that this addiction is a threefold illness of body, mind, and soul. One pastor, who had been through the
addictive experience and therapy, calls alcoholism a "physical,
emotional and spiritual disorder" (Mehl, 1976: 118). In the meetings
of the National Clergy Council on Alcoholism there is frequent
discussion of the spiritual effects of alcoholism, the deterioration of the victim's relationship with God, even among the ministers
of religion. The active alcoholic person "dethrones God" (Sullivan,
1973).

The treatment of the alcoholic and his restoration to a normal
way of living apparently includes some kind, or degree, of spiritual
recovery. It is also a widely held conviction among recovering
alcoholics, especially those in the program of Alcoholics Anonymous,
that the maintenance of "quality" sobriety demands a constancy of
spiritual well-being. If recovering alcoholics know no other prayer,
they certainly know the prayer for serenity, and if serenity is a
rough equivalent for spiritual well-being, we ought to find spirituality among these men of prayer, the recovering alcoholic clergy.

For purposes of the present discussion, the concept of spirituality
denotes humility, dependence on God, and prayer. Its concrete
application to life is told in the words of a recovering alcoholic:
The first thing is to have a revulsion against myself and my
way of living. Then I must admit I was helpless, that alcohol had me licked and I couldn't do anything about it.
The next thing is to honestly want to quit the old life. Then
I must surrender my life to a Higher Power, put my drinking
problem in His hands and leave it there. After these things
are done, I should attend meetings regularly for fellowship
and sharing. I should also try to help other alcoholics.
(Anonymous, 1975)

LEVELS OF SPIRITUALITY

The attainment of spirituality is a relative process, with some people forging ahead and others lagging behind. By the use of certain logical criteria of measurement we were able to construct categories of different grades of spiritual well-being from the questionnaires answered by 677 clergymen who had gone through inpatient therapy for alcoholism at six accredited treatment facilities. We assume that the clergy are all spiritual men, but we make comparisons between the two polar categories, the 229 "super-saints" (33.8%) who appear now to be the most spiritual, and the 101 "mini-saints" (14.9%) who seem to be the least spiritual.

In the questionnaire we said that "the experience of alcoholism, and of recovery from it, seems to have different consequences in the lives of individuals." Then we asked to what extent the respondent had changed in three aspects of spirituality: (a) more dependence on God's grace, (b) better and frequent prayer, (c) a deeper sense of humility. By using these logical bench marks in combination, we decided that the super-saints are those who answered "very much" on all three items, while the mini-saints are those who gave this answer on none of the three. Those who answered "very much" on two of these are 197 "saints" (29.1%), and on only one of them are 150 "semi-saints" (22.2%). We omit these two intermediate categories from consideration here.

Why do these recovering alcoholic clergy turn out differently? At first we thought the difference could be attributed to the quality of the rehabilitation center at which they had been in treatment, but we found that approximately nine out of ten of both polar categories said that they were "very" or "quite" satisfied with their experience at the treatment facility. The respondents in these two contrasting groups were distributed proportionately in the six treatment centers, three of which were exclusively for clergy while the three others accepted lay people as well as clergy.

Table 1. Percentage Responses of Super-Saints and Mini-Saints on Preliminary Factors of Spirituality During Therapy

	Super-Saints	Mini-Saints
Had spiritual awakening	92.5%	49.5%
Therapy emphasized spiritual recovery	60.3	37.6
Concept of illness lessened guilt and shame	57.6	40.6

It is obvious from the comparisons in Table 1 that those who now exemplify a higher spirituality in their personal lives were also more likely to have had certain spiritual experiences in the process of therapy. Ever since the original story of Bill Wilson's "spiritual awakening,"the literature of Alcoholics Anonymous abounds in accounts of various kinds of personal renewal or regeneration. In Bill's extraordinary experience "he was aware first of a light, a great white light that filled the room, then he suddenly seemed caught up in a kind of joy, an ecstasy such as he would never find words to describe" (Thomsen, 1975: 223). One-fifth (21%) of all our respondents said that their recovery from alcohol addiction involved nothing like this. In other words, like all behavioral generalizations, this one is not universally applicable. We do find, however, that the great majority of the most spiritual clergymen say that they experienced a kind of spiritual awakening.

We assumed that the therapeutic process itself contained the seeds of general spiritual renewal and that these experiences were a factor in the present status of spiritual well-being. All of the treatment centers paid some attention to the spirituality of recovery, and a little more than half (53%) of the respondents said there had been "very much" emphasis on this. A much higher proportion of the super-saints gave this answer. Practically all respondents (92%) said that the concept of alcoholism as illness helped to remove their feelings of guilt, shame and humiliation. The percentages in Table 1 refer to those who said it removed these "completely."

SPIRITUALITY AND SOBRIETY

There is no permanent cure for alcoholism, but the primary prerequisite for rehabilitation is abstinence from alcoholic beverages. The illness cannot be arrested until, or unless, alcohol is removed from the diet of the addicted person. When we speak of spiritual recovery we tend to assume that the ability to refrain from drinking is in proportion to the degree of spirituality achieved. It is a cardinal principle of the A.A. program that the relationship with God, the dependence on the "higher power," is essential for the maintenance of sobriety. This spiritual principle is not necessarily shared by those who favor therapy through behavior modification by various types of aversion treatment (Bandura, 1969).

In the light of this basic "principle" of recovery, it is a surprise to discover that there is relatively little difference between the super-saints and mini-saints in their ability to stay away from booze. In other words, about one-third of both the most spiritual (32%) and the least spiritual (35.6%) admit that they have had one or more "slips" since leaving the treatment center. We asked them also when they had their last drink and found that only a slightly higher proportion of the most spiritual (75.5%) than of the least (70.3%) are successfully sober by our definition of sobriety, that is, being without a drink for four years during and/or since leaving the treatment facility.

There is overwhelming evidence in support of the generalization that spirituality helps one greatly to maintain sobriety, but there are enough exceptions to allow one to say that a person can stay sober without being very spiritual. In other words, the degree of spirituality achieved through the recovery process is not the single, all-important factor in returning the clergyman to sobriety. Everybody knows about the "wretchedly" sober people, those who are doggedly, but unhappily, staying away from alcoholic drinks. This appears to be the difference between simple sobriety and "quality" sobriety. It seems that quality sobriety includes spirituality, and that the combination of sobriety and spirituality makes it possible to lead a normal life again (Armour et al., 1976: 28; Pattison, 1966).

Two further pieces of evidence lend support to this generalization. We asked the respondents to rate themselves on a "scale" of serenity, and we found that the most spiritual were twice as likely (45.4%) as the least spiritual (22.8%) to place themselves at the highest rank of serenity. We asked them also what choice of an occupation or profession they would make if they had the chance to live their lives over again. A higher percentage of the most spiritual (90.4%) than of the least spiritual (74.3%) would again opt for the ministry.

IMPROVEMENT OF MINISTRY

One of the obvious benefits of their experience in alcohol therapy is not only that these men got a better understanding of themselves as vulnerable human beings but also a deeper appreciation of the frailties of the people they serve in the ministry. More than half of all respondents said that they are now "very much" more available to the people they serve (56.7%), have improved the quality of their ministry (60.8%), and have more compassion for people in trouble (72.9%). The comparative statistics in Table 2 show that the super-saints are proportionately much higher on all three items than are the mini-saints.

The inference from these comparisons is that the more spiritual a man is, the more likely is he to do a good job in the human relations aspects of his professional ministry. In other words, his interior practices of prayer, his deep humility, and his dependent relationship with God tend to carry over into a much more humane and responsible pastoral care for the people he serves.

Table 2. Percentage Responses of Super-Saints and Mini-Saints on Aspects of Their Relations with the Laity

	Super-Saints	Mini-Saints
More compassion for people in trouble	90.4%	36.0%
More available to the people served	82.5	24.0
Improved quality of ministry	82.4	26.0

This improvement of human relations in the ministry is reflected in responses to the question of whether these recovering alcoholic clergymen find satisfaction in the assignment they now have in the Church. More than half (56%) of all respondents say that they are very satisfied with their current assignment, but this proportion is considerably higher for the super-saints (66.8%) than for the mini-saints (35.4%). A further indication that their improved ministry has come to the attention of church superiors is in the fact of promotion to a better assignment. About three out of ten (28%) of all respondents report that they have had a promotion since returning from the treatment center, but this percentage is higher for those who are most spiritual (40%) than it is for the others (15%).

RELATIONS WITH THE CHURCH

One of the distinctions most frequently heard among recovering alcoholics is that between spirituality -- their relationship with God as we have been discussing it -- and religion, by which they mean the formal church organization to which they belong, or had belonged. Tiebout (1944: 11) remarked that
too often religion has been identified with its dogma and not with its essence of spirituality. It is not the form which religion takes, it is its function in achieving a frame of mind which is significant.
Often the Church is spoken of in derogatory terms as having provided no help when help was most needed. Thus they talk about spiritual recovery, rather than religious recovery, from alcoholism. Many of the priests we interviewed stressed that they had attained sobriety through spiritual experience gained "outside" the church structure.

Here we have an opportunity to compare religiosity with spirituality. We are able to test the extent to which the relationship

259

with their church has been maintained, or improved, by men who are in the professional employ of the church and who are now back in the service of the Lord and His people in an official ministry. In this regard the statistical contrast between the super-saints and the mini-saints is startling. On the several criteria of measurement we employed, we found that only a bare minimum of the least spiritual respondents have improved "very much" in this relationship.

Table 3. Percentage Responses of Super-Saints and Mini-Saints on Improved Relations within the Church

	Super-Saints	Mini-Saints
Stronger in theological beliefs	73.2%	5.0%
Greater loyalty to church tradition	69.0	4.0
Closer ties with fellow clergy	43.4	4.0

One would normally expect that a clergyman who serves in an official ministry has firm theological beliefs, a strong commitment to his church, and good relations with his fellow ministers of the Gospel. The low percentages of the mini-saints in Table 3 indicate their relative position on these three items. The question was whether they had experienced "very much" improvement in these areas after having gone through treatment for alcoholism. Many of them said they had improved "somewhat," so we cannot suggest that they are less religious than they were before.

Nevertheless, the comparisons in Table 3 indicate quite clearly that there is a close relationship between spirituality and religiosity. The super-saints are high on both spirituality and religiosity, while the mini-saints are low on both. This research finding calls into serious question the oft-repeated assertion among recovering alcoholics that the shift to a better relationship with God is accompanied by lower appreciation of organized religion (Fichter, 1977). The fact is that the recovering clergy who are least spiritual tend also to be those who do not find themselves stronger in either their beliefs or their church loyalty or in their relationships in clergy fellowship. It seems safe to assume that, if this phenomenon exists among the clergy, it is even more in evidence among lay people who are recovering alcoholics. The conventional pastor may not be satisfied until he "gets them back in the church" as regular parishioners.

MINISTRY TO FELLOW ALCOHOLICS

The alcoholic who goes for extended treatment is constantly
reminded that he must have an essential and permanent concern about
his own sobriety. Alcohol was his addiction, and alcohol was the
prime cause of his troubles. We asked our respondents to rank in
order of importance the three elements of their treatment that
they found personally most helpful to them. The result was as
follows: (a) learning about alcoholism, (b) individual counselling, (c) attendance at A.A. meetings.

Out of this knowledge and experience, together with their vocational thrust of ministering to others, many of the recovering
alcoholic clergy feel that they can themselves be of service to
active alcoholics. They have read in the "Big Book" that "practical
experience shows that nothing will so much insure immunity from
drinking as intensive work with other alcoholics" (Alcoholics
Anonymous, 1955: 89). These men are warned by their therapists
that their first duty is to themselves and that, if they do not
themselves maintain sobriety, they will not be of much help to
others. Relatively few go on for clinical training and become
full-time professional therapists. Many others become involved,
in varying degrees, in a kind of special apostolate to alcoholics.
This almost invariably includes active involvement with the fellowship of Alcoholics Anonymous.

The question arises whether the extent of later involvement in
the work of alcoholism is related to the degree of spirituality
which these men manifest. We asked them whether they consider
participation in A.A. both helpful and necessary for their personal
maintenance of sobriety; six out of ten of all respondents answered
in the affirmative. Among the super-saints this proportion rose
to seven out of ten (69%), and among the mini-saints it dropped to
half (51%). Faithful participation in A.A. means frequent attendance at the meetings. The most spiritual are twice as likely
(39.7%) as the least spiritual (19.8%) to report that they go to
A.A. meetings more than once a week.

There are probably some clergymen who feel that they can minister
to alcoholics without direct reference to the A.A. fellowship.
All of the respondents to this survey, however, were indoctrinated
in the A.A. philosophy and learned the A.A. procedures at the treatment centers where they resided. Even though a small minority
(11%) said that for themselves they found A.A. neither helpful
nor necessary, they probably recognized its value for other alcoholics. The questions we asked them about their ministry to alcoholics revolved around the extent to which they cooperated in
the tested procedures of A.A.

Table 4. Proportions of Super-Saints and Mini-Saints in Three Forms
and Ministry to Active Alcoholics

	Super-Saints	Mini-Saints
Do Twelfth-Step work	66.0%	40.6%
Alcoholics come for Fifth Step	55.9	33.6
Act as sponsor for alcoholic in A.A.	49.8	26.7

The twelfth and final step of the A.A. program is the following:
"Having had a spiritual awakening as the result of these steps we
tried to carry the message to alcoholics, and to practice these
principles in all our affairs." Although the message can be carried
through preaching and teaching, which are in themselves ministerial
functions, the practical procedure is to contact the suffering alcoholic who is in need of assistance. Visiting the sick is a normal pastoral activity which has special pertinence in the case of
the sick alcoholic, and it goes far beyond the parish boundaries.

In the fifth step of the A.A. program recovering alcoholics say
we "admitted to God, to ourselves, and to another human being, the
exact nature of our wrongs." In the "Big Book" the recommendation
is made that we may "do well to talk with someone ordained by an
established religion" (Alcoholics Anonymous, 1955: 74). This
disclosure of one's faults need not be made to a clergyman, but
since the man of God is trained to be a listener, a counselor,
and a confessor, it seems most appropriate that the recovering
alcoholic priest or minister will have people coming to him for
this service (Johnson, 1973: 163).

Sponsorship of a new "pigeon" in the A.A. fellowship is a demanding and time-consuming task which the clergyman finds difficult
to perform. Only one out of five (19%) of our respondents entered
A.A. under the sponsorship of a clergyman, but other former alcoholics also acted as sponsors. About six out of ten (62%) of
the super-saints, as compared to four out of ten (41%) of the mini-
saints, had sponsors who helped to involve them in A.A. The fact
is that the more spiritual a man is, the more likely is he to act
as sponsor. This requires that he "shepherd" the newly recovering
alcoholic to the point where he no longer needs such help and can
himself become a guide of another alcoholic.

CONCLUSIONS

We start with the assumption that religious professionals are by training and inclination spiritual men, but that degrees of spirituality can be ascertained from their responses to this survey. We are thus able to make comparisons between the most spiritual, the "super-saints," and the least spiritual, the "mini-saints."

Approximately the same proportion of complete abstainers is found in both types of recovering alcoholic clergy. This finding questions the generalization that the maintenance of sobriety depends largely on one's spirituality.

The research data show, however, that high spirituality ties in with quality sobriety; that is, the more spiritual they are, the more likely are they to enjoy serenity, have satisfaction with their work, and be satisfied with their life's profession.

The more spiritual they are, the better performers they are in dealing with people in trouble and carrying on humane relations with lay people.

The contrast between spirituality and religiosity does not show up in this survey. Those who have the lowest regard for their church are also the lowest in spirituality. Those who are high in spirituality are also high in religiosity.

Finally, the more spiritual they are, the more are they involved in the ministry to fellow alcoholics and in the fellowship of Alcoholics Anonymous.

THE CHRISTIAN'S SPIRITUAL WARFARE

Finally, be strong in the Lord and in his mighty power. Put on the full armor of God so that you can take your stand against the devil's schemes. For our struggle is not against flesh and blood, but ... against the spiritual forces of evil in the heavenly realms. -- The Bible, Ephesians 6: 10-11, NIV.

Chapter 21

RELIGIOUS WOMEN'S COMMUNITIES AND

SPIRITUAL WELL-BEING

Regina Marcum, O.S.F.

Most people have found some way to cope with questions of ultimate reality. Often there is no conscious calling to mind of our
solutions; rather, abrupt changes force us to consider how we cope
with the unexpected. Some Roman Catholic women have selected the
life style of the religious community as their way of handling the
questions of life. Fifty-three percent of the sisters in this
study felt that their primary reasons for remaining in religious
life were that they felt called to this life; they were convinced
that this was their personal vocation; it was their way for finding
God. For another two percent the fear of the unknown and fear of
going against God's will were indicated as the primary reasons for
remaining in religious life.

One task of students of religion is to identify religion where
it is present. But where is the religious to be found? This essay
looks to an invisible aspect of religion, namely, spiritual well-
being among religious women.

What variables can possibly be used to identify this dimension
of religion? Glock and Stark (1965) offer us an interesting and
informative collection. King (1967) proposes dimensions, and Yinger
(1969) and Nudelman (1971) hoped to find some universal themes
which would open up the study of religion and release it from cultural and denominational boundaries. Additionally, Nudelman (1971)
suggests that better analysis of the dimensions of religiosity
could reduce the number of variables used to describe it.

Some writings help us to see what type of characteristics mark
the spiritually mature, and/or spiritually well, Christian.
Duncombe (1974) believes that the four expressions of a mature
(spiritually well) Christian can be identified behaviorally. These
characteristics are 1) freedom from self-deception, 2) honest expressions, 3) undistorted perception of the world, and 4) demands
are given an appropriate response, not a rigid one. Duncombe's

concept of the spiritually mature person was limited to the Christian. No attempt was made to investigate the non-Christian nor the non-believer, and he provided no subcategories among Christians.

Freedom from self-deception indicated that the person had no illusions about himself. There was no false humility. Personal virtues were seen as grace. This led to honest expressions about one's own spiritual condition to oneself as well as others in the world about one. The world is seen as the work of God's hands, yet at the same time one experiences a tension caused by the temptations of the world. Demands made on oneself by God and others are not responded to in a rigid manner, conforming to rules and regulations without regard for the appropriateness of the response. In all, Duncombe's (1969) characteristics are limited by Christianity, but they are broadened by seeing spiritually mature persons in light of their personal response, rather than by specific virtues or attitudes defined from outside the person.

Kosicki (1976) suggests that ten characteristics mark the renewed religious life. These could well indicate the spiritually well person and/or community. They are a common commitment to Christ as Lord, agreement on rules, horizontal as well as vertical authority patterns. Additionally, asking and receiving forgiveness, Eucharist which celebrates and nourishes community, the gifting of time through celibacy, and mutual support are seen as important. A sense of being dispossessed but rich in the Lord is a contemporary expression of leaving all to follow Christ. Companionship in discipleship and apostolate, witnessing to what it means to be Christian, and, lastly, a faith sharing in prayer marks the religious person.

Neal (1967) stated that in true community people are refreshed and reinforced to do their work. Motivation is received to experiment with richer forms of human encounter, and communal experience offsets frustrations and anxieties.

In a study on spiritual growth (Edwards et al., 1974), clergy were asked to identify persons in their congregations whom they considered to be spiritually mature and to describe the characteristics they used as their criteria. The sample was small and methodology weak, but despite those limitations, there were some interesting findings.

The values of those selected were diverse and complex. However, seeking God and his presence was subordinate to sharing and caring for one's neighbor. On the whole, the religious experience of the group was not extraordinary. It was assumed that they were probably no different from a cross-section of their particular congregations. The respondents seemed to be selected more for being "mature" than for being "spiritual."

Such a conclusion was the result of the hidden meanings of

spiritual maturity held by the researchers themselves. They had
divergent views on it as well. One identified spiritual maturity
as a transformed consciousness which made one attentive to the
movement of the Spirit. Another said the openness to the mystery
of human life, a multi-faceted reality, marked the spiritually
mature. A recognition of the uniqueness of one's person and a
simplicity of expression about one's essence through his personality
was another view. The last of the researchers said that spiritual
maturity suggests a life marked by the pilgrim stance, which strives
to be responsive to, and to integrate the tensions rising out of,
everyday life and the values arising from faith.

Moberg (1971b)identifies the spiritual as one's inner resources.
It is the basic value or ultimate concern that guides one's conduct.
Non-theologically, it is the totality of the non-material dimen-
sions of man's nature.

The enormous variety of responses about the area of spiritual
well-being provides an interesting sociological "dig." However,
the term "spiritual well-being" itself provides mere questions
than light. Does our culture give us any clues to the combination?
Is there to be more emphasis on "spiritual" or on "well-being"?
Once the indicators are identified and listed, is there anything
left? Is spiritual well-being merely a sociological construct or a
reality? Is whether spiritual well-being exists a concern of the
sociologist, or is it his responsibility only to study how it
affects human interaction?

Another problematic is whether it is even possible to measure
spiritual well-being sociologically, let alone develop a survey to
uncover its dimensions. Is it simply a reification? Is there a
magic number of indicators that one possesses and thereby has spiritual well-being? Does it have degrees or rank? Is it constantly
in process, so that the very best that can be done is to identify
its particular incidence at a given moment? Is it a condition
which has static, measurable dimensions? The variable is indeed
elusive, perhaps transcendent.

The working definition of spiritual well-being used in this
paper is that spiritual well-being is a meaningful, purposeful
relationship with God through man. How does this definition emerge
from this group of religious women?

METHODOLOGY

Various methodologies might have been used to determine what
constitutes the spiritual well-being of sisters in religious communities. The most satisfactory form for attaining information of this
type might have been the focused interview (Merton and Kendall,
1946; Schroeder, 1977) or a comparative study (Swatos, 1977).
However, for purposes of exploration, a survey method was acceptable.

At one time in the history of women religious' communities, any sample of sisters might well have been representative of sisters in general. Perhaps the best that can be said today is that diversity is the characteristic which all sisters hold in common.

The population sampled in this survey consists of four groups: (1) the Sisters of St. Francis, Stella Niagara, New York Province, to which 366 questionnaires were sent and 219 returned before the deadline (59.8% return rate); (2) the Wisconsin Region of the National Sisters Vocation Conference, 229 sent, 159 returned (64.4%); (3) women who had left the first community, 64 sent, 13 undeliverable by post office, 26 returned (40.6%), and (4) women who had left a variety of other communities, 22 sent, 16 returned (72.7%).

At an early date, an item by item breakdown of the responses of the two categories of women who had left religious community indicated that in only 8 of 91 variables did the two groups differ significantly (p = .001). This high level of similarity, in spite of the smallness of the sample, made it appropriate to identify both together as one group.

A general description of the women in this study shows that the median age is 44.6. They are well-educated with a median of 14.1 years compared with 12.2 years of education for all women over 25 years of age in the 1970 Census of Population. They have been in the community over a quarter century on the average. Seventy-three percent of them live in convent type residences and 24% in apartments. Fifty-three percent are in teaching or educational administration occupations; 17% in community administration, formation, and maintenance; 12% in health services, and the remaining 18% in a broad variety of fields.

FACTOR ANALYSIS

Factor analysis of data about religious attitudes and behaviors has a respectable history (Cline and Richards, 1965; Brown, 1966; King, 1967; Keene, 1967; Lenski, 1961; Yinger, 1969; Hudelman, 1971, to mention but a few of its applications). Religion is very complex, involving beliefs, behaviors, experience, and faith. Some aspects of it can be objectively measured, such as belief or practices. Religious experience, faith, and attitudes present much more difficulty.

In looking at informal patterns created by Pearsonian correlations using these data, the intercorrelation ranges from .00 to .50 with only two exceptions. These correlations show that the variables are not identical, nor are they all independent of each other.

Item 65 (see Appendix) on prayer support and item 58 on spiritual

268

well-being as a strong awareness of God correlate moderately (less than .50) on many of the same items, tending to make us believe in the substantive correlation between prayer and an awareness of God. Item 41, identifying the need for adaptation to meet contemporary changes, correlates moderately (less than .50) with several other items that identify some specific adaptations. This need for adaptation was highly significant in the variance in women who left religious communities.

Accepting a multi-dimensional approach to the definition of religion, a factor analysis was performed to discover the patterns that emerge. Separate analyses, using the principal components (eigen value and eigen vector) solution with a varimax rotation were run on each group of respondents. All factors having an eigen value greater than unity were retained in the rotation. Fifteen to seventeen factors emerged for each group. Not all were clear enough even to label tentatively.

Perusal of the unrotated factor matrix could have suggested rotating fewer factors and thus simplified the process of identification of a spiritual well-being variable. However, the study was not made to test hypotheses nor to confirm preconceived ideas, but rather simply to explore the dimensions of such a variable. Therefore finding fifteen to seventeen factors was acceptable.

Factor analysis on the responses to attitudinal questions on the questionnaire (Appendix) in this study shows several factors which load significantly (.30 or higher) on items that might be used to create a spiritual well-being variable. An examination of the first five factors that emerged for each group indicates the following results.

Sisters of St. Francis

Factor I (Table 1) loads significantly on eleven questions and accounts for 26% of the common variance. Those questions seem to focus on the area of openness to change, ability to be flexible and adaptable, and a person-centered orientation. This factor may be seen as primarily psychological. This does not necessarily exclude it from the realm of a spiritual well-being variable. However, traditionally the churches have not identified the psychological with the spiritual. Latently, however, social and psychological adjustment have been present in church programs and activities (Moberg, 1971b).

Factor II includes questions 32, 33, and 35 (15% of the common variance). The questions clearly identify the factor as being focused on the responsibility to share and work together. It suggests the communal aspect of religious life. This could be spiritual well-being in religious women, but it also appears in those surveyed who left religious communities.

269

Table 1. Factor Analysis of Beliefs and Attitudes about Religious Life: Sisters of St. Francis

ITEM***	UNROTATED*						ROTATED**				
	I	II	III	IV	V		I	II	III	IV	V
17			11						39		
18			09						-34		
19	47						44				
21			08						37		
22			31						62		
23			36						50		
24			27						35		
25	45						31				
30	48				-01		32				30
31					06						36
32		46			05			47			34
33		37						87			
34	58				-07		43				33
35		35						60			
37				38						-35	
38					-30						60
40	21						38				
41	47						48				
43	38						55				
44	24						44				
45	52						51				
55					-08						55
56			41						31		
58					11						35
59	50						32				
60					-18						63
61					-17						68
62					04						42
65					-05						40
66	26						43				
68				-32						53	
70				-36						44	
71				-45						54	

*Decimal points have been omitted.
**Only factor loadings greater than .30 have been included on rotated factors.
***See Appendix.

Factor III (8.4% of the common variance) focuses on attitudes about chastity and poverty. These concepts traditionally and according to Canon Law are an essential part of religious community life. It is well understood that there are discrepancies between attitudes and behavior. The addition of question 56 concerning lack of responsibility requires a new look at the factor. It would be possible to read it as a dependency on others; therefore, this factor may be difficult to use to create a spiritual well-being variable.

The components of Factor IV (7.1% of the common variance) are a personal identification of possessing spiritual well-being and personal attitudes about meditation and scripture inspiration in meditation and thinking. This factor loads primarily on feeling one has spiritual well-being and the interior life of prayer. A significant negative loading on a question directed to identifying anomie adds an interesting dimension. This clarifies the factor as focusing on personal responsibility for action to develop a good quality of spiritual life.

The quality of spiritual life is the focus of Factor V (6.0% of the common variance). It identifies many of the components ordinarily associated with the spiritual life of persons in a religious community. Questions concerning the Eucharist, prayer, focus on the interior religious life, and community and personal responsibility for spiritual well-being are some of the components of the variable.

National Sisters Vocation Conference

Table 2 gives the factors emerging for the Wisconsin Region of the National Sisters Vocation Conference. Note that no items repeat significant loadings (.30 or higher) on any of the first five factors. Factor I accounts for 19.5% of the common variance and bears a strong resemblance to Factor V of the Sisters of St. Francis data; namely, it suggests a quality of religious life factor, even though it contains fewer items.

Factor II accounts for 10.7% of the common variance and is defined primarily by the need to accept personal responsibility and to revamp the decision-making processes in order to require accountability of all members.

Factor III loads significantly on anomie items. Assuming a lack of personal initiative, this factor could relate to the third factor of the Sisters of St. Francis data, which also marks a dependence on others in regard to the traditional form of religious life. This factor accounts for 10.1% of the common variance.

Factor IV is similar to the Sisters of St. Francis' Factor II, namely, working and sharing together. This factor loads highest

Table 2. Factor Analysis of Beliefs and Attitudes about Religious
Life: Wisconsin Region of the National Sisters Vocation
Conference

ITEM***	UNROTATED*					ROTATED**				
	I	II	III	IV	V	I	II	III	IV	V
18		-20					48			
19				05					59	
20			-43						72	
25		-30					46			
26		-00					54			
28		-05					53			
34				-22					66	
37			44					51		
38					-28					44
39			11					72		
41		-14				30				
42			47					61		
57	40					34				
58	40					70				
59	40					71				
60	49					53				
68					-09					37
70					-05					33
71					-13					68
73					14					44

*Decimal points have been omitted.
**Only factor loadings greater than .30 have been included on ro-
tated factors.
***See Appendix.

on searching together for meaningful ways to serve others. The
St. Francis Factor II loads highest on working together for the
community itself. This Factor IV accounts for 7.9% of the common
variance.

Factor V accounts for 6.5% of the common variance and revolves
around the interior life of prayer. It corresponds with the
fourth factor of the St. Francis data. This factor, identified
as the quality of religious life variable, could be related to
devotionalism.

Table 3. Factor Analysis of Beliefs and Attitudes about Religious Life: Women Who Have Left Religious Community Life

ITEM***	UNROTATED*					ROTATED**				
	I	II	III	IV	V	I	II	III	IV	V
18		-38				39				
21		05				33				
23			16				76			
24			31				76			
26	40					43				
27			39				76			
28	48					64				
29			08				61			
30	56					47				
31		20					45			
32	51					35				
33		-07					82			
34		-22					65			
35		-51					75			
36		-02					51			
37			40					56		
38	57					52				
39	71	-25				76	34			
41	43					80				
42	72					70				
57	55			-02		40			52	
58					06					32
59					-07					36
60					38					84
64		-37		21				53		35
65				39						90
66				-16				73		
67				-15				81		
68				-01				36		
70	64					42				
71	33	17				50	-33			
72					-27					37

*Decimal points have been omitted.
**Only factor loadings greater than .30 have been included on rotated factors.
***See Appendix.

In the third group (Table 3), composed of women who have left religious community living, a still different pattern of factors emerged. Three can be identified with factors that emerged in the other two groups. Factor II, working and sharing together, accounts for 10.8% of the common variance; Factor III, dependence on others, 9.2%; and Factor V, the quality of religious life, 7.1%.

Factor IV explains 7.4% of the common variance and is similar to the National Sisters Vocation Conference Factor II, which identifies decision-making skills. It loads highly on ability to handle tension and security in making one's own decisions.

Factor I, 26% of the common variance, is relatively unique to this group in regard to the way in which items loaded. It is defined primarily by the need for a new structuring of religious life and by a feeling that one's personal responsibility and initiative has not been allowed to play an important role in bringing about the adaptation.

The comparison (Table 4) of these three groups is made using no mathematical formula but rather the researcher's best judgment, maximum objectivity, and familiarity with the data.

Some items and factors can be found in all three groups surveyed. It is a question of priorities. Nearly all items were mutually exclusive in the five factors; nonetheless, they were not so among the three groups. Therefore, in this study, spiritual well-being in religious women is marked by prayer and having one's thinking and meditating directly inspired by Scripture. This leads me to identify spiritual well-being with the religious woman's prayer life. This factor failed to appear in the control group of women who left religious community. The items did appear in the factors for that group, but they were scattered among four of the factors, and none grouped with the item identifying oneself as having spiritual well-being.

DISCUSSION AND CONCLUSIONS

Some of the respondents expressed concern that the questionnaire did not reach to the theological depth of religious community life. They felt that much which is essential in light of the spiritual was missing. Berger (1974) has some interesting second thoughts on the substantive vs. the functional definitions of religion. In the past, his attitude toward different definitions of religion was one of

...relaxed ecumenical tolerance. It is an attitude that I would like to revise now. I have become more militant in my opposition to functional definitions.

Table 4. Comparison of Factors: Sisters of St. Francis, National Sisters Vocational Conference, and Women who Left Religious Community

SISTERS OF ST. FRANCIS	VOCATIONAL CONFERENCE	WOMEN WHO LEFT
1. Person-oriented (11)*		
2. Working and sharing together (3)	4. Working and sharing together (3)	2. Working and sharing together (10)
3. Dependence on others (7)	3. Dependence on others (3)	3. Dependence on others (5)
4. Prayer in spiritual life (4)	5. Prayer in spiritual life (5)	
5. Quality of religious community life (12)	1. Quality of religious community life (4)	5. Quality of religious community life (6)
	2. Decision making skills (5)	4. Decision making skills (4)
		1. Need for adaptation of religious community and personal involvement (11)

*The number preceding each descriptive label is the order in which the factors were produced by the analysis. The number in parentheses is the number of items on which those factors loaded .30 or higher.

275

The functions approach to religion serves to provide quasiscientific legitimations of a secularized world view. It achieves this purpose by an essentially simple cognitive procedure: the specificity of the religious phenomenon is avoided by equating it with other phenomena. The religious phenomenon is "flattened out." Finally, it is no longer perceived. Religion is absorbed into a night in which all cats are grey. The greyness is the secularized world view of reality in which any manifestations of transcendence are, strictly speaking, meaningless, and therefore can only be dealt with in terms of social or psychological functions that can be understood without reference to transcendence (pp. 127-129).

The whole issue of spiritual well-being is problematic. Some respondents wondered how they could say whether they had spiritual well-being, and no one would say with absolute certainty how she could tell what characteristics of it were her own. Others said that it was one thing to have awareness of God and another to implement that awareness in their lives, one thing to have scripture as the basis of prayer and another to base one's life on scriptural values.

This factor analysis has sought an underlying pattern of relationships, a discovery of new concepts which could lead to a possible reduction in data. There is little that is unique among the three groups. The group which acted as a control is definitely limited; it would be desirable to have still another group of women who have not been sensitized by religious community living. Also problematic is whether the variable of spiritual well-being which surfaces is what is characteristic of religious women or is simply representative of Roman Catholic theology. No Episcopalian, Lutheran, etc. religious women were included in the survey.

So what constitutes spiritual well-being in religious communities? Perhaps it can be reduced to several items, namely, the place of prayer in one's life, the emphasis given to the interior life, coupled with the importance of assuming personal responsibility for one's spiritual health. Further study is yet to be made using these data, for if the sociologist of religion is not to be simply a technician for a particular religious institution, he must realize that quantifying the religious gives only the appearance of objectivity. It does not unbias the research. A holistic approach states that all facets of man are interrelated. He can be divided only analytically. Survey research and quantitative methods can provide us with leads which can act as catalysts for greater in-depth analysis of human interaction, especially in the realm of the spiritual.

(All of the questions except 68-73 had an answer range from strong
agreement to strong disagreement.)

17. The life of virginity is an angelic life on earth.
18. The traditional way of presenting chastity in religious life
has allowed for the development of isolation and false mysticism among sisters.
19. The sister must be willing to take the risk involved in form-
ing deeply personal and truly human friendships.
20. This generation of religious is being asked to rediscover
evangelical poverty. This means a realistic search for ways
to be meaningfully poor and with the poor here and now.
21. As long as a sister is personally poor, I think that it is
good for the community to be financially secure.
22. Unless a community was founded for that special purpose, I
do not feel religious have any particular obligation to work
with the poor.
23. Vowed poverty means dependence on superiors such that the use
of all things falls under the authority and control of those
who are set over the common life.
24. I feel that the essence of religious poverty is dependence
on the community for whatever a sister needs and uses.
25. One of the main characteristics of the new poverty will be
openness and liberality of mind and heart and goods, and the
dwelling of a group of religious will be a place where persons
will feel welcome, accepted, and put at ease.
26. I feel that one of the dangers of the traditional way obedience has been presented in religious communities is that sisters
have not been formed to accept personal responsibility.
27. By establishing oneself in the religious state, one gives up
one's independence and sets aside one's liberty.
28. I think that contemporary religious communities must drastically revamp their decision-making processes to include all
members of the community.
29. By the grace of office, superiors express the will of God for
me.
30. The vow of obedience is a promise to listen to the community
as it speaks through many voices.
31. Sharing the Eucharistic celebration is essential to community.
32. Praying the Office together, at least some hours, is essential
to community living.
33. Sharing the housekeeping and cooking and buying chores is
essential to community living.
34. Talking seriously and candidly about spiritual matters as they
are personally experienced by the individual members, including
the anguish of doubt, suspicions, aspirations and longings,
is essential to community living.
35. Sharing the responsibility of financing the residence is

essential to community.
36. The essential nature of religious life is to be of service.
37. It seems to me that other people find it easier to decide what is right to do than I do.
38. The central focus of our renewal effort should be on the interior life.
39. I feel that the way obedience is practiced in our community has been an excuse for me to dodge real responsibility.
40. The trouble with the world today is that people really don't believe in anything.
41. Adaptation to contemporary life calls for a new structure of religious life.
42. I feel any initiative on my part is stifled.
43. All authentic law is by its very nature flexible and can be changed by the community in which it is operative.
44. The only purpose for a religious rule is to allow for the channeling of human energy into the fulfillment of the gospel in a radically Christian way.
45. The community in which the sisters live must strive to develop that openness to the other that should characterize every Christian living-together group, if it is to be a form of Christian witness needed in the world today.

55. Spiritual well-being is a process -- you can have more or less of it. You have to work at developing it.
56. Spiritual well-being is a condition -- you either have it or you don't. You are not responsible for getting it.
57. Spiritual well-being is both process and condition.
58. Spiritual well-being is a strong awareness of God.
59. It is a strong openness to the giftedness of others.
60. It is a good sense of reality which is grounded in prayer.
61. The community is responsible for maintaining an atmosphere conducive to spiritual well-being.
62. Each sister is responsible for her own spiritual well-being, thereby giving spiritual well-being to the community.
63. Spiritual well-being is a gift of God not dependent on others or outside conditions.

How do you handle the tension between stability and change?

64. Through the support of my friends.
65. Through the support of prayer.
66. You welcome the tension, learn to live with it and laugh at the mistakes.
67. I am secure in my own ability to make decisions, therefore, change does not produce tension.

68. Do you personally have spiritual well-being?
   1) yes   2) no   3) not sure
69. Which is the most important characteristic of your own spiritual well-being?

1) a strong awareness of God
2) a strong openness to others
3) a good sense of reality grounded in prayer
4) all of these
5) none of these
6) #1 and #2
7) #1 and #3
8) #2 and #3
9) don't have spiritual well-being

70. How do you feel about meditation?
1) I really enjoy it, looking forward to it every day.
2) I value it deeply but have to work hard at it.
3) It's a burden to me, though I accept it willingly as a necessary part of my spiritual life.
4) My response is uneven. Sometimes it's fine; sometimes a burden.

71. How much of your thinking and meditating derives its inspiration directly from scripture?
1) a great deal
2) a moderate amount
3) directly, very little

72. How important is it to you as an active religious to have periods of retreat in which you go apart completely from your service work for a lengthy period of time to spend a period in contemplation, e.g., a week or more?
1) Important
2) Because of kind of person I am, not really important
3) Because of the nature of my work, not really important at all
4) None of these

73. How frequently do you go apart for shorter periods of recollection, e.g., a day or a weekend?
1) at least once a month
2) about every two to three months
3) about every four to six months
4) none of these

SPIRITUAL WELL-BEING IN NURSING

The nursing process is an ongoing cycle of observing, interpreting, planning, implementing and evaluating ... . Perhaps more than in any other dimension of human need, spiritual needs are discerned through the interpretation of observations and the testing of hypotheses. ... Assessing spiritual needs requires a sensitive ear and a willingness to respond to tiny clues. ...if we have a commitment to caring for the whole person we cannot claim lack of competence, lack of interest or lack of responsibility in the area of spiritual needs (Fish and Shelly, 1978: 59-61).

Chapter 22

SPIRITUAL WELL-BEING AND INTEGRATION IN TAIWAN

Larry M. Hynson, Jr.

The spiritual nature of man has been neglected by social
scientists for many reasons. Besides the lack of interest in
the topic and the historical influence of separation of church
and state is the more difficult problem of methodology (Moberg,
1971b: 3-4). Moreover, the ontology issue about the nature of
man may even take precedence over the problem of conceptual clarity
and the methodological issue of exactly how social scientists
are to empirically measure this phenomenon. Because of these
special problems and the lack of empirical work in the area of
the spiritual, this paper includes 1) a discussion of the importance and the conceptualization of the spiritual, 2) a literature
review of related research, and 3) a presentation of the research
findings on this topic.

SPECIAL PROBLEMS

The fact that the spiritual reality of man cannot be proven
or that it is difficult to measure should not exclude it from
worthy consideration and research. It has been argued that at
the core of human experience, community life, and cultural values
is the spiritual dimension. Thus, the spiritual pertains
  to man's inner resources, especially his ultimate concern,
  the basic value around which all other values are focused,
  the central philosophy of life -- whether religious,
  anti-religious, or nonreligious, which guides a person's
  conduct, the supernatural and nonmaterial dimensions of
  human nature (Moberg, 1971b: 3).
This assumption that man is a spiritual being cannot be proven nor
can it be denied. For this research it is assumed to be a valid
and useful concept in spite of the many problems.

In trying to conceptualize spiritual well-being Moberg (1974b)
has suggested using other observable phenomena as indicators,
such as a satisfactory philosophy of life, satisfactory relationships, a good self-image, preparedness to die, a proper orientation

toward losses, and ethical and moral conduct. Since the spiritual dimension is non-observable, this approach seems both logical and appropriate. When the concept is viewed from this conceptual framework, it overlaps with the main stream of sociological research and writings. Special attention should be given to this classical tradition in developing this new concept. For example, Weber, Durkheim, and Marx were all concerned about religious belief, moral behavior, and social structure. Implicit at the micro-sociological level, however, has been the notion of a philosophy of life, a self image, and beliefs about death, losses, and interpersonal relationships.

Tiryakian (1976) credits Weber with constructing the most appropriate macro-sociological theory relevant to the American society. In this analysis Weber saw a special relationship between Protestant sects, voluntary associations, and the social structure. The belief system as seen in Weber's idea of the Protestant ethic was of major importance. This ethic referred "to the existential and cultural foundations of any society committed to the mastery of this world through intensive discipline and consensual organization of personal and social orders" (Nelson, 1973: 83).

Likewise, Durkheim's concern for moral behavior has been detected by many (Tiryakian, 1962; Wallwork, 1972; Bellah, 1973; Kemper, 1975). Specifically Durkheim believed that morality was at the center of social bonding. Ideals, obligations, and religions were thought to be closely linked with moral behavior. While moral behavior develops from religious institutions, it is nevertheless distinct from them. Once formed, morality includes two aspects, namely the ideal and obligations. This means that belief about the ultimate in turn affects the sense of obligations one has toward others. Consequently, morality has a social impact and shapes the social structures.

In contrast with Weber and Durkheim, Marx analyzed society from a conflict perspective. Within this context, revolution and violence received special attention. Even though they emphasize a materialistic perspective, Marxists have ascribed an important role to religion. Religion, and more specifically religious belief, does influence people's attitudes and actions toward violence and revolution. For some people a particular religion has provided the impetus for violent and rapid change. Third world countries have demonstrated that this can be the case (Beach, 1977). However, for most Western countries the reverse holds true. Here there is found an inverse relationship between adherence to historic Christian beliefs and violent action (Glock and Stark, 1965: 185-226; Wuthnow, 1973; Beach, 1977).

Even the Marxian tradition has something in common with the traditional writings of Weber and Durkheim. Basic to all these sociological traditions is the idea that religious belief and morality provide an integrative function for society. This is the variable relationship that is examined. With the exception of a study by Nelson (1974), not much research has been done on these kinds of variable relationships. On the basis of earlier sociology writings and some empirical research, it is predicted that spiritual well-being varies directly with functional integration.

METHODS

After defining the spiritual and recognizing problems of conceptualization, the next issue concerns operationalization of the two variables, spiritual well-being and integration. The basic approach used was secondary analysis of previously collected data; this somewhat restricted the way these two concepts are operationalized.

The data are from a study undertaken by Professor Wolfgang L. Grichting and the National Taiwan University in 1970. The sociology faculty and its Chairman, Dr. Lung Kwan-hai, assisted in the interview stages. Care was taken to insure that each respondent was interviewed in his own dialect. All interviewers, 16 male and 16 female sociology students, were trained before conducting the interviews. Later seventy students helped to code the data and translate the information. The sampling design included both a random and a stratified approach. Samples were drawn from four types of residences, provincial cities, prefectual cities, townships, and rural areas. The data were distributed in computerized form by the Inter-University Consortium for Political and Social Research, Ann Arbor, Michigan. Because the original study concerned the value system in Taiwan, secondary analysis for the present research was more adaptable to the data, than might otherwise have been the case.

The original study contained over 475 questions about religious belief, as well as basic demographic data. Various questions were first selected on the basis of face validity and the suggestions of Moberg (1974b) about observable phenomena related to spiritual well-being. Initially six items were used as indicators of spiritual well-being. These, with abbreviations used in Table 1, are as follows:
1. It's no good to mix religion with life's everyday problems. (Mix religion)
2. Man has a soul that does not die after the death of the body. (Soul lives on)
3. The value of any religion can best be assessed according to its usefulness for life's everyday problems.(Rel....useful)
4. Without religion, life does not make sense. (Rel....meaning)
5. Intelligent people don't need religion. (Rel. not needed)

283

6. God exists? (Belief in God)
   1) I know God really exists and have no doubts.
   2) While doubts, I feel that I believe in God.
   3) I find myself believing in God sometimes.
   4) I don't know whether there is a God and I
      don't believe there is a way to find out.
   5) I don't believe in God.
   6) I have never bothered to ask this question.

In items 1-5, the responses were given in Likert categories, such
as strongly agree, agree, don't know, disagree, and strongly
disagree.

Six items were also selected initially as a measure of integration. These included both attitudinal and behavioral measures:
1. Friendship means
   1) Often visit one another in each other's homes.
   2) Frequent casual chatting as we see each other.
   3) Occasional chatting as we run into each other.
   4) Hardly know my neighbors.
2. How many close friends have you?
   0) no friends
   1) one
   2) two, etc. (up to over 20 friends)
3. In order to be really happy, one must do good to all people
   one knows.
4. A person who loves his enemy makes a fool of himself.
5. Respondent's cooperation
   1) good from beginning
   2) began good, but weak
   3) began weak, but good
   4) average
   5) weak
6. Interview quality
   1) high
   2) average
   3) questionable

These items have face validity and also resemble the items used
in Nelson's (1974) study of integration. Moreover, this measure
also contains data about actual behavior; items 5 and 6 record the
interviewer's evaluation of the respondent. It is possible that
certain interviewers obtained cooperative respondents with high
quality interviews. On the other hand, the main advantage of
these items is that the actual, not merely reported, behavior pattern is measured. Overall, these items indicate the degree to
which an individual has strong relationships with others and, in
turn, is integrated into society.

Factor analysis was used for data reduction and exploration purposes. An attempt was made to isolate the source variables underlying the interrelationships in the data. Principal factoring with

Table 1. Factor Loadings for Spiritual Well-Being

Items	Factor 1	Factor 2
1. Mix religion	.142	-.166
2. Soul lives on	.501	.234
3. Religion is useful	.479	-.529
4. Religion gives meaning	.495	.085
5. Religion not needed	.015	.373
6. Belief in God	.492	.229

iterations was applied to the two measures discussed above. The factor loadings for spiritual well-being are presented in Table 1. Items 2, 3, 4, and 6 loaded reasonably high at or near .500 for factor 1, while only item 3 loaded that high for factor 2. Since item 3 also loaded high for factor 1, these four items (2, 3, 4, 6) were selected as the empirical indicators of spiritual well-being.

The factor loadings for the initial indicators of integration are shown in Table 2. Again, principal factoring with iterations

Table 2. Factor Loadings for Integration

Items	Factor 1	Factor 2
1. Meaning of friendship	.000	.186
2. Number of close friends	.332	.196
3. Meaning of happiness	.091	.464
4. Fools love enemy	.152	.302
5. Cooperation	.580	.009
6. Quality of interview	.729	.076

was employed. It should be remembered that items 5 and 6 are a measure of the degree of integration as perceived by the interviewer. Both loaded rather high on factor 1. Also loading high on this first factor was the number of close friends one has (item 2). Factor 1 taps the person's ability to establish quality interaction with those around him and thus reflects a measure of integration. Factor 2 contains only two items (3 and 4) that loaded reasonably high; it was not used in any further analysis.

In addition to specifying the relationship between spiritual well-being and integration, there are controls for the covariates of city size, socioeconomic status (SES), age, marital status, and sex. These control variables were significantly related to the variables in certain other research (Chasin, 1971; Nelson, 1974). Multiple classification analysis (MCA) was used to evaluate the net effect of the two variables for each religious group while the covariates are simultaneously controlled. The MCA gives a grand mean for the dependent measure and also provides the adjusted deviations for the main effect with controls for the covariates. Consequently, the magnitude of the main effect can be determined after the covariate effects have been partialled out.

FINDINGS

Once the two variables of spiritual well-being and integration were operationalized, the next step involved measuring the degree of association between them. In order to accomplish this, the scores for each of the measures were trichotomized into a low, medium, and high category. These divisions were made so that approximately one-third of the total number would fall into each of the categories.

Table 3. Spiritual Well-Being and Integration

| Integration | Spiritual Well-Being | | | | | |
| | Low | | Medium | | High | |
	N	%	N	%	N	%
Low	288	37.8	331	39.0	232	37.9
Medium	233	30.6	302	35.6	244	39.9
High	240	31.5	216	25.4	136	22.2
Total	761	99.9	849	100.0	612	100.0

$x^2 = 20.3$ $P < .01$ gamma = -.06

286

The cross tabulations for the two variables are presented in Table 3. While the chi square was significant, the gamma of -.06 reveals no relationship whatsoever. The low correlation substantiates the independence of the two measures. Obviously something different is being measured for each variable.

Since the predicted association was not valid for the total sample population, the next approach was to use various modes of elaboration. In Taiwan there is an interesting mixture of religions, both east and west. If spiritual well-being is related to religious institutions but independent of them, then specifying the original variable relationship by religion should prove helpful and provide additional insights about spiritual well-being.

Table 4 contains the integration score by degree of spiritual

Table 4. Integration Score* By Spiritual Well-Being and Religion

Religion[b]	N	Grand Mean	Spiritual Well-Being[a]		
			Low	Medium	High
Buddhism	950	2.22	2.25	2.20	2.23
Taoism	20	2.13	1.63	2.50	1.90
Pai Pai	761	2.20	2.17	2.20	2.25
Catholicism	66	2.00	2.11	2.13	1.84
Protestantism[c]	92	1.85	2.43	1.71	1.75
None	295	1.92	1.87	2.07	1.71

* The lower the score the higher the level of integration.
a Adjusted scores controlling for the covariates of city size, SES, age, marital status (dummy variables), and sex (dummy variables).
b F tests were significant at the .05 level for all covariates in all categories of religion except Protestant.
c Main effect with covariates controlled was significant at the .02 level (F test).

well-being for each religious category. The largest number of respondents by religious identity were in Buddhism (950), Pai Pai (761), and None (295), while the smallest numbers were in Taoism (20), Protestantism (92), and Catholicism (66). Several other

287

religious categories in the original study were dropped because of the small number of persons interviewed. The average integration score for each religion is the grand mean. In comparing the grand mean, the first three categories are the highest and the last three the lowest on the integration scale. The findings suggest that the measure of functional integration is strongest among Protestants, Catholics, and those without religious commitments.

In the right half of Table 4 are seen the integration scores by level of spiritual well-being. These scores are adjusted for covariate effects. The statistical analysis provides an F-test for each covariate and the main effect variable. In all cases the covariates had a statistically significant relationship with the integration score. However, the main effect of spiritual well-being was significantly related only to the Protestants. Another F-test also showed that Catholics exhibit this same trend, but it was not quite statistically significant.

CONCLUSIONS

This study provides an empirical base for the concept of spiritual well-being and extends support for further research efforts. Although problems of conceptualization and operationalization remain, it demonstrates that ways can be found to refine the concept and its measures.

It was found that the association between spiritual well-being and integration may not hold up for all religious groups. But evidently aspects of the Christian tradition as contained in Catholicism and more especially Protestantism strengthen this particular association. The significant finding about the relationship is that the specification by these religions holds true in a cross-cultural setting. The Taiwanese and Chinese historically have not adhered to these religious commitments.

There are limitations to this study. First, it is based upon secondary analysis of previous data. More serious is the fact that the researcher superimposed a measure of spiritual well-being upon each of the subjects rather than explicitly allowing their feelings and beliefs to come out. Survey data does not lend itself to this approach. Perhaps a verstehen or in-depth analysis of case studies would be the best approach. Finally, the items selected for empirical indicators were those which showed factor analysis inter-relationships. Obviously, with each new selection of items the factor loadings would change. Thus this research represents an exploratory study.

There is a body of literature in sociology that overlaps the subject area of spiritual well-being. The classic writers, Weber,

Durkheim, and Marx, sought answers to the problem of integration. They saw religions, moral behavior, and social structure as significantly related. Yet little research has been done on a macro-sociological level to evaluate the significance of these relationships. More cross-cultural studies like the present one should be pursued.

Hopefully this research fills the gap and represents a step toward grounding the concept of spiritual well-being with empirical indicators. Whatever methodologies are used in the future, attempts must be made to evaluate its significance. The present study indicates that further work also may yield significant insights about social life.

In conclusion, Tiryakian (1976: 19-30) viewed the manifestations of the Protestant influence for America in two significant areas. First was the idea of wilderness where nature as wilderness must be conquered, and second was the idea of voluntarism. The linkage at least for the American Puritan subculture is between the impetus for scientific investigation, responsibility for this world, and the establishment of strong community life. This latter idea finds expression in George Herbert Mead's writings, as Tiryakian (1976) has pointed out. According to Mead, society is not static, but rather dynamic. In society people meet the demands of life, and social action establishes group life. The quest for the dynamics of society must be continued: one fruitful, but difficult, path may be through investigation of the spiritual.

THE SHEPHERD'S SONG

Now as they were going along and talking, they espied a boy feeding his father's sheep. The boy was in very mean clothes, but of a very fresh and well-favoured countenance, and as he sat by himself he sung. 'Hark,' said Mr. Great-heart, 'to what the shepherd's boy saith.' So they hearkened, and he said,

He that is down, needs fear no fall,
He that is low, no pride:
He that is humble, ever shall
Have God to be his guide.

I am content with what I have,
Little be it, or much:
And, Lord, contentment still I crave,
Because thou savest such.

Fullness to such a burden is
That go on pilgrimage:
Here little, and hereafter bliss,
Is best from age to age.

Then said their guide, 'Do you hear him? I will dare to say, that this boy lives a merrier life, and wears more of that herb called hearts-ease in his bosom, than he that is clad in silk and velvet ...'
(Bunyan, 1970b: 289-290).

Chapter 23

THE MANIFESTATION OF RELIGIOUS COMMITMENT

WITH REGARD TO DIVERGENT REALITY DEFINITIONS

Jan K. Coetzee

There has already been quite a lot of speculation regarding the place and function of the present day church within a dynamically changing society. This cannot be otherwise because the established church finds itself in a world in which it becomes all the more difficult for it (the church) to function. The church cannot remain untouched by or protected against the streams and trends of the modern world. Nor should it be one of its characteristics to be constantly prepared to conform uncritically to the demands of the dynamic society. The church can never get away from the fundamental principle to which it is subject: it remains in this world, yet it may never be of this world. The incessant pressure to which the modern world subjects the church is not the only factor which has an effect on the functioning of the church. The individual church member, in his so-called emancipated position, also makes his demands when he himself wishes to judge to what extent he wants to identify himself with certain aspects of church services, or whether he simply does not accept them.

If the actual situation, on the one hand, is that the functioning and service of the church cannot simply rely on the uncritical "yes and amen" of its members, and if, on the other hand, we look at the structural problem brought about by the large organizational framework within which the church of our day figures, then it would seem that what Vrijhof (1970: 27-28) has to say about the church and secularization is a true reflection of reality. According to his statement, secularization means that religion and church have lost their meaning and relevance. A discrepancy or tension is found increasingly between real and feigned meaning. Herberg (1962: 152) discusses this phenomenon as well when he speaks of an increasing division between "operative religion" (which operates in the person and society) and "conventional religion" (which points to institutional restraints). The church cannot constitute religion simply as ultimate and overall reality which gives meaning to human existence. Spiritual well-being can be accomplished only when religion becomes the foundation and ultimate meaning of and for human living together.

If the church cannot make spiritual well-being "true," there is bound to be tension between the marginal position and central pretense of the church. If the church wants to be the originator of spiritual well-being, the following questions will have to be central and they will have to be answered: How can the church truly and reliably transmit spiritual well-being? How can the church, through its message, bring the individual and society to a definite choice which can lead to spiritual well-being? Does the church offer the member the opportunity to experience spiritual well-being within the church?

RESEARCH DESIGN

The Research Group

All members of a new congregation of the Dutch Reformed Church (DRC) in Pretoria (Lynnwood Ridge) were involved in a survey. The congregation is situated in a fairly recent suburb (six years since the first house was erected), inhabited mainly by a new generation that has grown up in and is to a considerable extent part of a prosperous culture. This research group has 409 respondents (about 75% of all the members of the Lynnwood Ridge congregation) and can be regarded as being representative of a new and indicative facet of the urban church situation. With the economic boom of the late sixties and seventies, the DRC acquired various congregations which arose as a result of rapid suburban expansion in larger centres. An analysis of the biographical details of the research group reveals that 65.2% are not yet 40 years of age. More than half (55.3%) follow occupations which may be classified as professional, administrative, or executive. Furthermore, the average family income is exceptionally high according to general standards. Because of the free availability of opportunities, most members can be put into the higher-middle and higher socio-economic categories.

Hypothesis

Because of the apparent homogeneity of the research group, another factor (or factors) had to be sought in order to account for, in a meaningful way, mutual differences in the religious commitment and involvement of members. As the identifiable variables remained fairly constant, that variable (or those variables) could be more easily investigated in order to account for the different opinions of members. These differences relate directly to the meaning each individual gives to his life-world and have to be found on a more abstract value-level. In studying spiritual well-being as it can be brought about within the institutionalized church, an attempt is made to understand how members, as participants of this situation, constitute meaning for themselves in regard to their religious involvement.

The meaning a specific action or involvement holds for the individual could become clear once the researcher has some idea of each individual's definition of the situation in which he (the individual) finds himself. It is this principle of constant defining of reality which becomes important in studying spiritual well-being. In the same way as each individual church member, by virtue of his church membership, has to account to himself for the meaning of this commitment, church groups have to give collective meaning to this commitment. The collective or joint definition of reality offers, then, an overall or all-embracing reality within which each individual member has to give meaning to his personal commitment to the church (Berger and Berger, 1972: 336). The possibility of spiritual well-being is constituted within this dialectical articulation of directives found, on the one hand, in the expectations of the church and, on the other hand, the way in which each member reacts to these expectations.

Much attention is paid to the influence religion has on people's opinions and attitudes. When divergent orientations of reality are studied within one particular church, the problem is reversed. The central question in this paper is thus: What influence has a specific orientation of reality (value-orientation) on the possibility of experiencing spiritual well-being within the institutionalized church?

Categories in Terms of Reality-Orientations

Any meaning or definition given to the overall or all-embracing reality within which we have to live our everyday life can be placed somewhere on a scale or continuum. The general factor underlying this continuum is conservatism. It has even been said that conservatism underlies the whole scope of social attitudes (Wilson, 1973: 3) and it can therefore be assumed that it also underlies all religious behavior. Conservatism functions only as an ideal-type concept; members have only been classified somewhere on a scale or continuum with conservatism at one end of the continuum and progressiveness, or a tendency to change, at the other end.

The conservative person (ideal-type) could be described as someone who experiences religion as a dogmatic or fundamentalist act. The absolute authority of the established church is accepted without much ado, as well as the literal truth of scripture. Such a person is likely to show preference for the maintenance of the status quo in his political involvement, even though this should happen as a result of pressure or strict censorship. Individual behavior has to be directed by strict rules and punitive measures. Because of this person's general resistance to change, one finds that the conservative person will be in favor of the traditional and conventional regarding art, music, literature, and clothing

(Wilson, 1973: 5-9).

These directives regarding the so-called conservative person
have been used to place the individual members of the research
group somewhere on a continuum. This has been done by means of
responses to a number of items centered on conservatism. The
one end of the continuum represents the conservative member, while
the progressive (liberal) member has been placed at the other end
of the continuum. A middle group consisting of members who keep
to a more moderate view of reality is found between these two
extremes.

The individual score of each member's reality orientation is
based on the answers to each of these items:
Must there be more alternation in the traditional pattern of public
    worship (e.g. music services, discussion services, etc.)?
Do you find the theory of evolution acceptable?
Ought Afrikanership and everything that is associated with it,
    still to be strongly emphasised today?
Ought legislation concerning abortion to be made more lenient?
Generally speaking, do you feel that the direction which clothing
    fashions are taking is cause for concern?
Do you think it is necessary to be loyal to your people and country
    in every aspect?
Is the action taken against so-called undesirable publications
    too strict in the RSA?
Should the church have more authority over the lives of members?
Is the compliance with strict rules one of the best ways in which
    order in society may be maintained?
Ought films in the RSA be subject to less censorship?
Should national festivals commemorating historic occasions be
    attended faithfully?
Is the inherent conscience of each person the most important
    criterion whereby matters must be judged?
Must divorce be made easier to obtain?
Can ministers hold services without their togas and white ties?

Each of these items could have been marked yes, perhaps, or
no. Depending on the connotation of each item, a conservative
response was allocated 3, a "perhaps" response 2, and a progressive
liberal response 1. The sum total of the marks for each item is
calculated for each respondent. The following points of intersection were decided on in order to obtain the same number of
members for each of the three broad classifications. The conservative group consists of 123 members, the sum total of their
response being 34-42. The sum total of the moderate middle group
(147 members) was between 24 and 33, while the 139 members classified in the liberal progressive group obtained between 14 and 23.

The decision concerning the size and points of intersection of
each of these groups may be regarded as arbitrary. No claim is

made that these three groups represent watertight categories, however. Grouping was affected solely to demonstrate tendencies relating to the reality orientation apparent in the opinions and attitudes of members of a particular church. These tendencies were correlated with their religious commitment and involvement. In this manner, the influence of the way each individual gives meaning to the reality of his life-world on the way in which he experiences religion and church life may be seen. Thus orientations in the practice of religion may be identified.

Statistical Calculations for Analysis of Data

In every case where possible, a test of independence was applied. Chi-square was used in this case to check whether or not there was a correlation between the findings in a two-dimensional table. Because the chi-square itself does not give an indication of the strength of the correlation, but only indicates whether there is a correlation between two variables, the coefficient of contingency (C) was calculated to show the strength of the correlation. The maximum value of the C-coefficient is always smaller than one, and this maximum value was calculated in each case. The correlation between the calculated value of the C-coefficient and the maximum value it could have was also spelled out (by dividing the calculated C by the maximum C.) Thus it is possible with each item to see if there is a correlation between the findings, how strong the correlation is, and how strong the correlation is in comparison with any other item.

FINDINGS

The original research (Coetzee, 1978) involved five dimensions of the ecclesiastic-religious life-world of the members. Thirteen items deal with the dimension of personal devotion. Another thirteen items relate to church participation. Seven items elucidate religion as an experience of koinonia, while eight items deal with the critical function of the church. The last dimension (eight items) relates to actual religious acts. As to whether or not there is a correlation between a variable (e.g., age, sex, socio-economic income, and reality orientation) and an item can be demonstrated on the basis of the statistical calculations (X^2 and C). Just how strong this correlation is in comparison with all other items can also be demonstrated (calculated C/maximum C). The reality orientation of the research group was brought into correlation with all 49 items of the research. The strength of the correlation between the three-fold reality orientation and each item was established and compared. In this way it was possible to arrange the 49 items in order of the strength of correlation (the correlation between the item and the reality orientation of the research group).

The main finding was that the twelve items which showed the

strongest correlation with reality orientation center mainly on
the extent to which the church functions as reference group for
its members. Reference groups are those groups to which one
turns, either literally or symbolically, when one must choose
among alternative attitudes or courses of action (Goodman et al.,
1978: 193). The church's frame of reference is to present the
member with a specific background to reality according to which a
choice may be made. It has always been accepted that man consciously
or unconsciously refers to a frame of reference whenever he has to
evaluate his life situation. The findings help to focus on the
way in which the institutionalized church functions as a frame of
reference for members who hold divergent reality orientations. Two
of the twelve items that showed the strongest correlation with the
reality orientations of the research group deal respectively with
(i) the necessity that parents who intend having their children
baptized be Christians by conviction, and (ii) the right of a
church council to refuse baptism to a member's child.

The functioning of the church as frame of reference, which runs
through all the other items, centered round various aspects of
the structure and system of the church. These aspects throw light
on different facets which are directly related to the meaningful
functioning of the church and to the possibility it offers the
members to experience spiritual well-being. Each of these aspects
is subsequently illustrated briefly on the basis of the ten
items of the research data which showed the strongest correlation
to the reality orientation of the 139 progressives, 147 moderates,
and 123 conservatives in the research group.

Participation

Individual members' continued participation in the activities of
the church, as well as the theoretical possibility it offers for
experiencing spiritual well-being, is related to a number of factors.
The participation has to have meaning for the participants, and any
alternative to the way in which members participate in church
activities has to be regarded as subordinate (Cohen, 1971: 134).
Church attendance has, for example, to function as an act through
which the participant acquires religious meaning. There should be
a link or bond based on personal meaning or gain which entails
lasting participation.

It appears from the data relating to these three items in Table 1
that church participation occupies a less central position, particularly with regard to the progressively oriented members. If
religion were defined as the service to and of God, in and through
human society and not as the individual inner possession of religious
convictions of individuals, then the question should arise as to
whether the ecclesiastic-religious life-world of man ought not to
come to the fore in visible form. There is indeed more to the life
of the church than just the public worship or any other religious

act. The attitude toward participation in institutionalized forms of religion indicates the possibility which the institutionalized church offers its members for ensuring spiritual well-being.

Table 1. Participation (in percentages)

Reality Orientation	The necessity of regular church attendance by a religious person:		
	No	Perhaps	Yes
Progressive	54.7	16.5	28.8
Moderate	35.4	17.7	46.9
Conservative	21.1	12.2	66.7

X^2: 41.3; P <.01; C: 0.303; calculated C/maximum C: 0.371

Reality Orientation	Need for greater involvement in church activities:		
Progressive	41.0	28.1	30.9
Moderate	18.4	28.6	53.1
Conservative	13.0	26.8	60.2

X^2: 37.6; P <.01; C: 0.290; calculated C/maximum C: 0.355

Reality Orientation	The possibility of leading a religious life as Christian without belonging to a church:		
Progressive	30.9	30.2	38.8
Moderate	51.0	27.9	21.1
Conservative	65.9	22.0	12.2

X^2: 38.4; P <.01; C: 0.293; calculated C/maximum C: 0.359

Cohesion

Here the emphasis shifts from the question "What is the relationship of church members to their participation in activities within the church?" to "Why do members remain within the church and congreation?" This question embraces resistance to dissension or separation (Cohen, 1971: 135-139). Mutual interests and dependence are prominent.

In the case of the church one would expect that there would be a greater measure of group cohesion among members. Loyalty and devotion to greater unity (the church) have a better opportunity of existing where corporate witness and symbolism are found to establish a common bond.

297

Table 2. Cohesion (in percentages)

| Reality Orientation | The extent to which it is felt that bonds with the church could be broken without much trouble: | | | | |
	No, definitely not	No, not really	Uncertain	Yes, rather	Yes, definitely
Progressive	41.0	35.3	5.8	12.9	5.0
Moderate	61.2	24.5	4.8	8.2	1.4
Conservative	75.6	14.6	2.4	6.5	0.8

x^2: 35.4; $P < .01$; C: 0.282; calculated C/maximum C: 0.346

	Permissibility of member's deflection from doctrine:				
Progressive	23.7	9.4	25.2	13.7	28.1
Moderate	39.5	14.3	28.4	10.9	17.0
Conservative	69.1	9.8	11.4	2.4	7.3

x^2: 65.8; $P < .01$; C: 0.372; calculated C/maximum C: 0.456

	The extent to which members have a strong affiliation for fellow members:				
Progressive	7.2	48.2	9.4	25.9	9.4
Moderate	3.4	36.1	9.5	39.5	11.6
Conservative	2.4	22.0	6.5	39.8	29.3

x^2: 41.2; $P < .01$; C: 0.303; calculated C/maximum C: 0.371

In theory there exists an overall reality within the church in which meaning can be given to religious behavior. Common belief, acceptance of a common normative structure (biblical principles), and participation in a common ideal (the spreading of God's kingdom) are some aspects which should lead to social cohesion. The data, however, seem to show that group loyalty or common fate shared by the community cannot be taken for granted (Table 2).

Solidarity

Solidarity in the church is found in the willingness to act together for the sake of specific goals. This concept relates specifically to the communal conviction of the members. This feeling of belonging is based on an experience of strong involvement in and loyalty to the church. Solidarity rests to a great extent on identification with the church. Emancipation of the members' way of thinking and decision-making is evident from the data in Table 3.

Table 3. Solidarity (in percentages)

Reality Orientation	The experience of strong involvement in church events:				
	No, definitely not	No, not really	Uncertain	Yes, rather	Yes, definitely
Progressive	15.8	36.7	10.1	21.6	15.8
Moderate	2.0	31.3	8.2	38.1	20.4
Conservative	2.4	16.3	14.6	28.5	38.2

X^2: 59.2; P<.01; C: 0.356; calculated C/maximum C: 0.435

	The acceptance of a church pronouncement above personal conscience:		
	No	Perhaps	Yes
Progressive	71.9	19.4	8.6
Moderate	47.6	35.4	17.0
Conservative	29.3	36.6	34.1

X^2: 54.8; P<.01; C: 0.344; calculated C/maximum C: 0.421

Consensus

In looking at the concepts of participation, cohesion, and solidarity we find that a certain principle runs through the whole discussion. This principle is the willingness of individual members to act in accordance with the broad, enveloping frame of reality in which the church functions. The absence of a common disposition makes the occurrence of consensus improbable (Table 4).

Table 4. Consensus (in percentages)

Reality Orientation	Consensus of opinion with fellow church members:				
	No, definitely not	No, not really	Uncertain	Yes, rather	Yes, definitely
Progressive	2.9	21.6	27.3	42.4	5.8
Moderate	1.4	11.6	20.4	54.4	12.2
Conservative	2.4	10.6	8.9	61.8	16.3

X^2: 30.7; P<.01; C: 0.264; calculated C/maximum C: 0.324

	The church's authority over the members' way of life:		
	No	Perhaps	Yes
Progressive	49.6	21.6	28.8
Moderate	30.6	36.7	32.7
Conservative	15.4	22.8	61.8

X^2: 52.0; P<.01; C: 0.366; calculated C/maximum C: 0.411

Members' willingness or readiness to act according to the normative demands of the church stresses two aspects, i.e., the member's
inner motivation and the external pressure exercised by the church.

CONCLUSION

If one is to judge the stability or instability of religious
commitments from the church's point of view, attention must be
paid to the degree of conformity between the attitudes of the members and the norms and teachings of their church. It is precisely
with reference to this that divergences concerning the reality
orientation of members and the way in which the church functions as
a frame of reference come to the fore. When the church no longer
acts as a frame of reference for the member, the church ceases to
figure in the life-world of the member and no longer contributes
to spiritual well-being.

If the progressively oriented member no longer experiences affiliation as far as participation, cohesion, solidarity, and consensus
are concerned within the frame of reference of the church, it must
be assumed that the church plays only a slight role in the consti-
tution of an overall reality within which he has to live his everyday life. When the church similarly plays a marginal role, the
question of the system integration of the church also becomes relevant. This raises the question of the meaningful survival of the
church.

For the member involved in the church in this way, the church
has not succeeded in structuring or influencing the reality orientation of the member. The involvement of this member in the church
remains incomplete because it does not penetrate to the level of
motivation. The involvement of the progressively oriented members
in the church is also incomplete because it does not penetrate the
level of meaning. If the church functions only minimally or not
at all as frame of reference, institutionalized religion loses
its purpose and meaning. This results in the church's exercising
only a slight influence on the spiritual, meaning-giving center
of the life-worlds of such members.

PART VI. CONCLUSION

Chapter 24

THE FUTURE OF RESEARCH ON SPIRITUAL WELL-BEING*

David O. Moberg

We have seen that spiritual well-being is a significant topic for sociological investigation. It reflects many of the basic interests of classical sociological theorists. It focuses attention around central issues of the sociology of religion. It contributes to numerous insights about individual and institutional behavior. It can be studied by all of the research methods at the disposal of social and behavioral scientists, and it already has been studied in a wide variety of religious and national contexts.

Investigations into spiritual well-being are fraught with rich possibilities for contributing to the quality of human life. They contribute to the objectives of professional people in all of the occupations which are oriented toward helping to meet human needs in a wholistic frame of reference. The work of sociologists on this subject therefore overlaps with the theoretical, ideological, descriptive, and methodological findings, concerns, and efforts of scholars in numerous other disciplines.

This chapter sketches a few of the basic research challenges that lie ahead of scientists and scholars who aim to broaden the horizons of our knowledge and strengthen the foundations of our understanding of spiritual well-being. It mentions some significant examples of relevant work that has not been described elsewhere in this book, and it suggests the promising possibilities of future collaborative research.

BASIC RESEARCH PROBLEMS

As is typical in the development of most subjects when they are first introduced into the social and behavioral sciences, many significant issues related to spiritual well-being still must be

---

*Portions of this chapter are reprinted from Sociological Analysis, vol. 40, no. 1, Spring 1979, as concluding parts of the article reprinted in Chapter 1 of this book.

resolved. Some of these pertain to basic values and philosophical assumptions, others to conceptual, theoretical, and empirical topics. The significant progress already made on many of these topics provides a foundation upon which to base the next steps.

Only if we assume that the concept of the spiritual nature of humanity is ontologically based are we likely to engage in research to seek evidences of it. If one assumes that it is merely a reification or hypostatization, the assumption constitutes a self-fulfilling prophecy, for the result will be failure to seek any evidences of it and even the inability to recognize such evidences when they emerge serendipitously. We ought, therefore, to be skeptical of the reductionistic perspective that interprets observable evidence of the spiritual as constituting nothing but reflections of other phenomena. This temptation to yield to the fallacy of reductionistic "nothing buttery" (MacKay, 1974: 40-45) is particularly strong on subjects related to religion (Moberg, 1978a). We may at times have doubts about the possibility of incorporating the concept of spiritual well-being and its analogues into sociology, but we need to realize that premature negative conclusions will definitely cut off even the possibility of doing so. Such judgment ought not to be accepted until after substantial effort has been expended in an attempt to bring the subject into the domain of both qualitative and quantitative sociology.

Values obviously intrude in regard to specification of the criteria by which it can be determined that people possess or lack spiritual well-being. Each major ideological school has its own implicit or explicit definitions and criteria. Religious bodies have their traditional theologies and scriptures. Theoretical schools of both the sciences and the helping professions have their own sets of interpretations. It is entirely possible that some of the criteria of spiritual well-being specified by certain groups may be considered symptoms of spiritual illness by others.

The respective groups sometimes are anxious to give authoritative definitions couched in the language and ideology of their own specific faith commitments. Some of these may involve a creedal approach, emphasizing the importance of correct beliefs. Some are experiential, accentuating the attainment of certain emotional feelings, affects, sentiments, and sensations. Some are ritualistic, holding that through rites of passage or sacraments one can become spiritually well. Intellectual, dispositional, mystical, behavioral, and communal interpretations may also be identified (Moberg, 1977a: 10-11).

As a result of this diversity of conceptual interpretations, much initial work toward the construction of an index of spiritual well-being may of necessity have to be confined within particular ideological frames of reference. As a result, relatively independent and different indexes may be constructed for use in the contexts of Charismatic Catholicism, Traditional Catholicism,

Protestant Fundamentalism, Evangelical Christianity, Liberal
Protestantism, Mormonism, Orthodox Judaism, Reform Judaism, Marxism,
and the various branches of Hinduism, Buddhism, and Islam, to
mention but a few major possibilities.

After extensive research has been done within each of several
value-orientations, it will be possible to determine the extent to
which and the manner in which these varying definitions, together
with their supporting criteria and indicators, overlap with each
other. Possibly the overlap can lead to constructing a general
Index of Spiritual Well-Being which will be useful in all ideological groups and sociocultural settings. That Index can then be
used to study a broad range of topics and test numerous hypotheses,
including those which relate spiritual well-being to social justice,
personality development, mental health, religious education, and
effective socialization.

The conceptual issue is also complicated by the difficulty of
defining "health." Even in the area of physical and mental conditions, most definitions are couched in a negative manner; that is,
they define health as the absence of illness (Leach, 1975; Susser,
1974). It is possible that the same will apply in the area of
"spiritual health." If so, a major focus in the development of an
Index of Spiritual Well-Being will need to be upon "Spiritual Illness."
Of course, it may be inadvisable to adopt the health model because
of its negativistic connotation and its traditional orientation
toward treating illnesses more than toward fostering and sustaining
good health.

The manner and degree to which wholistic well-being (that of the
total person) can be analyzed in terms of component parts (e.g.,
physical, mental, material, and spiritual) is also a problem that
deserves explicit consideration. As with other topics, diverse
theoretical commitments and philosophical assumptions will lead to
varying conclusions by the nominalists and realists, functionalists
and conflict sociologists, and empiricists and ethnomethodologists,
to mention but a few examples of frequently clashing perspectives.

All of the problems of defining "religion" are evident also in
connection with defining "spiritual well-being" (Berger, 1967: 25-28,
175-178; 1974; Towler, 1974: 10-19; Weigert, 1974). The context
and purpose of any given theoretical, practical, or methodological
application of the concept are basic to determination of the usefulness, desirability, and validity of any given definition (see Machalek,
1977).

Although many Christian religious groups have had their own criteria to classify persons as lacking or possessing spiritual well-
being (whatever its label may be), these have frequently been flawed
by problems of hypocrisy, excessive judgmentalism, legalism, sub-
jectivism in applications of the criteria, and other significant

303

problems. These difficulties have contributed to the elimination of specific character standards for being members in good standing in many groups. Nevertheless, examination of the criteria which prevailed in the past and of the crude operational definitions that were used in their enforcement can reveal the implicit "indexes" of spiritual well-being and parallel concepts which were applied.

Other questions which are both conceptual and theoretical pertain to the problem of whether spiritual well-being is a dichotomous (either-or) phenomenon or a continuous variable, whether it is a condition or an on-going process, whether it is basically qualitative or quantitative, whether it is a strictly "religious" or "secular humanistic" concept, and whether it can be objectively identified or is only an interiorized, subjective phenomenon.

Some will raise the issue of the danger of imprisoning people in a three-dimensional universe and failing to recognize that the human spirit transcends space, time, and matter. We must avoid the reductionistic "nothing-buttery" temptation (MacKay, 1974: 40-45), common among social scientists and other scholars, to assume that when we have "explained" something within our own frame of reference, we have explained it away (Claerbaut, 1977).

Obviously, there also are pragmatic problems of finding the appropriate resources for investigations of spiritual well-being. Since the subject overlaps considerably with religion, the biases of funding agencies against allocating financial support to "religious" projects is likely to extend also to a bias against funding research on this subject. Again, however, if we succumb to a defeatist attitude in this regard, the self-fulfilling prophecy mechanism will guarantee a lack of success.

FUTURE PROSPECTS

We have reviewed the scientific and applied needs for social indicators of spiritual well-being, the progress, that has been made toward the development of an Index of Spiritual Well-Being, conceptual and theoretical studies, exploratory descriptive and analytical research on spiritual well-being and related topics, and significant problems which must be confronted in research on the subject, to mention but a sample of the rich coverage of this book.

All of the best qualitative and quantitative methodologies of sociology can be directed toward resolution of the numerous issues which continue to demand our attention. Cross-national research, as well as research within each cultural, ideological, and theoretical frame of reference, is essential in order to attack this subject on a broad scale and not be limited to some narrow, culturally limited, parochial, or insular approach. Important as such narrow approaches are in the early stages of the research, it is essential to keep moving toward the broader perspective with the goal of covering the spiritual well-being of the entire scope of humanity.

As most of the authors of this book have intimated, the subject of spiritual well-being ranges far and wide; it is not a microscopic topic of little relevance beyond its own immediate religious or pseudo-religious domain. It is important to recognize also that sociology is but one discipline among many which are interested in various aspects of spiritual well-being. It would be tragic if scholars and scientists in other fields or areas of specialization would refrain from working on the subject in the mistaken assumption that it now is a part of the domain of the sociologists of religion, hence outside their own. Such a pattern of action -- really inaction! -- occasionally has contributed to major gaps in human knowledge in the overlapping or boundary areas of the respective social sciences (Lynd, 1939: 151-152).

Much relevant work by others already has been done or is in progress. Possibly the most significant research on the psychological aspects of spiritual well-being is by Ellison and Paloutzian (1978). Many of the studies from the National Conference Integrating Christianity and Mental Health (Donaldson, 1976) have a direct bearing on our subject, as does the work of Unger (1976) and to some extent Pettersson (1975) in Sweden. Research related to the discovery that about one-third of the adult population of the U.S.A. have had one or more mystical experiences (Bourque, 1969; Greeley, 1974, 1975; Greeley and McCready, 1975; Hood, 1977a; Thomas and Cooper, 1978) undoubtedly is relevant, as is that which pertains to the ultimate values for which people live (McCready and Greeley, 1976).

The Nurses Christian Fellowship has stimulated both research and the development of professional guidelines by which nurses can help to satisfy the spiritual needs of patients in the context of caring for the whole person (Fish and Shelly, 1978). Many medical doctors, like William Standish Reed (1969), Director of the Christian Medical Foundation International in Tampa, Florida, are finding their work to be more effective when they give explicit attention to the spiritual nature and needs of their patients. The evaluation research which has accompanied the development of the Wholistic Health Centers (Tubesing, 1976) under the leadership of Granger Westberg (Tubesing and Strosahl, 1976) comprises another important building block in the edifice of knowledge about spiritual well-being. All of the work on "holistic health care" which is truly holistic, including attention to the spiritual nature of people, is directly relevant to our quest (see, e.g., Swaim, 1962; Kelsey, 1973; von Gagern, 1954; Belgum, 1967), as are the scholarly interpretations of the numerous branches of the human potential movement (see Hulme, 1978).

The studies mentioned here and elsewhere in this book are but samples of significant efforts by people in numerous disciplines which are relevant to the sociological study of spiritual well-being.

The work of theologians on spirituality and of artists, historians, literary scholars, philosophers, and others in the humanities who are concerned with enrichment of the human spirit similarly has much to contribute, even though most of it is not explicitly scientifically oriented. Experiences of the clergy and clinical insights from studies by spiritually sensitive persons in psychiatry, psychology, social work, medicine, and the counseling professions can be rich sources of insights into spiritual well-being. Experimental research on the efficacy of prayer in physical, mental, and spiritual healing and in the reconstruction and rehabilitation of personalities (Parker and St. Johns, 1957) constitutes supportive evidence.

All of this demonstrates that communication and cooperation with representatives of anthropology, psychology, philosophy, history, linguistics, literature, theology, and many other disciplines, as well as with the practitioners and researchers in clinical and counseling psychology, psychiatry, other medical and paramedical vocations, marriage and family counseling, social work, education, pastoral care, and many other professions, can help us to develop this subject on a much broader front than is represented by sociology alone (Moberg, 1978b). Even though the sociology of religion is becoming multiparadigmatic (Moberg, 1978a: 2), our frame of reference is still limited. No discipline can be completely holistic, covering every aspect of the complex realities of human life. We need others, and they need us.

Through synergistic cooperation with each other, we can mutually round out the totality of work that is being done in such manner that all of us will enrich all the others. Therefore it may be advisable to develop funding proposals for cooperative research -- national and cross-national, disciplinary and interdisciplinary, inter- and intra-faith oriented -- on spiritual well-being. Even if such efforts fail, however, we can remain in communication with each other and on occasion cooperate cross-nationally in the collection and analysis of data. This will make our work of far greater value than if each of us were working all alone.

As we have seen, rising popular interest, human needs, scientific capabilities, and pioneering progress which already has been made combine to indicate that the time has come for extensive, systematic investigations of spiritual well-being. The potential contributions of such work to the body of knowledge and theoretical perspectives of the respective academic disciplines, policy sciences, and "helping professions" are great. Greater still is their potentiality for improving the quality of human life through giving explicit attention to the all-too-frequently-neglected spiritual nature and needs of the whole person.

CONTRIBUTORS

To conserve space we have abbreviated the names of some of the most frequently mentioned professional associations and journals:

ASA   American Sociological Association
ASR   Association for the Sociology of Religion
CISR   International Conference for the Sociology of Religion
ISA   International Sociological Association
JSSR   Journal for the Scientific Study of Religion
RRA   Religious Research Association
RRR   Review of Religious Research
SSSR   Society for the Scientific Study of Religion

EILEEN BARKER is Lecturer in Sociology, London School of Economics (Houghton St., Aldwych, London WC2 2AE, England), from which she earned the B.Sc. (Hons. First Class) degree in 1970. She won the Hobhouse Memorial Prize in 1970 and is currently convenor of the Sociology of Religion Group in the British Sociological Association. Her articles have been published in Inquiry, Archives de Sciences Sociales des Religions, Group Analysis, Interdisciplinary Science Reviews, Contact, Philosophy of the Social Sciences, Times Newspapers, and other periodicals.

NORMAN W.H. BLAIKIE is Senior Lecturer in Sociology, Monash University (Clayton, Victoria 3168, Australia), from which he received the Ph. D. degree in 1973. He is the Australian and New Zealand Delegate to the ISA Council. He is the author of CONVERT, CARE OR CHALLENGE: CONFLICTS AND DILEMMAS OF AUSTRALIAN CLERGY (University of Queensland Press, 1979) and articles in JSSR, Sociology, the Sociological Review, and the Australian and New Zealand Journal of Sociology.

CARROLL J. BOURG is Professor of Sociology, Fisk University (Nashville, TN 37203, USA). His Ph. D. degree was conferred by Brandeis University in 1967. He has previously taught at Boston College and Woodstock College and in 1974 was a fellow in the Institute for Ecumenical Research, Collegeville, MN. He is editor of Sociological Analysis, President-elect of ASR, and a member of ASA, SSSR, and Fellowship of Reconciliation. He is the author of THE MOBILITY OF THE ELDERLY IN A SOUTHERN METROPOLITAN AREA (Nashville: Center for Community Studies Publication, 1972).

EARL D. C. BREWER is Professor of Sociology and Religion in Emory University's School of Theology (Atlanta, GA 30322, USA), having

previously served from 1938 to 1945 in pastoral and special appoint-
ments in the Western North Carolina Conference of the Methodist
Church. He earned his Ph. D. in 1951 from the University of North
Carolina. A past-president of RRA and of the Atlanta Chapter of the
World Future Society, he also is a member of ASA and SSSR. He is
the author of LIFE AND RELIGION IN SOUTHERN APPALACHIA (with W. D.
Weatherford; NY: Friendship Press, 1962) and THE MENTAL HEALTH
COUNSELOR IN THE COMMUNITY (with David S. Shapiro et al.; Springfield,
IL: Charles C Thomas, 1968); editor of TRANSCENDENCE AND MYSTERY
(NY: IDOC/NA, 1976), and contributor of articles in Social Forces
and RRR.

D. WAYNE BROWN, JR. is a Graduate Assistant and Instructor, Family
Studies Program, Brigham Young University (Provo, UT 84602, USA),
where he previously served as a Graduate Assistant in the Department
of Sociology. He earned his M.S. degree there in April 1979,
and earlier he was a summa cum laude graduate of Howard Payne University (B.A., 1976) and a Presidential Scholar at BYU (Winter 1977).
He is a member of AAMFT and National Council on Family Relations.

RICHARD DAVID CHRISTY is Assistant Professor of Sociology, Wilfrid
Laurier University (75 University Ave. West, Waterloo, Ontario N2L
3C5, Canada). His Ph. D. degree was conferred by the University of
Toronto in 1977, where he had the honor of receiving the University
Sociology Grant in 1973 and the Ontario Graduate Fellowship in 1970.
He is a member of ASA, ASR, and the Canadian Sociology & Anthropology
Assn. He is a contributor to A READER IN SOCIOLOGY: A CHRISTIAN
PERSPECTIVE (Charles deSanto & W. L. Smith-Hinds, eds., Scottdale,
PA: Herald Press, 1979).

JAN K. COETZEE is Senior Lecturer in Sociology, University of South
Africa (P.O. Box 392, UNISA, Pretoria 0001, Republic of South Africa).
Previous to 1974 he was a Research Officer in the Human Sciences
Research Council. He earned his D. Phil. degree from the University
of Pretoria in 1973 and has published six articles in the South
African Journal of Sociology.

JAMES TAYLOR DUKE is Professor of Sociology, Brigham Young Univer-
sity (Provo, UT 84602, USA), having previously taught at Idaho
State University, University of Utah, and Utah State University.
His Ph. D. was conferred by the University of California at Los
Angeles in 1963. In 1971 he was Professor of the Year at BYU. He
is a former president of the Utah Sociological Society and a member
of ASA, ISA, Pacific Sociological Assn., and Western Social Science
Assn. He is the author of CONFLICT AND POWER IN SOCIAL LIFE (Brigham
Young University Press, 1976) and of articles in Social Forces,
Western Sociologist, and THE DEMOCRATIC REVOLUTION IN THE WEST
INDIES (edited by Wendell Bell, New York: Schenkman, 1967).

HAROLD FALLDING is professor of Sociology, University of Waterloo
(Waterloo, Ontario N2L 3G1, Canada). Previous teaching and research

appointments were in the University of Sydney, Dept. of Agricultural Economics, and University of New South Wales in Australia and at Rutgers University in the USA. His Ph. D. degree was conferred by Australian National University in 1957, and he was honored by membership in Clare Hall, University of Cambridge, in 1971-72. He is a member of ASA, ASR, SSSR, and Canadian Sociology & Anthropology Assn. He is the author of THE SOCIOLOGICAL TASK (Prentice-Hall, 1968), THE SOCIOLOGY OF RELIGION (McGraw-Hill Ryerson, 1974), and DRINKING, COMMUNITY AND CIVILIZATION (Rutgers University Press, 1974).

JOSEPH H. FICHTER, S. J., is Professor of Sociology, Loyola University (New Orleans, LA 70118, USA). He also has taught at the University of Chicago, Harvard University, and the State University of New York in Albany. His Ph. D. is from Harvard University, 1947. He has served as president of SSSR, council member of ASA, and vice-president of the Southern Sociological Society. Among his numerous books are ORGANIZATION MAN IN THE CHURCH (Schenkman, 1973), ONE-MAN RESEARCH (Wiley, 1974), and THE CATHOLIC CULT OF THE PARACLETE (Sheed & Ward, 1975).

WILLIAM R. GARRETT is Associate Professor of Sociology, St. Michael's College (Winooski, VT 05404, USA). His Ph. D. in Sociology of Religion was conferred by Drew University in 1968. He is an associate editor of Sociological Analysis and a member of ASA, ASR, Eastern Sociological Society, RRA, SSSR, and American Academy of Religion. His articles have appeared in Sociological Analysis, JSSR, and SOCIOLOGY: AN INTRODUCTION (Reece McGee, ed., NY: Holt, Rinehart & Winston, rev. ed., 1977).

PAOLO GIURIATI is a teacher of Sociology and Sociology of Religion, Theological Dept. of North Italy -- See of Padua (Priestly Seminary of Padua, Seminario Vescovile, Via Seminario 29, 35.100 Padova, Italy). His doctoral degree in social sciences was earned at Gregorian University, Rome, 1975. His articles have appeared in Studia Patavina and Il Santo.

LARRY M. HYNSON, JR. is Associate Professor of Sociology, Oklahoma State University (407 Business Bldg., OSU, Stillwater, OK 74074, USA). Previous teaching appointments were at the University of Tennessee and Trinity College, Deerfield, IL. He earned his Ph. D. from the University of Tennessee in 1972. He is a member of Alpha Kappa Delta (the national sociology honor society), chairperson of the community development program committee in the American Society for Training and Development, and a member of the Southern Regional Demographic Society and the Cooperative Education Assn. His articles have appeared in Family Coordinator, JSSR, Rural Sociology, Practical Sociology, RRR, Omega, Free Inquiry, and Urban Education.

J. HOWARD KAUFFMAN is Professor of Sociology, Goshen College (Goshen, IN 46526, USA), where he has taught since 1948. His Ph. D. was conferred by the University of Chicago in 1960. He is vice-president of the Indiana Council on Family Relations and a member of ASA, ASR, ISA, and National Council on Family Relations. He is author (with Leland Harder) of ANABAPTISTS FOUR CENTURIES LATER (Scottdale, PA: Herald Press, 1975).

GARY PAUL KELSEN is a postgraduate student at Monash University (Dept. of Anthropology & Sociology, Clayton, Victoria 3168, Australia). His B.A. (Hons.) was earned at Monash University in 1975.

DAVID LYON is Senior Lecturer in Sociology, Ilkley College (Ilkley, West Yorkshire, LS29 9RD, England). He has previously taught at Wilfrid Laurier University and Regent College in Canada and earned his Ph. D. from the University of Bradford. He is the author of KARL MARX: A CHRISTIAN APPRECIATION OF HIS LIFE AND THOUGHT (London: Lion Books, 1979) and CHRISTIANS AND SOCIOLOGY (London: Tyndale Press, 1975; Downers Grove, IL: InterVarsity Press, 1976).

OTTO MADURO is Professor of Sociology, University of Los Andes (Apartado 349, Merida, Venezuela). He was a social worker at the Venezuelan Council on Childhood, 1967-69. His Ph. D. was conferred by the Catholic University of Louvain, Belgium, in 1978. His book on MARXISMO Y RELIGION (Caracas: Monte Avila editores, 1977) won him the Best Essay award of the National Council on Culture in May 1978. He is a board member of the Sociology of Religion Research Committee in the ISA and a member of the ASR, SSSR, Council on the Study of Religion (USA), CISR, and AFSR (France).

REGINA MARCUM, O.S.F., is Assistant Principal and Teacher, Buffalo Academy of the Sacred Heart (3860 Main St., Buffalo, MY 14226, USA). She earned the M. A. degree in Sociology from Marquette University in 1977. She is a member of ASR, Catholic School Administrators Assn. of New York State, and the National, New York, and Niagara Frontier Councils for the Social Sciences.

DAVID ALFRED MARTIN is Professor of Sociology, London School of Economics (Houghton St., Aldwych, London WC2 2AE, England). He earned the Ph. D. degree in 1964. He is president of the CISR, former editor of A SOCIOLOGICAL YEARBOOK OF RELIGION IN BRITAIN, and author of A GENERAL THEORY OF SECULARISATION (Blackwell, 1978) and other publications, including articles in the British Journal of Sociology, Encounter, Times Literary Supplement, and New Statesman.

PATRICK H. McNAMARA is Associate Professor of Sociology, University of New Mexico (Albuquerque, NM 87131, USA). He previously taught in the University of Texas at El Paso and California State College in Los Angeles. His Ph. D. was earned at the University of California in Los Angeles, 1968. He is a member of the ASA, ASR, RRA, SSSR, and Southwestern Social Science Association. He edited RELIGION AMERICAN STYLE (Harper & Row, 1974) and is author of articles in JSSR, Sociological Analysis, and Social Science Quarterly.

DAVID O. MOBERG is Professor of Sociology, Marquette University (Milwaukee, WI 53233, USA). He previously taught at the University of Washington in Seattle, Bethel College in Minnesota, and in Fulbright professorships at the University of Groningen, Netherlands, and Muenster University, West Germany. His Ph. D. degree was conferred by the University of Minnesota in 1952. He is a member of the Alpha Kappa Delta and Pi Gamma Mu honor societies and is listed in WHO'S WHO IN AMERICA, WHO'S WHO IN RELIGION, and numerous other directories. He is a former president of ASR and the Wisconsin Sociological Society and a former editor of the Journal of the American Scientific Affiliation, RRR, and ADRIS Newsletter (Assn. for the Development of Religious Information Systems). He is a member of the board of Christian Sociologists and of the Sociology of Religion Research Committee in the ISA, as well as a member of ASA, ASR, RRA, CISR, SSSR, Gerontological Society, Association for Humanist Sociology, and Midwest Sociological Society. He is the author of THE CHURCH AS A SOCIAL INSTITUTION (Prentice-Hall, 1962), INASMUCH: CHRISTIAN SOCIAL RESPONSIBILITY IN THE TWENTIETH CENTURY (Eerdmans, 1965), THE GREAT REVERSAL: EVANGELISM AND SOCIAL CONCERN (Lippincott, rev. ed., 1977), THE CHURCH AND THE OLDER PERSON (with Robert M. Gray, Eerdmans, rev. ed., 1977), and articles in a wide range of sociological and religious journals.

LARRY F. RENETZKY is Executive Director of Niles Family Service, Village of Niles and also is in private practice as a Consultant and Counselor (637 Webster, Algonquin, IL 60102, USA). He has previously held administrative positions in the Dept. of Children's and Family Services for the State of Illinois, the Illinois Valley Economic Development Corporation (OEO), and Peaceful Valley Youth Ranch. His M.S.W. degree was earned at the George Warren Brown School of Social Work, Washington University, 1963. He has been a member of the Academy of Certified Social Workers since 1965 and was first listed in WHO'S WHO IN THE MIDWEST in 1972. He is president of the Fox Valley Chapter of the National Association of Social Work and a member of the national board of NACSW (National Association of Christians in Social Work). He is a former president of the Midwest Chapter of NACSW, the suburban Family Agency Assn. of Metropolitan Chicago, and the Northwest Suburban Welfare Council, and he is a former vice president of the Illinois Branch of the AAMFC. His articles have been published in CAPS Bulletin (Christian Assn. for Psychological Studies) and The Paraclete (journal of NACSW).

KULDIP KUMAR ROY is Editor of Religious Consultancy (55, Gariahat Road, P.O. Box 10210, Calcutta 700019, India). His previous positions were editorships of Religious Book Review Index and Bibliographia Asiatica. He earned his B.A. (Hons.) in Punjab, India, and his D. Litt. from the University of Canberra, Australia. He won the Valor Award in New York City in 1966, the Bruce Hartmann Trophy in Sydney, Australia, in 1971, and the Edward Hatton Award in London, 1972. He is a Fellow of the Royal Asiatic Society, London; Theosophical Society, Adyar, Madras; Royal Society of Medicine, London; Asiatic

Society, Calcutta, and the International Research Society for Children's Literature, Stockholm. He was the organising secretary of the International Assn. for the History of Agriculture. His publications include THE SWAMI AND THE COMRADE: A HINDU-MARXIST DIALOGUE; THE MYSTICS: SIKH & SUFI, and ANTHOLOGY OF MYSTIC LITERATURE OF THE PUNJAB.

ARTHUR ST. GEORGE is Assistant Professor of Sociology, University of New Mexico (Albuquerque, NM 87131, USA). He has previously taught at Sacramento State University and the University of California in Davis. His Ph. D. was conferred by the University of California in Davis in 1974.

DEMOSTHENES SAVRAMIS is Professor fuer Religions- und Kultursoziologie, University of Koeln, and Lehrbeauftragter fuer Kultursoziologie, University of Bonn (Masurenweg 8, 5300 Bonn-Tannenbusch, Federal Republic of Germany). He has previously held research and teaching positions in Greece and at the University of Bonn. He holds three doctoral degrees: Dr. phil. (Bonn, 1956), Dr. rer. pol. (Koeln, 1960), Dr. theol. (Athens, 1962), and he is a bearer of the Order of St. Andreas in Gold. He is a member of the ISA, CISR, Deutsche Gesellschaft fuer Soziologie, Deutsche Sektion der Internationalen Gesellschaft fuer Religionswissenschaft, and Deutsche Gesellschaft fuer Wissenschaftliche Sexualforschung. He is an editor of the INTERNATIONALEN OEKUMENISCHEN BIBLIOGRAPHIE and DRITTEN WELT and is a contributor to several radio programs. Among his numerous publications are AUS DER NEUGRIECHISCHEN THEOLOGIE,1961; ZUR SOZIOLOGIE DES BYZANTINISCHEN MOENCHTUMS, 1962; DIE SOZIALE STELLUNG DES PRIESTERS IN GRIECHENLAND, 1968; THEOLOGIE UND GESELLSCHAFT, 1971; RELIGIONSSOZIOLOGIE: EINE EINFUEHRUNG (2d ed.,1977); RELIGION UND SEXUALITAET, 1972, and THE SATANIZING OF WOMAN: RELIGION VERSUS SEXUALITY, 1974. He also has five books in the Greek language and numerous articles in Greek, English, and German journals, lexica, and encyclopedias.

REFERENCES

AA. VV.
1977 S. Antonio di Padova fra storia e pietà. Padova, Italy: Edizioni Messaggero.

Acquaviva, Sabino
1964 Der Untergang des Heiligen in der industriellen Gesellschaft (trans. from Italian by E. Kenngott). Essen, Germany: Ludgerns.

Ahmed, Farosh
1962 Iqbal's Concept of Self and the Belief in the Hereafter. Karachi, Pakistan: Iqbal Review.

Alcoholics Anonymous
1955 Alcoholics Anonymous. New York: A.A. World Services.

Allport, Gordon W.
1961 The Individual and His Religion. New York: Macmillan.

Anderson, Lavina Fielding
1977 "What Are Nonmembers Interested In?" The Ensign, October: 73-76.

Andrews, Frank M. and Stephen B. Withey
1976 Social Indicators of Well-Being: Americans' Perceptions of Life Quality. New York & London: Plenum.

Anonymous
1975 Twenty-Four Hours a Day. Center City, MN: Hazelden.

Appel, Kenneth E. and Edward A. Strecker
1958 Discovering Ourselves, 3rd ed. New York: Macmillan.

Arberry, Arthur J.
1956 Sufism: An Account of the Mystics of Islam. London: Allen & Unwin.

Argüelles, José and Miriam
1972 Mandala. Berkeley, CA: Shambhala.

Argyle, Michael
1959 Religious Behavior. Glencoe, IL: Free Press.

Armour, David, J. Michael Polich and Harriet Stambul
1976 Alcoholism and Treatment. Santa Monica, CA: Rand.

Atchley, Robert C.
1976 The Sociology of Retirement. New York: Wiley.

Aurobindo, Sri
1949 The Life Divine. Calcutta: Arya.

Avyaktananda, Swami
1972 Universal Meditation. London: Somerset.

Bahr, Howard M.
1978 Mormon Families in Comparative Perspective: Denominational Contrasts in Divorce, Marital Satisfaction, and Other Char-

acteristics. Provo, UT: Family Research Institute, Brigham
Young University.
Bahr, Howard M., Lois Franz Bartel, and Bruce A. Chadwick
1971 "Orthodoxy, activism, and the salience of religion." Jour.
for the Scientific Study of Religion 10: 69-75.
Balswick, Jack and Dawn Ward
1976 "The nature of man and scientific models of society." Jour.
of the Amer. Scientific Affiliation 28: 181-185.
Bandura, Albert
1969 Principles of Behavior Modification. New York: Holt,
Rinehart & Winston.
Barker, Eileen
1978 "Living the Divine Principle: Inside the Reverend Sun Myung
Moon's Unification Church in Britain." Archives de Sciences
Sociales des Religions 45 (1): 75-94.
Bates, Frederick L. and Clyde C. Harvey
1975 The Structures of Social Systems. New York: Wiley.
Bateson, Gregory et al.
1956 "Toward a theory of schizophrenia." Behavioral Science 1:
251-264.
Bauer, Raymond (ed.)
1966 Social Indicators. Cambridge, MA: MIT Press.
Baum, Gregory
1975 Religion and Alienation. New York: Paulist Press.
Beach, Stephen W.
1977 "Religion and political change in Northern Ireland."
Sociological Analysis 38: 37-48.
Beckford, James A.
1975 Religious Organization. The Hague, Netherlands: Mouton.
Belgum, David (ed.)
1967 Religion and Medicine: Essays on Meaning, Values, and
Health. Ames, IA: Iowa State University Press.
Bellah, Robert N.
1970 Beyond Belief. New York: Harper & Row.
1973 Emile Durkheim on Morality and Society (ed.). Chicago:
University of Chicago Press.
1976 "New religious consciousness and the crisis in modernity."
Pp. 333-358 in Glock and Bellah.
Benson, Purnell H.
1960 Religion in Contemporary Culture. New York: Harper.
1966 "An introspective approach to psychological theory."
Paper presented at the annual meeting of the Amer. Psychological Assn., Sep. 4 (copies available from author).
Benz, Ernst
1971 Neue Religionen. Stuttgart, Germany: Ernst Klett Verlag.
Berger, Peter L.
1967 The Sacred Canopy. Garden City, NY: Doubleday.
1973 Zur Dialektik von Religion und Gesellschaft. Frankfurt,
Germany: Fischer Verlag.
1974 "Some second thoughts on substantive versus functional definitions of religion." Jour. for the Scientific Study of

Religion 13: 125-134.
1977 Pyramids of Sacrifice. Harmondsworth, England: Pelican.
Berger, Peter L. and Brigitte Berger
1972 Sociology: A Biographical Approach. New York: Basic Books.
Berger, Peter L., Brigitte Berger and Hansfried Kellner
1974 The Homeless Mind: Modernization and Consciousness. New
York: Vintage Books; Harmondsworth, England: Pelican
Berger, Peter L. and Thomas Luckmann
1967 The Social Construction of Reality. Garden City, NY:
Doubleday.
Bergson, Henri
1935 The Two Sources of Morality and Religion. New York:
Doubleday.
Berkowitz, Leonard
1956 "Group norms among bomber crews." Sociometry 19: 141-153.
Bible, The
n.d. Any of the numerous translations of the Christian Scrip-
tures which have the standard chapter and verse numbers.
LB refers to the Living Bible (Wheaton, IL: Tyndale House;
London: Coverdale House, 1971). NIV refers to the New Inter-
national Version (Grand Rapids, MI: Zondervan, copyright by
the New York International Bible Society, 1978).
Binstock, Robert H. and Ethel Shanas (eds.)
1976 Handbook of Aging and the Social Sciences. New York: Van
Nostrand, Reinholt.
Birnbaum, Norman and Gertrud Lenzer (eds.)
1969 Sociology and Religion: A Book of Readings. Englewood
Cliffs, NJ: Prentice-Hall.
Blaikie, Norman W.H.
1974 "The dialectics of sociological research, or, where should
I begin?" Pp. 131-139 in J. Sherwood Williams and Walter
G. West (eds.), Sociological Research Symposium IV. Richmond,
VA: Virginia Commonwealth University.
1978 "Towards an alternative methodology for the study of occupa-
tional prestige: A reply to my reviewers." Australian &
New Zealand Jour. of Sociology 14(1): 87-95.
Bonnet, Serge
1976 Prières secrètes des Francais d'aujourd'hui. Paris: Ed.
du Cerf.
Bourque, Linda B.
1969 "Social correlates of transcendental experiences." Sociological Analysis 30(3): 151-163.
Bradburn, Norman M.
1969 The Structure of Psychological Well-Being. Chicago: Aldine.
Brewer, Earl D.C. (ed.)
1975 Transcendence and Mystery. New York: IDOC/North America.
Brown, L.B.
1966 "The structure of religious belief." Jour. for the Scientific Study of Religion 5(2): 259-272.
Bryant, M. Daroll and Herbert W. Richardson (eds.)
1978 A Time for Consideration: A Scholarly Appraisal of the

Unification Church. New York: Edwin Mellin Press.
Buber, Martin
  1958 I and Thou. New York: Scribner's.
Bunyan, John (1628-1688)
  1970a Grace Abounding to the Chief of Sinners. Menston, England:
         Scolar Press.
  1970b The Pilgrim's Progress (edited with an introduction by Roger
         Sharrock). Harmondsworth, England: Penguin.
Campbell, Angus and Philip E. Converse (eds.)
  1972 The Human Meaning of Social Change. New York: Russell Sage
         Foundation.
Campbell, Angus, Philip E. Converse and Willard L. Rodgers
  1976 The Quality of American Life. New York: Russell Sage Founda-
         tion.
Campbell, Douglas F. and Dennis W. Magill
  1968 "Religious involvement and intellectuality among university
         students." Sociological Analysis 29: 79-93.
Campbell, Thomas C. and Yoshio Fukuyama
  1970 The Fragmented Layman. Philadelphia: Pilgrim Press.
Campolo, Anthony, Jr.
  1971 A Denomination Looks at Itself.
         Valley Forge, PA: Judson Press.
Capps, Donald, Lewis Rambo and Paul Ransohoff
  1976 Psychology of Religion: A Guide to Information Sources.
         Detroit: Gale Research Co.
Capra, Fritjof
  1975 The Tao of Physics. Berkeley, CA: Shambhala.
Cardwell, Jerry D.
  1969 "The relationship between religious commitment and premarital
         sexual permissiveness: A five dimensional analysis." Socio-
         logical Analysis 30: 72-80.
Chasin, Barbara
  1971 "Neglected variables in the study of death attitudes."
         Sociological Quarterly 12: 107-113.
Cherlin, Andrew and Leo G. Reeder
  1975 "The dimensions of psychological well-being: A critical
         review." Sociological Methods & Research 4: 189-214.
Chisti, Yusif Salim
  1962 God and the Concept of Self. Karachi, Pakistan: Iqbal
         Review.
Church of Jesus Christ of Latter-day Saints
  1830 The Book of Mormon (trans. by Joseph Smith, Jr.). Salt
         Lake City, UT: The Church.
  1833 The Doctrine and Covenants. Salt Lake City, UT: The Church.
  1858 The Pearl of Great Price. Salt Lake City, UT: The Church.
Cipriana, Roberto
  1977 "La religiosità popolare nel Sud." Pp. 427-437 in AA. VV.
Claerbaut, David
  1977 "Religion in the sociological perspective: A form of reduc-
         tionism." Paper presented at the annual meeting of the Mid-
         west Sociological Society, Minneapolis, MN, April 14.

Clarke, William G. and W.A. Wright (eds.)
 1952 The Plays and Sonnets of William Shakespeare. Chicago:
      Encyclopaedia Britannica.
Clayton, Richard R.
 1968 "Religiosity in 5-D: A Southern test." Social Forces 47:
      80-83.
 1971 "Religiosity and premarital sexual permissiveness: Elaboration
      of the relationship and debate." Sociological Analysis 32:
      81-96.
Clayton, Richard R. and James W. Gladden.
 1974 "The five dimensions of religiosity: Toward demythologizing
      a sacred artifact." Jour. for the Scientific Study of
      Religion 13: 135-143.
Clayton, Richard R. and William L. Tolone
 1973 "Religiosity and attitudes toward induced abortion: An
      elaboration of the relationship." Sociological Analysis
      34: 26-39.
Cline, Victor B. and James M. Richards, Jr.
 1965 "A factor-analytic study of religious belief and behavior."
      Jour. of Personality & Social Psychology 1: 569-578.
Cock, Peter H.
 1977 A Study of Alternative Communities in Australia. Ph.D.
      dissertation, Anthropology & Sociology Dept., Monash Univer-
      sity, Melbourne, Australia.
Coe, George A.
 1916 The Psychology of Religion. Chicago: University of Chicago
      Press.
Coetzee, Jan K.
 1978 'n Kerk in die kollig. Pretoria, South Africa: NG Kerk-
      boekhandel.
Cohen, P.S.
 1971 Theorie van de Samenleving. Alphen aan den Rijn, Netherlands:
      Samson.
Cole, W. Owen and Piara Singh Sambhi
 1978 The Sikhs: Their Religious Beliefs and Practices. New Delhi,
      India.
Cook, Thomas C., Jr.
 1977 The Religious Sector Explores Its Mission in Aging. Athens,
      GA: National Interfaith Coalition on Aging.
Cook, Thomas C., Jr. and James Thorson (eds.)
 1979 Spiritual Well-Being of the Elderly. Springfield, IL:
      Charles C Thomas.
Cooley, Charles H.
 1956a Human Nature and the Social Order. Glencoe, IL: Free Press.
 1956b Social Organization. New York: Scribner.
Curle, Adam
 1972 Mystics and Militants: A Study of Awareness, Identity and
      Social Action. London: Tavistock.
Cygnar, Thomas E., Cardell K. Jacobson, and Donald L. Noel
 1977 "Religiosity and prejudice: an interdimensional analysis."
      Jour. for the Scientific Study of Religion 16: 183-191.

317

Dahm, Karl-Wilhelm, Niklas Luhmann and Dieter Stoodt
    1972 Religion - System und Sozialisation. Darmstadt, Germany:
          Neuwied.
Davis, Arthur K.
    1953 Review of Robert A. Nisbet, For Community. Amer. Sociolo-
          gical Review 18: 443-444.
DeCoppens, Peter R.
    1976 Ideal Man in Classical Sociology: The Views of Comte, Pareto,
          Durkheim and Weber. University Park, PA: Pennsylvania State
          University Press.
DeJong, Gordon F. and Joseph E. Faulkner
    1967 "The church, individual religiosity, and social justice."
          Sociological Analysis 28: 34-43.
DeJong, Gordon F., Joseph E. Faulkner and Rex H. Warland
    1976 "Dimensions of religiosity reconsidered: Evidence from a
          cross-cultural study." Social Forces 54: 866-889.
De la Cruz, San Juan (1542-1591)
    1940-52 Saemtliche Werke. Munich: Koesel.
Delooz, Pierre
    1977 "Rapports entre saint réel et saint construit. La sainteté
          comme construction sociale." Pp. 421-426 in AA. VV.
Demerath, Nicholas J. III
    1965 Social Class in American Protestantism. Chicago: Rand McNally.
Deschner, Karlheinz
    1972 Abermals kraehte der Hahn. Reinbek, Germany: Rowohlt.
    1974 Das Kreuz mit der Kirche. Deusseldorf, Germany: Heyne.
Deutsch, Morton
    1973 The Resolution of Conflict: Constructive and Destructive
          Processes. New Haven, CT, & London: Yale University Press.
Dittes, James E.
    1961 "Impulsive closure as reaction to failure-induced threat."
          Jour. of Abnormal & Social Psychology 63: 562-569.
Donaldson, William J., Jr. (ed.)
    1976 Research in Mental Health and Religious Behavior. Atlanta,
          GA: Psychological Studies Institute.
Donne, John (1572-1631)
    1912 The Poems of John Donne (edited with introductions and
          commentary by Herbert J. D. Grierson), 2 volumes. Oxford,
          England: Clarendon Press.
    1953-62 The Sermons of John Donne (edited with introductions and
          critical apparatus by George R. Potter and Evelyn M. Simpson),
          10 volumes. Berkeley, CA: University of California Press.
Douglas, Jack D. (ed.)
    1970 Understanding Everyday Life. Chicago: Aldine.
Douglas, Mary
    1970 Natural Symbols: Explorations in Cosmology. London: Barrie
          & Rockcliff.
Duke, James T.
    1976 Conflict and Power in Social Life. Provo, UT: Brigham Young
          University Press.

Duncombe, David C.
  1969 The Shape of the Christian Life. Nashville, TN: Abingdon.
Durkheim, Emile (1858-1917)
  1915 The Elementary Forms of the Religious Life (trans. from
        French by Joseph Swain). London: Allen & Unwin.
  1947, 1965 Ibid. New York: Free Press.
Duvall, Evelyn M.
  1957 Family Development. Philadelphia: Lippincott.
Eckhart, Meister (ca. 1260-1328)
  1956-63 Die deutschen und lateinischen Werke: Predigten und
        Traktate. Stuttgart: Kohlhammer.
Edwards, Tilden H., Jr., Loren B. Mead, Parker J. Palmer and James
        P. Simmons
  1974 Spiritual Growth: An Empirical Exploration of Its Meaning,
        Sources and Implications. Washington, DC: Metropolitan
        Ecumenical Training Center.
Eliade, Mircea
  1959 The Sacred and the Profane. New York: Harper.
  1963 Patterns in Comparative Religion. New York: Meridian
Elio, Franzin
  1977 "Oral Interventions." Pp. 230-233, 454-455 in AA. VV.
Eliot, Thomas Stearns
  1970 The Complete Poems and Plays of T.S. Eliot. London: Faber
        & Faber.
Ellison, Craig W. and Raymond F. Paloutzian
  1978 "Assessing quality of life: Spiritual well-being and lone-
        liness." Paper presented at the annual meeting of the Amer.
        Psychological Assn., Toronto, Aug. 29.
Erikson, Erik H.
  1963 Childhood and Society. New York: Norton.
Etzioni, Amitai
  1961 A Comparative Analysis of Complex Organizations. New York:
        Free Press.
Express Information
  1974 Soviet Sociological Literature. Moscow, USSR: Dept. of
        Information & Advertising.
Fallding, Harold
  1958 "Towards a definition of the term 'spiritual'." Jour. of
        Christian Education 1 (June): 29-44.
  1967 "Evaluation, social systems and human needs." Pp. 455-463
        in Nicholas J. Demerath III and Richard A. Peterson (eds.),
        Systems, Change and Conflict. New York: Free Press.
  1968 The Sociological Task. Englewood Cliffs, NJ: Prentice-Hall.
  1974 The Sociology of Religion: An Explanation of the Unity and
        Diversity in Religion. Toronto: McGraw-Hill Ryerson.
  1978 "Made in the Likeness of God." Paper presented at the Ninth
        World Congress of Sociology, Uppsala, Sweden, August.
Faulkner, Joseph E. and Gordon F. DeJong
  1966 "Religiosity in 5-D: An empirical analysis." Social Forces
        45: 246-254.
  1969 "On measuring the religious variable: Rejoinder to Weigert

and Thomas." Social Forces 48: 263-267.

Fichter, Joseph H.
1972 "The concept of man in social science: Freedom, values and second nature." Jour. for the Scientific Study of Religion 2: 109-121.
1977 "Spirituality, religiosity and alcoholism." America 136: 458-461.

Finner, Stephen L.
1970 "New methods for the sociology of religion." Sociological Analysis 31: 197-202.

Finner, Stephen L. and Jerome D. Gamache
1969 "The relation between religious commitment and attitude toward abortion." Sociological Analysis 30: 1-12.

Fish, Sharon and Judith Allen Shelly
1978 Spiritual Care: The Nurse's Role. Downers Grove, IL: InterVarsity Press.

Fletcher, Colin
1975 The Person in the Sight of Sociology. London & Boston: Routledge & Kegan Paul.

Fowler, James W.
1976 "Stages in faith: The structural-developmental approach." Pp. 173-211 in Thomas Hennessay (ed.), Values and Moral Development. New York: Paulist Press.

Fox, George (1624-1691)
1911 The Journal of George Fox (edited from the ms. by Norman Penney), 2 volumes. Cambridge, England: Cambridge University Press.

Frankl, Victor
1963 Man's Search for Meaning. Boston: Beacon Press.
1965 The Doctor and the Soul. New York: Knopf.

Friedrichs, Robert W.
1961 "Sociological man: An inquiry into assumptions." University College Quarterly 6 (May): 23-30.
1970 A Sociology of Sociology. New York: Free Press.

Frost, Robert C., M.D.
1965 Aglow with the Spirit. Plainfield, NJ: Logos International.

Fuerstenberg, Friedrich (ed.)
1964 Religionssoziologie. Neuwied/Berlin, Germany: Luchterhand.

Gaede, Stan
1976 "A causal model of belief-orthodoxy: Proposal and empirical test." Sociological Analysis 37: 205-217.

Gallup Opinion Index
1975 Religion in America, 1975. Princeton, NJ: AIPO.
1977 Religion in America, 1977-78. Princeton, NJ: AIPO.

Gamboso, Vergilio
1977 "Dal s. Antonio della storia al s. Antonio della pietà popolare." Pp. 83-109 in AA. VV.

Gardavsky, Vitezlav
1969 Gott ist nicht ganz tot. Munich: Kaiser Verlag.

Garrett, William R.
1973 "Politicized clergy: A sociological interpretation of the

'new breed'." Jour. for the Scientific Study of Religion 12: 384-399.
1975 "Maligned mysticism: The maledicted career of Troeltsch's third type." Sociological Analysis 36: 205-223.
Gaustad, Edwin S.
1973 Dissent in American Religion. Chicago: University of Chicago Press.
Geertz, Clifford
1960 The Religion of Java. New York: Free Press.
Gehlen, Arnold
1940 Der Mensch: Seine Natur und seine Stellung in der Welt. Berlin: Junker & Duennhaupt.
Gerard, Harold and Jacob M. Rabbie
1961 "Fear and social comparison." Jour. of Abnormal & Social Psychology 62: 586-592.
Gerson, Elihu M.
1976 "On 'Quality of Life'." Amer. Sociological Review 41: 793-806.
Gerth, Hans and C. Wright Mills
1953 Character and Social Structure. New York: Harcourt, Brace.
Gibbs, David R., Samuel A. Mueller and James R. Wood
1973 "Doctrinal orthodoxy, salience, and the consequential dimension." Jour. for the Scientific Study of Religion 12: 33-52.
Gibbs, James O. and Kelly W. Crader
1970 "A criticism of two recent attempts to scale Glock and Stark's dimensions of religiosity: A research note." Sociological Analysis 31: 107-114.
Giddens, Anthony
1976 New Rules of Sociological Method. London: Hutchinson.
Gill, Robin
1975 The Social Context of Theology. London: Mowbrays.
Giuriati, Paolo
1977a "Elementi per una indagine sulla devozione popolare a s. Antonio di Padova in area europea." Pp. 201-210 in AA. VV.
1977b "Invocazioni a s. Antonio di Padova e preghiere segrete dei Francesi contemporanei." Il Santo: Rivista Antoniana di Storia, Dottrina e Arte 17: 227-241 (Padova, Italy: Centro di Studi Antoniani, Basilica del Santo).
1977c "La devozione popolare a s. Antonio Abate e a s.Antonio di Padova in area abruzzese e veneta." Il Santo: Rivista Antoniana di Storia, Dottrina e Arte 17: 323-333.
1977d "Sondaggio esplorativo pluridimensionale sulla devozione popolare a s. Antonio di Padova." Pp. 321-396 in AA. VV.
Glaser, Barney G. and Anselm L. Strauss
1967 The Discovery of Grounded Theory. London: Weidenfeld & Nicholson.
Glock, Charles Y.
1976 "Consciousness among contemporary youth: An interpretation." Pp. 353-366 in Glock and Bellah.
Glock, Charles Y. and Robert N. Bellah (eds.)

1976 The New Religious Consciousness. Berkeley: University of California Press.

Glock, Charles Y., Benjamin B. Ringer and Earl Babbie
1967 To Comfort and to Challenge. Berkeley: University of California Press.

Glock, Charles Y. and Rodney Stark
1965 Religion and Society in Tension. Chicago: Rand McNally.

Godin, Andre
1971 "Some developmental tasks in Christian education." Pp. 109-154 in Strommen.

Goffman, Erving
1959 The Presentation of Self in Everyday Life. Garden City, NY: Doubleday.
1969 Strategic Interaction. Philadelphia: University of Pennsylvania Press.

Goodman, N. et al.
1978 Society Today. New York: CRM/Random House.

Gouldner, Alvin W.
1970 The Coming Crisis of Western Sociology. London: Heinemann.

Greeley, Andrew M.
1972 The Denominational Society. Glenview, IL: Scott, Foresman.
1974 Ecstasy: A Way of Knowing. Englewood Cliffs, NJ: Prentice-Hall.
1975 Sociology of the Paranormal: A Reconnaissance. Beverly Hills, CA: Sage Publications.
1977 The American Catholic. New York: Basic Books.

Greeley, Andrew M. and William C. McCready
1975 "Are we a nation of mystics?" New York Times Magazine (Jan. 26): 12-25.

Green, Doyle L.
1970 Meet the Mormons. Salt Lake City, UT: Deseret Book Co.

Gustafson, James M.
1961 Treasure in Earthen Vessels. New York: Harper.

Habermas, Juergen
1969 Technik und Wissenschaft als "Ideologie." Frankfurt am Main: Suhrkamp.
1976 Legitimation Crisis. London: Heinemann.

Hadaway, Christopher Kirk
1978 "Life satisfaction and religion: A reanalysis." Social Forces 57: 636-643.

Hadaway, Christopher Kirk and Wade Clark Roof
1978 "Religious commitment and the quality of life in American society." Review of Religious Research 19: 295-307

Hampden-Turner, Charles
1970 Radical Man. Cambridge, MA: Schenkman.

Happold, R.C.
1967 Mysticism. Baltimore: Penguin.

Harris, Thomas A., M.D.
1973 I'm O.K., You're O.K. New York: Harper & Row.

Harrison, Paul M.
1959 Authority and Power in the Free Church Tradition. Princeton, NJ: Princeton University Press.

Havighurst, Robert J.
1953 Human Development and Education. New York: Longmans, Green.
Herberg, Will
1962 "Religion in a secularized society." Review of Religious
Research 3: 145-158.
Heynen, Ralph
1973 The Art of Christian Living. Grand Rapids, MI: Baker.
Himmelfarb, Harold S.
1975 "Measuring religious involvement." Social Forces 53: 606-
618.
Hirsch, Marielies
1972 "Jesus und Freud: Das Heil und das Wohl des Menschen, Seelsorge
und Psychotherapie -- nicht scheiden, aber unterscheiden."
Deutsches Allgemeines Sonntagsblatt 10(March 5): 9.
Hoellinger, Sigurd
1972 "Das Verhaeltnis der Jugend zur Religion am Anfang der
siebziger Jahre." Pp. 353-366 in J. Woessner (ed.),
Religion im Umbruch: Soziologische Beitraege zur Situation
von Religion und Kirche in der gegenwaertigen Gesellschaft.
Stuttgart, Germany: Enke Verlag.
Hoffman, Martin L.
1971 "Development of internal moral standards in children."
Pp. 211-263 in Strommen.
Hoge, Dean R.
1972 "A validated intrinsic religious motivation scale." Jour.
for the Scientific Study of Religion 11: 369-376.
1976 Division in the Protestant House. Philadelphia: Westminster.
Homans, George
1964 "Bringing men back in." Amer. Sociological Review 29:
809-818.
Hood, Ralph W., Jr.
1977a "Differential triggering of mystical experience as a function
of self actualization." Review of Religious Research 18:
264-270.
1977b "Eliciting mystical states of consciousness with semi-
structured nature experience." Jour. for the Scientific
Study of Religion 16: 155-163.
Hopkins, Gerard Manley
1967 The Poems of Gerard Manley Hopkins, 4th edition (W.H. Gardner
and N.H. Mackenzie, eds.). London: Oxford University Press.
Hopper, Earl I.
1979 Insatiability and Social Mobility. Oxford, England:
Blackwell.
Hulme, William E.
1978 Your Potential Under God: Resources for Growth. Minneapolis,
MN: Augsburg.
Hutschnecker, Arnold A., M.D.
1974 The Will to Live. New York: Cornerstone Library.
Huxley, Julian
1948 Evolution: The Modern Synthesis. London: Allen & Unwin.
James, William (1842-1910)
1936 The Varieties of Religious Experience: A Study in Human

(1902) Nature. New York: Modern Library (original ed., New York:
Longmans, Green, 1902).
1950 Principles of Psychology, 2 volumes. New York: Dover
(1890) (original ed., New York: Holt).
Johnson, Vernon
1973 I'll Quit To-morrow. New York: Harper & Row.
Johnson, William A. (ed.)
1974 The Search for Transcendence. New York: Harper & Row.
Jung, Carl G. (1875-1961)
1939 The Integration of Personality. New York: Farrar & Rinehart.
1958 Psychology and Religion: West and East. New York: Pantheon
Books.
1960 "The Stages of Life." Pp. 387-403 in The Collected Works of
Carl G. Jung, vol. 8. New York: Bollingen Foundation.
1968 "The Symbolism of the Mandala." Pp. 95-223 in The Collected
Works of Carl G. Jung, vol. 12. Princeton, NJ: Princeton
University Press.
Kahn, Robert L. and Daniel Katz
1953 "Leadership practices in relation to productivity and morale."
Pp. 612-628 in Dorwin Cartwright and Alvin F. Zander (eds.),
Group Dynamics, Research and Theory. Evanston, IL: Row,
Peterson.
Kamali, A.H.
1960 The Nature of Experience in the Philosophy of Self. Karachi,
Pakistan: Iqbal Review.
Kauffman, J. Howard and Leland Harder
1975 Anabaptists Four Centuries Later: A Profile of Five Mennonite
and Brethren in Christ Denominations. Scottdale, PA:
Herald Press.
Keene, James J.
1967 "Religious behavior and neuroticism, spontaneity, and worldli-
mindedness." Sociometry 30: 137-157.
Kelley, Dean M.
1972 Why Conservative Churches Are Growing. New York: Harper &
Row.
1977 Ibid., revised edition.
Kelsen, G. Paul
1975 Access and Motivation to Join the Divine Light Mission of
Melbourne by the Member-to-be. Fourth Year Honours Disser-
tation, Anthropology & Sociology Dept., Monash University,
Melbourne, Australia.
Kelsey, Morton T.
1973 Healing and Christianity. New York: Harper & Row.
Kemper, Theodore D.
1975 "Emile Durkheim and the Division of Labor." Sociological
Quarterly 16: 190-206.
Kersten, Lawrence K.
1970 The Lutheran Ethic. Detroit, MI: Wayne State University
Press.
Keyes, Ken, Jr.
1972 Handbook to Higher Consciousness. Berkeley, CA: Living

Loving Center.

Kierkegaard, Søren A. (1813-1855)
1941 The Sickness unto Death. London: Oxford University Press.

Kimball, Edward L. and Andrew E. Kimball, Jr.
1977 Spencer W. Kimball. Salt Lake City, UT: Bookcraft.

King, Morton
1967 "Measuring the religious variable: Nine proposed dimensions."
Jour. for the Scientific Study of Religion 6: 173-190.

King, Morton and Richard A. Hunt
1969 "Measuring the religious variable: Amended findings."
Jour. for the Scientific Study of Religion 8: 321-323.
1975a "Measuring the religious variable: National replication."
Jour. for the Scientific Study of Religion 14: 13-22.
1975b "Religious dimensions: Entities or constructs?" Sociological
Focus 8: 57-63.

Kinsey, Alfred C., Wardell B. Pomeroy and Clyde E. Martin
1948 Sexual Behavior in the Human Male. Philadelphia: Saunders.

Kohlberg, Lawrence
1974 "Education, moral development and faith." Jour. of Moral
Education 4: 5-15.

Kohli, Mohindar Pal
1969 Influence of the West on Punjabi Literature. Ludhiana,
India: Lyall Book Depot.

Kolb, William L.
1961 "Images of man and the sociology of religion." Jour. for
the Scientific Study of Religion 1: 5-29.

Kosicki, George
1976 "Renewed religious life: The dynamics of re-discovery."
Review for Religious 35: 14-28.

Krishnamurti, Jidhu
1953 Education and the Significance of Life. New York: Harper.

Kroll, Wilfried (ed. and commentator)
1971 Jesus Kommt! Report der "Jesus-Revolution" unter Hippies
und Studenten in USA und anderswo. Wuppertal, Germany:
Aussaat Verlag.

Kuldip, Kumar
1971 Waris Shah, 1730-1790. Calcutta: Intertrade Publications.

Laing, Ronald D.
1961 The Self and Others. Harmondsworth, England: Penguin.
1965 The Divided Self. Harmondsworth, England: Penguin.

Lanczkowski, Guenter
1974 Die neuen Religionen. Frankfurt, Germany: Fischer.

Land, Kenneth C. and Seymour Spilerman (eds.)
1975 Social Indicator Models. New York: Russell Sage Foundation.

Leach, Edmund
1975 "Society's expectations of health." Jour. of Medical Ethics
1: 85-89.

Lenski, Gerhard
1953 "Social correlates of religious interests." Amer. Sociological Review 18: 533-544.
1961 The Religious Factor. New York: Doubleday.

Lowenthal, Marjorie F. et al.
    1975 Four stages of Life. San Francisco: Jossey-Bass.
Luckmann, Thomas
    1967 The Invisible Religion. New York: Macmillan.
Luhmann, Niklas
    1977 Funktion der Religion. Frankfurt am Main: Suhrkamp.
Lundberg, George A.
    1939 Foudations of Sociology. New York: Macmillan.
    1963 Social Research, 2d ed. New York: Longmans, Green.
Lynd, Robert S.
    1939 Knowledge for What? Princeton, NJ: Princeton University
          Press.
Lyon, David
    1978 "Image of the person in theology and sociology." Crux
          14(2):15-39.
Machalek, Richard
    1977 "Definitional strategies in the study of religion." Jour.
          for the Scientific Study of Religion 16: 395-401.
Macintosh, Douglas C.
    1919 Theology as an Empirical Science. New York: Macmillan.
MacIntyre, Alasdair
    1969 "The Christian-Communist rapprochement: Some sociological
          notes and queries." Pp. 173-186 in David Martin (ed.),
          Sociological Yearbook of Religion in England 2. London:
          SCM Press.
MacKay, Donald M.
    1974 The Clock Work Image: A Christian Perspective on Science.
          Downers Grove, IL: InterVarsity Press.
Marangon, Paolo
    1977 "Tradizione e sviluppo della devozione antoniana." Pp.
          165-178 in AA. VV.
Marcuse, Herbert
    1967a Der eindimensionale Mensch. Neuwied/Berlin: Luchterhand.
    1967b Triebstruktur und Gesellschaft. Frankfurt am Main: Suhrkamp.
Marx, Karl H. (1818-1883)
    1970 The German Ideology (C.J. Arthur, ed.). London: Lawrence
          & Wishart.
Maslow, Abraham
    1962 Toward a Psychology of Being. Princeton, NJ: Van Nostrand.
    1970 Religions, Values, and Peak-Experiences. New York: Viking.
    1971 The Farther Reaches of Human Nature. New York: Viking.
Masters, Roy
    1964 How Your Mind Can Keep You Well. New York.
Matson, Floyd W.
    1964 The Broken Image. New York: Anchor Books.
    1976 The Idea of Man. New York: Delacorte Press.
Mattellini, Celso Giuseppe
    1977 "Il 'Santo die miracoli': Valori e ambivalenze." Pp. 281-
          289 in AA. VV.
McCall, Storrs
    1975 "Quality of life." Social Indicators Research 2: 229-248.

McCready, William C. and Andrew M. Greeley
1976   The Ultimate Values of the American Population.   Beverly
       Hills, CA: Sage Publications.
McNamara, Patrick H. and Arthur St. George
1978   "Blessed are the downtrodden? An empirical test." Socio-
       logical Analysis 39: 303-320.
Mead, George Herbert
1963   Mind, Self, and Society. Chicago: University of Chicago
       Press.
1967   Philosophy of the Act. Chicago: University of Chicago Press.
Meditation
1969   Ramakrishna Mission. Calcutta, India: Ramakrishna Order.
Mehl, Duane
1976   No More for the Road. Minneapolis, MN: Augsburg.
Mendel, Gérard
1972   "De la régression du politique au psychique." Pp. 11-63
       in Gérard Mendel (ed.), Sociopsychoanalyse 1. Paris: Payot.
Mensching, Gustav
1938   Volksreligion und Weltreligion. Leipzig, Germany: Hinrichs.
1941   Vergleichende Religionswissenschaft. Heidelberg, Germany:
       Quelle & Meyer.
1947   Soziologie der Religion. Bonn, Germany: Roehrscheid.
1949   Allgemeine Religionsgeschichte. Heidelberg, Germany:
       Quelle & Meyer.
1957   Das Wunder im Glauben und Aberglauben der Voelker. Leiden,
       Netherlands: E.J. Brill.
1959   Die Religionen: Erscheinungsformen, Strukturen und Lebensge-
       setze. Stuttgart, Germany: Curt E. Schwab Verlag.
1966   Soziologie der grossen Religionen. Bonn, Germany: Roehr-
       scheid.
1967   "Weltreligion, Weltkultur und Weltzivilisation." In Richard
       Schwarz (ed.), Menschliche Existenz und moderne Welt,
       Part 2. Berlin: Walter de Gruyter.
1974   Der offene Tempel: Die Weltreligionen im Gespraech miteinander.
       Stuttgart, Germany: Deutsche Verlags Anstalt.
Merleau-Ponty, Maurice
1967   The Phenomenology of Perception. London: Routledge &
       Kegan Paul.
Merton, Robert K.
1968   Social Theory and Social Structure, rev. ed. New York: Free
       Press.
Merton, Robert K. and Patricia L. Kendall
1946   "The focused interview." Amer. Jour. of Sociology 51:
       541-547.
Merton, Thomas
1968   Zen and the Birds of Appetite. New York: New Directions.
Messer, Jeanne
1976   "Guru Maharaj Ji and the Divine Light Mission." Pp. 52-
       72 in Glock and Bellah.
Miller, Perry
1964   Errand into the Wilderness. New York: Harper.

Miyamoto, S. Frank
  1969 "The impact on research of different conceptions of role."
        Pp. 111-123 in Stephen P. Spitzer (ed.), The Sociology of
        Personality. New York: Van Nostrand Reinhold.
Moberg, David O.
  1967a "The encounter of scientific and religious values pertinent
        to man's spiritual nature." Sociological Analysis 28:
        22-33.
  1967b "Science and the spiritual nature of man." Jour. of the
        Amer. Scientific Affiliation 19: 12-17.
  1971a "Religious practices." Pp. 551-598 in Strommen.
  1971b Spiritual Well-Being: Background and Issues. Washington,
        DC: White House Conference on Aging.
  1974a "Spiritual well-being: Discussion notes for Luncheon Round-
        table No. 71." Handout for program at the annual meeting
        of the Amer. Sociological Assn., Montreal, Aug. 27.
  1974b "Spiritual well-being in late life." Pp. 256-279 in Jaber
        F. Gubrium(ed.), Late Life. Springfield, IL: Charles C Thomas.
  1977a "Spiritual well-being and quality of life indicators."
        Paper presented at the annual meeting of the Amer. Psycho-
        logical Assn., San Francisco, Aug. 26.
  1977b "Spiritual well-being: An elusive goal for social work."
        Pp. 27-53 in Proceedings of the annual meeting, Southern
        Baptist Social Service Assn., New Orleans, Sep. 25-28.
  1978a "Presidential address: Virtues for the sociology of religion."
        Sociological Analysis 39: 1-18.
  1978b "Spiritual well-being: A challenge for interdisciplinary
        research." Jour. of the Amer. Scientific Affiliation 30:
        67-72.
  1978c "Spiritual well-being and the quality of life movement: A
        new arena for church-state debate?" Jour. of Church and
        State 20: 427-449.
Moberg, David O. and Patricia M. Brusek
  1978 "Spiritual well-being: A neglected subject in quality of
        life research." Social Indicators Research 5: 303-323.
Mol, Hans
  1976 Identity and the Sacred. New York: Free Press.
Mollis, M.
  1977 Models of Man. Cambridge, England: Cambridge University
        Press.
Musgrove, Frank
  1977 Margins of the Mind. London: Methuen.
National Interfaith Coalition on Aging
  1975 "Spiritual well-being definition: A model ecumenical work
        product." NICA Inform 1(Aug. 25): 4.
Neal, Marie Augusta
  1967 "The value of religious community." Pp. 128-170 in Eugene
        E. Grollmes (ed.), Vows But No Walls. St. Louis, MO:
        Herder.
Nee, Watchman
  1965 The Release of the Spirit. Cloverdale, IN: Sure Foundation.

1977 The Spiritual Man. New York: Christian Fellowship, Inc.
Nelson, Benjamin
1973 "Weber's Protestant Ethic: Its origins, wanderings,and foreseeable futures." Pp. 73-130 in Charles Y. Glock and Phillip E. Hammond (eds.), Beyond the Classics: Essays in the Scientific Study of Religion. New York: Harper & Row.
Nelson, L.D.
1974 "Functions and dimensions of religion." Sociological Analysis 35: 263-272.
Nelson, L.D., and Russell R. Dynes
1976 "The impact of devotionalism and attendance on ordinary and emergency helping behavior." Jour. for the Scientific Study of Religion 15: 47-59.
Neugarten, Bernice L. and Gunhild O. Hagestad
1976 "Age and the life course." Pp. 35-55 in Robert H. Binstock and Ethel Shanas (eds.), Handbook of Aging and the Social Sciences. New York: Van Nostrand Reinhold.
Niebuhr, H. Richard
1929 The Social Sources of Denominationalism. New York: Holt
(1957) (reprinted by Meridian Books, New York, 1957).
1945 "The ego-alter dialectic and the conscience." Jour.of Philosophy 42: 352-359.
1960 The Meaning of Revelation. New York: Macmillan.
1963 The Responsible Self. New York: Harper.
Nudelman, Arthur E.
1971 "Dimensions of religiosity: A factor-analytic view of Protestants, Catholics, and Christian Scientists." Review of Religious Research 13: 42-56.
O'Dea, Thomas F.
1957 The Mormons. Chicago: University of Chicago Press.
1966 The Sociology of Religion. Englewood Cliffs, NJ: Prentice-Hall.
Osborne, C.
1973 The Art of Understanding Yourself. Grand Rapids, MI: Zondervan.
Otto, Rudolf (1869-1937)
1936 Das Heilige. Munich: Beck'sche Verlagsbuchhandlung (40 Aufl. 1973).
1958 The Idea of the Holy. New York: Oxford University Press.
Oyle, Irving
1975 The Healing Mind. Millbrae, CA: Celestial Arts.
Panteghini, Gabriele
1977 "Problemi che la devozione popolare ai santi pone alla teologia." Pp. 475-483 in AA. VV.
Parker, William R. and Elaine St. Johns
1957 Prayer Can Change Your Life: Experiments and Techniques in Prayer Therapy. Carmel, NY: Guideposts Associates.
Parsegian, V.L.
1973 This Cybernetic World: Of Men, Machines and Earth Systems. Garden City, NY: Doubleday.
Parsons, Talcott

1937   The Structure of Social Action. New York: McGraw-Hill.
1951   The Social System. New York: Free Press.
1961   "Comment." Jour. for the Scientific Study of Religion 1:
       22-29.
Pattison, E. Mansel
1966   "A critique of alcoholism treatment concepts: With special
       reference to abstinence." Quarterly Jour. of Studies on
       Alcoholism 27: 29-71.
Peale, Norman V.
1974   Favorite Stories of Positive Faith. Pawling, NY: Foundation
       for Christian Living.
1978   The Power of Positive Thinking. Pawling, NY: Foundation for
       Christian Living.
Pettersson, Thorleif
1975   The Retention of Religious Experiences. Uppsala, Sweden:
       Acta Universitatis Upsaliensis, Psychologia Religionum
       No. 3.
Petty, Jo
1962   Applies of Gold. Norwalk, CT: C.R. Gibson Co.
Pfuetze, Paul E.
1961   Self, Society, Existence. New York: Harper.
Phillips, Derek L.
1978   "What's one to believe?" Review of Frank M. Andrews and
       Stephen B. Withey, Social Indicators of Well-Being. Con-
       temporary Sociology 7: 392-395.
Phillips, J.B.
1961   Your God Is Too Small. New York: Macmillan.
Piaget, Jean and ·Barbel Inhelder
1969   The Psychology of the Child. New York: Basic Books.
Pike, Kenneth L.
1971   Language in Relation to a Unified Theory of the Structure of
       Human Behavior. The Hague, Netherlands: Mouton.
Possehl, Gregory L.
1977   Ancient Cities of the Indus. New Delhi, India
Post, W.
1969   Kritik der Religion bei Karl Marx. Munich, Germany:
       Laetare/Imba Verlag.
Prem, Sri Krishna
1976   Yoga of the Kathopanishad. Bombay, India
Purce, Jill
1974   The Mystic Spiral. New York: Avon.
Rector, Hartman, Jr. and Connie Rector
1971   No More Strangers, Vol. 1. Salt Lake City, UT: Bookcraft.
Reed, William Standish, M.D.
1969   Surgery of the Soul. Old Tappan, NJ: Revell.
Rex, John
1974   Approaches to Sociology. London & Boston: Routledge &
       Kegan Paul.
Richards, LeGrand
1950   A Marvelous Work and a Wonder. Salt Lake City, UT: Deseret
       Book Co.

Riesman, David
1971 The Lonely Crowd. New Haven, CT: Yale University Press.
Ritschl, Albrecht (1822-1889)
1901 The Theology of Albrecht Ritschl (A.T. Swing, ed.). New York: Longmans.
Riva, Anna
1977 "S. Antonio modello di identificazione spirituale per il devoto?" Pp. 251-261 in AA. VV.
Robertson, Roland
1975 "On the analysis of mysticism: Pre-Weberian, Weberian, and post-Weberian perspectives." Sociological Analysis 36: 241-266.
1976 "How is religion possible? Simmel on religion as life world." Paper presented at the annual meeting of the Assn. for the Sociology of Religion, New York City.
Roethlisberger, Fritz J. and Dickson, William J.
1961 Management and the Worker. Cambridge, MA: Harvard University Press.
Roof, Wade Clark and Richard B. Perkins
1975 "On conceptualizing salience in religious commitment." Jour. for the Scientific Study of Religion 14: 111-128.
Ruppel, Howard J., Jr.
1969 "Religiosity and premarital sexual permissiveness: A methodological note." Sociological Analysis 30: 176-188.
Ruysbroeck, John of (1293-1381)
1916 The Adornment of the Spiritual Marriage. The Sparkling Stone. The Book of Supreme Truth (trans. from the Flemish by C.A. Wynschenk, Dom.; edited with introduction and notes by Evelyn Underhill). London: J.M. Dent & Sons.
St. John of the Cross (1542-1591)
1908 The Dark Night of the Soul (trans. by David Lewis, with corrections and introduction by B. Zimmermann). London: Thomas Baker.
Sartre, Jean-Paul
1956 Being and Nothingness (trans. by Hazel E. Barnes). New York: Philosophical Library.
Savramis, Demosthenes
1967 "Das Vorurteil von der Entchristlichung der Gegenwartsgesellschaft." Koelner Zeitschrift fuer Soziologie und Sozialpsychologie 19: 263-282.
1968 Religionssoziologie: Eine Einfuehrung. Munich: Nymphenburger (Second ed., Bonn: Bouvier, 1977).
1969 Entchristlichung und Sexualisierung -- zwei Vorurteile. Munich: Nymphenburger.
1970 "Wertsysteme in traditionalen und industriellen Gesellschaften." Pp. 7-44 in Religionen im sozialen Wandel: Internationales Jahrbuch fuer Religionssoziologie, vol. 6. Opladen,Germany: Westdeutscher Verlag.
1971 Theologie und Gesellschaft. Munich: List.
1972 Religionen. Duesseldorf, Germany, & Vienna: Econ.

1973a "Die Religionssoziologie als Rettungsanker der Religion?"
Pp. 327-335 in Guenter Albrecht, Hansjuergen Daheim and
Fritz Sack (eds.), Soziologie: ...Rene Koenig zum 65.
Geburtstag. Opladen, Germany: Westdeutscher Verlag.
1973b Jesus ueberlebt seine Moerder. Munich: List.
Scapin, Pietro
1975 "Dimensione sacrale della devozione a s. Antonio." Il
Santo: Revista Antoniana di Storia, Dottrina e Arte 15:
216ff.
1977 "Dimensioni del fenomeno antoniano." Pp. 65-79 in AA. VV.
Schachter, Stanley
1959 The Psychology of Affiliation: Experimental Studies of the
Sources of Gregariousness. Stanford, CA: Stanford University
Press.
Schachter, Stanley et al.
1951 "An experimental study of cohesiveness and productivity."
Human Relations 4: 229-238.
Schaer, Hans
1950 Religion and the Cure of Souls in Jung's Psychology. New
York: Pantheon Books.
Scheler, Max (1874-1928)
1960 On the Eternal in Man. New York: Harper.
1963 "Ueber oestliches und westliches Christentum." Pp. 111-112
in Max Scheler, Schriften zur Soziologie und Weltanschauungs-
lehre. Bern, Switzerland & Munich: Francke Verlag.
Schlette, Heinz Robert
1971 Einfuehrung in das Studium der Religionen. Freiburg,
Germany: Rombach.
Schroeder, W. Widick
1977 "Measuring the muse: Reflections on the use of survey methods
in the study of religious phenomena." Review of Religious
Research 18: 148-162.
Schuller, Robert H.
1969 Self Love: The Dynamic Force of Success. New York: Hawthorn
Books.
Schutz, Alfred
1963 "Concept and theory formation in the social sciences."
Pp. 231-249 in Maurice Natanson (ed.), Philosophy of the
Social Sciences. New York: Random House.
1967 The Phenomenology of the Social World. Evanston, IL:
Northwestern University Press.
Schutz, Alfred and Thomas Luckmann
1973 The Structures of the Life-World. Evanston, IL: Northwestern
University Press.
Sears, Robert R. and S. Shirley Feldman (eds.)
1973 The Seven Ages of Man. Los Altos, CA: William Kaufmann.
Seashore, Stanley
1954 Group Cohesiveness in the Industrial Work Group. Ann Arbor,
MI: University of Michigan Press.
Sedgwick, Peter
1972 "R.D. Laing: Self, symptom and society." In Robert Boyers

and Robert Orrill (eds.), Laing and Antipsychiatry. Harmondsworth, England: Penguin.
Sekida, Katsuki
  1975 Zen Training. New York: Weatherhill.
Shakespeare, William (1564-1616)
  1953 The Complete Works (C.J. Sisson, ed.). London: Odham's.
Sheehy, Gail
  1974 Passages. New York: Dutton.
Shils, Edward A. and Morris Janowitz
  1948 "Cohesion and disintegration in the Wehrmacht in World War
        II." Public Opinion Quarterly 12: 280-315.
Simmel, Georg (1858-1918)
  1950 The Sociology of Georg Simmel (ed. by Kurt A. Wolff).
        New York: Free Press.
  1971 On Individuality and Social Forms (ed. and with introduction
        by Donald H. Levine). Chicago: University of Chicago Press.
Smith, Houston
  1958 The Religions of Man. New York: Harper & Row.
Smith, W. Robertson (1846-1894)
  1957 The Religion of the Semites. New York: Meridian.
Solomon, Charles R. (ed.)
  1977 Handbook to Happiness. Wheaton, IL: Tyndale House.
Sorokin, Pitirim
  1947 Society, Culture, and Personality. New York: Harper.
Spencer, Sidney
  1963 Mysticism in World Religion. Baltimore: Penguin.
Stark, Rodney and Charles Y. Glock
  1968 American Piety: The Nature of Religious Commitment. Berkeley,
        CA: University of California Press.
Steeman, Theodore M.
  1975 "Church, sect, mysticism, denomination: Periodical aspects
        of Troeltsch's types." Sociological Analysis 36: 181-204.
Strommen, Merton P. (ed.)
  1971 Research on Religious Development. New York: Hawthorn.
Strommen, Merton P., Milo L. Brekke, Ralph C. Underwager, and Arthur
        L. Johnson
  1972 A Study of Generations. Minneapolis, MN: Augsburg.
Strumpel, Burkhard (ed.)
  1974 Subjective Elements of Well-Being. Paris: Organization for
        Economic Co-operation and Development.
Sturzo, Luigi (1871-1959)
  1947 The True Life: Sociology of the Supernatural (trans. from
        Italian by Barbara Barclay Carter). London: Geoffrey Bles.
Sudnow, David
  1967 Passing On: The Social Organization of Dying. Englewood
        Cliffs, NJ: Prentice-Hall.
Sullivan, Paul
  1973 "The spiritual effects of alcoholism." The Blue Book 25:
        32-36.
Susser, Mervyn
  1974 "Ethical components in the definitions of health." Interna-
        tional Jour. of Health Services 4: 539-548.

Swaim, Loring T., M.D.
1962 Arthritis, Medicine and the Spiritual Laws. Philadelphia:
      Chilton Book Co.
Swatos, William H.
1977 "The comparative method and the special vocation of the
      sociology of religion." Sociological Analysis 38: 106-114.
Talmage, James E.
1913 The Articles of Faith. Salt Lake City, UT: Church of Jesus
      Christ of Latter-day Saints.
1915 Jesus the Christ. Salt Lake City, UT: Church of Jesus
      Christ of Latter-day Saints.
Tapp, Robert B.
1971 "Dimensions of religiosity in a post-traditional group."
      Jour. for the Scientific Study of Religion 10: 41-47.
Tauler, John (ca. 1300-1361)
1901 The Inner Way: Being Thirty-six Sermons for Festivals (a
      new translation from the German, ed. with introduction by
      A.W. Hutton). London: Methuen & Co.
Teilhard de Chardin, Pierre (1881-1955)
1961 The Phenomenon of Man. New York: Harper.
Thakar, Vimala
1976 Meditation: A Way of Life. Bombay, India
Thomas, L. Eugene and Pamela E. Cooper
1978 "Measurement and incidence of mystical experiences:An
      exploratory study." Jour. for the Scientific Study of
      Religion 17: 433-437.
Thomsen, Robert
1975 Bill W. New York: Harper & Row.
Tiebout, Harry
1944 Conversion as a Psychological Phenomenon. New York: National
      Council on Alcoholism.
Tiger, Lionel and Robin Fox
1972 The Imperial Animal. London: Secker & Warburg.
Tillich, Paul
1961 Wesen und Wandel des Glaubens. Berlin: Ullstein.
1969 My Search for Absolutes. New York: Simon & Schuster.
Tiryakian, Edward A.
1962 "Neither Marx nor Durkheim...perhaps Weber." Amer. Jour.
      of Sociology 81: 1-33.
1976 Sociologism and Existentialism. Englewood Cliffs, NJ:
      Prentice-Hall.
Titchener, Edward B. (1867-1927)
1929 Systematic Psychology. New York: Macmillan.
Tournier, Paul
1962 Guilt and Grace. New York: Harper & Row.
1964 The Whole Person in a Broken World. New York: Harper & Row.
1968 A Place for You. New York: Harper & Row.
1973 The Meaning of Persons. New York: Harper & Row.
Towler, Robert
1974 Homo Religiosus: Sociological Problems in the Study of
      Religion. New York: St. Martin's Press.

Triplett, Norman
1898 "The dynamogenic factors in pacemaking and competition."
      Amer. Jour. of Psychology 9: 507-533.
Troeltsch, Ernst (1865-1923)
1931 The Social Teaching of the Christian Churches (trans. by
      Olive Wyon). London: Allen & Unwin.
Tubesing, Donald A.
1976 Whole Person Health Care, An Idea in Evolution: History of
      the Wholistic Health Centers Project 1970-1976. Hinsdale,
      IL: Society for Wholistic Medicine.
Tubesing, Donald A. and Sally G. Strosahl
1976 Wholistic Health Centers: Survey Research Report. Hinsdale,
      IL: Society for Wholistic Medicine.
Tucci, Giuseppe
1961 The Theory and Practice of the Mandala. London: Rider.
Turner, Victor
1969 The Ritual Process. Ithaca, NY: Cornell University Press.
1974 Dramas, Fields and Metaphors: Symbolic Action in Society.
      Ithaca, NY: Cornell University Press.
1977 "Process, system and symbol: A new anthopological synthesis."
      Daedalus 106(3): 61-80.
Unger, Johan
1976 On Religious Experience: A Psychological Study. Uppsala,
      Sweden: Acta Universitatis Upsaliensis, Psychologia
      Religionum No. 6.
United Press International
1974 "Individualism worries Soviets." Milwaukee Journal, April
      1(Part 1): 9.
United States Dept. of Health, Education, and Welfare
1969 Toward a Social Report. Washington, D.C.: U.S. Government
      Printing Office.
Van der Leeuw, Gerardus
1963 Religion in Essence and Manifestation, 2 volumes. New York:
      Harper.
Van Gennep, Arnold
1960 The Rites of Passage. Chicago: University of Chicago Press.
Vecchi, Alberto
1977 "Miraculorum prodigia." Pp. 111-158 in AA. VV.
Venkataraman, T.N.
1966 Talks with Ramana Maharshi. Tiruvanamalai, India.
Vergote, Antoine
1977 "Interprétation psychologique du 'phénomène antonien'."
      Pp. 237-249 in AA. VV.
Vernon, Glenn M.
1962 Sociology of Religion. New York: McGraw-Hill.
Visentin, Pelagio
1977 "Celebrazioni del mistero di Cristo e celebrazione dei
      santi nell'anno liturgico." Pp. 463-473 in AA.VV.
Von Gagern, Frederick, M.D.
1954 Mental and Spiritual Health (trans. from German by Meyrick
      Booth). Paramus, NJ: Paulist Press Deus Books.

Vrijhof, P.H.
  1970 Bijdragen tot de Sociologie van Godsdienst en Kerk. Meppel,
        Netherlands: Boom.
Wach, Joachim
  1951 Types of Religious Experience. Chicago: University of
        Chicago Press.
Wallwork, Ernest
  1972 Durkheim: Morality and Milieu. Cambridge, MA: Harvard
        University Press.
Ward, Professor
  n.d. Antiquity of Hinduism (apparently adapted from William Ward,
        Account of the Writings, Religion, and Manners of the Hindoos,
        4 vols. Serampore, India: Mission Press, 1811, or one of
        at least five subsequent editions -- editor).
Warner, W. Lloyd
  1937 A Black Civilization. New York: Harper.
Warshay, Leon H.
  1975 The Current State of Sociological Theory. New York: McKay.
Weber, Max (1864-1920)
  1920 Gesammelte Aufsaetze zur Religionssoziologie, Vol. 1.
        Tuebingen, Germany: J.C.B. Mohr (Paul Siebeck).
  1947 The Theory of Social and Economic Organization (trans. by
        A.M. Henderson and Talcott Parsons). New York: Oxford
        University Press (reprinted by Free Press, New York).
  1958 The Religion of India (trans. by Hans H. Gerth and Don
        Martindale). New York: Free Press.
  1963 The Sociology of Religion (trans. by Ephraim Fischoff).
        Boston: Beacon Press.
Weigert, Andrew J.
  1974 "Functional, substantive, or political? A comment on Berger's
        'second thoughts on defining religion'." Jour. for the
        Scientific Study of Religion 13: 483-486.
Weigert, Andrew J. and Darwin L. Thomas
  1974 "Secularization and religiosity: A cross-national study of
        Catholic adolescents in five societies." Sociological Analysis
        35: 1-23.
Weinberg, Gerald M.
  1975 An Introduction to General Systems Thinking. New York: Wiley.
Weizsaecker, Carl Friedrich von
  1977 Der Garten des Menschlichen. Munich: Carl Hanser Verlag.
Wesley, Charles (1707-1788)
  1762 Short Hymns on Select Passages of the Holy Scriptures, 2
        volumes. Bristol, England: E. Farley.
Wesley, John (1703-1791)
  1909-1916 The Journal of John Wesley: Enlarged from Original
        Mss., with notes from Unpublished Diaries (Nehemiah Curnock,
        ed.). London: Culley
White, Ralph and Ronald Lippitt
  1960 "Leader behavior and member reaction in three 'social
        climates'." Pp. 527-553 in Dorwin Cartwright and Alvin F.
        Zander (eds.), Group Dynamics, Research and Theory. Evanston,

       IL: Row, Peterson.
Wilson, Bryan R.
  1969 "A typology of sects." Pp. 361-383 in Roland Robertson (ed.),
       Sociology of Religion. Harmondsworth, England: Penguin.
Wilson, Glenn D.
  1973 The Psychology of Conservatism. London: Academic Press.
Wolff, Kurt H.
  1974 Trying Sociology. New York: Wiley.
  1976 Surrender and Catch: Experience and Inquiry Today. Dordrecht,
       Netherlands: D. Reidel Co.
Wrong, Dennis
  1961 "The oversocialized concept of man in sociology." Amer.
       Sociological Review 26: 183-193.
Wuthnow, Robert
  1973 "Religious commitment and conservatism." Pp. 117-132 in
       Charles Y. Glock (ed.), Religion in Sociological Perspective.
       Belmont, CA: Wadsworth.
  1976 The Consciousness Reformation. Berkeley, CA: University of
       California Press.
Yinger, J. Milton
  1963 Sociology Looks at Religion. New York: Macmillan.
  1969 "A structural examination of religion." Jour. for the
       Scientific Study of Religion 8: 88-99.
Zahn, Gordon C.
  1970 "The commitment dimension." Sociological Analysis 31:
       203-208.

INDEX OF NAMES

AA. VV.,192,196,199,313
Abraham,28
Acquaviva, Sabino,120,313
Ahmed, Farosh,41,313
Albrecht, Guenter,332
Alcoholics Anonymous,261,262,313
Allport, Gordon W.,240,247,313
Anderson, Lavina Fielding,180,182,313
Andrews, Frank M.,173,229,236,313,330
Anonymous,255,313
Appel, Kenneth E.,228,313
Arberry, Arthur J.,41,313
Argüelles, Jose,103,313
Argüelles, Miriam,103,313
Argyle, Michael,247,313
Armour, David J.,258,313
Atchley, Robert C.,100,101,102,313
Attali,Jacques,205
Aurobindo, Sri,41,313
Avyaktananda, Swami,43,313

Babbie, Earl,247,248,322
Bach, Johann C.,208
Bach, J. S.,208
Bahr, Howard M.,176,240,313,314
Balswick, Jack,92,314
Bandura, Albert,257,314
Barker, Eileen,153,163,307,314
Bartel, Lois Franz,240,314
Bates, Frederick L.,102,314
Bateson,Gregory,201-203,314
Bauer, Raymond,103,314
Baum, Gregory,109,314
Beach, Stephen W.,282,314
Beckford, James A.,74,314
Beethoven, Ludwig van,209
Belgum, David,305,314
Bell, Wendell,308
Bellah, Robert N.,1,53,108,134,135,
   136,145,282,314,321
Bellow, Saul,45
Benedict,Saint,16
Benson, Purnell H.,51,53,55,58,314
Benz, Ernst,119,314
Berger, Brigitte,116,293,315
Berger, Peter L.,76,87,103,116,131,
   134,274,293,303,314,315,336
Bergson, Henri,17,21,315
Berkowitz, Leonard,25,315
Berlioz,Louis H.,209
Binstock, Robert H.,102,315,329
Birnbaum, Norman,55,315
Blaikie, Norman W.H.,133,141,307,315

Bonnet, Serge,194,315
Bothel, Karen Moore,1
Bourg, Carroll J.,15,307
Bourque, Linda B.,305,315
Bradburn, Norman M.,3,173,315
Brekke, Milo L.,333
Brewer, Earl D.C.,12,99,107,307,315
Britten, Benjamin,212
Brown, D. Wayne, Jr.,173,308
Brown, L. B.,268,315
Brown, Sharon,44
Browne, William,207
Brusek, Patricia,1,3,106,173,238,244,328
Bryant, M. Daroll,163,315
Buber, Martin,79,316
Buddha,35,140,45,46
Bunyan, John,30,290,316

Campbell, Angus,3,103,173,229,230,231,232,
   235
Campbell, Douglas F.,238,243,248,316
Campbell, Thomas C.,248,316
Campolo, Anthony, Jr.,248,316
Capps, Donald, 60,316
Capra, Fritjof,105,316
Cardwell, Jerry D.,250,316
Cartwright, Dorwin,324,336
Chadwick, Bruce A.,240,314
Chalker, John,211
Chasin, Barbara,286,316
Cherlin, Andrew,3,316
Chisti, Yusif Salim,41,316
Christy, Richard D.,91,308
Cipriana, Roberto,198,316
Claerbaut, David,304,316
Clarke, William G.,99,317
Clayton, Richard R.,239,240,243,250,317
Cline, Victor B.,268,317
Cock, Peter H.,135,136,317
Coe, George A.,67,317
Coetzee, Jan K.,291,295,308,317
Cohen, P.S.,296,297,317
Cole, W. Owen,41,317
Converse, Philip E.,103,173,229,230,231,
   232,235,236,316
Cook, Thomas C.,Jr.,5,103,317
Cooley, Charles H.,67,317
Cooper, Pamela E.,305,334
Crader, Kelly W.,239,243,321
Curle, Adam,149,317
Cygnar, Thomas E.,250,317

Daheim, Hansjuergen,332

339

341

343

Body, natural, 132
  spiritual, 132
Book of Mormon, 174n
  cited, 175,179,185,188
Brahman, 45
Brahmaviharas, 43
Brazil, 181
Brethren in Christ, 240,241
Buddhism, 26,27,29,35,43,45,47,108,119,
  138-151,287,303
Business, 31
Byzantine tradition, 206

Calvinism, 206
Canada, 241
Cancer, 44
Capitalism, 108,114,115,119,127,145,160
Career, 29
Carols, 212
Catholic
  churches, 206
  clergy, 201-203
  religious women, 265-279
  rites, 195
  traditions, 19
Catholics, 287-288,302
  American, 74
Center for Anthonian Studies, 192
Chakras, 46
Change, 129
  openness to, 18,134
  social, 136
Chaplains, viii,5
Character formation, 116; see Personality
  development; Socialization
Charisma, 149,162
Charismatic movement, 119,138
Charismatic path, 143-151
Chastity, 271
Childhood, 100-102
Chile, 181
Chinese, 288
Choice, 33
Choir, 210,212
Choral societies, 212
Christ, 42,64,117,174,185,195
  acceptance of, 66-68,189
  as God, 64
  commitment to, 11
  example of, 68-70
  faith in, 8,9
  second coming, 59,166
  teaching of, 68-70

Christian life, 62
Christian Medical Foundation
  International, 305
Christianity, 26,27,29,36,58,59,61,91,
  108,119,120,121,127,149,165,183,215,
  287-288
Christians, 29,59,165,215,223,264
  born again, 72,216
  former, 150
  mature, 237-254,265-266
Christlike, 58
Church, 113,291
  attendance, 230,231
  dilemmas of, 117
  individual and, 117-118
  as institution, 85,126,259,296
  local, 75-84,88,117
  membership, 10,230,235,291
  service in, 11
  type, 114,148-149,248
  see Associationalism; Participation
Church of Jesus Christ of Latter-day
  Saints, 173-189
Churches, conservative, 4
Circumcision, 28
Cistercians, 16
Civic sentiment, 210-212
Civil religion, 108
Civil rights movement, 136
Civilization, 27,48
  Indus Valley, 42
  sensate, 113
Clan, 123
Clergy, viii,250,266,306
  Catholic, 201-203
  Evangelical Protestant, 11
  Promotion of, 259
  Recovering alcoholic, 255-263
Cognitive dissonance, 139
Cohesion, 297-298
Collective representations, 108
Collectivism, 123,124
Collectivity, linkage to, 16
Commitment, 82,247,248,291-300
Communal(ism), 136,139,161,239,
  241,242,251,266,269
Communication, 59,199
Communion, Holy, 9,191,193,194
Communism, 119,127,160
Communist Party, 1
Communitas, 21,109
Community, 77
  of believers, 161

346

347

Dissonance, cognitive, 139
Divine Light Mission, 138-151
Divine Principle, 163
Doctrine and Covenants, 174n, 175,176
Doctrines, 59,238
Domain satisfactions, 230-235
Dominicans, 16
Double bind, 201-203
Dreams, 163
Drug subculture, 136
Drugs, 120
Dutch Reformed Church, 292
Dying, 18

Ecclesiology, vii
Ecstasy, 119,205,257
Ecuador, 181
Eden, 166
Education, 306
Ego, 36,43,80,116,140
  integrity, 101
Ekstasis, 114
Elites, religious, 85
Emic, 94-95
Emotions, 107
Energy, 218
England, 181,205-213
Enlightenment, 43,140
Environment, 1,105,178
  pollution of, 117
Epistemology, 156
Ergriffensein, 122
Eschatology, 127,163
Esprit-de-corps, 37
Eternity, 178
Ethicalism, 239
Ethics, 69,251
Ethnomethodology, 91,94
Etic, 94-95
Eucharist, 266,271
Evaluation, 2
  research, 4,305
Evangelicals, 136,303
Evangelism, 242,246-249,253
Evil, 27,92,95,122,123,125,126,128,129,
  130,131,176,264
Evolution, 33,46,114,118
Excommunication, 187
Exercise, 1
Existential(ism), 17,42,128,137,159,166
Exodus, 77
Expectancy, 34

Experience, 60-61,79
  Christian, 58
  faith, 128
  of God, 65,66,143
  mystical, 108
  religious, 60-61,63-66,199,238,
    241,242,246-249,251,253-254,
    266
  subjective, 155
Experimentation, 60
Exploitation, 127
Exteriority, 17
Extrinsic religion, 240

Factor analysis, 245-246,268-276,
  284-286
Failure, 27
Faith, 30,32,62,81,82,83,100,110,
  122,128,186,223,230,231
  authentic, 75,80
  in Christ, 8,9
  in God, 223,226
  healing, 222
  in mysticism, 49
  in people, 8,222-226
  in power beyond self, 222-227
  in self, 222-226
  stages, 100-102
  transcendent, 88
Fall, the, 93,97
Family, 101
Fasting, 176
Feedback loops, 108
Fellowshipping, 181,184
Finland, 181
Flood, the, 28
Folk song, 212
Forgiveness, 186,187,188
Fourth dimension, 215-228
France, 194
Franciscans, 16,196,197
Freedom, 40,47,93,97,147,155,189
Friends, 10,35-36,182,214
Friendship, 239,284-286
Frustration, 27,34,171
Fulfillment, 30,35,40,51,57,60,62,
  70,135,154,158,180,216-222
Functional alternatives, 18,79
Functionalism, 93,113,179,230,274,
  276,282-283
Fundamentalism, 63,118
Future, 34,45,108,144,219

National Taiwan University, 283
Nationalism, 208
Natural resources, 26
Nature, 205,210-212,219,289
Negotiation, 73
Neighbor, 266
Neurosis, 40
New consciousness, 1
New man, 1,2
Ninth World Congress of Sociology,
   viii-ix,13
Nirvana, 43
Nomos, 154,164
Normlessness, 164
Norms, 76,300
Norway, 181
Nothing-buttery, 90,302,304
Numinal(-ous), 79,198
Numinosum, 65
Nuns, 184,265-279
Nurses, viii,152,305
Nurses Christian Fellowship, 305
Nursing, 280

Obedience, 129,173-189
Objectivism, 52
Occult, the, 1
Old age, people, 14,100,102,111,178
Ontology, 281,302
Opera, 207,208,209,210
Operationalization, 24
Opiates, 165
Optimism, 25
Options, 19
Oratorio, 208
Order, 96-97
Ordination, 186
Organizations, types of, 86
Orgies, Tantric, 43
Orthodoxy, 29,85
   doctrinal, 238,241,242-243,245,
   247-249
Ostracism, 77
Overself, 36

Padua, Italy, 191-200
Pai Pai, 287
Palladianism, 208
Pantheon, 207
Paradise, 45,127
Paradox, 26,45
Participant observation, 54-55

Participation, 22,295-297; see
   Associationalism
Particularism, 239
Pastoral care, 4,258,306
Patient, 152
Peace, 30,31,140,143
   with God, 8,9
   inner, 8,9,51
Peak experiences, 79,82,107
Pearl of Great Price, 174n
Pentecostals, 119
Perception(s), 52,115
Perfection, 34
Personal resources, 231
Personal Well-Being X-Ray,
   217-219
Personality development, 101
   Christian model, 66-70
   sociopsychological model of,
   51-71
Personhood, 91-98,106; see Indi-
   vidual
Pessimism, 97
Phenomenology, 3,5,42,97,103
Philippines, 181
Philosophy, 62,66,71,306
   of life, 282
   of religion, vii
   speculative, 57
Piety(-ies), 9,148,195,242,244
Pilgrim(age), 82,191,193,194,198
   267,290
   Saint of, 196
Plausibility, 134,135
Plausibility structure, 87,150
Pleasure-seeking, 30-31,57
Pluralism, 116,130-131,133,135,
   150
Pluralization, 20
Poetry, 22,211
Polarization, 96
Politics, 117,145,202,210,251
Polity, 84
Portugal, 181
Positive thinking, 49
Poverty, 271
   inner, 50
Power, 30,89,115n,117,169-170
   blocs, 85
   within, 216-222
Practicality, 26
Prana, 42-44,46

352

world, 131
Religiosity, 9,81,113,236
  churchlike, 248-249
  defined, 237-238
  dimensions of, 238-240,243-244,251-252
  of masses, 124
  measures of, 3,229-236,237-254
  model of, 85,88
  sectlike, 248-249
  and spirituality, 259-260
Religious activity, 177,295
Religious communities, Catholic, 12,
  265-279
Religious deafness, 207
Religious education, vii
Religious experience, see Experience,
  religious
Religious Experience Research Unit, 159
Religious life, questions, 277-279
Religious Life Scale, 237,244-246,247-249,
  250,252-254
Religious-mindedness, 231,232-235
Religious movements, 114,133-151
Religious orders, 16
Religious practices, 51,238
Religious preference, 230
Renaissance, 206
Renunciation, 35
Repentance, 30,173-189
Research Foundation for Eastern Wisdom
  and Western Science, 42
Researchers, personal equations of, 52-53
Responsibility, 96
Restitution, 186,187-188
Resurrection, 132,174,175
Retirement, 100-102, 110
Revelation, 76,129
Revival of religion, 119
Revolution, 208,282
Righteous living, 179,189
Rites de passage (of passage), 21,109
Ritual, 238
Ritualistic path, 143-151
Role analysis, 19-20
Role strain, 73-89
Roles, 19-20,74,80,143,171
  female, 217
  male, 216-217
  negotiated, 20
  religious, 219
Roman Catholic Church, 117
  Canon Law, 271
Rule, 16

Russia, 120

Sabbath, 69
Sacralization, 15
Sacrament(-al), 17
Sacred, the, 15,78,79,80,86,
  137-138
Sacredness, 111
Sacrifice, 35
Saint, 45, 192
  mini-, 255-263
  super-, 255-263
  thaumaturgical, 194

Saint Anthony of Padua, 191-200
St. Anthony of Thebaides, 194,19
Salience, 240
Salvation, 23,32,34,35,56,65,72,
  118,122,123,124,126,128,129,1
  143,162
  models of, 124-126
  paths to, 148
Samadhi, 43,46
Sanctification, 93,229-235
Sat Sang, 138,139,145
Satan, 165,176; see Devil
Satchidananda, 47
Satisfaction, 103,229-235,259
Schizophrenia, 40,201
Science, 24,39,51,55,64,66
  metaphysical, 41
  physical, 53
  social, see Social science
Scripture, 274,276
Second Coming, 59,166
Sect(s), 46,77,78,88,114,117,
  120-121,134,148,248
Secularization, 15,120,121,153,
  159-160,207,248,276,291,310
Security, 160,274
Self, 33,34,46-50,77,105-106,
  116,134,141,156,221
  Abundant, 47,50
  Effluent, 47,50
  locating, 133-151
  strength of, 32
Self-actualization, 17
Self awareness, 155
Self conception, 141
Self-concern, 36-38
Self-consciousness, 23,36-38,12
Self-deception, 179,266
Self-discovery, 41

Self-education, 43
Self-existence, 123
Self-fulfillment, 36,47,49,160
Self-giving, 30
Self-God dyad, 79
Self-image, 185-186,282
Self-isolation, 37
Self-location, 30,142-143,148,149
Self-love, 219-221
Self-realization, 140,154,164
Self-respect, 185
Self-seeking, 35,50
Self-transcendence, 113-114,153,154
Self Wheel, 217,219-222
Selfishness, 35,92
Semantics, 12
Sensuousness, 18
Serendipity, 87
Serenity, 43,47,49,255,258
Seriousness, 26,27
Service, 11,188,272,296
Sex(ual), 42,159,202,206
  attitudes toward, 250
Sex differences, 248
Sexologists, 57
Shepherd's Song, 290
Significant other, 142
  divine, 78-84
Sikh, 47
Sin(s), 26,27,92,94,174,176-177,189
  forsaking, 186,187,188
  forgiveness for, 12,30,38,185,188
  human condition, 97
  original, 166
  penalties for, 187
  universal, 93-94
Sisters, 265-279
  departed, 268,273-274,275
Sisters of St. Francis, 268,269-271,
  272,275
Sobriety, 255,257,261,263
Social activism, 134
Social bond, 123,282
Social class, 248-249,252
Social constraint, 84
Social control, 32,77-78,84-85,86
Social distance, 250-251
Social engineering, 116
Social illness, 128
Social indicators, 173,236
  defined, 2
  economic, 2

movement, viii
of spiritual well-being, 1-13
Social justice, 2
Social psychology, 6,51-71,113,134
Social psychology of religion, vii,
  63-66
Social reconstruction, 93
Social reform, 118
Social science (scientists), 56,
  135,281,301
Social services, 215-228
Social structure and spiritual ex-
  perience, 113-118
Social work(ers), viii,4,5,306
Socialism, 120
Sociality, 75,82
Socialization, 74,79,82,142
  anticipatory, 76
  religious, 12,76-77
Society, 108,113,118,156
  American, 149,282,289
  industrialized, 20,106
  caricatures of, 157-160
  perfection of, 18
  pluralistic, 116,133
  western, 153
Sociology, 6,15,52,53-55,91,92,
  154-157,267,282-283,302
  Morale in, 25
  Schools of, 61,134
  Soviet, 1
  and theology, 94,96,98,155-157
  Theory in, 3,73-131,166,179,301
Sociology of religion, vii,54,113,
  119,133,230,237,276,301,305,306
Solidarity, 21,36,37,86,298-299
Soul, 32,37,43,45,47,130,131
  realized, 44
South Africa, 136
  Pretoria, 292
Speech communities, 12
Spirit, 114,155,304
  Eternal, 156
  fruit of, 11,70,226,244
  of God, 204; see Holy Ghost, Holy
  Spirit
Spiritual, 1,2
  definition of, 14,215,281
Spiritual advice, 71
Spiritual awakening, 256-257,262
Spiritual body, 132
Spiritual community, 63,162,163

355

357

2354